Blazing Splendor

The Memoirs of the Dzogchen Yogi
Tulku Urgyen Rinpoche

Erik Pema Kunsang

Marcia B. Schmidt

Rangjung Yeshe Books • www.rangjung.com

PADMASAMBHAVA
 Dakini Teachings • *Advice from the Lotus-Born*

PADMASAMBHAVA & JAMGÖN KONGTRÜL
 Light of Wisdom, Vol. I • *Light of Wisdom, Vol. II*

YESHE TSOGYAL • *The Lotus-Born*

GAMPOPA • *The Precious Garland of the Sublime Path*

DAKPO TASHI NAMGYAL • *Clarifying the Natural State*

TSELE NATSOK RANGDRÖL
 The Heart of the Matter • *Mirror of Mindfulness*
 Empowerment • *Lamp of Mahamudra*

CHOKGYUR LINGPA • *Ocean of Amrita, Ngakso Drubchen*

JAMGÖN MIPHAM RINPOCHE
 Gateway to Knowledge, Vol. I • *Vol. II* • *Vol. III*

TULKU URGYEN RINPOCHE
 Blazing Splendor • *Rainbow Painting* • *As It Is, Vol. I* • *Vol. II*
 Vajra Speech • *Repeating the Words of the Buddha*

KHENCHEN THRANGU RINPOCHE
 Crystal Clear • *Songs of Naropa* • *King of Samadhi* • *Buddha Nature*

CHÖKYI NYIMA RINPOCHE
 Present Fresh Wakefulness • *Indisputable Truth* • *Bardo Guidebook*
 The Union of Mahamudra & Dzogchen • *Song of Karmapa*

TSIKEY CHOKLING RINPOCHE • *Lotus Ocean*

TULKU THONDUP • *Enlightened Living*

ORGYEN TOBGYAL RINPOCHE • *Life & Teachings of Chokgyur Lingpa*

TSOKNYI RINPOCHE
 Fearless Simplicity • *Carefree Dignity*

COMPILATIONS
 Quintessential Dzogchen • *Dzogchen Primer* • *Dzogchen Essentials*
 A Tibetan Buddhist Companion

DICTIONARIES
 The Rangjung Yeshe Tibetan-English Dictionary of Buddhist Culture CD

Blazing Splendor

The Memoirs of the Dzogchen Yogi
Tulku Urgyen Rinpoche

As told to
Erik Pema Kunsang &
Marcia Binder Schmidt

Foreword by Sogyal Rinpoche
Introduction by Daniel Goleman
Edited with Michael Tweed

Rangjung Yeshe Publications
Boudhanath, Hong Kong & Esby
2005

Rangjung Yeshe Publications
Flat 5a, Greenview Garden,
125 Robinson Road, Hong Kong

Address letters to:
Rangjung Yeshe Publications
p.o. box 1200,
Kathmandu, Nepal
blazing@rangjung.com
www.rangjung.com

© 2005 Erik Hein Schmidt & Marcia Binder Schmidt

All rights reserved. No part of this book may be reproduced without written permission from the publisher.
Distributed to the book trade by:
Publishers Group West / North Atlantic Books

1 3 5 7 9 8 6 4 2

First edition 2005
Printed in the United States of America on recycled acid-free paper

Publication Data:
Schmidt, Erik Hein; Schmidt, Marcia Binder.
Blazing Splendor: The Memoirs of the Dzogchen Yogi Tulku Urgyen Rinpoche. Compiled, translated and edited by Erik Pema Kunsang and Marcia Binder Schmidt, with Michael Tweed. Foreword by Sogyal Rinpoche. Introduction by Daniel Goleman.
Includes glossary with geographical and bibliographical references.
isbn 962-7341-56-8 (alk. paper.)
1. Eastern travels. 2. Biographies. 3. Tibet—Dzogchen (Nyingma).
I. Title.

Cover art detail: Fortress Peak (Dzong-go Ling), Nangchen; Erik Pema Kunsang
Cover and text designed by Rafael Ortet

Contents

List of Illustrations	vii
Foreword by Sogyal Rinpoche	ix
Introduction by Daniel Goleman	xiii
Preface	xviii
Prologue	xi

Part One • Spiritual Roots

Grandmother's Mission	3
Tibet, a Buddhist Land	6
Gampopa and the Early Barom Masters	10
The Treasures of the Lotus-Born	25
My Great-Grandfather, the Treasure Revealer	27
Two Sublime Masters	41
Khyentse	41
Kongtrul	49
Lord of Activity, the Fifteenth Karmapa	53
Spiritual Sons	62
Karmey Khenpo	62
Wangchok Dorje	66
Tsewang Norbu	70
My Precious Grandmother	79
My Guru, Samten Gyatso	86
My Father, the Performer of Miracles	103
Two Special Uncles and Their Teachers	122
Uncle Sang-Ngak	122
Tersey Tulku	124
Shakya Shri, the Lord of Siddhas	129
The Master-Scholar Katok Situ	135

Part Two • Early Years

My Childhood	141
The Nunnery of Yoginis	157

Receiving My First Teachings	163
An Extraordinary Speech	166
My Previous Life	170
My Monastery and Enthronement	176
The Young Karmapa	186
Grandmother's Death	193
The Colorful Chokling of Tsikey	204
Transmission at Surmang	215
The Master in the Hollow Tree	219
An Eccentric King	226
My Last Days with Samten Gyatso	231
My Guru's Passing	234
Meetings with a Remarkable Teacher	247

PART THREE • CENTRAL TIBET

At Tsurphu with the Karmapa	263
Brilliant Moon	280
My Last Visit to Central Tibet	290
Amazing Masters in Lhasa	297
DZONGSAR KHYENTSE	297
DUDJOM RINPOCHE	303
SHECHEN KONGTRUL	307

PART FOUR • IN EXILE

Leaving Tibet	319
Sikkim	325
Nepal	337
The Chokling of Neten	340
The Hearing Lineage from Bomta Khenpo	347
Conclusion	354

Afterword	359
Acknowledgements	364
Art Credits	367
Appendix: The Lineage of the New Treasures	368
Endnotes	372
Glossary	398
Activities and information connected to the lineage of Tulku Urgyen Rinpoche	433

List of Illustrations

1. Tsewang Chokdrub Palbar—Blazing Splendor xxii
2. Trisong Deutsen—the great Dharma king 7
3. Samye—the castle of the early Dharma 7
4. Chimphu—a view from the caves above Samye 7
5. Padmasambhava—the Lotus-Born master 8
6. Vajradhara—the dharmakaya buddha 10
7. Gampopa—the forefather of the Kagyu masters 11
8. Chokgyur Lingpa—the revealer of hidden treasures 27
9. The lotus crown of Chokgyur Lingpa 28
10. The Lotus Crystal Cave—sacred place of the Three Sections 28
11. Kala Rongo—where the Tukdrub was revealed 28
12. Yeshe Tsogyal—the great dakini disciple of the Lotus-Born 38
13. Longchenpa—the great Dzogchen master 44
14. Vairotsana—the great translator of Buddhist scriptures 49
15. Mipham—the famous scholar 50
16. The Great Dakini of Tsurphu 56
17. King Jah—the master of Mahayoga 66
18. Tara—the female buddha of compassion 82
19. Fortress Peak—the lofty hermitage 89
20. Tsewang Dechen—the tulku of Samten Gyatso 102
21. Tsechu monastery in Nangchen 108
22. Shakya Shri—the Lord of Siddhas 129
23. Druk Kharag Yongdzin Rinpoche 130
24. Cool Grove charnel ground in India 133
25. On the road from Lachab to Dechen Ling 144
26. Dechen Ling 148
27. Tsangsar County—on the road to Dechen Ling 149
28. View of Fortress Peak from the road to Lachab 152
29. Gebchak Gompa—the nunnery of meditators 158
30. Gebchak nuns sitting in their meditation box 161
31. The Derge royal family 166
32. The Situ of Palpung 168
33. Pages from the writings of Chowang Tulku 172
34. Lachab monastery 174
35. View from Lachab monastery 177
36. On the road from Fortress Peak to Lachab 178
37. The sixteenth Karmapa—a willful incarnation 187
38. The terma site above Tsikey and the present tulku 193
39. Karsey Kongtrul—the son of the fifteenth Karmapa 194
40. The tulku of Karsey Kongtrul 197
41. Tsikey monastery 207
42. The king of Nangchen 226
43. Prince Achen of Nangchen 227
44. The young Karmapa 263
45. Mural of Tsurphu monastery 264
46. Lotus Garuda Fortress above Tsurphu monastery 265
47. Shri Singha—the early master of Dzogchen 269
48. The young Dalai Lama 272
49. The inner retreat room at Lachab 278
50. Dudjom Rinpoche—flanked by Dordrak Rigdzin and Minling Chung 279
51. A tulku named Rabsel Dawa, Brilliant Moon 280
52. Early photo of Dilgo Khyentse Rinpoche 281
53. Pawo Rinpoche of Nenang monastery 291
54. The Moon Cave at Drak Yerpa 294
55. View from the Moon Cave 294
56. The young Dudjom Rinpoche 295
57. Dzongsar Khyentse Rinpoche 297
58. Dilgo Khyentse Rinpoche in Lhasa 301
59. Dudjom Rinpoche 303
60. Chatral Rinpoche 304
61. The Kongtrul of Shechen 307
62. Chökyi Nyima, Chokling and their mother Kunsang Dechen 319

63. Tulku Urgyen Rinpoche early photo 320
64. The family in Sikkim 326
65. The Vajra Throne in Bodhgaya 328
66. Dzongsar Khyentse under the Bodhi Tree 329
67. Dzongsar Khyentse Rinpoche 333
68. Trinley Norbu Rinpoche with his wife and the tulku of Dzongsar Khyentse 333
69. The sixteenth Karmapa 334
70. Trulshik, Dudjom and Tulku Urgyen, Rinpoches 335
71. Dudjom and Nyingma lamas in exile 336
72. The Great Stupa in Boudhanath 338
73. Swayambhu Stupa 338
74. Lama Tashi Dorje of Nubri 339
75. The third Chokling of Neten—Pema Gyurmey 340
76. The Chokling of Neten with his oldest son Orgyen Tobgyal Rinpoche 341
77. The fourth Chokling of Neten 341
78. Chökyi Nyima and Chokling, Rinpoches 342
79. View of Nagi Gompa 344
80. Bomta Khenpo 347
81. Nyoshul Khen Rinpoche 348
82. Khenpo Ngakchung 349
83. Vimalamitra—the Dzogchen master 349
84. The Black Crown ceremony of the Karmapa 353
85. The Boudha Stupa and Ka-Nying Shedrub Ling Monastery—old air photo by Toni Hagen 354
86. The sixteenth Karmapa with the tulkus at Ka-Nying Shedrub Ling Monastery 355
87. The sixteenth Karma & King Birendra of Nepal at the inauguration 355
88. Chatral, Dudjom and Dilgo Khyentse, Rinpoches 356
89. Enacting the drama of Padmasambhava, Shantarakshita and King Trisong Deutsen—Dilgo Khyentse, Trulshik & Chökyi Nyima, Rinpoches 356
90. Lamas at the Boudha Stupa, at the end of the transmission for the New Treasures 356
91. Five lamas in Boudha—Tulku Urgyen, Trulshik, Dilgo Khyentse, Dabzang and Depuk, Rinpoches 357
92. Dilgo Khyentse Rinpoche with lamas at the Yak & Yeti 357
93. Dilgo Khyentse Rinpoche with Tulku Urgyen Rinpoche's family 358
94. Tulku Urgyen with Tsoknyi and Mingyur, Rinpoches, and their mother Sonam Chodron at Nagi Gompa 361
95. Tsoknyi Rinpoche with Adeu Rinpoche of Nangchen 361
96. Yongey Mingyur Rinpoche—the youngest son 361
97. Tenga Rinpoche with Tenpa Yarpel 361
98. Ka-Nying Shedrub Ling monastery in Boudha 362
99. The temple at Asura Cave in Parping 362
100. Ngedon Osel Ling monastery 362
101. Chatral and Tulku Urgyen, Rinpoches, with Kunsang Dechen and Phakchok Tulku 362
102. Chokling Rinpoche with his first son—Phakchok Tulku 363
103. Chokling Rinpoche with his second son—the incarnation of Dilgo Khyentse Rinpoche 363
104. The fourth Chokling of Tsikey in Nepal 363
105. The fourth Chokling of Tsikey in Kham 363
106. Tulku Urgyen Rinpoche with Tsikey Chokling, Dechen Paldron and the incarnation of Dilgo Khyentse Rinpoche 363
107. Neten Chokling and Tsikey Chokling 363
108. Three sons and Phakchok Tulku at Nagi Gompa 363
109. Marcia Binder Schmidt in Nangchen 2003 365
110. Tulku Urgyen Rinpoche and Erik Pema Kunsang at Nagi Gompa 365

Foreword
by Sogyal Rinpoche

Here in this book, you will read about extraordinary practitioners of meditation and exponents of the teachings of Buddha, about great masters whose compassion, understanding and capacity defy ordinary criteria, and about a world in which a very particular definition prevails, quite different to the one promoted all around us today, of what is possible to be achieved by a human being. However, you will not learn so much in these pages about the author of these memoirs, the Tibetan master Kyabje Tulku Urgyen Rinpoche. This is inevitable, because of his humility and his discretion. And yet he is the heart of this book, not only because it is his eyes witnessing these amazing events, his voice recounting them and his mind making sense of them for us, but also because he was of the very same caliber as the exceptional individuals he is describing. He inherited their wisdom completely, and he embodied their incredible qualities. Tulku Urgyen Rinpoche was, in fact, one of the greatest masters of meditation of the twentieth century, and one of the most outstanding and prolific teachers of the Dzogchen and Mahamudra teachings that lie at the heart of the Buddhist tradition of Tibet.

I first met Tulku Urgyen Rinpoche when I was very young, because, as he explains in this book, he came many times to receive teachings from my master Dzongsar Khyentse, Jamyang Khyentse Chökyi Lodrö. When, years later, I requested Tulku Urgyen Rinpoche for teachings, he recalled how he had always seen me at the side of Jamyang Khyentse, and our mutual bond through our proximity to this great teacher gave us both a deep feeling of closeness. In the Nyingma and Kagyü schools of Tibetan Buddhism, Tulku Urgyen Rinpoche was an immensely important lineage master, and was the teacher and representative of the 16th Gyalwang Karmapa. He also passed on transmissions to the greatest lamas of the Nyingma tradition, Kyabje Dudjom Rinpoche and Kyabje Dilgo Khyentse Rinpoche. Both of them, along with Nyoshul Khenpo Jamyang Dorje and so many other great holders of the teachings, held Tulku Urgyen Rinpoche in the highest regard, as someone who had fully realized the view and practice of Dzogpachenpo, the Great Perfection.

As a teacher, Tulku Urgyen Rinpoche was unique, in a class of his own. One fact that struck you straight away was that whatever he taught was saturated with the flavor of Dzogchen. Of course, he possessed a complete mastery of all aspects of the Buddhadharma; he specialized, for example, in carrying out Vajrayana practices with extreme precision and authenticity; he had meditated since the age of four and spent over twenty years of his life in retreat; and he was renowned as someone to whom many great masters would go for his priceless clarification on difficult points in the teachings. But when it came to introducing the essential, innermost nature of mind, Tulku Urgyen Rinpoche was unparalleled. I remember how, at Nagi Gompa in Nepal, he would always give the pointing out mind instructions, introducing people to the essence of mind whenever they requested teachings—whether they were students of Dharma or just trekkers visiting the Himalayas. When people asked for the pointing out mind instructions, in one session, he would somehow just give them everything, the whole teaching, even if it was a large group of people. It was uncanny: he would keep on and on introducing the nature of mind, until they got it. Tulku Urgyen Rinpoche must have introduced thousands of people to the Buddhadharma and allowed them to experience, if only fleetingly, the innermost nature of their mind. They would come away from their meeting with him with a fervent inspiration to practice, and to pursue this new and nascent understanding of their minds by taking up the path of Dharma.

On his world tour in 1980-1, Tulku Urgyen Rinpoche gave precious instructions to my students in London, and in 1988, he gave the pointing out instructions to a much larger group who had traveled to Nepal to see him and Kyabje Dilgo Khyentse Rinpoche. After that, I endeavored to return every winter to Nagi Gompa to receive teachings from him. I count myself extraordinarily fortunate to have been able to do so. His teachings, which were simply amazing, went straight to my heart, and had a deep and powerful effect on the manner in which I taught. I remember well the encouragement he gave me too; it was he, in fact, who showed me in many ways the importance of what I was seeking to do in teaching the Dharma in the West. Everybody, from the highest lama to the most ordinary person who knew him in Nepal, remarked on Tulku Urgyen Rinpoche's kindness, and in his character and his dealings with people, it is true that he enacted to the letter the spirit of 'The Way of the Bodhisattvas'—the *Bodhicaryavatara*. He possessed all the naturalness, simplicity and ease of a great Dzogchen yogi, and I believe it is no way an exaggeration to call him a mahasiddha, a contemporary saint. At his cremation, the sky was clear, and the air above the land completely still, which the Dzogchen tantras denote marks the passing of someone with the greatest realization, whose practice was 'without attributes'. As they say, the sign is that "there are no clouds in the sky above; no dust upon the earth below".

Tulku Urgyen Rinpoche's style of teaching was so fresh, so unpretentious and yet so effective. People were utterly disarmed by his warmth, his directness and his sincerity, the atmosphere that he seemed to conjure around him, and the way he would coax you, and guide you, step by step, into an experience of the nature of mind. He would unveil the mind essence from every possible angle; it was almost as if he were drilling it into you, until you had glimpsed it. And because his words came directly from his experience and his wisdom mind, whenever he gave the pointing out instructions, it was never the same. I used to reflect on how, when a master like Tulku Urgyen Rinpoche, with his incredibly human kindness and grace, gives you the pointing out instructions, what he is introducing you to is nothing less than the wisdom mind of the buddhas. He is personally connecting you with the wisdom of all the masters. This is exactly what we mean when we speak of the extraordinary 'blessing' of the master, and his 'incomparable compassion'. When all is said and done, what greater kindness could there be? The master turns towards you the human face of the truth, as the personification of your innermost nature, and in the case of Tulku Urgyen Rinpoche it was so easy to see how his very being communicated everything about the essence of the teachings. I feel that just having met a master like him means that your precious human life is not wasted, and has achieved its meaning and true purpose.

Compassion, wisdom, devotion and the innermost nature of the mind—all of these you will read about in this book. After all, they comprise the Buddhadharma, and they are what we all aspire to understand, master and realize. But the place in which they are all drawn together, and all exhibited most perfectly, most personally, most directly in front of us, is in the master, in a master such as Tulku Urgyen Rinpoche. When I think of him, it brings home what Jamyang Khyentse said in his striking account of who the master really is:

> It is not only at this present moment, now, that the *tsawé lama*, the root master, is with us. In all his kindness, he has never been apart from us in any single one of our lives throughout beginningless time, because he is the manifestation of our mind's true nature, appearing externally in all kinds of guises, pure and impure, in order to help us, either directly or indirectly. Right now, on account of all the merit we have accumulated in the past, he has taken on the form of our spiritual friend, and because of this powerful karmic connection, we have been able to meet him, he has given us the nectar of the profound and vast instructions, and he has enveloped us in his tremendous kindness. From now on too until enlightenment, he will never be separate from us for even a single instant.

We could be immeasurably sad now that this great master Tulku Urgyen Rinpoche is lost to the world, and yet, more and more, we can feel joyful, not only because he lives on, in our minds and deep within our hearts, 'never separate from us, for even a single instant', but also because he succeeded in ensuring the continuity of his heritage, the teachings that he embodied so completely. His sons, Chökyi Nyima Rinpoche, Tsikey Chokling Rinpoche, Drubwang Tsoknyi Rinpoche and Yongey Mingyur Dorje Rinpoche are all fully qualified holders of his lineage and his vision, each one displaying their own individual qualities, different and yet extraordinary, and yet each one also bearing the stamp of Tulku Urgyen Rinpoche. Just like him, their familiarity with mind-essence bubbles contagiously just beneath the surface, ready to spring out at any moment. Tulku Urgyen Rinpoche had many wonderful western students, among them scientists and Buddhist teachers who are intimately involved in presenting the Dharma to the modern world. His beloved students, Erik and Marcia, have been a source of constant delight to so many people with the books, such as this, which they have created over the years, and I pray that they may continue, without any obstacles.

Finally, what do they all imply, the stories and memories that you will find in this book? Two things. First, that spiritual realization or enlightenment is actually *really* possible, if only we dedicate ourselves to it, with consistency and with ardor. Second, this is not simply ancient history, a phenomenon that happened in the past in India or in Tibet. Thanks to masters like Tulku Urgyen Rinpoche and his disciples, this living tradition of wisdom and spiritual awakening continues right now in the present, and thanks to them, these teachings of Buddha, with their precious pith instructions, are readily available to people everywhere.

I pray for the fulfillment of all of Tulku Urgyen Rinpoche's aspirations; may his emanation appear, just as wonderful and powerful as he was, if not more so, to rise to the challenges of this time. May his sons and his disciples continue his work, without the slightest obstacle, and may his magnificent vision come to pass, of awakening countless beings, and pointing them towards their true nature, the essential innermost nature of their minds!

Introduction
by Daniel Goleman

Tulku Urgyen Rinpoche was among Tibetan Buddhism's greatest masters of the 20th century. *Blazing Splendor* invites us to his side as he looks back over a life that put him at the center of an unparalleled spiritual abundance. Through his unblinking eyes we meet the remarkable contemplative adepts of old Tibet—as friends and teachers. And through the lens of his awakened awareness, we see the world from a fresh, eye-opening perspective.

Like the Dalai Lama a *tulku*, or reincarnate master, Tulku Urgyen was among the most renowned and influential modern teachers in the Dzogchen (Great Perfection) tradition, highly instrumental in first bringing this now-popular practice to the West.

"Blazing Splendor"—referring to the qualities of a realized master—directly translates the name Tulku Urgyen was given by the Karmapa, head of Tibetan Buddhism's Kagyu order. *Blazing Splendor*, his spiritual memoir, offers an intimate glimpse into his remarkable reality—and a fascinating journey through a lost culture. In these pages we become familiar with Nangchen, his homeland and a kingdom of spiritual richness, a land where everyone from shepherds to kings were dedicated practitioners.

The world Tulku Urgyen knew was one in which today's conventional values were turned upside-down: instead of fame, fortune or celebrity being the marks of "success", it was inner realization that counted, one where the mark of a life fulfilled was leaving a spiritual legacy for others. And Tulku Urgyen was uniquely positioned to know—and share with us—people who inhabited this landscape of sacred values. Yet his message for readers is not that realization is reserved for an elect few, but something that each of us can move toward, no matter where we begin.

A theme central to *Blazing Splendor* is that of *terma*—a sacred teaching from a mystical source dating back a millennium—which enriches the life and spirit of those who connect to it. Tulku Urgyen's stories cast a special light on these treasures designed to transform us. They are jewels of our human heritage hitherto largely unknown in the Western world. Tulku Urgyen was the bearer of such treasures, carrying them in his heart and mind over the Himalayas and then transmitting them in the world beyond to thousands of people from every walk of life.

Blazing Splendor covers more than the years of Tulku Urgyen's life, from his birth in 1920 to his death in 1996; it weaves a rich tapestry from his family history, and from the contemplative lineages that he himself came to hold. The result is not just a personal memoir, but a spiritual history of Tibet itself. We hear about the teachers who brought the Buddhist teachings to Tibet in the 9th century, and the unbroken line of masters who passed its secrets on through the ages to Tulku Urgyen himself.

Through Tulku Urgyen's eyes, we meet some of the most realized and genuine spiritual practitioners of the 20th century Tibet. Not only was he a friend and personal confidant of many of the great religious figures of contemporary Tibet, but his relatives and ancestors were some of the most influential figures in Eastern Tibet over the past centuries.

Tulku Urgyen's life spanned an exceptional period in Tibetan history; throughout the story, an ominous drumbeat in the background heralds the coming of the Communists from the East, and the ultimate devastation of the Tibetan culture and all its richness. We get a telling, up-close look at the treachery of Lhasa politics during this endgame, as Tulku Urgyen tells of his days as envoy of the Karmapa to the Tibetan government in its last gasp. And finally, we see how the spiritual greatness that was once Tibet managed to resurrect itself in the world beyond, as Tulku Urgyen—reading ill auguries of what is to come—fled Tibet a year before the Dalai Lama himself.

Blazing Splendor gives us this access in an earthy, candid and entertaining narrative style: Tulku Urgyen's own voice. What may be most striking is Tulku Urgyen's natural humility. Calling no attention to himself or his own stature, he lets us see the world—and a fascinating pantheon of characters—just as he does: with blunt, often wry, candor.

The book's voice reflects the cozy circumstances in which this tale was first told—a feeling of sitting at the master's side, as Tulku Urgyen shared these chapters in his life with his closest Western students. Here they have been organized into a sweeping account that shares with readers a world where miracles, mystery, and deep insight are the order of the day—a world as reflected through the open, lucid quality of Tulku Urgyen's mind.

His students, Erik and Marcia Schmidt, were moved to write this book in part because the unique lifestyle and culture of old Tibet was inexorably changed by the Communist takeover in 1959. Tulku Urgyen was widely recognized within Tibetan Buddhist circles as one of the most outstanding lamas to survive the tragedy of the Chinese takeover in Tibet. As the years take their toll, one after another of the great masters who were trained under Tibet's classical spiritual system have passed away.

In an effort to keep the spirit of this tradition alive, the authors felt compelled to present these first-person accounts by one of the last of a dying breed.

However miraculous many of the events related within these pages seem, recent scientific studies indicate such miracles may not be the stuff of imagination. For example one of the more intriguing aspects of these tales relates to recent findings on the beneficial ways long-term meditation shapes the human brain. While these studies are still in their preliminary stage, they nevertheless have yielded several eye-opening results on the very meditation methods applied by the masters of Tulku Urgyen's lineage—particularly those undertaken during years of intensive retreat.

For instance, brain imaging using functional MRI while lamas meditate on "boundless compassion" reveals that their brains show remarkable levels of activation in two areas: the site that generates happiness and bliss, and that for readiness to take action. These eight lamas had put in from 10,000 hours of practice time up to 60,000 hours, and the longer they had done so, the stronger their brain's activity level. While ordinary volunteers who practiced the same meditation for a month had 10% increases in these brain regions, the lamas had, on average, ten times more activity. And for some lamas, the jump was as much as 80 times greater.

As William James, a founder of modern psychology, suggested in his classic *The Varieties of Religious Experience*, our experiences while we register a temperature of 98.6 F may not give us the fullest account of reality. In other words, alternate states of brain function—and so consciousness—might allow perceptions of the universe that are just not discernible from the vantage point of everyday awareness.

Religious traditions around the world offer accounts of altered realities by visionaries ranging from Meister Eckhardt and St. Teresa of Avila to Black Elk. Of course we don't know what altered brain activity or extraordinary states might have allowed such visions (and we must acknowledge our own scientific bias in assuming that special brain states need be involved at all), but we do know that in every case the visions came after years of focused spiritual efforts. And neuroscience now tells us that the brain responds to sustained retraining by reshaping its own circuitry.

We have yet to understand what the upper limits of basic mental functions like attention, visualization and memory might prove to be—for modern science is in its infancy in studying how training the mind can rewire the nervous system. On the other hand ancient spiritual traditions, like that of Buddhism in Tibet, have systematically urged practitioners to spend years honing their sensibilities through sustained training.

What's particularly intriguing about the stories in *Blazing Splendor* is the sheer length of time put into these practices by the masters of Tibet. While the lamas studied in modern labs have done at least three to six years of intensive retreat, it seems to have been routine for masters of Tulku Urgyen's generation to have done three or four times that amount. Tulku Urgyen himself, for example, appears to have spent more than 20 years in intensive retreat, as was true of his late peer, the great Dilgo Khyentse. But some of the masters who lived their entire life in Tibet often did even more: Tulku Urgyen's father put in 33 years of meditation retreat over the course of his life.

Science has now verified how powerful just three years of retreat can be in sharpening mental faculties. We can only guess what 20 or 30 years might do. From that perspective, we might do well to suspend our judgments about the seeming "miraculous" powers routinely ascribed to these Tibetan masters of the past. Who knows what might be possible for a mind so highly and exquisitely trained?

What might be possible remains further obscured by another element of Buddhist tradition, the remarkable humility about their own achievements that marks many highly accomplished practitioners. Thus Tulku Urgyen himself, who was venerated as a teacher by many of the most revered masters of his day (including the 16th Karmapa), repeatedly asserts that he is nothing special—just an ordinary person. This humble stance has another wrinkle: Tulku Urgyen's line holds to the tradition of the "hidden yogis," who routinely camouflage their spiritual attainments. Western readers, unaccustomed to this strong tradition of humility about one's spiritual stature, might misread its signs, inferring instead an absence of accomplishment rather than its veiled presence.

The reader confronts yet another dilemma: how to regard the many matter-of-fact accounts of what, from a modern mindset, are improbable or impossible events, even miracles. Some readers may simply dismiss them as embellishments, while others choose to take them all at face value, or to set aside a dismissive criticism for the time being—or simply being open to their possibility without coming to any firm judgment.

For those steeped in the assumptions of rationality, these events are enigmatic, raising questions that cannot be readily answered. Are these accounts mere legends and folktales? Are they recounted as metaphors or teaching stories whose details or veracity are less important than the point they make? Did some of these seemingly impossible events actually occur only in the mind of those who tell of them? Or could it be they partake of a range of experience beyond the everyday "trance" created by our thoughts and fantasies, memories and daydreams?

Each of us will have to decide for ourselves. But all of us stand to benefit richly in expanding the horizons of our own spiritual aspirations.

A note to readers:

I would urge the serious reader to take the time to go through the endnotes as you read along. Much rich context, detail and explanation will be found in the notes and the glossary, which in themselves could stand as a partial tutorial in the Vajrayana tradition of Buddhism. Reading the notes will make the narrative itself much richer. And for those new to this perspective, the notes offer an essential background, bringing clarity where otherwise there could be some confusion.

Mendocino, California
November, 2004

Preface

This is not a traditional narrative of an enlightened master's life in the Tibetan Vajrayana tradition. In fact, Tulku Urgyen rarely if ever spoke much about himself or his accomplishments. At most he occasionally might tell a 'teaching story' from his past in order to convey a specific point to a particular person at a particular time. He would only mention details about his life when urged, and so this memoir results from Tulku Urgyen Rinpoche telling us stories about his life at our request, over a period of fourteen years.

From these tales we've strung a storyline, piecing together vignettes he told at different times, much like beads on a rosary. The resulting mosaic offers a rich narrative of Tulku Urgyen Rinpoche's tradition and ancestors, tales of masters he knew or heard about, and many details of his life. We cannot claim that Tulku Urgyen Rinpoche wrote this, as he did not set out to narrate an autobiography. He simply responded to our requests by telling these stories, and he did so only after I promised that the main emphasis would be not on himself, but on the remarkable people he met or was connected to through other masters.

When I asked him about the contents, he replied: "Just stick to the stories. Don't fill it with photos of me. In Kham we call that self-aggrandizement. Include many photos of realized lamas, but there's no need to include common people. Sacred places are very good too. It is beneficial for people to see sacred places like Bodhgaya if they haven't been there themselves."

He also gave a suggestion for a title: "Devotional summary of the life-examples of sublime masters."

I feel we have stayed true to that spirit.

In the course of looking for the thread that tied everything together one theme became paramount and that is the vital continuity of lineage. As the reader will see, the *New Treasures*—the revelations of Tulku Urgyen Rinpoche's great-grandfather—and the transmission from one generation to the next play an important role in this book. And in the end all streams of transmission converge in the ocean of the supreme incarnation.[1] The teller of these tales was such an incarnation. *"Blazing Splendor"* is a mystical adventure story, a journey into eras, places, and situations unlike anything most of us have experienced. At the same time, it is a down-to-earth, human story, vividly told and, at times, heart-wrenching.

Tulku Urgyen's narrative tells of remarkable accomplishments of the human spirit, supported at times by divine intervention. It is no fairy tale, yet it is replete with magic and epic triumphs of wondrous magnitude. It describes spiritual achievement at its best—and human folly at its worst. Tibetans will find this biography unlike most others in their traditional genre, for it fails to mention almost any of the important details of this master's life, his miraculous feats and his extraordinary level of realization. Western readers may find that many of the stories seem to be sheer fiction or at least demand the suspension of their critical attitude. Yet what is presented, though at times challenging to normal conventions and perceptions, is for the most part verifiable.

Nobody could tell an anecdote like Tulku Urgyen Rinpoche. Not only could he perfectly recall tales told him as a child long ago and repeat them verbatim; he could invite you into his memory's landscape and describe exactly what took place in vivid detail, as if casting a spell. He offers events and conversations with a captivating emotional depth that transports us into his experience.

Still, in an odd way, this memoir is not really about Tulku Urgyen Rinpoche, his incredible works or his legendary special teaching style, which could ignite the listener's hidden potential for attaining liberation and complete enlightenment. Rather, it shares with the reader what he witnessed and, perhaps most profound, how he perceived his world.

And what a world Tibet was before the communist invasion! In that world, sacred exploits were the yardstick of success. Love and appreciation of the great gift of the Buddha's teachings and for the masters who upheld those teachings were paramount. That was a legacy even the communists could not destroy; it was carried far and wide in the hearts of those who escaped the wanton destruction and devastation of their culture. *Blazing Splendor* recounts their fortitude—a victory of the strength of mind in the face of overwhelming odds.

The main themes that permeate Tulku Urgyen's story are the depth of veneration of the Buddhist teachings, their preservation and dissemination through unbroken lines of transmission, unfaltering courage in following one's teacher's commands, the unparalleled respect that masters had for one another, and the inescapable impermanence of any situation.

The inconceivable damage that took place in Tibet cannot be denied or ignored. History bears witness to what happened. Yet, out of that devastation many precious masters and teachings survived. And the fact that these teachers were forced into exile has meant that those of us born into materialistic cultures can meet with this extraordinary tradition.

So, we invite you to enter a world that once was and glean the atmosphere. Let your heart open and connect with the sublime. Don't get lost in the details of place and time; just experience the spiritual ambiance. And, to be sure, deep meaning interweaves these pages—heart advice and spiritual teachings that just might set you on your own personal spiritual quest.

We offer this all to you with unimpeded love and devotion for our amazing teacher and with the heartfelt aspiration that you will be greatly benefited in both the short and the long term.

In telling his story, Tulku Urgyen Rinpoche placed the greatest emphasis on a landscape of people rather than physical places. Those people who inspired him most emerged as the main focus for this book. We have used the sequence of his spiritual ancestry and his life as the thread for these wonderful stories, each a jewel of timeless value strung together by Rinpoche's memory. We present this garland of tales here for you to savor.

Erik Pema Kunsang & Marcia Binder Schmidt
Nagi Gompa, 2005

Prologue

Since you have asked so many times, I will tell a bit about my life. In our Tibetan tradition, we begin a life story by tracing back one's family to its origins. My family name is Tsangsar. My other name, as I am considered a reincarnation of a yogi, is Chöwang Tulku.

I was born in Central Tibet, taken to Kham, then went back and forth between the two several times.[2] I fled the communists to Sikkim and finally moved to Nepal, where I am now living as an old man. That's my life in a nutshell. I haven't accomplished any great deeds. Mostly it's just one sad event after another.

Whenever I tell a story, I always avoid the two shortcomings of exaggeration and denigration—neither adding any extra qualities that someone does not possess nor refusing to acknowledge qualities that are truly present. As I am not the type of person who remembers specific dates, don't look for any clear chronology here.

I can, however, tell you some of the stories I have heard, many of which come from my grandmother.

Part One
Spiritual Roots

1

Grandmother's Mission

As my grandmother, Könchok Paldrön, supervised the loading of her yaks for the long, hard journey from Kham to Lhasa, she was in a hurry. She was an elderly woman now, and too much time had already gone by since she had last seen her son, who was living in Central Tibet—a two-month journey. She was determined to start searching for him.

My grandmother made her feelings very clear, lamenting: "My father was Chokgyur Lingpa, the great revealer of hidden treasures,[3] and no matter where he went, people gathered around him like iron filings around a magnet. During my father's short life, his fame and glory, his influence and the number of his disciples seemed to surpass even those of the eminent Karmapa. Yet for all that, he left his body behind and me along with it.

"Then my mother and brother passed on, too. Everyone I love has abandoned me. Who could be more cheerless than a lost orphan like me? Even my youngest child, Tersey Tulku, has discarded me to stay with his illustrious master in Central Tibet. People say he is unfurling the four enlightened activities among the nobles in Lhasa.[4] Even the king of Bhutan caters to him—the king gave my Tersey so many presents that fifty pack animals were needed to carry them. He nurtures a flock of eight hundred disciples—but he leaves me, his mother, all alone here in Kham.

"The travels of my father, Chokgyur Lingpa, were like a wave sweeping through the land, pulling everyone in its wake, no matter how learned or accomplished they might be. And no matter what school they belonged to, all the masters of his time received his teachings. Having witnessed such greatness, how can I be impressed by anything these days? I hear all kinds of stories about the so-called great deeds of Tersey Tulku, yet compared to the activities of his grandfather, they seem no more than foam on water.

"And now here I am, Chokgyur Lingpa's only remaining child, all alone. Tears have flowed from my eyes day and night, so that my pillow is moist with tears. I feel that all things beautiful and positive are no more than flowers in an autumn meadow—they are splendid but don't last long."

What triggered my grandmother's outburst? Uncle Tersey was extremely learned in her father's tradition of the *New Treasures,* the forty thick volumes of teachings revealed by Chokgyur Lingpa. From an early age, Tersey had had many visions and received prophecies, but, being a "hidden yogi," one who never flaunts his accomplishments or realization, he rarely spoke of them.

One day, Uncle Tersey left Kham to go on pilgrimage. A very strong man, he carried his own provisions on his back, unlike most travelers in the steep terrain of Tibet. He didn't have a single pack animal, just two trusted attendants, each carrying a backpack of their own. They traveled everywhere, even to the holy places in India. It was during this pilgrimage that he became a disciple of the illustrious Shakya Shri.[5]

Word reached Kham that "the bearded Tersey Tulku was living the untroubled life of a lama-yogi," and the stories were quite impressive. But none of this fooled my grandmother, who always responded to such news with "That too will pass!"

And she began to worry about her youngest son. "I can't sleep as long as he is floundering about Central Tibet," she said, "I must go fetch him. He is my youngest and the reincarnation of my brother who met an early death. Tersey has stayed in Central Tibet too long. If he won't return to Chokgyur Lingpa's seat to assume his responsibilities, I'll have to go and bring him back myself!"

Since they couldn't let their elderly mother travel the long journey to Central Tibet alone, her three eldest sons had to prepare to accompany her.

Our family eventually found Uncle Tersey at Kyipuk, where Shakya Shri had lived and taught. When they asked him to return with them to Kham, he replied, "Sure, I'll come back, but first I must finish my pilgrimage." Five years passed before they were all able to return home to Kham.

It was during this journey that I was born.

❧

My grandmother was a very self-assured lady. It was from her that I heard most of the tales that I will tell here. My uncle Samten Gyatso had said several times, "Mother has so many stories to tell." And she sure did!

This remarkable lady never forgot anything; she was able to discuss events from long ago as though they had just taken place. People often wondered how such an old lady could be so lucid. She could give a detailed explanation on any topic that piqued my curiosity, and she knew an incredible number of interesting tales.

    I adored spending time with her. I was especially fond of stories about her father, Chokgyur Lingpa, many of which never found their way into his official biography.[6] She accompanied her father, the *tertön*, on many of his journeys and saw with her own eyes what happened. She also knew many of his visionary experiences and personally witnessed many of the *terma*s being revealed. With her virtually perfect recall, she could give an impeccable eyewitness account of the whole event. Whenever she told a story, it sounded as if she were still right there.

2

Tibet, a Buddhist Land

The Buddha's teachings were transmitted to the people of Tibet with the patronage of an ancient lineage of kings. It is said that a semi-divine being from the Punjabi royal lineage, who had descended to live among human beings, fled north into the Himalayas. Eventually, he emerged from the high mountains and entered the Yarlung region of Tibet. The people of the area believed he was a miraculous being who had fallen from the sky, and they carried him on oxen yokes placed on their shoulders to crown him as their first monarch. For this reason he became known as King Nyatri, the "yoke-throned" king.

The first Buddhist scriptures miraculously arrived in the Land of Snow after thirty-five generations of these kings had ruled in an unbroken line from father to son. At that time, everyone was illiterate, a fact that filled the reigning king with sorrow. He prayed fervently to end his people's ignorance. Due to the blessings of the buddhas, three scriptures of the enlightened ones fell from the sky, landing on the roof of his palace. Although no one could read them, the mere presence of these sacred texts transformed the environment so that harvests were plentiful and the evil forces in the country were somewhat pacified. It was as though the dense darkness of night had been broken by dawn's first glimmer.

Five generations later, Songtsen Gampo took the throne and invited the first Buddhist teachers to Tibet. Through his enormous merit, he managed to acquire two of the three main statues located in the temple in Bodhgaya, the place of the Buddha's enlightenment in India. These statues were brought to Tibet as bridal gifts from the two foreign princesses he married. One statue accompanied the daughter of the Chinese emperor, while the second statue was brought by the daughter of the king of Nepal. To continue the analogy, the period of Songtsen Gampo's reign was like the first sliver of the rising sun illuminating the morning sky. The Dharma was beginning its spread throughout the land.

After another five generations King Trisong Deutsen made a great vow to fully establish Buddhism throughout Tibet, and this was like the sun finally rising high in the sky. During his reign, he invited 108 great masters to Tibet from their native countries, mainly India. In those days, spiritual guides, teachers, and masters were called *pandita*s, learned scholars. Those who received the teachings and translated them into Tibetan were called *lotsawa*s, translators.

2. Trisong Deutsen—the great Dharma king

The first important master invited to Tibet during this period was the renowned Khenpo Bodhisattva, also known as Shantarakshita. The king had grand plans to build a group of temples in Central Tibet, the complex that today is known as Samye. But a powerful *naga* spirit loathed the bodhisattva, saying, "If these Indians start bringing Buddhism here, we will suffer. Let's all gang up and make trouble." All the eight classes of spirits agreed to try their best to stop Buddhism from spreading in Tibet by preventing the construction of Samye. Whatever was built during the daytime the gods and demons of the land destroyed that night.

Now, Shantarakshita was a great bodhisattva with a tremendously loving and peaceful heart. But because of his peaceful nature, he was unable to subjugate the local spirits around Samye. It seemed Shantarakshita was going to fail in his mission so the king became increasingly depressed by the lack of progress.

"I'm only a bodhisattva," Shantarakshita told him. "I can't handle all the powerful spirits of this region. But don't despair; there is a way. In India lives a being who is exceptional in every way. He was not even born from a human womb; his name is Padmasambhava, the Lotus-Born. Any gods or demons who oppose the true teachings become terror-stricken and powerless simply from hearing his name. Invite him to Tibet, and our problems will end."

"How can we invite him?" the king asked.

3. (left) Samye—the castle of the early Dharmas

4. (right) Chimphu—a view from the caves above Samye

5. Padmasambhava—the Lotus-Born master

The Indian bodhisattva replied, "We three share a vow from our former lives, when Your Majesty, Padmasambhava, and I were brothers who helped erect the great stupa in Boudha, Nepal.[7] Since we vowed at that time to spread Buddhism to the north, the Lotus-Born master will certainly accept our invitation; we need only ask him to come."

Padmasambhava possessed tremendous power, enough to subjugate all evil forces. Being the single embodiment of the activity of the buddhas, he was able to convert disciples in the dark country of Tibet as well as subjugate all the hostile forces. Because of his mystical proficiency, the temple complex of Samye was finally erected.

Other legendary masters who helped establish the Dharma in Tibet included Vimalamitra, who was said to have attained the extraordinary "vajra body of great transformation," beyond the reach of birth and death. There was the Tibetan translator Vairotsana, himself an emanation of a buddha. All together, 108 panditas arrived in Tibet.[8]

A great number of Tibetans were educated as translators during this period, so that the entire body of the Buddhist teachings, including numerous *sadhana* practices detailing entire spiritual paths, were translated into Tibetan and accurately codified.

During the reign of Trisong Deutsen, auspicious conditions occurred in Tibet. The king himself was an emanation of the great bodhisattva Manjushri, and some of his ministers were said to be divine emanations, as were the masters and panditas invited to Tibet and even the translators of that time. Due to these incredibly positive circumstances, the king was able to fulfill his vow of establishing Buddhism in Tibet.

The teachings from that remarkable period are now known as the Nyingma, or the Old School of the Early Translations, as opposed to the teachings imported from India during subsequent centuries, which are called the Sarma, or the New Schools of the Later Translations.

But all did not go smoothly. A while after King Trisong Deutsen's death, there was a period of religious persecution, in which the evil oppressor Langdarma, who had become king, almost succeeded in eradicating Buddhism. But a subsequent revival saw the beginning of the Sarma schools, introduced chiefly by the great translators Rinchen Zangpo and Marpa. These two—and many other great teachers—journeyed all the way to India, received instructions from the Buddhist masters there, and brought them back to Tibet. One of the kings of this early period, a great religious ruler named Ralpachen, a grandson of Trisong Deutsen, also invited many masters to Tibet.

Now, at that time there were two Sanghas, consisting of the congregation of ordained monks, recognized by their shaven heads and Dharma robes, and the congregation of *ngakpa*s, tantric practitioners distinguished by their long braided hair, white skirts and striped shawls. As a sign of his deep appreciation for these two congregations, the king would spread his two very long braids out upon the ground, and allow the revered practitioners to tread on and sit upon his own hair. He would even take pebbles from under their feet and place them on the crown of his head to show respect. The royal patronage, in conjunction with the king's great reverence for the teachings, created the circumstances for Buddhism to firmly take root and flourish in Tibet.

Finally, the Dharma was fully established throughout the country. Over the centuries, through the support of such devoted kings and the efforts of all these masters and translators, eight distinct lineages of teachings translated from their sources in India came to flourish in Tibet.[9] These eight schools are all, without a single exception, the teachings of the Buddha. Each taught without any conflict both the Sutra system, which includes Hinayana and Mahayana, and the system of Tantra which is Vajrayana.[10]

During these two periods of the first flourishing of Dharma in Tibet, masters and disciples—and even the disciples' disciples—attained a profound level of realization. Some displayed extraordinary signs of their accomplishment, such as soaring like flocks of birds through the sky. Wherever they took flight and wherever they landed, they left footprints in solid rock. This is not just a legend from the past; these imprints are visible even today, so you can go and look for yourself.

Such was the country where I was born.

3

Gampopa and the Early Barom Masters

As I mentioned, according to the Tibetan tradition of storytelling, a person should not simply appear out of nowhere. The tale should begin with the person's origins. We describe origins in two ways: family tree and spiritual lineage. So I will begin in the proper way, by telling you a bit about my family, who were often known by the lofty—and somewhat exaggerated—title "divine bloodline of Tsangsar." Our clan was for many centuries the rulers of two kingdoms: Tsangsar and Nangchen. According to oral history, our bloodline traces back to India. The story goes that a celestial being from the Brahma realm descended to earth to produce a child with a tigress in the Forest of Black Sandalwood in northern India.[11]

These are unusual ancestors, but we are not unique in this: tradition holds that the first person in the Drigung family line was fathered by a god, while the mother was a goat. The goat gave birth to a boy and his divine father then returned from the heavens to collect his child. But as he picked up the boy, the goat mother, heartbroken at losing her child, let out a "Baaahhhhh!" and out of compassion the god let her keep the child.

6. Vajradhara—the dharmakaya buddha

My ancestors are deeply connected to a spiritual lineage called Barom, one of the early Kagyu schools.[12] The word *Kagyu* means the teachings (*ka*) that are transmitted (*gyu*) in an unbroken lineage from the very beginning until today. It is said that this spiritual lineage traces a continuous line back to the celestial buddha Vajradhara, whose teachings passed through the Indian masters Tilopa and Naropa and then to their Tibetan successors Marpa and Milarepa. The famous yogi Milarepa had many disciples, but there is one who rose to the fore; today we know him as Gampopa, "the man from Gampo," the root of our Barom tradition.

Before he met Milarepa, Gampopa had studied and practiced the Buddha's teachings for quite a while and had reached proficiency in the meditative state of *samadhi*. One day, a beggar happened by and began talking about Milarepa, a great guru, right outside Gampopa's window. The moment Gampopa heard Milarepa's name, he was overcome with emotion and called the beggar inside.

"Where does this Milarepa live?" he asked.

7. Gampopa—the forefather of the Kagyu masters

The beggar told the master's life story: how he had been wronged as a child by his own relatives and suffered, how he mastered black magic and used it to take revenge, then how he had a change of heart, became a renunciate, and was now an amazing master yogi. The beggar ended by saying, "Right now he lives in the province of Ngari. I am one of his disciples."

"Could I meet him?" asked Gampopa.

"Of course," replied the beggar.

Gampopa felt a deep yearning to meet this yogi, and, wasting no time, the very next morning he headed for Ngari. He met Milarepa at a place named Auspicious Ridge. Upon merely seeing the master's face, Gampopa attained the warmth of blissful emptiness. Milarepa told him, "Sit down and train in *tummo*!"—the yoga of inner heat. After a short time of practice, as you can read in the *Life of Milarepa*, he showed profound signs of progress connected with the energy currents dissolving into the central channel.[13]

When Gampopa had gained a highly refined level of insight into Mahamudra, the awakened state of mind, his guru said, "You have spent enough time with me. You must now go to Mount Dakpo and practice in solitude, but before you leave I still have one final lesson for you."

On the day of departure, Milarepa walked with Gampopa for some distance. After he rested a while on a large boulder, it was time for the final good-bye. Then Milarepa stood up, lifted his yogi's skirt and showed Gampopa his buttocks. They were so worn down and callused that Gampopa could almost see the bones.

"Listen to me! When training in Mahamudra, do not busy yourself with virtuous deeds of body and speech," Milarepa explained, "because you risk losing thought-free wakefulness. It was by sitting on these buttocks that I attained realization. I have persevered in the two paths of means and liberation: Naropa's Six Doctrines and Mahamudra. Easy, comfortable practice won't get you anywhere!

"Forsake the aims of this life," he continued. "Practice with fortitude. One day, you will see this old father as a buddha in person. That is when genuine realization of Mahamudra will have taken birth in you. This is my final instruction."

Gampopa went to stay in a small meditation hut on Mount Dakpo, where he trained with tremendous perseverance, unconcerned with life or limb. Through this effort, his insight deepened until he realized the awakened state that is boundless like the sky. Gradually his following grew vast; five hundred of his disciples became masters in their own right, allowed to bear the parasol of the Dharma, signifying their status as lords of the Buddha's teachings—no small position. Thus he fulfilled the prediction of Naropa, who said, "My disciples will be more eminent than their teacher, but their disciples will be even more eminent." And sure enough, the practitioners who sprung from his lineage were as numerous as flocks of birds taking flight and filling the sky.[14]

Among Gampopa's foremost disciples was a man named Darma Wangchuk, who is counted as the first master of the Barom lineage. From early childhood he had no other thought than practicing the Buddha's sacred teachings; as he grew up, his sole aim was to find the best master to follow.

Eventually, the young Darma Wangchuk met a yogi and asked where he was headed.

"I'm going to Mount Dakpo, where the extraordinary Gampopa lives."

"Take me with you—I want to meet him too!" exclaimed Darma Wangchuk, having made up his mind that very moment. Off they went. Upon meeting Gampopa, Darma Wangchuk immediately became his disciple.

Where I come from, the word 'disciple,' is not used lightly. It means someone who practices full-time, who gives up everything to focus one-pointedly on attaining enlightenment in that same body and lifetime. People who merely received a few empowerments or a short teaching now and then were not necessarily counted as disciples.

Darma Wangchuk became the prime example of the kind of disciple who serves his master perfectly in thought, word, and deed. He even saved Gampopa's life several times.

We Tibetans are in the habit of showing our religious fervor by pushing one another aside to get close to the lama and receive blessings. It can become quite a scene, almost a stampede. Once, at a big market fair, word spread that Gampopa was there, and so everyone at the fair wanted to obtain his blessings—all at the same time, nearly crushing the master. Darma Wangchuk must have been quite a strong man because, the story goes, he lifted Gampopa on his back and carried him to safety.

Another time Gampopa and his following were moving along a steep, narrow trail in the high mountains. The yak Gampopa was riding slipped and fell into the abyss. But Darma Wangchuk was quick enough to catch hold of Gampopa and thereby saved his life.

One day, Gampopa told Darma Wangchuk, "You have served me for a long time and with great devotion. Now the time has come for you to benefit others. Go to the north, to a cave on sacred Mount Kangsar, and devote yourself one-pointedly to meditation practice." Gampopa then described the mountain and how to get there. Darma Wangchuk pleaded with him, saying that he would rather remain a humble servant, but Gampopa sent him off just the same.

Darma Wangchuk went where he was told and practiced with great diligence, having completely turned his back on striving for food, clothing or fame. The gods and spirits of the mountain brought him provisions, and he stayed there for thirteen years. At the end of his retreat, he could fly through the sky and move freely through solid rock, and he had the signs of an accomplished master.

Darma Wangchuk established his first center in Central Tibet,[15] near Mount Kangsar, northeast of Lhasa, where he had spent all those years. An increasing stream of faithful people with offerings, some coming all the way from China, began to find their way there. But after an avalanche buried his temple, he accepted an invitation from the king of Nangchen in eastern Tibet. There he established his second monastery, and over the generations the kingdom slowly became filled with meditators and yogis.

The word 'meditator' in my homeland of Nangchen is closely connected with the pointing-out instruction of Mahamudra, the most profound teaching in the Barom lineage. Almost everyone living in Nangchen received this instruction, which directly introduces the state of realization, and so they all became meditators. On every mountainside, in every valley, each family's house became a practice center. At the end of the day, even simple water-bearers used the leather straps on their yokes as meditation belts, as did shepherds with the ropes from their slingshots. It is said that almost everyone was a practitioner, and so the kingdom got the name *Gomde*, the Land of Meditators, a sign that the Buddha's teachings had firmly taken root there.[16]

In modern times, people often wonder why so many spiritual practitioners spent year after year in remote mountain dwellings. The answer is simple: They had an acute awareness of the grave facts of life—that we are mortal, that time is running out for each of us, and that we can use this precious life to secure a lasting attainment of liberation and enlightenment.

They saw worldly success and social recognition, even in dreams at night, as nothing but demonic attempts to seduce us away from the attainment of enlightenment. Seeing mundane pursuits as the futile chasing of a mirage, they removed themselves from the world like a wounded deer recovering from an injury, until they attained stability in the awakened state. Having attained the perfect stability of enlightenment, the masters among them engaged in work for others, by establishing monastic centers where the Buddha's teachings could be practiced and passed on.

It's amazing what a single authentic spiritual master can accomplish in terms of the common good. When you have the chance, try to read the biographies of the early Buddhist masters and the original founders of the major monasteries in Tibet. See how they went off and practiced with great dedication, and how they later built magnificent temples for the benefit of others. If you could have seen the number of beautiful statues of exquisite craftsmanship that existed before the communist destruction—gilded with the offerings of devoted people and created for over a thousand years—you would be quite impressed. Yet every single founder of this exquisite abundance had been a true renunciate, while regarding worldly honor and success as an attack by demonic forces.

The spiritual influence of a single enlightened being can spread into every corner of human civilization. There have been innumerable examples of this over the centuries. For instance, before he built the temple complex at Tsurphu in Central Tibet, where the Dharma flourished for centuries, the first Karmapa had already spent decades in meditation sheltered by nothing more than the overhang of a cliff. But there came a time when he reached such a level of realization that there were abundant signs of extremely high spiritual attainment.[17]

Like the Karmapa, there have been thousands upon thousands of practitioners who followed Milarepa's example. When someone stayed in an unpopulated valley or a remote cave, having abandoned futile involvements, and thereby had the time to awaken to true enlightenment—now, *that* impresses me!

❧

My family became linked to these early Barom Kagyu teachers through the master Tishi Repa, one of Darma Wangchuk's main disciples. Tishi Repa had four other gurus as well, and in their honor he fashioned a famous hat with five peaks— one at the center and one in each of the four directions.[18]

In Tishi Repa's time, a tradition of spiritual relationship between China and Tibet had begun whereby the Chinese emperors sought out and invited the most eminent Tibetan master to be the imperial guru. At regular intervals, a search party was sent to travel throughout Tibet to find the greatest master of the day. As his fame had spread far and wide, the lama with the five-peaked hat received an invitation from the emperor. That's how he became known as Tishi Repa—*tishi* being the Chinese title for the imperial preceptor, the highest religious rank. Below a tishi were two masters of the *pakshi* rank, and below each pakshi were two dignitaries with the position known as *goshir*. The tishi position also included an entourage of forty religious officials, all paid from the emperor's coffers.

While perusing the archives during my stay at Tsurphu, the main seat of the Karmapas, I came across ancient correspondence with China. A similar invitation from the imperial court to become a tishi was once sent to the third Karmapa. In those days, an invitation sounded more like a command.

One of the letters read: "To the west, no lama has been found to surpass you in spiritual qualities. The emperor has established this fact through his many emissaries. You alone must now be the imperial preceptor. If you fulfill his wish and come to China, the emperor will bestow every boon upon you in both spiritual and secular affairs. If you fail to fulfill the emperor's wish, you will never have another happy day."

Along with the document came a large seal of pure gold, a sign of exalted rank. Two high-ranking officials had personally carried the invitation to Tsurphu. The letter continued, "Commence your journey to China immediately, together with these two officials. Unnecessary delay of departure, even for a single day, will result in dire consequences."

Such an "invitation" required Tishi Repa to go to China—he simply had no choice. But he did so in a highly unusual manner. Perhaps he knew intuitively that traveling in the style of a grand master of Tibetan Buddhism would cost him his life or perhaps it was simply a personal choice, but he chose to dress as a wandering beggar.

"That attire is entirely inappropriate," the Chinese officials objected. "While traveling on imperial command, you must proceed in a dignified manner with the proper pomp and circumstance befitting a grand lama."

They negotiated back and forth, until it was agreed that the traveling party of the grand lama, including his own retinue of forty religious officials, would travel all the way to China in the traditional way. Tishi Repa, however, was permitted to accompany the caravan on foot dressed as a beggar in a simple cotton robe and carrying only a wooden walking staff. He walked the entire distance from Kham to the distant Chinese capital while everyone else rode on horseback.

There are written accounts of the miracles and other signs of accomplishment Tishi Repa displayed at the imperial court. But he also saw that the emperor's dynasty, which was of Mongolian descent, would last no more than thirteen years. When ten of those years had passed, Tishi Repa thought it best not to be in the capital when the dynasty fell, and so he made excuses to leave. But the imperial family categorically refused to let him return to Kham.

"Times are taking a turn for the worse," Tishi Repa thought. "The emperor's life is running out, and if I stay I will get caught up in warfare and internal strife. I must escape by stealth."

And so he slipped away. When the emperor discovered that Tishi Repa had fled, he sent out search parties in all directions. After two or three days, they caught up with him, and under strict guard Tishi Repa was marched back to the imperial court, where the emperor kept the master under lock and key.

"How will imprisoning me help you?" Tishi Repa asked. "You are the ones who are in trouble! Three years from now, both the dynasty and the crown prince will meet an untimely end. What can you do about that? I didn't want to be a witness to all that, so I decided to leave. You wouldn't let me, so I had to flee."

"Lama, do not speak in such a manner!" replied the emperor. "What you say couldn't possibly come true. Anyone who speaks as you do is to be punished! But since you have been my guru, I will excuse you. And if you really intend to leave, I will let you. In return, try your best to ensure that my life does not end."

So, with a change of heart, the emperor showered Tishi Repa with gifts and provided him an escort back to Kham. When the party arrived at the border, Tishi Repa's mount lay down and refused to stand up again. He told his escorts, "This is a sign that from now on I will return to being a wandering beggar." And he proceeded on foot.

Along the road, he met Sakya Pandita, the head of one of the main branches of Buddhism in Tibet, who was on his way to China. Sakya Pandita wanted to honor him by arranging an extravagant welcoming party. However, Tishi Repa replied, "There is no need for all that! Just treat me like the humble beggar that I am."

He continued on his pilgrimage and, taking a very long route home, visited Lhasa. A few days after finally arriving back in Kham, he passed away.

As he had been a guru of the emperor, Tishi Repa's passing was the cause of much attention and many ceremonies, and the news soon reached China. The new emperor sent emissaries to make offerings as well as to search for a suitable successor. They returned with a master named Repa Karpo, who was Tishi Repa's chief disciple. According to all written accounts, the greatness of this master defied all imagination; he was even more accomplished than Tishi Repa. Many people saw him emitting a resplendent light. He was given immense wealth by this new emperor and used it to build many temples. In particular, he built a huge temple in Nangchen with innumerable statues, the main being a replica of the Jowo Buddha statue in Lhasa. Eventually, he received the same spiritual rank as Tishi Repa from the emperor.

※

It is among Repa Karpo's disciples that we find my ancestor, Lumey Dorje of the Tsangsar clan. Earlier, during an empowerment ceremony with a huge gathering, Repa Karpo spotted Lumey Dorje in the crowd and called out, "Hey, you! Do you want to follow me?"

Lumey Dorje approached and replied, "Certainly. How kind of you to make it so easy for me—I don't even have to make the request." Then and there he became a disciple of Repa Karpo.

Before long, Lumey Dorje attained a high level of realization. He also built a monastery called Nangso Chenmo to which Nangchen owes its name. It had 115 pillars, making it extraordinarily large. When it came time for the consecration, he pitched a small tent and began practicing the instructions he had received from his guru.

During the ceremonies, some benefactors offered him *droma*, our traditional and auspicious but very rich dish of tiny sweet roots swimming in clarified butter. Lumey Dorje consumed one large pot after another, ten in all, and the word got around that the master had done something crazy and would die, or at least become seriously ill. But when everybody had gathered, he exuded all the butter through the pores of his body, leaving him even more radiant than before. Someone said, "That can't be an ordinary human body!" Another remarked, "Look! His body doesn't even cast a shadow! You can see right through it. He should be called Bodiless Vajra," which is what *Lumey Dorje* means. This master was truly a sublime being—like a lion among men.

When his guru Repa Karpo passed away, the funeral ceremony was a major event, a special occasion for his disciples to make lavish offerings to honor their guru's physical form. Soon after, the great Chögyal Pakpa, a master of the Sakya lineage, traveled through the region on his way to China and visited the monastery at Nangso Chenmo.[19] The followers of Repa Karpo told him, "We have been abandoned by our master, like a body without a head. You are a sublime being, the emperor's guru and the ruler of Tibet, and we would like to offer the monastery and the Nangchen kingdom to you."

Chögyal Pakpa replied, "This would be inappropriate because the head wouldn't fit the body. I am Sakya while you are Kagyu. It would be like putting a sheep's head on the body of a goat. I would rather choose the best of Repa Karpo's disciples. I have been entrusted with thirteen emblems of power to be given to thirteen people below me; the first of these I will offer to Repa Karpo's main disciple, giving him the rank of *lachen*, grand master. So, choose the one among you who is the foremost disciple, and I will invest him with this title so that he can take charge of your kingdom."

One of the disciples replied, "My Dharma brothers are all equal; there is no difference. It would be hard for us to choose who is best."

"Isn't there one who is just slightly better than the others?"

"Well, there is Lumey Dorje, whose bodily form resembles a golden offering lamp, but he has gone to Central Tibet. The rest of us are all equals."

"I am also going to Central Tibet. Send someone to find him and tell him to meet me there."

The messengers found Lumey Dorje near Lhasa, residing at the seat of a close disciple of Marpa.[20] They escorted him to Chögyal Pakpa, who enthroned him, giving him a golden seal and an insignia of precious brocade that symbolized the rank of lachen, one of the thirteen imperial priests. Upon receiving these honors, Lumey Dorje said, "I have had no other aim in my heart than to be a renunciate meditator, least of all a Dharma king, but I will not oppose your command. However, you must appoint me an effective Dharma protector."

Chögyal Pakpa then entrusted him with the Four-Faced Guardian, a Dharma protector from the Sakya lineage, together with the accompanying empowerment and instructions. Chögyal Pakpa then said, "You can rest assured that this guardian will follow you everywhere like a shadow follows a body."

This was not to be his only protector. Later Lumey Dorje had a vision of the female guardian Dusölma. She asked him, "What do you need?"

"I don't need anything!" Lumey Dorje replied.

"Nevertheless," she said, "I will protect your Dharma lineage for thirteen generations as if I were present in flesh and blood."

Lumey Dorje had also received many empowerments and instructions from a great lama in the Kadam tradition and a disciple of the famed Indian master Atisha.[21] When Atisha came up from Nepal to Tibet for the first time, a Dharma protector named Monkey-Faced Ganapati had followed him. At some point, Atisha entrusted this guardian to the lama, who later passed him on to Lumey

Dorje, saying, "This protector is half-wisdom and half-mundane; often his activity is mischievous."[22] So when Lumey Dorje returned to Kham as a Dharma king, he had an invisible following of not just one but three Dharma protectors.

⁂

It is interesting to note that Lumey Dorje—as well as his descendants, my own ancestors—had no real wish for secular power and fame but preferred the simple life of the renunciate. Perhaps because of this, eventually my paternal ancestors lost their position as the kings of Tsangsar to the ruler of Nangchen.

Lumey Dorje caused the Dharma to flourish throughout Nangchen. It was primarily through his spiritual influence that the kingdom became known as a land of meditators. Lumey Dorje remained on the golden Dharma throne for eighteen years and then he passed away—or, as we say in Buddhist terms, he "displayed the manner of transcending the world of suffering." For seven days, wonderful designs in rainbow colors appeared in the sky for all to see. On his bones, thirteen self-appeared images in the shape of the auspicious white conch were found. Even today people still retell the story of his cremation and all the wonderful, truly unbelievable signs.

By this time, Nangchen was a small country unto itself, and it was now necessary to choose Lumey Dorje's successor. The choice fell on Lumey Dorje's nephew, Jangchub Shönnu, who was a lama. He was a disciple of Lumey Dorje's and was living as a renunciate meditator in the area. Messengers found him and said, "You must leave your hermitage to be king. You can continue your spiritual activities from the golden throne of the Dharma."

"I don't wish to do anything but meditate in retreat," Jangchub Shönnu replied.

"What use is your meditation if you ignore the well-being of all those who live in the kingdom?" the messengers argued, and so Jangchub Shönnu became the successor to the throne.

On ascending the Dharma throne, Jangchub Shönnu received a high religious position from the Chinese emperor, along with many gifts from the imperial court. He decided to use his newfound wealth to build a magnificent castle-like palace in Nangchen. When he moved there, he transferred the three Dharma guardians as well, except for the monkey-faced protector, who vehemently refused to go to the palace, preferring to stay behind in the monastery at Nangso Chenmo.

Every morning Jangchub Shönnu would make a circumambulation of both castles and their temples. One morning, while he was walking around Nangso Chenmo, a dog attacked and bit him. People started talking. In the new castle, they said, "How can they let vicious dogs run around loose? Don't they feed the dogs over there? The manager there is so conceited he thinks he can use our lama as food for his mongrels!"

The servants in the other camp retorted, "He may be a great lama, but what is he doing running around alone every morning?" And the argument escalated from there. Words were flung back and forth. That was all it took to create a big rift. But we shouldn't be surprised that jealous rivalry abounds in the world of humans.

In the end, the high Sakya lama who had succeeded Chögyal Pakpa on the throne in Central Tibet was asked to mediate by the manager of the new castle. This manager must have been quite politically astute, because when he came back he brought a royal decree granting equal status to the two castles, which meant that the kingdom would have to be divided. Jangchub Shönnu didn't mind and said it was fine with him.[23]

From then on, there were two castles: one called Nangso Chenmo and the other Tsangsar. In time, each was to have its own king. In those days, the throne holders of the Dharma were simultaneously the ruler of a major region and oversaw both secular and spiritual affairs. Over the centuries, the surrounding areas were consolidated into the two kingdoms, which eventually comprised ten thousand family estates scattered over a sparsely populated area. In the following generations, many of these masters held high ranks bestowed by Chinese emperors: tishi once, pakshi twice, and goshir thirteen times.

As the Mongols came into power in China, they also gave the Nangchen kings official titles and positions. The title conferred upon the Nangchen kings was the position of *chinghu,* which is one rank below goshir but still higher than a *wang*. The whole western continent was divided under the power of four chinghu and eight wang. In our terms, we can equate the chinghu with an affiliated but independent ruler, while the position of wang is closer to that of a district governor. But the kings in the Tsangsar family—my ancestors—never received any such position and remained lamas.[24] In later centuries, the custom of the imperial court was to station its own representative in the various districts of Tibet. Just like the high-ranking Chinese official in Lhasa called an *amban*, there was a similar Chinese delegate in Nangchen and the neighboring kingdom of Derge.

Chinese from Ziling in the north had forced Tsangsar to relinquish most of its political power to Nangchen twelve or thirteen generations before mine, during the time of the master-poet Karma Chagmey. Then, about three generations ago, an important minister from the Nangchen court succeeded in forcing Tsangsar under the rule of the Nangchen king and imposed obligatory taxes. So, in the end, we lost our independence completely.

When I grew up in the Tsangsar mansion, our family line was no longer involved in politics, although we had a continuing spiritual lineage. There had been one *ngakpa* lama after another in my paternal line. The Tsangsar family line continued as lineage holders of the Barom Kagyu, while all the country's political affairs were handled by the Nangchen palace.

❧

This state of affairs—Nangchen as rulers and Tsangsar as lamas—went on harmoniously over the centuries, except for the reign of one king.

Sometimes worldly power goes to a person's head, and, one fine morning, the king of Nangchen looked toward the east and saw that the sun's warm rays were prevented from touching his palace by a mountaintop nearby.

He exclaimed, "I am the king! I want sunlight in the morning, so lop off the top of that mountain!" A huge labor force was mobilized and they began chipping away at the rock.

This was no small mountain, but they managed to take a fair chunk off the peak. Even today, if you climb that mountain, you can see the results of their labors.

But the work was overwhelming. Eventually, one of the workers said, "This is no good. We're dealing with this in the wrong way."

"What do you mean?" a coworker inquired.

"It's easier to chop off the ruler's head than to cut off the head of a mountain," the first replied.

"What are you saying?"

"Even if we continue for ten thousand years, we will still not finish this work. We have been given a horrible, endless task. Let's mobilize everyone and put an end to this senseless king!"

So that's exactly what they did: They cut off the king's head.

❧

Nangchen was divided into eighteen districts, each with a major monastery.[25] In the early days, all eighteen were Barom Kagyu, but the lineage waned in influence as the Karmapa's influence grew over the centuries and many of these monasteries began to follow his branch of the Kagyu. By the time I left Tibet, only a few small monasteries remained Barom Kagyu; one was my guru's monastery at Lachab.[26]

A bit more about my paternal line of ancestors, with its famous (and perhaps a bit pretentious) name, Divine Bloodline of Tsangsar. Ours was a family lineage of married Vajrayana masters who for many generations were politically independent of the Nangchen king. Over the generations, their estate and mansion were no longer vast, but they were not small either.

As I noted, my ancestors focused on spiritual works, not politics. At one point, there were eighteen Tsangsar brothers who together made eighteen sets of the *Kangyur*, the translated words of the Buddha, each written in pure gold. One set was offered to the head lama of the Sakya lineage, one to the Karmapa and another to Karma Gön, the Karmapa's main seat in Kham. When I was at Lachab, we still had one set and there was also one at a small temple under Tsangsar patronage. The pages were handmade of thick black paper and the script was a beautiful calligraphy in pure gold.

The wives and sisters of those eighteen brothers, a group of twenty-five, decided to create the merit of making twenty-five sets of the many *Prajnaparamita* sutras on transcendent knowledge, each written in pure gold on deep blue paper made from powdered azurite. During my time, one of these was still kept at the Tsangsar temple. Over the centuries, many people have seen the female protector Dusölma circumambulating and paying respect to these scriptures. There was also a profusion of artists connected with my family. Once when the Karmapa passed through between Tibet and China, he was given one thousand *tangka* paintings as an offering.

These Tsangsar ancestors all the way down to my great-great-grandfather were realized masters. There is almost no one, including my father, who didn't show some miracle or sign of great realization.[27] I heard that one of them was the leader of the army from Nangchen and was attacked by a gang of soldiers from Derge, but their muskets couldn't kill him.[28]

༄

A more recent and very important link in this Tsangsar family line was Orgyen Chöpel, my paternal grandfather. Being a married Vajrayana master, he dressed as an ordinary layperson. He married Könchok Paldrön—my grandmother and the only daughter of my illustrious ancestor, the great treasure revealer Chokgyur Lingpa—with whom he had four sons, all lamas, and two daughters.[29] These are all major figures in my family story. Remember, I was born on the journey when my grandmother went in search of Tersey Tulku.

When my grandmother was given in marriage to Orgyen Chöpel, his family's basic Dharma lineage was Barom Kagyu—but in name only. By that point, they were all following the Nyingma practices found in Chokgyur Lingpa's *New Treasures*, the forty volumes of teachings he revealed for these times. So, it seems the Barom seat had turned predominantly Nyingma.

That didn't mean they had completely abandoned the Barom teachings. The once-flourishing practice of the Six Doctrines from the Indian master Naropa had weakened long ago and was now maintained in only a few places. But by unifying Naropa's Six Doctrines with the liberating instructions of Mahamudra meditation, many early Barom Kagyu practitioners attained accomplishment—thirteen could run as fast as horses, another thirteen could run like the wind and there were many, many others. Their disciples spread far and wide, all over Nangchen.

The training in Mahamudra, on the other hand, had for the most part taken on the flavor of Dzogchen, the teachings of the Great Perfection. All that was left of pure Barom practice was a very particular ritual involving a way to invoke the guardian of the Buddha's teachings. This ritual was continued with very high regard—so much so that some monks would accumulate more recitations of this mantra than of their *yidam* deities. In the Tsangsar mansion where I spent my early years, there was a special shrine room for the lineage protectors, with huge masks covering all the walls. Every day, special petitions and offerings had to be performed in front of each. One of them, I remember, was said to give almost instant results; over the centuries, there have been many accounts of their protective powers.

These days, I am sorry to say, Barom is close to fading out, as very few lamas are left to uphold it. I, too, was supposed to do my part, but obviously I haven't done much. Of the Barom I have not practiced the Barom style of the Six Doctrines, but only the chanting for the Dharma protectors. Instead I have been steeped in Chokgyur Lingpa's terma treasures since I was a child. I haven't even had the chance to perform the practice connected to Chakrasamvara, the main deity of the Barom Kagyu.[30] So I am definitely to blame—shame on me!—for letting my forefather's Dharma lineage slip away as I occupied myself with Chokgyur Lingpa's termas. Actually, my father and one uncle did most of the Barom Kagyu practice in our family; they employed the practices for the Dharma protectors. But another uncle, Tersey, didn't chant even one syllable from the Barom Kagyu lineage; he followed the *New Treasures* one-hundred percent.

According to Khampa tradition, since the great tertön's sons had no children, his daughter's offspring were then highly respected as descendants and representatives of Chokgyur Lingpa. We speak of two kinds of grandchildren: "bone line" and "blood line." To be a grandchild from bone means being born in the family of a son, while a grandchild from blood would be in the family of a daughter.

The continuation of Chokgyur Lingpa's terma teachings was primarily due to my grandmother's having borne four sons, each of whom performed an immense service in propagating this lineage. My father was the second of the four sons; his name was Chimey Dorje. My mother's name was Karsa Yuri.

So that's a short history of both the spiritual and worldly aspects of the Tsangsar lineage and, particularly important, how it connects with Chokgyur Lingpa when his daughter, my grandmother, was given in marriage to Orgyen Chöpel of the Tsangsar family. At this point, you may wonder just who this Chokgyur Lingpa was and what his *New Treasures* are—and what exactly are terma teachings? Also, what's so important about propagating a Dharma lineage? All this will be my main topic in most of the following stories. And it is due to the kindness of my grandmother that I even know many of these tales.

4

The Treasures of the Lotus-Born

At the end of the eighth century, Padmasambhava, the Lotus-Born, arrived in Tibet. As the primary master of Vajrayana, he accompanies every one of the thousand buddhas of this eon.[31] He had twenty-five main disciples; in later incarnations those disciples were reborn as tertöns, who revealed teachings Padmasambhava had hidden to benefit people of coming times.

My root guru, Samten Gyatso, had incredible faith in Padmasambhava and would tell me how he marveled at the words of the Lotus-Born. Although Samten Gyatso was extremely erudite and had studied vast volumes of literature, he continued to find many fresh levels of meaning in Padmasambhava's teachings.

"There is no one greater than Padmasambhava," he would often say. "Of course, Buddha Shakyamuni is the root, but the Lotus-Born made the Vajrayana teachings spread and flourish throughout India—and especially in Tibet. If you look closely, you can see just how amazing his terma teachings are! And if you compare his terma revelations with any other treatise, you can see their unique quality. The reason is that they were from Padmasambhava himself.

"The beauty of their prose is astounding! It is very difficult for anyone to write with such beauty and depth as you find in terma practices. Unlike treatises by people who are merely learned, in a terma each word can be understood on increasingly deeper levels. That special quality of Padmasambhava's vajra speech means that whenever you read his teachings, you inevitably feel faith and devotion, trust and complete confidence!

"We see that similarly worded teachings appear in the revelations of several tertöns. The reason is they are all the unmistaken speech of Padmasambhava deciphered from the symbolic script of *dakini*s,"[32] he said, referring to female tantric deities. "One need not harbor any doubts. For instance, the *Seven-Line Supplication* starting with 'On the northwest border of the land of Uddiyana' appears in numerous different termas; the different revealers tapped the same source.

"Before he left Tibet, Padmasambhava concealed an abundance of termas containing teachings, precious stones and sacred articles for practitioners in later centuries to follow." Out of great kindness, the Lotus-Born concealed termas for the benefit of future beings—within solid rock, in lakes, even in the sky. Thinking of this immense kindness evoked my awe.

Yet, there are people who can't appreciate this kindness. These days some skeptics object saying, "Tertöns probably don't possess the unbroken lineage of empowerment and reading transmission from Padmasambhava for their teachings. They just dig up a few articles they themselves hid!"

But in fact, the tertöns who later appeared to reveal these treasures had, in their past life as his disciples, been blessed by the Lotus-Born master, receiving empowerment and reading transmission for those termas. Every tertön has already received the complete lineage—and in an authentic way far superior to the superficial manner empowerments so frequently are given these days, which bear only the semblance of blessings.

All the great tertöns were masters who, in body, speech and mind, were personally blessed, and empowered by the Lotus-Born. To claim they didn't have transmission is childish. Such statements demonstrate the speaker's ignorance of the seven traditional ways of transmission.[33] The terma teachings are amazingly profound and are concealed within the treasure chest of the *four modes and six limits*, ten levels of increasingly profound meaning at which each of the tantric scriptures can be explained. This is how Samten Gyatso introduced me to Padmasambhava's teachings.

"If you are interested in exploring them, the layers of meaning in a terma are vast. From childhood, a great tertön is unlike other children," my guru continued. "He has pure visions of deities, and realization overflows from within. Tertöns are not like us ordinary people who must follow the gradual path of study and practice. Ordinary people don't have instantaneous realization!"[34]

As another of my teachers, Dzongsar Khyentse, told me, "Termas are like crops that ripen in the autumn. Every year, there's a new crop, and each season it is freshly harvested and enjoyed, since that is the crop for use at that time. Terma teachings were concealed to be revealed at particular periods later in history, and they appear in forms most appropriate to the particular time periods in which they are revealed."

When the time came for the different terma teachings to be revealed, great tertöns would appear in this world. They were able to dive into lakes, fly up to impossible locations in caves and take objects out of solid rock.

My great-grandfather, Chokgyur Lingpa, was one of those masters who revealed the Lotus-Born master's hidden treasures.

5

My Great-Grandfather, the Treasure Revealer

Chokgyur Lingpa was born near the royal palace in Nangchen and grew up as a simple monk in the Tsechu monastery. Once during the annual tantric dances, he fell out of rhythm and danced on independently of the others. This upset the dance master who then wanted to give him a beating.

Present in the assembly was Adeu Rinpoche, who was the guru of the king of Nangchen. He also happened to be the son of the previous king and therefore a very powerful personage in the kingdom; during those days, there was no higher lama in Nangchen. Adeu Rinpoche, who had clairvoyant abilities, saw that the young tertön was participating in a dance of celestial beings taking place in the young monk's vision of Padmasambhava's pure realm—Chokgyur Lingpa had simply joined that dance instead.

Adeu Rinpoche came to Chokgyur Lingpa's rescue, saying, "Don't beat him! He has his own style. Leave him to himself."

Soon after, Chokgyur Lingpa asked permission to leave the monastery and Adeu Rinpoche consented, saying, "Yes, you can go. Travel freely wherever you like and benefit beings!"

Before leaving, Chokgyur Lingpa gave a statue as an offering to the king of Nangchen and requested a mount and provisions. But the king was a hardheaded character and not happy that he was leaving.

"That crazy monk has given me a statue of Padmasambhava that is neither clay nor stone," the king said, not realizing it was one of the extremely precious terma objects Chokgyur Lingpa had already discovered. "Give him an old horse and a saddle blanket." As a result of the king's lack of appreciation, Chokgyur Lingpa never settled in Nangchen.

8. Chokgyur Lingpa—the revealer of hidden treasures

9. The lotus crown of Chokgyur Lingpa

My great-grandfather had not gone through any formal studies, yet Old Kongtrul later called him a true pandita, a great scholar.³⁵ This change took place while Chokgyur Lingpa remained in a strict traditional retreat, lasting three years and three fortnights, at his residence above Karma Gön in Kham. During this retreat, he, to use his own words, "slightly unraveled the intent of the tantras, statements, and instructions," referring to the profound three inner sections of tantra—Maha, Anu, and Ati Yoga.³⁶

Chokgyur Lingpa was not just an authentic tertön; his revelations are pivotal to our lineage. He was the reincarnation of Prince Murub, the second son of the great king Trisong Deutsen, who established Buddhism in Tibet. Another of his former lives was Sangye Lingpa.³⁷ Chokgyur Lingpa was the "owner" of seven distinct transmissions and is often counted as the last of one hundred tertöns of major importance.

He is regarded as the "universal monarch of all tertöns," in part because no other tertön has revealed a teaching that includes the *Space Section* of Dzogchen. There are several *Mind Section* revelations and all major tertöns reveal the *Instruction Section*; but only Chokgyur Lingpa transmitted the *Space Section.* This is why his *Three Sections of the Great Perfection* is considered the most extraordinary terma he ever revealed.³⁸

⁂

Most of the stories I know about how Chokgyur Lingpa revealed termas I heard from my grandmother. Being Chokgyur Lingpa's daughter, she witnessed these events as a child. My grandmother was never known to lie or overstate anything; she was an extremely truthful person who didn't brag or slander.

She told me how Chokgyur Lingpa once revealed a terma before a crowd.³⁹ "Often my father would take a terma out in the presence of more than a thousand

10. (left) The Lotus Crystal Cave— sacred place of the Three Sections

11. (right) Kala Rongo— where the Tukdrub was revealed

people. It had to be this way, because Tibetans, especially those in the eastern province of Kham, were known to be extremely skeptical. They didn't blindly believe everyone who claimed to be a tertön. But Chokgyur Lingpa was beyond dispute, because he repeatedly revealed termas with numerous witnesses present.

"The purpose of revealing a terma publicly," she continued, "is to ensure complete trust, free from doubt or skepticism. There is no trickery involved; the terma is revealed before the eyes of everyone present. If it were just a magic trick, there would be no actual, material terma to show afterward, no representation of enlightened body or speech.[40]

"Otherwise, it was no simple feat to convince people that Chokgyur Lingpa was in fact an emissary of Padmasambhava. Khampas were even more hardheaded than Central Tibetans; they were much more suspicious. Among Khampas, the people from Derge were the most skeptical; there was no way in the world they would simply believe any impostor professing to be a tertön! They would only trust someone they had personally witnessed revealing a terma in public.

"We call such a revelation *tromter*, meaning 'public terma,' a terma revealed amid and witnessed by many people. When a terma treasure was about to be revealed as a tromter, it would first be announced: 'A terma will be revealed in public!' As word spread, a lot of people would gather to watch.

"A tertön would also miraculously receive a 'location-list,' which is like a key showing exactly where the terma is hidden. Such a text is necessary to be able to find the terma and take it out; and having received the location list—a mystical guidebook—the tertön can see in his mind's eye the layout of the landscape and the location of the mountains, valleys, rocks, caves and so on. This list also contains a description of the 'terma sign,' a certain mark placed by Padmasambhava or Yeshe Tsogyal, for instance the syllable HUNG. The terma site could be a certain rock or cave, a place described as looking like a gaping lion, a tortoise or another animal of a particular shape indicating the character of the location. The terma sign might be found at the throat, between the eyes, at the heart or at another such place on that particular animal.

"The location list will also indicate the proper time to reveal the terma and the particulars of the spirit guarding it. Sometimes three different spirits would be involved: *zhidag*, *neydag*, and *terdag*. The zhidag, the lord of the land, is, for example, like Maheshvara, who guards the entire Kathmandu valley, while the neydag, the lord of the locality, is, for instance, like Tarabhir, who guards the sacred place of the female buddha Tara near Nagi Gompa. The terdag,[41] the terma owner, is the particular spirit who was entrusted with the terma's safekeeping at the time it was concealed.

"How is it possible for anyone to steal a terma? Perhaps when Guru Rinpoche was concealing the terma he was seen by birds and other animals, who then knew where it was hidden. In one of their subsequent lives, they could become a terma thief. So the command would be, 'Don't allow a terma thief to take this! Don't let it fall into the hands of *samaya* violators! Entrust it to no one but the representative of me, Padmasambhava!'

"In this way, the guardian would already have been instructed by Padmasambhava to hand over the terma to the destined tertön. The treasure revealer however must then give a tribute in return, a kind of bribe. In addition, he must place something as a substitute, either a teaching or something precious, such as a sacred substance; he cannot just carry off the terma like a thief making off with some loot.

"As soon as the news spread that something amazing was about to take place, of course a lot of people would turn up—and why not! Sometimes five or six hundred people would be present, once even a thousand. But other times when the terma was revealed as a tromter there would only be a small group present consisting of seven, twenty-one or more people.

"On one such occasion, Chokgyur Lingpa presented a ritual drink to the guardian of the terma, accompanied by a request to release custody of the terma. He then drew a design on the surface of a rock, which opened up like the anus of a cow and the stone just poured out to reveal a cavity containing the terma. As the interior became visible, we saw that it was filled with scintillating rainbow light. We also noticed an unusually lovely fragrance that seemed to permeate the entire valley. A vast quantity of scarlet *sindhura* powder came spilling forth as well. Chokgyur Lingpa handed some of this powder out and people collected it for safekeeping.

My grandmother continued, "Everyone was slowly chanting the supplication to the Lotus-Born known as *Spontaneous Fulfillment of Wishes*:

> When revealing termas for destined people to benefit beings, ⸙
> With the courageous confidence of pure samaya, ⸙
> Free of hesitation and doubt, I supplicate you; ⸙
> Grant your blessings to spontaneously fulfill all wishes! ⸙

"Someone had already arranged a table nearby covered with a brocade cloth to place the precious articles on. The terma articles were often too hot to touch when taken out and my father was the only one who could hold them. Some were so hot in fact that they scorched the brocade"[42] My grandmother described these to me as "objects from which the heat of blessings had still not vanished." Sometimes this is used as a metaphor, but, in actuality, sometimes people did get burned. Once I actually saw some of these scorched pieces of red and yellow brocade in a box containing some of Chokgyur Lingpa's sacred belongings.

After the great tertön took out the terma, he blessed everyone. At this time he also gave an explanation of the terma's historical background, how and why Padmasambhava concealed it, with what particular aspiration it was buried, why it was revealed now, the benefits of receiving its blessings and so forth.

She said, "I saw the crowd weep out of faith and devotion, the air humming with crying. Even if you were a stubborn intellectual, all skepticism would melt away. Everyone was struck with wonder.

"After the revelation, he placed a substitute for the terma inside the rock cavity. For example, if there were two statues of Padmasambhava, then Chokgyur Lingpa replaced one of them. If the terma was a scroll of dakini letters, written in their symbolic script, he would place some other precious article in its place. Then he finished by walling up the cavity, sometimes with stones, sometimes even melting the rock as if coating it with plaster. If Chokgyur Lingpa simply set some rocks in the crack, people who later went back to check discovered that the surface had naturally 'healed,' all by itself."

My grandmother was not the only person I knew who actually saw Chokgyur Lingpa reveal termas. Once, while I was living at our Tsangsar family home, Pema Trinley, who had been the great tertön's servant, came to stay. He spent the last year of his life with us and was about ninety years old when he passed away. Being young and curious, I questioned him about his days with the tertön and he told me all that he remembered. Here is one of his stories:

"Once, while Chokgyur Lingpa was in a small village at the foot of beautiful Mount Karma, he was given the opportunity to reveal a 'cattle terma.' Believe it or not, he announced that he would bring forth real animals! Hearing this, many people gathered around him, proceeding with much commotion to a steep cliff that rose up the side of Mount Karma.

"In those days there were no matches, and Chokgyur Lingpa's cook, Lhagsam, had forgotten to bring along a fire kit of flint and steel. Without a fire kit, he couldn't make tea, so he sent his helper down to the village to fetch one. But all the villagers were out collecting wild, sweet droma potatoes on the hillsides, so the cook's helper had to return empty-handed.

"While the helper was heading back up the mountain, Chokgyur Lingpa had been at work in his tent in front of the cliff. Already people could hear cattle lowing and bellowing from deep within the mountain. It sounded as if the animals were just about to break through the surface of the rock. Everyone heard it—some were even frightened, thinking they were about to get trampled.

"Right then, the cook's helper yelled out, 'Hey, Lhagsam! I've got no fire kit! There was no one at the village!' The great tertön heard this from within his tent and asked, 'What did he say? They vanished? They are gone?' You see, in the Khampa dialect, the word for fire kit, which is *mesa*, and the cook's name, Lhagsam, can also sound like the word for 'vanished,' 'gone.' While Chokgyur Lingpa asked what was said, the sounds of the animals gradually vanished.

"Chokgyur Lingpa then exclaimed, 'The auspicious circumstance has passed! The cook's helper bungled it! We shouldn't stay here! Let's pack up and leave!' Everybody then left in a flurry. They didn't even have a cup of tea, since they couldn't start a fire."

~

My grandmother once told me why we in the lineage of Chokgyur Lingpa don't need to fear local spirits like Gyalpo Pehar or Samten Kangsar.[43]

On one of Chokgyur Lingpa's trips to Lhasa by the northern route, the party was caught in a terrible snowstorm on the vast plains. Even after the main storm subsided, a tremendous amount of snow continued to fall for a week or so, preventing them from continuing their journey. The travelers started to fear for their lives. They grew so desperate that they began to burn any flammable objects they could find—even the wooden frames of their saddles.

At an emergency meeting someone said, "We still have a long journey ahead of us. We haven't even crossed the pass. What's going to happen to us? With this snow I fear the worst. Let's ask the tertön for help; it's our only choice."

When the crisis was brought before the tertön, he responded, "The elemental forces of the valleys and the mountain spirits have ganged up to test us. They are taunting me, insinuating that I am not the lineage holder of Padmasambhava. But don't worry, just wait and see what happens. Divide the practitioners up into two groups: the ngakpas should stay with me in my tent and the monks should remain in Karmey Khenpo's charge. Prepare yourselves by training in the tummo yoga, for tonight we will perform the practice of the soaked cotton garments. It is the only way to deal with this."

The two groups began to practice the yoga that very afternoon and they produced so much heat that people outside could see clouds of vapor rising from both tents. At midnight the heavy snow clouds began to disperse and by morning the sky was clear, without even a wisp of cloud. Not only that, but all the snow around

Chokgyur Lingpa's tent had melted; you could see the stones on the bare ground. The sun rose in a blue sky to reveal splendid weather and the snow continued to melt across the entire plain. The streams became swollen to their banks with all the melted snow.

Chokgyur Lingpa suggested they stay for a few days and during that time the snow continued to melt. At one point he exclaimed, "I'm still not done with those guys! Samten Kangsar, Nyenchen Tanglha and some of the other spirits still seem to have their minds set on putting us through an ordeal. Samten Kangsar needs to be taught a lesson today. Please prepare a big white *torma* and bring it to me."

That afternoon, after the petitions to the guardians, Chokgyur Lingpa heated up the torma until the butter decorations on top melted down to its shoulder. Meanwhile, looking at Mount Samten Kangsar—from which the spirit has his name—in the distance, everyone saw that the snow on its peak had begun to melt and was gushing in streams down the mountainside. The next morning, large patches of black rock were visible.[44]

After Chokgyur Lingpa had subdued Samten Kangsar, the weather was brilliantly clear for three days straight; there was not a single cloud in the sky. The melting snow caused quite a flood in low-lying areas.

Wherever Chokgyur Lingpa traveled, he was accompanied by many learned and accomplished masters. His splendorous dignity and sphere of influence were comparable to those of the great Karmapa—so that even spiritual masters served as his attendants. One such was Karpo Sabchu, a yogi adept in Naropa's Six Doctrines and especially accomplished in the feat of swift walking. It was said that he could cover the distance from Kham to Lhasa—ordinarily a two-month journey—in a day, bringing back fresh vegetables.

Once, when she was still a girl, my grandmother was sitting outside the great tertön's tent with her mother, Lady Degah.[45] In the distance, they saw a man approaching on horseback. As he rode closer, they recognized him to be a Northerner, a balding old nomad with braided hair and glaring eyes, wearing an unusually short goatskin coat. His mount was an albino with bloodshot eyes. Such horses are rare and known to have bad eyesight in the snow.

Usually a visitor would, out of respect, dismount quite a distance from the central tent; but this man surprised my grandmother by riding straight up to Chokgyur Lingpa's tent, dismounting and going inside without looking right or left.

Lady Degah said, "Did you see that brazen Northerner heading straight for the tertön's tent? He was just about to ride right into it."

"He was staring straight ahead without the slightest glance right or left," commented my grandmother. "Doesn't he know he's supposed to see the *drönyer* first?" The drönyer is an attendant in charge of receiving guests.

As Chokgyur Lingpa was always in the company of his close disciples, the two women had no cause to worry about his safety and thought nothing more of the strange visitor. They went about their business.

Inside the tent, the great tertön was seated upon a makeshift throne of stone and wood collected from around the camp.[46] The visitor plopped himself down right in front of the tertön and just sat there without saying a word.

The servant Karpo Sabchu felt no suspicion and served him tea, thinking to himself, "These Northerners have no sense of etiquette, as we well know. Look at this brash old geezer; he's so pushy he didn't even wait to be let in."

In addition to being a yogi, Karpo Sabchu was also quite playful with people. He sat down next to the old man and rubbed his knees affectionately while remarking on how cold they were. The stranger was carrying a plain crooked stick in his belt that Karpo Sabchu tried to grab in fun, playing the fool with the old nomad.

At some point, the old man and Chokgyur Lingpa seemed to be making gestures and faces at each other. Suddenly the great tertön assumed an awesome air, raising his right hand high, quite majestically poised. The stranger let out a sharp howl and suddenly disappeared—vanishing completely into thin air. Karpo Sabchu looked outside, to reassure himself that he hadn't been hallucinating, but he discovered that the horse too had vanished without a trace.

As the day wore on, Karpo Sabchu began to feel sick to his stomach. Because Chokgyur Lingpa's close disciples knew to bring only the gravest of matters to his attention, Karpo Sabchu kept his mouth shut and quietly went to the kitchen to prepare for the meal. But before long he began to feel a gnawing pain, something like worms writhing about, eating away at his stomach. Although by now he felt extremely sick, he still didn't want anyone to tell Chokgyur Lingpa. As time went on, though, Karpo Sabchu became so ill he was certain he was going to die. Finally, he told someone to inform the great tertön.

My grandmother had heard Karpo Sabchu's cries of anguish. Soon she saw Chokgyur Lingpa and the drönyer heading for Sabchu's tent and tagged along to see what was happening. She poked her head in the door and saw Karpo Sabchu curled up on his bed, writhing in pain. She saw Chokgyur Lingpa frown, as he said, "He's sure to die. Who else would be foolish enough to touch—and even play around with—a demon? He even grabbed hold of the demon's stick and so he has lost his life force[47]. There's no doubt about it: he's not long for this world."

The others then beseeched the great master to do something, if anything could be done to save the life of the poor yogi. After some pleading, Chokgyur Lingpa finally growled, "Prepare a burnt offering outside; I'll take care of the rest."

When Chokgyur Lingpa came out of the tent, he threw some *tsampa* in the fire and blew on it, and immediately Karpo Sabchu's moans subsided. When Karpo Sabchu was well enough to get up, he slunk back to the tertön's tent. "I suddenly felt this worsening pain. It got so bad I couldn't stand on my feet. Then, just as suddenly, it went away. What on earth happened?"

"The old man who came to see me today," Chokgyur Lingpa explained, "is actually an infamous spirit with quite fierce powers. He had assumed a human form. Your days were numbered the moment you touched his walking stick. The spirit asked me, 'Aren't you the emissary of Padmasambhava? In all the snowy ranges of Tibet, there is nothing I need, no advice I seek. I am very powerful. Even so, I have one small problem: There are two other spirits who just won't leave me alone. They bother me at every opportunity. If it weren't for those two, I would be one of the greatest spirits in all Tibet. So how can I subdue them? If you will just give me some helpful instructions, I promise not to harm or bother anyone in your lineage.'

"I replied, 'Are you willing to constantly visualize the Lotus-Born guru above your head in the form of the glorious Subjugator of All Appearance and Existence, one inch in size?' I told him that if he answered yes, I would give him instructions.

"But the spirit replied, 'No, I definitely will not!'

"So, I said, 'Well, then, if that is the case, this is what the glorious Subjugator of All Appearance and Existence looks like in his full splendor!'

"But all you saw was me raising my hand. It was then that the old man gave out a yelp and disappeared without a trace. But before scaring him off, I extracted his promise never to bother my descendants, lineage holders or their followers."

※

One day, Chokgyur Lingpa was invited to the large monastery at Samye. The main courtyard was elaborately decorated with brocade and banners, and the master was requested to take his seat upon a lofty Dharma throne. People filled every inch of the courtyard, creating a multicolored array dominated by the maroon and yellow of monk's robes, just like at the famous prayer festivals in Lhasa.

This was no small event; it lasted for almost seven days and had great significance, both secular and religious. At some point, an elaborately dressed monk, wearing layers of brocade garments, approached the throne and engaged the master in conversation. As it happened, Chokgyur Lingpa's personal tea server and cook was the reincarnation of the great tertön Mingyur Dorje—which was not unusual, since his attendants were often tulkus.[48]

Mingyur Dorje saw the elaborately costumed monk talking with his master and thought, "Who is that proud old guy taking up our guru's time? He may be a dignitary—they are all so proud—but he has been here long enough and I need to serve tea." So under the pretext of serving tea to the master, he put his arm on the old monk to push him aside. The stranger, however, didn't yield; quite the contrary, he held his ground. A small scuffle broke out between the two.

Finally, after a while, the man turned and walked off. As he did so, Chokgyur Lingpa gave a command for him to be escorted through the tightly packed crowd and the man departed with great dignity into the main temple.

Not long after this incident, Mingyur Dorje felt sharp pains in his belly. They grew so acute he soon couldn't even stand up. Chokgyur Lingpa, of course, could not be approached about anything but important matters. So Mingyur Dorje just told the drönyer, "I'm not feeling well—I need to be excused. Please ask the master if he could give me his blessing."

Hearing this, Chokgyur Lingpa exclaimed, "What does he expect after trying to wrestle with Gyalpo Pehar? Doesn't he know that one shouldn't let one's shadow fall upon a powerful spirit? Not only did he cover Pehar with his shadow, but he tried to manhandle him as well—all for the sake of a cup of tea! It's a given that anyone who touches a spirit will lose his life."

So, though Mingyur Dorje was in unbearable pain, instead of being consoled, he was scolded—like Karpo Sabchu, who had fooled around with that spirit masquerading as an old Northerner—and told that he was soon going to drop dead!

The drönyer acted as a go-between for Mingyur Dorje, asking Chokgyur Lingpa if anything could be done. Chokgyur Lingpa, softening, told him to get a certain text and chant four particular lines about "undoing the web" and "untying the knots" and to accompany this with an offering at the temple to Gyalpo Pehar. They carried out his instructions—and sure enough Mingyur Dorje recovered.

My grandmother told me this story when I was a child. She added that Chokgyur Lingpa was not in the habit of bragging about seeing supernatural beings. On the contrary, he mentioned it only on rare occasions, when specifically asked. Indeed, he rarely volunteered a word about any of his exceptional powers, such as clairvoyance. There were a few rare exceptions, however, as the following story shows.

One fine day, the tertön and his following were riding up the Tölung valley on their way to Tsurphu. As my grandmother rode along behind him, she heard him tell stories of the political infighting and skirmishes that occurred between the factions of the two potential successors to the fifth Dalai Lama, Sangye Gyamtso and Lhabsang.

The two men were excellent friends, and each insisted the other should rule the country—they didn't want a struggle. So finally they agreed to settle the shift of power with a throw of the dice. Sangye Gyamtso, who was skilled in astrology, picked a favorable day for the event to take place, but the calculations showed that everything had to be settled and completed on that same day. He told Lhabsang, "If I win, you have to pack up and leave with your entire following and all your possessions. If you win, I promise to immediately do the same."

The dice were thrown and fell in Sangye Gyamtso's favor. Lhabsang went to prepare to leave, but soon he returned to say, "My wife is pregnant, and it appears she is soon to give birth."

So Lhabsang stayed on, and during that time political intrigues began to fester. As you know, the wish for political power can exert a tight grip on people's heart, one not easily relinquished. What happened next would be a long and involved tale, but the long and the short of it is that, at some point, the fledgling regent Sangye Gyamtso found himself alone on horseback trying to escape a band of Lhabsang's soldiers.

"They caught up with him right there where the road bends," said Chokgyur Lingpa, pointing at the roadside to everyone's amazement, "I'm the only one now who knows what happened, since that was one of my previous lives. In those days, important captives were not brought back home but immediately beheaded. See that row of *mani* stones? That's where my body fell. My head rolled all the way over there."

Wide-eyed and amazed at her father's clairvoyance of past lives, my grandmother rode past the site and continued on to Tsurphu.

Karmey Khenpo told my grandmother the following story: Chokgyur Lingpa decided to go to the marketplace in Lhasa. On one street, all the butchers line up their meat on tables, and all you can see is blood and guts. They hack the flesh off the carcasses and sell it right on the spot.

"Off by herself was a tall woman with a strange look in her large eyes. I thought she had a bluish hue to her face, and in her hand she wielded a large knife. With great skill, she carved off large chunks of meat that she sold to the customers who were lined up.

"What occurred next really took me by surprise. Before we knew what was happening, the tertön had not only walked up to her but bowed his head, and her large hand covered the crown of his head. This was something we had never seen before, and we wondered what he could be up to now. Not only was he asking a woman to bless him, but a butcher at that!

"'My oh my! How inauspicious!' I thought. We were flabbergasted, and it wasn't until we had headed on that I had the chance to ask the tertön who the woman was.

"'What do you mean, who is she?' the tertön asked. 'It seems no one among us is as fortunate as I, for I was the only one to be blessed by the female buddha Vajra Varahi in human form. You could so easily have received her blessing too, but not one of you even thought of asking.'

Karmey Khenpo was a very strict monk who rigorously upheld his vows, including the vow not to touch women. As he later told my grandmother. "There's no way in the world I would have asked a woman for a blessing!"

~

My great-grandmother Dechen Chödrön was known as Lady Degah. Chokgyur Lingpa's personal consort, she was the daughter of one of the twenty-one district governors of Derge. Lady Degah was also regarded as an emanation of Yeshe Tsogyal, the closest disciple of Padmasambhava.

I don't like saying this, for it may sound like I'm bragging about my family line, but there are scriptures in which the Lotus-Born predicted that Chokgyur Lingpa's three children would be emanations of the three chief bodhisattvas: Avalokiteshvara, Manjushri, and Vajrapani. The Manjushri emanation was supposed to be his son Wangchok Dorje; the Avalokiteshvara emanation his other son by a different consort, Tsewang Norbu; and the Vajrapani emanation my grandmother.

Lady Degah could be quite wrathful. On several occasions, she set her will against the great tertön—not too seriously, but she was sometimes stubborn enough to start a squabble. She was strong-headed and liked to have a drink now and then, which didn't bother Chokgyur Lingpa. But he didn't appreciate her drinking from a *garuda* claw that he had discovered when revealing a terma. One day, he said, "I didn't go to the trouble of recovering this rare garuda claw for you to use as a shot glass! I won't stand for you pouring liquor into it—it's only for sacred substances!"

12. Yeshe Tsogyal— the great dakini of the Lotus-Born

Lady Degah retorted, "Whether it's made from a garuda's claw or a yak's horn, it holds a drink really well! And that's what I'm going to use it for!" And she immediately poured herself a drink.

Chokgyur Lingpa fired back, "How easy do you think it is to come by the claw of a real garuda? Such a bird lives only on the summit of the fabulous Mount Sumeru. Padmasambhava concealed it in a terma for the benefit of this time. Its real purpose is to help cure epidemics caused by naga spirits. But day and night, you with your brazen attitude use it for nothing better than having a drink."

Someone later said that it was Lady Degah's obstinacy that caused their second child, my grandmother, to be born a girl. But I still feel that my grandmother's life—whether she had been a boy or a girl—fulfilled the Lotus-Born master's prophecy that she would be an emanation of Vajrapani. It was thanks to her having four sons, who performed immense service for the continuation of Chokgyur Lingpa's terma teachings, that they are so widespread today. This stems from her being an emanation of a bodhisattva.

Truly remarkable!

Karmey Khenpo told Könchok Paldrön this story as well:

"During one journey, Chokgyur Lingpa was passing through an area that lies on the road between Lhasa and Kham that was well known as a favorite spot for bandits and thieves to prey on travelers and pilgrims. At this point, the road forks off to the Amdo region, leading into another area full of bandits.

"The leaders of the gangs from each region held a meeting, and for a good reason. 'We have received news that a large caravan of seven or eight hundred Khampas are coming our way. Some of them are rich and have many pack animals. We must combine our forces and strip them of all their valuables,' proposed one of them.

"As a result, we saw a gang of bandits following us, but they never came closer. Each day, a dozen or so would appear on a hilltop to keep an eye on us; we felt like goats being stalked by a leopard. Chokgyur Lingpa was kept abreast of developments with regular reports.

"Among his revealed treasures, Chokgyur Lingpa had a particular practice—from his past life as the chief disciple of Sangye Yeshe of Nub—that was a certain way of calling upon the Dharma protectors. So Chokgyur Lingpa summoned me to his tent and said, 'Take up your pen; we need to teach those bandits a lesson once and for all! Write down what I say.' Chokgyur Lingpa then dictated the full practice that he had learned in his previous life from Sangye Yeshe. It contained lines on how the great Nubchen master commanded the guardians of the Dharma, including instructions on how to blow their bone trumpets in a particular way. When I had finished writing the practice down. Chokgyur Lingpa asked us to perform this ritual together with a torma offering.

"That night, the bandits made their move, but they found the camp encircled by a pack of ravenous wolves! The roles of predator and prey were suddenly reversed, and they found themselves fleeing the gaping jaws. The story spread far and wide that two or three bandits weren't fast enough and were torn apart.

"But some bandits were still around and decided to try again the following night. That night we performed this ritual again and we had barely completed it, in fact the bone trumpets had only sounded a couple times, before the bandits began closing in on the camp. One of the bandits yelled, 'You see, there's nothing to be afraid of!'

"Then, all of a sudden the bandits saw Chokgyur Lingpa's trident catch fire, and his tent burst into flames. To their amazement, the flames grew and spread until the entire camp was engulfed in a raging sea of fire.

"Not a single bandit dared walk into the inferno. Instead, they sat down and waited. They later claimed that the fire continued blazing the entire night. Most of the bandits lay down to sleep and, to their surprise, when they woke up in the morning they saw that the camp was totally intact with people milling about, packing up.

"The bandit leader told his second-in-command, 'These Khampa lamas are more than we can handle! Put out the word to let them go back where they came from—the sooner the better!' Word proceeded the caravan and so they never encountered another bandit the rest of the way to Lhasa.

"While we were in Lhasa," Karmey Khenpo added, "news of what the bandits had experienced began to arrive—how some were eaten by wolves and others consumed by flames. With that, the bandits' faith grew, and, one by one, they came to receive Chokgyur Lingpa's blessing."

༄

Terma predictions had described how Chokgyur Lingpa's remains should be enshrined in a golden stupa upon his death and Old Khyentse personally came to supervise the enshrinement. The stupa had been gilded in gold that the great tertön had revealed from his termas. It was a very large stupa; I remember it to be unusually high, approximately three stories in fact. Chokgyur Lingpa's body was placed inside as the main relic.

6

Two Sublime Masters

Khyentse

Let me tell you about two outstanding masters whose role in the *New Treasures* is inextricably interwoven with that of my great-grandfather, Chokgyur Lingpa. Their connection goes back a thousand years to the time when Buddhism reached Tibet. When the magnificent Samye, Tibet's first major monastery, was under construction, great masters were invited from India: Padmasambhava, Vimalamitra, Buddhaguhya, and others. Their chief Tibetan disciples included the translators Vairotsana and Yudra Nyingpo. All these masters, disciples, and translators helped the teachings of the Buddha to flourish like the rising sun.

During the time of Khyentse, Kongtrul, and Chokgyur Lingpa, those twenty-five foremost disciples of the Lotus-Born who had gathered around him at Samye almost a thousand years earlier all returned in simultaneous incarnations. As one of my teachers, Dzongsar Khyentse, put it, "The twenty-five disciples of the Lotus-Born came back together like a throng of sheep and goats running out of a barn. These disciples reappeared as masters with incredible experience and realization, learning, and accomplishment. Their personal disciples and their disciples' disciples were equally amazing."

In fact, throughout Kham and the rest of Tibet, tulkus of all twenty-five were identified and recognized. Paradoxically, this flowering was a portent that the time for Tibet's role as a field of influence to benefit beings was just about to run out.

There had been a prediction from Padmasambhava pertaining to two of these masters: "You possess the karmic link of father and son." The father was the great Khyentse and the son was Chokgyur Lingpa. The prediction also said, "Their minds will mingle into oneness"—meaning they would be identical in their level of experience and realization—"like the torrential rivers of summer." That image referred to their meeting, exchanging pith instructions and awakening their karmic potential.

The great Kongtrul was enthroned by Khyentse and Chokling as the authentic incarnation, or conscious rebirth, of the Tibetan translator Vairotsana. When you compare these three masters—Chokgyur, Khyentse, and Kongtrul—Chokgyur Lingpa regarded both the great Khyentse and Kongtrul as his teachers. But Khyentse received the entire New Treasures transmission from Chokgyur Lingpa, so in this regard Chokgyur Lingpa is one of his teachers. The great Kongtrul definitely accepted Khyentse as his master—there is no question about that—as he did Chokgyur Lingpa. So, in fact, all three were one another's teachers and disciples. They were connected to each other as "mingled minds." In this way, the three masters assisted each other. Their mutual benefit for the Buddha's teachings and all beings was like that of the sun of Dharma once again rising in the sky.

❦

Early in his life, Chokgyur Lingpa made the journey to the kingdom of Derge. There he met with Kongtrul, who showed great fondness for the young tertön and for his terma writings. One of Kongtrul's letters mentions this: "When you see the terma teachings of this man who doesn't even know his grammar, it is most amazing! It's really strange that such wonderful writing can come through a man who cannot even spell!"

In those days, one needed a letter of introduction in order to gain an audience with a lama of high standing, so Chokgyur Lingpa requested such a letter, saying, "I want to go see Jamyang Khyentse Wangpo; please give me a petition letter." The great Khyentse was then known by the name Venerable Shabdrung; a *shabdrung* corresponds in level to the *vajra master* in charge of tantric ceremonies, a religious rank two steps below the highest hierarch of the Sakya school.

So Kongtrul replied, "Of course I'll write a letter introducing you to Venerable Shabdrung!" With the letter in hand, Chokgyur Lingpa then proceeded to Khyentse's residence.

Prior to this, Khyentse had written down a mind treasure containing the complete teachings of the famous terma *Tukdrub Barchey Kunsel*. Now, Chokgyur Lingpa arrived, also bringing a version of the *Tukdrub*, which had been revealed to him at the sacred place of Khala Rong-go. He had kept it secret for eight years.

Chokgyur Lingpa explained to Khyentse the story of his revelation, including the time and place of its discovery and the nature of the terma teaching. While comparing the two versions of the terma, they found them to be totally identical, without even one word of difference. After a careful examination of the two,

Khyentse burned his own, saying, "Since the words and the meaning are identical, what is the use of having two! Yours, being an earth terma," a physical object the tertön discovers, "is more profound and will be more effectual than my mind terma," one that unfolds in the tertön's mind.

Thus, the blessings of two lineages, earth terma and mind terma, were fused into a single stream. This remarkable coincidence was a major reason for the profound trust they had in each other as authentic tertöns. After their first meeting, they both had many auspicious dreams and visions. The great Khyentse accepted Chokgyur Lingpa as his disciple, conferring several important empowerments upon him.

Chokgyur Lingpa then returned to see Kongtrul at his residence, located at the famous Tsari-like Jewel Rock, on the slope above the Palpung monastery in Kham. Kongtrul had fallen seriously ill and was unable to see. Chokgyur Lingpa gave him the empowerment for the deity Vajrapani from his terma treasure called *Vajra Club of the Lord of Secrets* and told him to do some recitations of the mantra. That was their first Dharma connection.

Chokgyur Lingpa insisted, "You must do this practice—nothing else will help you regain your eyesight!" After Kongtrul had completed a retreat reciting the mantra of this tantric deity, he fully recovered from his disease.

When Kongtrul recounted the story of his recovery, Chokgyur Lingpa responded, "Of course you recovered. In your past life as the great translator Vairotsana, you put a curse on the infamous Lady Margyenma, that troublemaking queen of King Trisong Deutsen.[49] Now you had to suffer the ripening of that karmic deed. In keeping with the severity of your former action, the karmic ripening corresponded to the seriousness of the disease with which your retinas were afflicted. This disease was influenced by the naga spirits. Accordingly, Padmasambhava designed this special sadhana of Vajrapani to cure you. That's why I gave you that particular empowerment."

From then on, Kongtrul and Chokgyur Lingpa gained even stronger confidence in each other, further fortified by several auspicious dreams and visions.

Khyentse, Kongtrul and Chokgyur Lingpa went on several journeys together, during which they discovered many terma teachings. The most famous of these was the *Light of Wisdom*, which later played an important role in my own education.[50]

~

Khyentse was born in the kingdom of Derge in Kham. The name Derge means "virtue and happiness." This area was traditionally saturated by the practice of

Buddhism, a virtuous and perfect place for the Dharma ruled by kings in accordance with spiritual principles. Over the centuries, these kings had promoted the most favorable conditions for the Buddha's teachings. For example, they saw to the carving of woodblocks for printing the entire vast Buddhist canon—consisting of the many hundred volumes of the translated words of the Buddha, the *Kangyur*, and the translated treatises, the *Tengyur*—a task that had until then proved insurmountable even for the government in Central Tibet.

Here's how that enormous task began. One day, while King Tenpa Tsering of Derge was walking to his bathroom, the thought suddenly arose in his mind, "Maybe I could get woodblocks carved for the entire body of the Buddha's teachings."

Later, when the king was visiting with his guru Situ Chökyi Jungney, he felt he should bring up his new idea. So he said, "Today I had a thought."

"What was that?" the master asked.

"I formed the wish to carve blocks for both the *Kangyur* and *Tengyur*. What do you think? Will it be successful?"

Situ Chökyi Jungney replied, "Don't ever give up this thought!"

"Very well," the king agreed, "If I arrange for the carving, can you do the proofreading?"

"I will take care of the proofing," the great Situ promised.

No more conversation than that took place. Eventually, the king did have the entire Buddhist canon carved and printed. Situ, who was renowned as a great scholar, proofread the woodblocks thirteen times—a gigantic task in itself. This is why even today we regard the Derge edition of the canon as being of the highest standard.

It was in such a spiritual environment that the great Khyentse took birth.

13. Longchenpa—the great Dzogchen master

Old Khyentse was the combined reincarnation of Vimalamitra, King Trisong Deutsen, Longchenpa and the omniscient master Jigmey Lingpa—all in one body. Like Chokgyur Lingpa, he was renowned as the lord of seven transmissions. Yet Khyentse didn't start out as the head of a large monastery, but as an ordinary monk at a Sakya monastery in Derge.[51]

In the early part of his life, Khyentse went to Central Tibet, where he received a vast number of teachings from numerous masters. Slowly his talents led him to become a teacher, then vajra master, then shabdrung and finally abbot. During his second visit to Central Tibet, he transmitted most of these teachings back to others. And so people said, "Before he was a disciple; now he is a master!"

At one point, Khyentse had a deep spiritual experience involving a vision of the great master Chetsun Senge Wangchuk, after which he put in writing the precious teaching known as the *Heart Essence of Chetsun.* At the main Sakya monastery in Central Tibet, he did a retreat on Manjushri and had the experience of dissolving into the heart of his yidam so the "great treasure mine of courageous eloquence" overflowed from within his state of realization. Thus, he became like a king of all learned and accomplished masters.

Old Khyentse later built a hermitage, which he gave the splendid name Gathering Palace of Sugatas. He lived there in the latter part of his life.

༄

Old Khyentse had developed unimpeded clairvoyance. Tashi Özer, the great scholar of Palpung monastery, was one of his main disciples, and he told one of my teachers many stories about the great Khyentse. Here is one of them:

"One day," Tashi Özer recounted, "Khyentse exclaimed to me, 'Oh, my, Khenpo, what trouble you have! From morning until night, you have to do all these tasks.' He started mentioning all the different things I had to do. He knew everything, every little detail—including things no one else but me could have known about. 'You are really burdened by all these demands; you have no free time at all.' It was true, I was busy from morning till evening.

"Another day, Khyentse Wangpo, as he was known at the time, suddenly cried out, 'Oh, no, how terrible!' I asked him what was wrong. 'Far away a bald monk just fell over the side of the cliff. While he was falling, I heard him shout my name. Then, while I was thinking about this, somehow he became stuck in the branches of a tree. Now the other monks are trying to pull him up with ropes. Yes … now they got him up.'

"The next morning, a bald-headed monk came to visit Khyentse. 'Last night I had a strange accident,' he said. He went on to explain that as he was walking with a stick and a load, he fell over the side of the cliff, at which point he shouted out, 'Khyentse Wangpo! Khyentse Wangpo!' He didn't fall all the way down but became caught in some branches and was then pulled up with a rope.

"One night, I wanted to see for myself how Old Khyentse slept. So I hung around outside his door and took an occasional peek throughout the night. Khyentse did not seem to go to sleep at all. But late at night he loosened his belt, relaxed in his seat and exhaled. Then he just sat there with wide-open eyes, still breathing deeply. He might have been asleep or not, but he didn't move for an hour, still with open eyes. Then he cleared his throat loudly and his breathing went back to normal. The sound was enough to signal his attendant to prepare morning tea. That was how Old Khyentse passed his nights."

※

Near where the great Khyentse lived was a Sakya monastery, and it happened that one of their lamas passed away. The monks of the monastery trusted that Khyentse truly could see past, present and future as clearly as something placed in the palm of his hand—without a flicker of error or confusion. He was consulted about the lama's rebirth.

The monks kept insisting, "We must find him! By all means, we must find his tulku!"

"You might as well forget about it," replied Khyentse. "I promise you it won't help you to know."

"We will never give up our search for him!" retorted the monastery's representative, who wasn't one to take no for an answer. "Our teacher was so precious; please give us some unmistakable details regarding his whereabouts."

"All right!" said Khyentse. "Go to such-and-such place near Derge, where there is a rich family with plenty of cattle. Stand near their house and call out your lama's name at the top of your voice. It will be clear to you where your 'tulku' is."

The party went off in the prescribed direction and reached the rich man's property. There they began calling their lama's name as loud as they could. As they were yelling, the calf of a huge cross-bred yak and cow let go of its mother's teat, bellowed "Moooooooo!" and ran toward them. It walked around them and wouldn't leave. The monks were at a loss as to what to do. On their return, they stopped to see the great Khyentse once again.

"What did I tell you? Didn't I say it would be useless? Nonetheless, you did find your 'tulku.'"

※

Old Khyentse had the habit of asking every visitor one particular question. I know this from old people in Nangchen, because everyone there without exception who could afford the time to make the pilgrimage over to Derge had been to visit him and pay their respects. My mother's uncle, a lama who was quite old when I was a child, told me this story about one such visit he had.

"Well, well, where are you from?" Khyentse would first say. Then, "why are you here?"

"I came to meet you, Rinpoche," replied this old lama.

"There is nothing special in meeting me," said Khyentse. "Have you seen the Jowo in Lhasa?"

"No, I haven't," replied the old lama.

"What a pity! What a waste of a human life. Well, then, have you received the reading transmission for the *Kangyur*?"

"No, I haven't, Rinpoche!"

"Oh, no! What a terrible shame! In this day and age, the Buddha is represented by the Jowo statue and the *Kangyur*. That's what he has left behind. If one dies without meeting those two, I would consider it just as if one had returned from a jewel island empty-handed. If a big sinner, even someone who has killed eighteen people, receives the reading transmission for the Buddha's *Kangyur*, this old man here swears that such a person will not go to the lower realms."

Khyentse said that to almost every person who came to visit him.

⁂

Once, in the later part of his life, Khyentse was served poison mixed in curd by a malicious old man from eastern Tibet. He accepted the bowl and drank it on the spot. As the man was leaving, Khyentse called out to him, "Hey, you! Are you satisfied now that I've swallowed your evil drink?"

The old man panicked and began to cry with great remorse.

"Please vomit it out immediately!" the old man wailed. "I don't know what vicious spirit took hold of me, but all of a sudden I had this thought to poison your food and didn't seem able to resist. The moment you drank the bowl, it was as though I woke up from a dream. Please, purge yourself of this poison!"

"No," Khyentse said. "I have repaid a karmic debt to you, so I won't vomit—there is not enough to kill me. I drank it to help you."

Earlier in his life, Khyentse had been very handsome and stout. People said he looked like Longchenpa. But soon after being poisoned, he fell ill and never totally recovered; his skin turned slightly dark. The toxin had also injured his throat, and every so often he would have to clear his throat with a loud hacking noise, even during teachings. "It is from being poisoned, but it didn't kill me," he would explain to the curious.

⁂

Grandmother, who had met the two masters as a child, once told me, "The great Kongtrul was neither tall nor fat, but he did have a prominent nose, very straight and square. Old Khyentse, on the other hand, was very large, with big eyes."

My father later added, "After Chokgyur Lingpa and his son Wangchok Dorje had both passed away, I too went with Lady Degah, my mother and some siblings to visit Old Khyentse. When we approached his quarters, we discovered that the great master had come outside holding the traditional incense and white scarf to receive Lady Degah—an unusual sign of deep respect. Led by Old Khyentse bearing incense, we were escorted inside his rather tiny room. Samten Gyatso and your uncle Tersey were both there as well. I remember Khyentse as having a bigger-than-life, majestic presence in that small room."

My father continued, "Khyentse was conducting an empowerment for my grandmother. Next to him was a little portable hearth, with a big kettle perking away on top. There was a Khampa-style bellows made of hide, and every once in a while during the empowerment Khyentse would reach over and fan the fire. He had a large bowl, and during the empowerment he put a couple of spoonfuls of tsampa—parched barley flour—and dried cheese into his bowl. Then he poured some hot tea on top and, using his large bone spoon, had a meal right there and then. He didn't drink butter tea, just black tea." As you may know, it is the tradition in Tibet that while a lama drinks tea during a ceremony, he always takes off his hat—but Old Khyentse was a yogi and left his hat on while he ate.

"He was such an imposing figure in that small room," my father added. "The fire was making it quite warm, and I sat near the hearth. He just went about his business and looked very comfortable eating and drinking at his leisure."

❧

Khyentse was a great *siddha*, incredibly realized. Yet probably because he held the position of "king of Dharma," ruling over a vast domain of spiritual activity, he did not manifest a rainbow body upon his departure.[52]

Instead, here is how he passed away.

All his life, Old Khyentse never sat idle; at the very least he would usually have a rosary in his left hand, chanting various mantras. One day, he told his servant, "One's final words should be like those of Terdag Lingpa, the great master of Mindrolling."

"And what were they?" his attendant asked.

> Sights, sounds, knowing—deva, mantra, dharmakaya—
> Play of kayas, wisdoms, boundlessly they merge.
> In this deep and secret practice of great yoga,
> Be they of one taste, nondual sphere of mind!

While chanting the last line, Old Khyentse rolled up his rosary, put it in its proper place, straightened his back and stopped breathing.

❧

Kongtrul often said of his friend Old Khyentse, "Jamyang Khyentse Wangpo is the only one who can truly distinguish between what is Dharma and what is not." Kongtrul would turn to him for advice in all matters of importance, calling him "the ultimate pandita". In this sense, the most important of the three amazing masters—Khyentse, Kongtrul, and Chokgyur Lingpa—was Khyentse.

So when Khyentse passed away, Kongtrul exclaimed, "The omniscient Dorje Ziji has left us!" using another name for Khyentse. "Now we are left behind in pitch-black darkness, not knowing right from wrong!" Khyentse had made it clear that he didn't want anyone to preserve his body after he died. He had explained, "Don't keep my body around. I want it cremated, because in this degenerate age, one should no longer keep an entire body as *kudung* (sacred remains). Of course, in earlier times it was the custom to do so with some masters. But from now on, I think all lamas should be cremated."

With Chokgyur Lingpa, who had died before Old Khyentse, he had made an exception. The reason was that Padmasambhava's terma predictions had described how Chokgyur Lingpa's remains should be embalmed and enshrined in a golden stupa, which was done exactly as indicated.

However, Khyentse and Kongtrul were both cremated, as were Karmey Khenpo, Tashi Özer, the great Mipham and all the other great lamas of the day in Kham. I believe this change was an early indication that everything was soon to be destroyed by the Chinese communists. But Khyentse didn't mention that. He just said to never keep a kudung.

14. Vairotsana—the great translator of Buddhist scriptures

Kongtrul

Kongtrul is considered a reincarnation of Vairotsana, the eminent translator of the Buddha's teachings when the Lotus-Born master came to Tibet.[53] Vairotsana, in turn, was regarded as an emanation of Buddha Vairochana.

Kongtrul had the ability to reveal a vast number of terma treasures; he once found a prophecy by Padmasambhava predicting that he, Kongtrul, was to compose five great treasuries of teachings. In his view, the older termas had great value, and he wished to gather them all into a collection to be called the *Treasury of Precious Termas,* covering the three inner tantras: Maha, Anu, and Ati Yoga.[54]

So Kongtrul sent a message to Chokgyur Lingpa: "You often meet the Lotus-Born in person. Could you please ask him if I may compile the *Treasury of Precious Termas?*"

Chokgyur Lingpa soon sent back this reply: "I asked Padmasambhava. He said, 'Excellent!' Since that is the case, you must definitely undertake this task."

While Kongtrul was in the process of collecting these treasure texts, the lineage for many of the termas of former tertöns had disappeared, some of them centuries before. Khyentse revived them as 'rediscovered treasures' and in this way supplied the important missing parts for the *Treasury of Precious Termas,* while Chokgyur Lingpa was the one who asked the Lotus-Born master for permission. Thus, the incredibly important collection now renowned as the *Treasury of Precious Termas* was a combined effort of all three masters.[55]

Old Kongtrul's reincarnation, Karsey Kongtrul, the famous son of the fifteenth Karmapa who was also one of my teachers, was in charge of the library at Tsari-like Jewel Rock. He still had this exchange of letters in which Kongtrul requested Chokgyur Lingpa to ask Padmasambhava about the *Treasury.* Once, while Karsey Kongtrul transmitted this very same *Treasury of Precious Termas,* he told me the above story in the presence of the sixteenth Karmapa.

⁂

15. Mipham—the famous scholar

In terms of scholarship, Kongtrul was nearly unsurpassed, as a story about him and the learned Mipham shows. After Mipham had composed his *Summary of Logic,* a sophisticated and complex philosophical volume, he brought it to Kongtrul to get his opinion.

"It looks like a work of outstanding precision and clarity," remarked Kongtrul. "But honestly, I'm not the one to judge. I don't know much about Buddhist logic, since I never studied the subject. You are an expert in the art of validating knowledge; I'm sure it's very good."

Mipham wouldn't accept Kongtrul's modesty. So he made the request, "Please, Rinpoche, give me the reading transmission for it."

"How could I possibly do that?" replied Kongtrul. "You're the author. If I had written it, I could give the transmission. But you should read it to me instead."

So, obediently, Mipham read the text aloud. At the end, Kongtrul suddenly exclaimed, "Ha, ha! Let me try to explain it."

"Please do, Rinpoche," Mipham replied. "You may not have studied many words of logic, but you certainly know the meaning."

"No, no," Kongtrul insisted. "I am not well versed in either the words or the meaning. But today is a fine day and I'm in a good mood. Let me try explaining it."

When he had finished his explanation, Mipham was astounded. "Rinpoche, how could you give such a brilliant clarification without having studied logic?" Mipham asked.

Kongtrul explained, "Well, it's not exactly the case that I didn't study logic *ever*, since in a former life as Sakya Pandita I studied it extensively. In fact, it all came flooding back to me while you were reading. I don't usually have that ability, so I wanted to explain it to you while the glimpse lasted."

After this encounter, Mipham saw Kongtrul in a completely new light, and his admiration and trust in him grew. As Mipham explained, "Our intellectual understanding is completely different. That man's learning extends back through many lifetimes, completely unlike ordinary scholars who study a few books here and there in this life."

~

After the scholar Tashi Özer had studied with the renowned Paltrul, he remarked, "How can there be another lama of that kind on the surface of the earth? He is tremendously learned and accomplished!" Later, having studied with Khyentse, he said, "No one can possibly be more extraordinary!" Lastly, when he had studied with Kongtrul, he said, "Fantastic; this man is incomparable!"

One day, he had the chance to ask Khyentse, "Rinpoche, I'm a student of all three of you lamas, and I don't perceive anything other than great qualities in each of you. But tell me: If you were to compete, who would be the most learned?"

"Paltrul for sure is the most learned," Khyentse replied.

"Of the three of you, who benefits beings the most?"

Khyentse replied, "As the translator Vairotsana in human form, there is nobody who benefits beings like Kongtrul."

Again the scholar asked, "But among you three who has the highest realization?"

Khyentse raised his shoulders and head high and, without any hypocrisy or the least hint of smugness, declared, "Hey! The one with the highest realization? That's me! I'm the best."

～

When Old Khyentse passed away, the fifteenth Karmapa saw in a vision that instead of just a single reincarnation, twenty-five emanations would appear, each embodying one of the twenty-five aspects of fruition: five each for enlightened body, speech, mind, qualities, and activity. Among these, five principal incarnations were recognized and enthroned. That's why we see so many reincarnations these days with the name Khyentse.

It is said that the activity of these amazing Khyentse incarnations is unceasing, like the moon rising when the sun sets: when one passes away, another appears in his place. When he died, several tulkus appeared to take over his Dharma activities. Seen from our side, while one of them dissolves back into the buddhafield, another emanation appears, sometimes even more brilliant than the previous one. After the great Khyentse died, Dzongsar Khyentse appeared, who was equally amazing. Then when Dzongsar Khyentse set, Dilgo Khyentse rose.

Khakyab Dorje had a similar vision that after Kongtrul passed away there would be twenty-five reincarnations as well. The number of such tulkus—"magical forms" that appear to benefit beings—is inconceivable.

I don't know much more than this about Kongtrul and Khyentse. You can find the details of their lives in their respective biographies.[56] I haven't made up any of these stories myself; I've only repeated the words I have heard from my precious teachers.

7

Lord of Activity,
the Fifteenth Karmapa

After Khyentse and Kongtrul, no one performed a greater service for the propagation of Chokgyur Lingpa's *New Treasures* than Khakyab Dorje, the fifteenth Karmapa.

Before passing on, the Karmapas traditionally write a letter describing where their next incarnation will be born. And so it was that Khakyab Dorje was found as a young child in the Tsang province of Central Tibet by a search party of lamas who used as their guide a letter written by the previous Karmapa. Chokgyur Lingpa further confirmed his identity in an independent prediction that pointed to the same child.

From an early age, Khakyab Dorje was remarkable. While still quite young, he was asked to consecrate a monastery near his family home. "I'll do it on the first day of the twelfth month," he replied.

By that time, he was residing in Tsurphu, quite a long distance from the monastery he had been asked to consecrate. But instead of traveling there, on the morning of the chosen day he just asked for a covered basin. His attendants thought he was playing when he told them, "Today I am consecrating a monastery far away!"

They played along with him when he insisted that two attendants carry the basin around Tsurphu. The young Karmapa walked along throwing grains into the basin. Later, some people who lived near the distant monastery made the journey to Tsurphu and said that grain had fallen from the sky on that very day, just like a light rain.

~

As he grew up, Khakyab Dorje came to possess profound scholarship, but he also performed many miracles. He was a tertön who had access to both earth and mind treasures.

Sometimes terma objects just suddenly appeared in the Karmapa's hands, very hot and sometimes moving of their own accord. This happened once while he was on a visit to the Amnye region. He received a terma from a local spirit and it was still quite hot while he held it—so hot that when he put it on the table, other people couldn't touch it without being burned. All these terma objects were still kept at Tsurphu when I was there.

Instead of having to go out somewhere, like a cave, to find the terma, the Karmapa had many terma objects brought to him by the spirits who were keepers of the termas. The Dharma protectors would place terma caskets on the table right in front of him at Tsurphu.

I saw one such terma object that was kept in his sacred treasury box: an image of the Lotus-Born master, highly unusual in that half the body was bronze and the other half pure crystal. I have never seen another like it. I also saw many sacred *kilaya* daggers and other Padmasambhava statues and was told when and from whom he had obtained them. One kilaya dagger was of meteoric iron with a crystal top, also extraordinary. There were many such exquisite treasures, like nothing I have ever seen anywhere else.

Sometimes in his field of vision the Karmapa would suddenly see terma boxes appear, floating toward him in space. Occasionally these floating boxes were even seen by others. This happened once while the Karmapa was on pilgrimage to Yarlung, a few days from Tsurphu. As he was riding, terma boxes began to swirl around him in midair. Several of the servants saw them.

"Today there was a vicious attack of evil spirits," one of the servants later commented.

"I'm not sure how *vicious* it was," the Karmapa replied.

*

Because the Karmapa is an emanation of buddha activity, when a tertön connects with him, that in itself increases the propagation of the terma teachings. A look through the history of tertöns reveals again and again that if one of the Karmapas shows respect for a tertön, then the Karmapa's influence and blessings will make everyone accept the tertön and his teachings without doubt or dispute. This is why major tertöns need to link up with the Karmapa; otherwise, the tertön is at risk of being called crazy or a charlatan.

But although the Karmapa discovered many termas, he himself never seemed to write down the many texts connected to them. The Karmapa once explained, "With the abundance of revelations from Khyentse, Kongtrul and Chokling, there is no need for me to add any new termas."

At Tsurphu, in the inner chambers, there were forty boxes containing amazing representations of enlightened body, speech and mind given to him by the guardians of various termas. When showing these spiritual treasures to my uncle Samten Gyatso, the Karmapa once again emphasized, "There were teachings to write down, but I didn't—there is no way I need to compete with the three great tertöns. I find their termas neither incomplete nor in need of correction."

※

Samten Gyatso told me, "Khakyab Dorje was an inconceivably great master. I felt sure that he could perceive the three times as clearly as something placed in the palm of his hand." This remarkable clairvoyance made it possible for the Karmapa to identify close to one thousand tulkus during his lifetime.

Since Samten Gyatso and Khakyab Dorje were very close, my uncle had no qualms about asking even very personal questions. Once he asked the Karmapa how he knew where tulkus would be reborn. Although he had unimpeded clairvoyance, the Karmapa explained that he did not always have complete control over it. On the one hand, sometimes he would know when a lama was going to die and where he would be reborn without anyone first requesting this information. Then, when the disciples responsible for finding the tulku would come to inquire about the lama, he would already have written down the details of the tulku's death and rebirth.

In other cases, he could only see the circumstances of rebirth when a special request was made and certain auspicious circumstances were created through any of a number of practices. And in a few cases, he couldn't see anything, even when people requested his help. He would try, but the crucial facts would be "shrouded in mist." This, he said, was a sign of some problem between the dead lama and his disciples. For instance, if there had been fighting and disharmony among the lama's following, the whereabouts of his next incarnation would be vague and shrouded in haze.

"The worst obstacle for clearly recognizing tulkus," he explained, "is disharmony between the guru and his disciples. In such cases, nothing can be done, and the circumstances of the next rebirth remain unforeseeable."

※

The Karmapa was supposed to be a major tertön, so there was good reason for him to take a consort, which is necessary to "unlock the treasure chest" of the termas.[57] However, the Karmapas were usually monks, and so taking a consort was not readily accepted; in fact it was considered highly inappropriate. His reluctance to reveal termas or take a consort caused him to become seriously ill. Some say this was a punishment meted out by the dakinis to potential tertöns who fail to fulfill their mission.

Whatever the case, in the end, many great masters persuaded him to take a consort; if he didn't, they pleaded, he would die prematurely. His first consort was the eldest daughter of a noble family from Central Tibet. As predicted by Padmasambhava, she was to be his consort for revealing termas. Afterward, he also married his consort's younger sister.

Later still, when the Karmapa again fell ill, a prediction by the Lotus-Born appeared in a terma revealed by a tertön from Surmang.[58] It stated that if the Karmapa accepted a particular young woman, who was a dakini in human form, his life would be extended by three years.

The Karmapa sent out a search party, who identified her and invited her back to Tsurphu. She became known as Khandro Chenmo, which means "the great dakini."[59] He took her as his consort, and she did indeed seem to extend his life for three years. Any time the Karmapa fell ill, she was invited to visit him, and within a couple of days he would recover. This went on for three full years. The value of extending the life of the Karmapa is immeasurable.

Khandro Chenmo was very beautiful and she became a remarkable practitioner. She was loving and compassionate, full of devotion, and with an unfathomable spiritual depth. I knew her quite well in the last years of her life. We first met in Tsurphu when I was twenty-six, then again three years later and then later still in Rumtek, where she finally departed for the invisible realms two years after fleeing Tibet. She was a very special being, a true dakini. She spent almost all her time in retreat practicing sadhana and reciting mantra, and reached a profound level of experience and realization. This is not hearsay; I can bear witness to it myself.

16.
The Great Dakini
of Tsurphu

Samten Gyatso had immense respect for her and once told me, "When I went to visit the Karmapa, she was often there. It felt like meeting the female buddha Tara in person. She is Noble Tara among us in a human body, an authentic dakini." She, in her turn, was very fond of my uncle and each year would send a present to him in Kham.

Khandro Chenmo was treated with immense respect, as though she were a great lama. Word would spread wherever she went and thousands of people would go to meet her. She traveled to Bhutan at the invitation of the royal family and when she came to visit Dzongsar

Khyentse in Gangtok, he personally came out to greet her. At special ceremonies she was usually placed on a throne as high as Khyentse and Kongtrul. But she never made a big deal out of herself.

~

The great scholar Tashi Özer was Kongtrul's attendant for a time, and he told me about the Karmapa's last meeting with his teacher Kongtrul. The meeting took place at Kongtrul's retreat place above Palpung.[60]

"I have come here to pay my respects upon my departure," the Karmapa said.

"Well, well. If *you* are leaving, I may come and live for a while in your house," replied Kongtrul. The Karmapa thought Kongtrul might be implying that he would come back as the Karmapa's child, though he didn't say anything.

As I mentioned, according to tradition, a senior monk is dispatched from the monastery of a deceased lama to inquire of the Karmapa (or another highly realized master) where the tulku might be found. After Kongtrul's passing, this task fell by coincidence to Tashi Özer, who traveled all the way to Tsurphu to ask the Karmapa where Kongtrul's reincarnation was.

"Please give us some indication of where the tulku has been reborn," he requested.

Khakyab Dorje kept silent, so Tashi Özer tried again, "I'm one of his chief disciples—you must tell me! I am sure you know."

The Karmapa still said nothing, but this didn't dissuade the great scholar.

He kept insisting, until finally the Karmapa admitted, "Very well, the great Kongtrul has been reborn as my son. I cannot and do not dare send back the message that the rebirth of my root guru is my own child!"

Tashi Özer objected, "Don't you remember? I was present when our great vajra holder explicitly said he would 'come to stay at your house.' Didn't you hear that with your own ears? And isn't it true that you call Kongtrul your root guru? So tell me, are you going to go directly against his word?"

This was typical of Tashi Özer's persuasive, hard-to-refute manner. I don't know how long the argument dragged on. But in the end he succeeded in bringing the Karmapa's son back to Palpung in Kham where he was enthroned as the reincarnation of the old Kongtrul.

~

Samten Gyatso transmitted the *New Treasures* to the Karmapa or, in my uncle's words, he "presented it as a *mandala* offering,"[61] including the complete empowerments, readings, and instructions. At this point, there were several arrangements necessary—for liturgies as well as for empowerments—which, like this one, had been codified neither by Chokgyur Lingpa, his son Tsewang Drakpa, nor by Khyentse or Kongtrul.

As these arrangements were needed for extremely important and profound termas, Samten Gyatso requested the Karmapa to compose these texts. The Karmapa kindly agreed and dictated them to his close disciple, the outstanding lama Jampal Tsultrim.

While the Karmapa was giving the empowerments, everyone lodged at Lotus Garuda Fortress, the retreat center nestled on the cliff high above Tsurphu. Often they all stayed up talking until midnight, when Uncle Tersey and Samten Gyatso would go back to their own rooms.

At that time, the Karmapa had already written a letter predicting his own future reincarnation. But as his life had been extended for three years with the help of his third consort, he needed to write another.

One evening, they were engaged in conversation when Samten Gyatso suddenly asked, "In your prediction about your next incarnation, you stated that you would take rebirth in the area of Denkhog, in the Dilgo family. You were ill then, but you didn't die and have in fact recovered. However, you will die one day, so when you do, will you still be born in that same place? If not, where will you take birth?"

Uncle Tersey was sitting next to him and was quite upset by the question. He later told me, "He actually asked that! Such an inauspicious question! I got really upset, thinking, 'Why does he have to ask a question like that while the Karmapa is still alive? What is he thinking? What got into him? This is so inappropriate.'

"The Karmapa became totally quiet; the silence grew longer and longer. I thought he was angry, and why wouldn't he be? At that point, I felt really scared. We were just sitting there and the Karmapa had stopped speaking to us. He just sat there for the longest time, not saying a word.

"Finally, the Karmapa broke the silence: 'The previous coincidence of time and place has vanished. I will not be born into the Dilgo family.'"

Samten Gyatso's response to this was to simply join his palms and say, "Lasoh! I see!" Then he remained quiet, too, for a time. But then he asked once again, "Well, if that's the case, where will you be reborn?"

Uncle Tersey had tried to nudge Samten Gyatso's thigh to stop him from asking such an impertinent question once again, but it was too late. "How inauspicious to ask the Karmapa about his own death!" he thought.

But the Karmapa seemed unfazed. He answered matter-of-factly, "I will take rebirth to the east not far from there. If you know the area of Denkhog, you must also know that to the east of the Dilgo estate lies that of the influential Ado family. I will be born into that family."

Uncle Tersey just held his silence, but he kept the information in mind.

That was the kind of master the Karmapa was.

※

After Samten Gyatso left Tsurphu, the Karmapa summoned his close retinue: Jampal Tsultrim, Khenpo Lekshey and his main consort, Khandro Chenmo. He held up an envelope and told them, "One of you three should take care of this prediction letter. There will come a point when it will be indispensable. At that time, read it, but before then, just hold on to it."

"I can't take care of this. I'm too young for this responsibility," Khandro replied as she was only nineteen at the time.

Khenpo Lekshey said, "I don't dare to either."

The two of them turned to Jampal Tsultrim and said, "You keep it!"

So Jampal Tsultrim put the letter inside the reliquary box he wore around his neck and kept it there.

A year or so later the great Karmapa finally left his body. There were many ceremonies during the first forty-nine days. Jampal Tsultrim was subsequently invited to Mindrolling to give the reading transmission of the *Collected Works of Khakyab Dorje*. Afterward, he went straight to Golok, his home region far away to the northeast, for four or five months.

In the meantime, the government in Lhasa had sent a representative to Tsurphu asking to be shown the prediction letter, "According to your tradition, the Karmapa always leaves an exact description of where he will take his next rebirth. We would like to see it!"

They found the earlier prediction letter but noticed that the Karmapa had added a sentence at the bottom, "The coincidence for this has dissolved." A frantic search for another letter began.

Jampal Tsultrim was gone; Khenpo Lekshey, having entered strict retreat, was incommunicado; and Khandro Chenmo was devastated. Nobody thought to even ask her about the letter. The search team rifled through every single one of Khakyab Dorje's books. They even tore open his mattress. But, of course, they came up with nothing—Jampal Tsultrim was unsuspectingly wandering about in distant Golok with the letter in the box around his neck.

Finally, the Tsurphu officials were forced to admit that they had no letter. Soon after, the thirteenth Dalai Lama's office issued a formal statement that the Karmapa's reincarnation had been born as the son of one of the cabinet ministers in Lhasa.

This news reached all the way to Golok. Hearing it, Jampal Tsultrim cut his stay short and hurried back to Tsurphu. As soon as he arrived, he exclaimed, "What do you mean there is no prediction letter? I have it right here!" And he opened his reliquary box and showed it to the general secretary at Tsurphu.

"You enemy of the Dharma! How could you do something like this?!?" exclaimed the general secretary angrily. "You should be immediately tossed into prison!"

"Throw me into prison if you like, if it will help in any way. The letter, however, is right here in my hand. There is no mistake."

"This is a disaster! The government of Tibet has already nominated another tulku. What are we going to do?" the general secretary asked, perplexed.

A messenger was immediately sent at top speed to the great Situ of Palpung in faraway Kham. And as the Karma Kagyu and Drukpa Kagyu were enjoying very harmonious relations at the time, another messenger was sent to the Drukchen Jamgön to ask his advice. The counsel of other respected lamas was also sought.

One lama stressed the importance of being in harmony with the Tibetan government. But the Drukchen reportedly differed, saying, "If the Karmapa is not the right one, then the chances are nil that future Kagyu tulkus will be accurately identified."

So he suggested that all the monasteries perform extensive ceremonies petitioning the Dharma protectors for their blessings. At the same time, a delegation was sent to Lhasa informing the government of the newfound letter, with the message, "We have found the Karmapa's prediction letter and it is authentic."

The officials at the central government replied, "First you say there is no letter and now you say there is. The office of the Dalai Lama has already issued a position. It cannot be changed."

The petitioning and refusal went back and forth for an entire year. Then one day, while playing on a rooftop near the Potala, the cabinet minister's son fell and broke his pelvis. In those days, such injuries were very serious and the boy soon died of complications. Now the Tsurphu office was asked to send out a search party for another candidate.

As the Karmapa had written the prediction letter in beautiful poetry with extremely precise details, Tsurphu only submitted a single candidate—the one identified in the letter. The Lhasa government replied, "You cannot submit just one candidate. That's the same as you deciding who the tulku is. If you are asking us to decide, which is the tradition, you must submit two or three different choices and we will decide which one it is."

Again Tsurphu was in major turmoil and one meeting followed another.

But the Khyentse of Palpung, another important lama from Kham, was not only very wise but also very clever. He came up with an idea to circumvent the proud officials in Lhasa. "Make one candidate's name the son of the father," he suggested, "and the 'other' candidate, the name of the son of the mother." So they wrote down two different names for the same boy, sent them to the government and awaited their reply. When it finally came, it said, "The correct tulku is the son of the mother, not the son of the father."

This was how the authentic tulku of the fifteenth Karmapa was established at Tsurphu after many trials and tribulations.

When I think of the fifteenth Karmapa, Khakyab Dorje, I am struck with amazement! To have such far-reaching powers of clairvoyance!

8

Spiritual Sons

Karmey Khenpo

Among the many remarkable masters who were disciples of Chokgyur Lingpa, one of the foremost was the learned scholar Karmey Khenpo. He was regarded as a reincarnation of Shantarakshita, the great pandita from Sahor in India who was the very first master invited to Tibet for the construction of Samye monastery.

Karmey Khenpo started out as a Kagyu practitioner and the main *khenpo*-preceptor—abbot and chief teacher—at Karma Gön, one of the three seats of the Karmapa.

He was no ordinary person, and an ancient terma by Padmasambhava predicted he would become Chokgyur Lingpa's main disciple. He became a very devoted follower and extremely realized. Yet he usually served as Chokgyur Lingpa's attendant, even though he was said to be as learned as the renowned fifteenth-century master Karma Chagmey. The erudite Dudjom Rinpoche—one of the most outstanding masters of recent times—was amazed by Karmey Khenpo's writings and once told me, "It's so wonderful that someone like Karmey Khenpo could possibly exist in this world."

My grandmother told me, "When I was young and went to see my father, if Karmey Khenpo was in with him, I would complain to my mother, 'Now we have no chance of seeing Daddy. Karmey Khenpo just slipped in and for sure he'll stay in there for at least an hour or two!'

"He seemed to have endless questions, and he always carried a silver ink pot, a bamboo pen and some blank paper, so that when he asked Chokgyur Lingpa questions he could write down the answers on the spot.[62] He was an extraordinary master; he looked like one of the sixteen arhats in the traditional fresco paintings."

Karmey Khenpo adhered strictly to the rules for a monk: during his entire life he never let meat or alcohol touch his tongue. It was also said that his hand had never even grazed a woman nor had he ever allowed a lie to cross his lips.

Even though he was so gifted and close to Chokgyur Lingpa, Karmey Khenpo never had the good fortune to receive the *Three Sections of the Great Perfection* from the great tertön in person. He was a bit upset at not receiving it. "Chokgyur Lingpa had *so* many termas," Karmey Khenpo would lament, "but the one I regard as the real essence I haven't had the good fortune to receive." I was told he agonized over it. But after the tertön passed away, Karmey Khenpo had a vision of Chokgyur Lingpa's wisdom-body and received the complete empowerments and transmissions of the *Three Sections* then. This restored his self-confidence.

"Even though I was never lucky enough to receive the *Three Sections* while Chokgyur Lingpa was alive, my transmission is unique," he later told the Chokling of Tsikey, a reincarnation of Chokgyur Lingpa.[63]

"After Chokgyur Lingpa dissolved into the basic space beyond form," he explained, "his immaculate wisdom-body appeared before me and transmitted the *Three Sections* to me in full. As I am the only one to have received this transmission mind-to-mind, it is not just unique but of a higher level than yours. Because of that, this lineage I now hold should not be broken. I could pass it on to whomever requests it, but I won't. Since you are the tertön's reincarnation, you should possess both lineages, so I will give the empowerment to you and you only."[64]

"Karmey Khenpo was that kind of person," added Tsikey Chokling when he told me the story.

༄

When it came to debating, Karmey Khenpo was a match even for Old Khyentse.[65] Sometimes at the end of a philosophical argument, Karmey Khenpo would act like the big winner, and Khyentse would play at being depressed, as if he had lost something of immense value. Khyentse would bemoan his defeat and shed crocodile tears, making everyone laugh.

There are many stories of Karmey Khenpo being thrashed by Old Khyentse. Once Khyentse even threw a torma at him, hitting him right in the head!

But it was all an act they were staging, one that made it look as though they could almost never talk without getting into an argument. Seen from the outside, they seemed to be picking a fight with each other. But from the inside, for anyone who really knew, they used this game to clarify subtle points of understanding, dispel hindrances and enhance progress on the path.

༄

My teacher Samten Gyatso was one of Karmey Khenpo's disciples, and he told me many stories about him, such as the following.

Once a year in Lhasa, a large tent was set up where all the major scholars, particularly from the three main monasteries—Sera, Ganden and Drepung—would gather to debate, to see who was the best that year. They would sit in rows of twenty facing one another in front of the head of Ganden monastery, who sat on a large throne. Each debate was judged until one scholar emerged as the champion.

One year, Karmey Khenpo happened to be in Lhasa at the time of these grand debates. He did not belong to any of the three prestigious participating monasteries, but one morning he had a strong sense that he should go and join the debating contest. He announced this plan to his attendants.

"Why do you want to do that?" one of them asked. "Won't it inconvenience you?" This was a polite way of discouraging him—the attendant thought it would be embarrassing for Karmey Khenpo to lose.

"No, I must do it," insisted the khenpo. "There's no way around it."

Karmey Khenpo then took a set of wooden plates of the kind used as book covers and tied them on his chest and back with some string. This was to symbolize that his body was the scripture and that he embodied the Dharma. Then he tossed his monk's shawl over the wrong shoulder, held his rosary in the wrong hand and instead of wearing his hat with a peak like the other scholars, he flattened it on top of his head. He visualized Chokgyur Lingpa at the crown of his head and himself as the Lion of Speech, a particular form of Padmasambhava indivisible from Manjushri. Confident that he was undefeatable, he entered the debate grounds.

As his turn came, he beat one opponent after the other. When he had finally defeated them all, he found himself in front of the throne holder of Ganden, who declared, "You have won—you are victorious!"

This was quite an extraordinary feat; I doubt any Khampa had ever won before. Tradition has it that all one's opponents must lay their yellow hats on the ground and then the winner walks over them as a sign of victory. But at that moment Karmey Khenpo thought, "One is supposed to respect even the tiniest shred of religious robes, so if I trample these hats I will be breaking my vows."

So, instead of taking his "victory march," he walked over into the shade, bowed his head, covered his face with his hand and slowly walked out. Still, he felt pretty good about himself, for not only had he beaten all the *geshe*-scholars, but he had also upheld the precepts.

Back in Kham, Karmey Khenpo met the great Khyentse, who was visiting Tsangsar Gompa at the time. After exchanging greetings, he said, "I have some really good news!" and proceeded to tell the story about the debate. He concluded by proudly stating, "And I didn't even walk on their yellow hats!"

At that, Khyentse snatched up one of his vajras and whacked Karmey Khenpo on the head with it. "You faint-hearted coward! Instead of clinging to the idea of monastic precepts, you could have made the Kagyu and Nyingma teachings famous. What happened to your Khampa courage? Don't you have any confidence in the view of the inner yogas? You're supposed to be a Vajrayana practitioner! Your body is a deity, your voice mantra and your mind samadhi, so how can you cling to such low attachments? You are an utter good-for-nothing!"

Then he smacked him again. The khenpo slunk out and wasn't seen for a while.

Just before his death, Karmey Khenpo said, "Khyentse Rinpoche beat me again and again, sometimes even knocking me to the ground with all his slaps and thrashings. Time and time again he hauled me over the coals. But by beating me he removed the obstacles to a long life; now I'm so old I can't see—and I'm still unable to die!"

It sounded like a complaint when he said it, but actually it was praise.

༄

Karmey Khenpo lived, I believe, into his early eighties and passed away at his hermitage above Karma Gön. He was then reborn as the son of my aunt.

There had been a prediction from the Lotus-Born master that both Karmey Khenpo and Kongtrul would manifest the rainbow body at the time of death, a sign of great realization. Perhaps it was due to their extensive efforts to benefit others—they were always busy with their many disciples—that neither ended up manifesting the rainbow body.

There are many factors involved in whether a practitioner attains the rainbow body. Karmey Khenpo, for instance, did reach the level at which all mental phenomena dissolve back into the basic nature of reality: the exhaustion of concepts and phenomena. But even though at that exalted level he should have displayed the rainbow body—the outward sign of this state of realization—he did not do so.

Likewise, the terma revelations of Chokgyur Lingpa predicted that Kongtrul would leave in a rainbow body when he passed away. But this was prevented because his activities on behalf of sentient beings were too encompassing. One major reason for this is that when there are a lot of disciples, then there are sure to be some broken *samayas* by some of them; broken samayas have consequences for the teacher and so can prevent the manifestation of a rainbow body. The tantric teachings describe the "rainbow body with remainder," an occurrence that depends upon the purity of samaya of disciples and benefactors.

But there are exceptions: not too long ago, Nyagla Pema Dudul attained the rainbow body when he died in the middle of his camp of five hundred disciples; it seems none of them managed to prevent it. Still, most other teachers with the same level of realization, and who have taught openly and widely to numerous disciples, typically do not attain a rainbow body, despite the possibility that they would have done so if they had had fewer students.

That is probably why it is taught, "If you want to attain the rainbow body, don't have too many disciples."

Wangchok Dorje

Wangchok Dorje was one of Chokgyur Lingpa's three children. One of our chant texts describes him as the "magical display" of King Jah, meaning that he was a reincarnation of the Indian king who, right after the Buddha's passing, received the *Eighteen Mahayoga Tantras* from Vajrapani, the timeless lord of the tantric teachings. Wangchok Dorje and my grandmother, Könchok Paldrön, were born from the same mother, Lady Degah. The mother of the third child, Tsewang Norbu, was a niece of Old Khyentse.

After chanting hundreds of thousands of Manjushri mantras, and due to his training in former lives, Wangchok Dorje developed an incredibly sharp intelligence; his insights left people speechless. I have been told that his realization—where he was on the path and the levels he attained—was higher than even that of his tertön father. Wangchok Dorje was still very young when, entirely on his own, he spontaneously recognized the nature of mind.

17. King Jah—the master of Mahayoga

Later, when people would ask him for meditation teachings, he would reply, "I'm not the kind of person who can guide you to the nature of mind. I didn't get up on the roof by climbing the stairs one at a time. I got here in one leap. Even if I were to describe my meditation state, you wouldn't be able to grasp it."

It had been prophesied that Wangchok Dorje would reveal all the remaining termas among the

New Treasures that hadn't yet been revealed by his father and ensure their propagation. He was of that caliber.

From childhood he could see the magical script of the dakinis as though it were right in front of his eyes and he could transcribe it, along with the connected teachings, at will, as they arose in the expanse of his mind. But despite the prophecy, this ability was never put to its fullest use.

❧

People found Wangchok Dorje incredibly handsome; some even said he had the features of a god and that they had never seen anyone so beautiful. He was quite tall and very strong, with a noble bearing. His hair was very unusual; he wore it long, braided and wrapped around his head. It was described as a "magnetizing tiara," which meant that it had never been cut and that a dakini dwelled in every strand. His hair shone with a dark blue luster and when he washed it, it never tangled, even if he didn't comb it.

Being both the son and the lineage holder of Chokgyur Lingpa, Wangchok Dorje by tradition was supposed to have sons to carry on the family and the lineage. People say he had one hundred lovers. Wherever he went, word went around that girls who wanted a "body connection"—a very physical blessing—with the handsome tulku could just come by to see him. The young women would literally line up, waiting at his quarters each evening.

But Wangchok Dorje was also an accomplished yogi who had reversed the flow of the white essence and, unlike ordinary men, who ejaculate, he never made anyone pregnant. I don't know whether this was good or bad, but that's the way it happened. On the other hand, how often in the old days did you hear of someone who had one hundred girlfriends, yet never made even one of them pregnant?

❧

Chokgyur Lingpa had immense confidence in the great master Paltrul and all his children—including Wangchok Dorje—became Paltrul's disciples. After Chokgyur Lingpa passed away, Wangchok Dorje journeyed to Paltrul's encampment. Since many of his disciples were masters in their own right, it was said throughout Kham that his camp was like a den of snow lions, who later spread the roar of the sacred Dharma in all directions.

Being the son of the great tertön, Wangchok Dorje arrived at the camp with great pomp and circumstance, on horseback and with a large retinue.

By contrast, Paltrul was a dedicated monk and of course had no consort. Rather, he would often speak about being "a child of the mountains, wearing the mountain mist as one's garments" and about the virtues of following the simple lifestyle of the early practitioners of the Kagyu lineage.

One day, Paltrul spoke of following their example by giving up elaborate involvements. "To practice the true Dharma, one should always take the lower seat and wear castaway clothing," Paltrul told the gathering. "It has never been said that one should put oneself above others and dress up in brocade."

Inspired, Wangchok Dorje thought, "That's fine by me!" So he shed all his brocade garments and wore a simple cloak made of inexpensive felt instead. He also dismissed his entourage and sent all his horses back to Chokgyur Lingpa's monastery, keeping but a single attendant. He then shaved off all his hair and took monk's vows from Paltrul. He remained there for three years, having abandoned all possessions.

But after he took the pledge to be a wandering renunciate with no possessions and had shaved off all of his wondrous hair, his majestic presence and splendor faded; he became just like an ordinary person. He turned pale and frail, and his back started to bend.

This austere way of life seemed to have a very negative effect on his status as the holder of the terma teachings. In particular, cutting off his hair broke a samaya bond with the dakinis. In order for a tertön to transcribe the sign script of a terma, the syllables have to hover clearly in his vision. But now, he found, they were blurred, darted about, and became smaller and smaller. As a result, he was unable to decode and write down a single terma.

Wangchok Dorje's journey home was in stark contrast to his imposing arrival—in his father's fashion—in the company of forty horsemen and a herd of yaks. Instead, he walked on foot all the way from Golok in the northeastern part of Kham, carrying only a staff like a mendicant beggar. He traveled with just two attendants and a single hornless yak as pack animal. All they carried were a few books and the makings for tea.

As they were walking down toward Dzongsar monastery in Derge, Wangchok Dorje fell ill. It must have been quite a severe illness, because in only five or six days he passed away at Khyentse's mountain retreat, the famous Gathering Palace of Sugatas. No one in the world could prevent this sad event. A procession carried the body back to Chokgyur Lingpa's seat. The tertön's cook Pema Trinley, whom I knew as a small kid, was present when Wangchok Dorje passed away. He was then the monastery's bursar and got stuck with the task of delivering the sad news to the great Khyentse, who was staying nearby.

Pema Trinley, who passed away near the age of ninety, gave me every detail of this story. Upon hearing of Wangchok Dorje's death, Khyentse was deeply displeased. Feeling that there had been no need for the son of a realized ngakpa to cut his hair,[66] he cried out: "Damn! Crazy Paltrul made Wangchok Dorje cut his hair and turned him into a renunciate—and now look what has happened! How tragic! This proves how little merit there is in the present age of decline. Padmasambhava himself made the prophecy that this son of the tertön would have spread his termas from the Chinese border in the east all the way to Mount Kailash in the west, benefiting beings like unfurling an immense sheet of white cloth. Now crazy Paltrul has messed everything up!"

Khyentse then slapped his fists against his chest, expressing despair in typical Khampa fashion. "The auspicious coincidence didn't hold up," he moaned with a very morose expression. "He was supposed to be the one to reveal and propagate the remaining termas."[67]

Pema Trinley presented an offering on behalf of the deceased and said, "Rinpoche, please give us an indication of where we can find his rebirth. I have given you an offering and I need to return with the information."

"Goodness!" replied Khyentse. "Before they were sister and brother; now they may be son and mother."

The great Khyentse continued to look upset and beat his chest. That was all he said by way of prediction.

No more than a year had passed when Khyentse confirmed that in fact my grandmother Könchok Paldrön's newborn son was Wangchok Dorje's reincarnation.

"Listen up!" Old Khyentse said. "Isn't it true that Könchok Paldrön has just given birth to a boy? I tell you, there is no doubt that he is Wangchok Dorje!"

Then Old Khyentse ratified it in writing.

Old Khyentse continued, "Her second son doesn't have a long life, but naming him Immortal Vajra will provide an auspicious circumstance for prolonging his life." And that is how my father got his name: Chimey Dorje.

⁓

Chokgyur Lingpa's collected works—apart from the forty volumes of his termas—comprised two volumes and Wangchok Dorje's writings a single thick volume. Both had been laboriously written out by hand rather than printed with woodblocks. I kept one copy of both these collections. After I left for Central Tibet, I wrote my monastery asking them to send me these texts. Later I heard that the caretakers of my monastery refused to send anything of value.[68] You might wonder what they were thinking! The precious handwritten texts were left in Kham, but what was the use? This is what happens when woodblocks aren't made!

A few years after the Chinese invasion, news went around of a coming boon to humankind: something called a "cultural revolution." This deceit was what the hordes of liars who followed the invading soldiers propagated. Sure enough, when the wave of the Cultural Revolution swept over our country, enormous changes occurred: our monasteries were destroyed and all our literature was reduced to ashes.

Wangchok Dorje's writings were probably destroyed, as most Buddhist scriptures were thrown into the flames. The Chinese communists were so menacing that they were able to coerce the villagers to gather all their books and toss them into a big fire. Then the occupation officials announced, "From this moment onward, if we find a single book in your house, the owner will be hanged. Each volume of scripture shall cost one life."

At that, many frightened people threw their precious books into the rivers. But some were buried in the ground with the hope that they would one day be retrieved—but when they were later dug up unfortunately they had rotted away. Still, our country is so huge that I wonder if some won't eventually turn up.[69] In fact, one very beautiful text that Wangchok Dorje wrote when he was only sixteen, called *Inexhaustible Garland of Lightning*, did survive; we still use it daily in our monasteries. How wonderful it would be if even just a few more like that have survived.

Tsewang Norbu

Tsewang Norbu's mother was Old Khyentse's niece.[70] The Lotus-Born master had also foretold that this consort would give birth to a reincarnation of Yudra Nyingpo.[71]

Since the *Three Sections* was the heart essence of Vairotsana, it was entrusted to his foremost disciple in Kham, Yudra Nyingpo. That is also why Yudra Nyingpo's reincarnation, Tsewang Norbu, had to be the first to receive the empowerment. As Padmasambhava's prophecies tend to be very precise, it was even predicted in the terma itself that "within one to three years he should be given this terma."[72]

Tsewang Norbu was quite humble; he once told Samten Gyatso, "I'm nothing special, not at all. I don't have any great qualities, not a single one, except for one thing: even though I was just six months old at the time, I clearly remember receiving the *Three Sections* from the two great treasure masters." As a matter of fact, the *Three Sections* had just then been revealed.⁷³

Twenty-five people were present at this event, including Khyentse and Karmey Khenpo. The moment the terma was revealed Chokgyur Lingpa called out to the child's mother, "Bring the kid here!"

She brought the baby over, wrapped in blankets, and sitting on a tray of woven reeds covered with a layer of dried sheep droppings and then with a couple of layers of cloth. This was all in typical Khampa style for an infant, leaving the child free to pee whenever need be.

Tsewang Norbu sat right between Khyentse and Chokling while he received the empowerment. Chokgyur Lingpa first conferred the empowerment on the baby and only then upon Khyentse. But because of the command that this empowerment only be given one on one, no one else received it—not even Kongtrul. That is also why the many lineages for the *Three Sections* all went through Tsewang Norbu. Later on, he came to be the one who did the most to ensure the propagation of Chokgyur Lingpa's termas.⁷⁴

Until Tsewang Norbu was about a year old, an eagle perched on the roof of his parents' house every single day. Later, the great Khyentse said this was the Eagle-Winged Goddess who guards the *Three Sections*.

~

Like his siblings, Tsewang Norbu was a disciple of the great Paltrul. Once in Kham, he had gone up on the mountainside near Paltrul's encampment to spend ten days in a cave. As he didn't intend to stay long, he only took a small bag of tsampa with him.

One night, there was a heavy snowfall and he was snowed in. The snow kept falling and falling. He failed to return; after a couple of months, word spread in Paltrul's camp that Tsewang Norbu must have passed away. Finally, his death was taken for granted, and virtuous actions were done in his name, including the traditional burnt offerings of food to nurture the spirit of the deceased.

Six months later, the snow finally thawed. One day, someone let out a scream: Tsewang Norbu's corpse was walking into camp! People began scattering right and left to get out of its way, afraid of being touched by the *rolang*, a Tibetan-style zombie.

"Don't worry, it's just me!" Tsewang tried to assure them.

Finally, after things settled down, someone had the chance to ask, "How is it you didn't starve to death?"

"Why would I starve to death?" he replied, "When I was thirsty I ate snow and when hungry I ate from my bag of tsampa. You don't starve if you have provisions."

Later he explained that he had survived on a mere spoonful of tsampa a day. In other words, he wouldn't admit to a thing. The truth was he had attained mastery in yoga, including full control over the subtle channels and energies, and so he probably spent most of the time in samadhi.[75]

He also mentioned one interesting point, "It seems there is good reason to burn offerings of tsampa and other foodstuffs during the seven weeks after someone's demise. I personally found it quite helpful as I felt neither hungry nor cold during those forty-nine days. Even inside my cave I could sometimes smell the smoke from the offerings being made for me at the monastery."

❧

Tsewang Norbu was also extremely learned—the equal of Karmey Khenpo. He claimed that his scholarship was merely due to spending his early years with the great Khyentse. As Tsewang Norbu was Old Khyentse's grandnephew, he could easily spend long periods of time with the master. So Tsewang Norbu received most of his early teachings at the feet of Khyentse.

"Staying with Khyentse when I was young made me a wealthy man—rich with teachings," he would say. "Old Khyentse didn't teach much during the day; he preferred just to relax with his disciples. At best, you might be able to ask a question or two during the day. But when evening fell and everyone heard the ring of the bell, they would gather at his hermitage. The empowerment began during the night.

"An hour or so before dawn, he would say, 'Now it's time for the old man to get some sleep. You better go and do the same.' Only then would all of us disciples leave his room."

❧

Tsewang Norbu was eccentric and, like many a yogi, spontaneous and direct. One distinctive peculiarity of his was never to do what a dignitary or high lama told him to. For instance, not even Khakyab Dorje, the fifteenth Karmapa, had been able to force Tsewang Norbu to give him the transmissions for the *New Treasures*.

The Karmapa's attendant and close disciple Jampal Tsultrim was an important teacher in his own right, as well as one of the chief disciples of the Karmapa. So Karmapa chose him to go to Lhasa, to try his best to compel Tsewang Norbu to give the sought-after empowerments.

"Since you're the son of Chokgyur Lingpa, the Karmapa is sending you this white scarf and telling you to give him the transmissions," he said.

"No way!" Tsewang Norbu replied, "Do you want a dog to put a paw on a human's head? You're talking nonsense. Don't even bring it up, you little monk."[76] Thus, he compared the Karmapa to a mere human being and himself to a dog—and even called this important and famous lama "little monk." In short, Tsewang Norbu couldn't be coerced by anyone.

Jampal Tsultrim later said he had "never met anyone as stubborn as Tsewang Norbu. Karmapa is Avalokiteshvara in the flesh, so who wouldn't rejoice in giving him Chokgyur Lingpa's termas as an offering?" But Tsewang Norbu still wouldn't cave in to such pressure.

Some years later, Samten Gyatso (who was Tsewang Norbu's nephew,) went to Central Tibet to fulfill the Karmapa's wish.

༄

Tsewang Norbu was a monk during the first half of his life, but that didn't last. At one point Old Khyentse told him, "You must go to Mindrolling and stay there." So off he went, staying for eight years in one of the most important centers for learning in Central Tibet.

Despite his standing as the only living son of the great tertön, Tsewang Norbu's style was to arrive unannounced, without the slightest pomp. So he enrolled at Mindrolling as a common monk to pursue his studies. But he must have made himself count somehow, since we find his name in the records of lineage masters who transmitted important teachings at Mindrolling. Without him, those teachings might have been lost.

Tsewang Norbu was not pushy, and he was a monk at heart—so during those eight years at Mindrolling the thought of marrying the head lama's daughter never even entered his mind. So despite the terma prophecy, after eight years he returned to Kham, still a monk.

But when he returned to Kham, he was scolded by Khyentse: "You useless good-for-nothing, you didn't do your job!"

"What do you mean I didn't do my job?"

"A descendant of Chokgyur Lingpa was supposed to replenish the bloodline at Mindrolling. That's why I sent you! But you're useless!"[77]

"How am I supposed to replenish their bloodline? They are humans, but I am just a dog. It never occurred to me that humans and dogs marry."

Still, Old Khyentse was set on Chokgyur Lingpa's son having descendants one way or another. So he forced Tsewang Norbu to give back his monk's vows and become a ngakpa. Moreover, Khyentse arranged for him to have a consort from a devoted family, but they didn't have any children.

After that, another consort from a family in Derge was arranged, still with the same lack of results.

Sometimes Tsewang Norbu would complain with his wry sense of humor, "Darn! I'm totally useless. I didn't keep the monastic precepts and so I'm a fallen monk. But I also haven't produced any children. My life has been wasted—I'm a total failure!"

Some lamas, hearing this, would become quite unsettled by his deadpan humor. And in Nangchen there is now a saying about being "as useless as Tsewang Norbu" and not accomplishing any worldly or spiritual achievements.

In the later part of his life, Tsewang Norbu went to live in Central Tibet, where he became known for his strange behavior. While he was there, it happened that the thirteenth Dalai Lama went to India.[78] One sign of Tsewang Norbu's status was that the Tibetan government in Lhasa requested him to perform a ritual for repelling foreign invasions. He performed it meticulously at the Ramoche temple in Lhasa, which contains one of the two most famous Jowo statues in all of Tibet.

Although Tsewang Norbu had held the position of a very high lama in Kham, after going to Central Tibet he changed his ways radically. He would often invite beggars in for tea, long conversations and a few laughs—he was that kind of master. And in other ways he was known to act contrary; as the saying goes, "If they said HUNG, he would say PHAT."

He usually wore a very simple sheepskin coat. But one day he put on a fine brocade robe. "Rinpoche, why are you dressing up like that?" his servant asked. "You never dress up."

"Quiet!" Tsewang Norbu said. "Today we are going to meet the king of all tantric yogis in this world."

"And who might that be?" the servant asked.

"Khakyab Dorje, the Karmapa," was the reply. "I'm supposed to be a ngakpa, so today is a good day to dress the part."

And he rode off to Tsurphu with great dignity. But the moment they got back to Lhasa, he immediately put his sheepskin coat back on.

When he was quite old, head chanter Trinley, who had been one of Tsewang Norbu's disciples, told me the following story:

"Sometimes I just couldn't understand what Tsewang Norbu was up to—I even wondered whether my teacher had gone crazy or something. Early one morning, Tsewang Norbu declared, 'Today we are going to hold a great feast! Go to the meat market and invite as many slaughterhouse shepherds as you can.'

"These particular slaughterhouse shepherds were a motley crew; they were very poor and quite grimy. Their only job was to lead animals to the chopping block. After a while, fifty or sixty of them were standing in the courtyard. In the meantime, Tsewang Norbu's disciples had set up a large table for food.

"Tsewang Norbu came out and told them all to sit down in lines, as if they were monks in a temple. First they were served a lavish meal, with Tsewang Norbu sitting right there among them, at the head of the row. He then asked for a text and, while they were all sitting in line eating, he started chanting the liturgy for the terma *Embodiment of Realization*.[79]

"These shepherds, to say the least, were unused to sitting in an organized group practice like a bunch of monks. They were trapped there, fidgeting a lot—but nevertheless enjoying the food.

"At the end, after the guests had left, I asked, 'What are you up to, Rinpoche? In all of Lhasa, there are no worse people than those guys—they are the ones who lead the animals to slaughter. They push the poor animals the last few steps and afterwards help chop up the wretched animals' carcasses. Why are you spending so much money on people like that?'

"'Hey! Don't talk like that,' Tsewang Norbu replied. 'Today I performed the feast offering in the company of several perfect bodhisattvas. Besides me, who has the merit to do so these days? I don't have a flicker of doubt about this. Today was an auspicious day.'"

That's just one example of the strange kinds of things Tsewang Norbu would do.

⁂

Tsewang Norbu also had amazing clairvoyant powers—to such an extent that he frightened people. Trinley, the head chanter, also told me this story:

One day, Tsewang Norbu went to perform a big smoke offering ritual for the longevity of a household in Lhasa. The father of the house had great faith in Tsewang Norbu; at the end of the ceremony he approached and asked, "I wonder how our luck and health will be next year."

"Oh, yeah! Your luck and health?" Tsewang Norbu proclaimed, "You'll be dead next year and not one month will pass before your wife will be dead too."

"But what about our son? What will he do?" the man gasped.

"He won't stay here without you; he'll be distraught and leave. Next year your house will be empty," Tsewang Norbu declared.

"Oh, no, here he goes again!" Trinley thought to himself, "Why did he have to go and do that? This is so inauspicious."

The following year, Trinley heard that the man had died, then about a month later that the wife had died and, finally, that the son had left, leaving the house empty.

~

Though I never met him when I was young I saw a photograph of Tsewang Norbu that had been taken in Bhutan; it hung in Samten Gyatso's private room at Fortress Peak. He was tall and stout like Dilgo Khyentse, and he was strikingly handsome.

At Tsikey monastery, Tsewang Norbu would often go for a walk outside by himself; in the afternoon he could be seen sitting for long stretches of time near the bank of the Kechu River.[80]

As a young boy, my father and some friends once saw the imposing frame of a man sitting very straight and alone by the river. My father, the leader of this gang of small monks, made a proposal:

"This big guy comes here every day to kill the poor fish. Let's hit him on the head with a stone to teach him a lesson. Keep quiet now . . ."

They snuck closer—but just when they were about to throw the stone, Tsewang Norbu gave a loud cough, almost as though in warning. They immediately recognized who it was and fled in all directions.

"If he hadn't coughed, I would surely have hit him right in the neck," my father later said. "I was that wild. If it hadn't been for Tsewang Norbu's clairvoyance, I would have been responsible for hitting him with a stone! How would I have lived with that?"

~

A lot of what we now call Chokgyur Lingpa's termas actually appeared through the combined efforts of Khyentse, Kongtrul and the tertön himself. They passed a lot of transmissions among themselves, but all these streams merged in Tsewang Norbu.

Once Khyentse and Kongtrul were requested to confer the empowerments for the *Treasury of Precious Termas* at Riwoche monastery, in the Chamdo province between Lhasa and Kham. Riwoche was a major center for the Dharma, so this was no small occasion.

"The *Treasury* is the quintessence of all the terma revelations of the hundred major tertöns," the lamas at Riwoche repeatedly insisted. "We must receive this transmission."

When told that Khyentse couldn't come, they asked Kongtrul instead. But both Khyentse and Kongtrul were too old at this point. So the two masters discussed the invitation with each other and agreed to send Tsewang Norbu as their substitute.[81]

Tsewang Norbu went to Riwoche and transmitted the entire *Treasury of Precious Termas.* At the end, he continued right on transmitting all the *New Treasures.* The two reincarnations of Chokgyur Lingpa—Tsikey Chokling and Neten Chokling—both attended, as did Samten Gyatso and Uncle Tersey.

One of the last empowerments was for the *Three Sections of the Great Perfection.* Prior to conferring it, Tsewang Norbu said, "The *Three Sections* cannot be given in public nor even in small, private groups. There is a strict command of secrecy, the breaking of which will have severe consequences—as dangerous as picking something from inside the mouth of a poisonous viper. I can only give it to one of you at a time."

He then made each of them hold on to his shawl and swear an oath, telling them, "You must only pass this sacred teaching on as a lineage restricted to a single recipient at a time!"

Tsewang Norbu also told the lamas, "After my death, people will search for my reincarnation. It may happen that someone will try to pin my name onto some unfortunate *bardo* spirit who has been floundering around and has just managed to come into a human body for the first time in a long while. Doing so will ensure his rebirth in the lower realms with no chance of escape. Don't search for my tulku!

"If my next incarnation does serve Chokgyur Lingpa's teachings, he will do so either directly or indirectly. You should definitely not try to find him! Take hold of my shawl and promise me that, all four of you!" He emphatically prohibited any recognition of his tulku, and so the four of them had no choice but to swear not to look for one after his death.

None of his main disciples dared to try to find him. I have heard that there have been some attempts lately to find a present incarnation, but thinking of that oath, I personally wouldn't dare to ask any master for his location.

༄

When he died, Tsewang Norbu was staying in Nyemo in the district of Tsang, to the west of Lhasa. I believe he was in his sixties. Just before his death, he told his attendant, "The main seat of my brother and me was Tsikey monastery. Send all my possessions there together with this note. And while you are at it, you might as well take along any bones from my cremated body.

"I have managed to compile a complete set of the *New Treasures*, so do not let anyone pilfer from it. My father's reincarnation, as well as my brother's rebirth, both live at Tsikey—you must hand-deliver this collection directly to them. And this note is my final will and testament. I do not have a single word to add besides what is written here, except that you must spread the word that 'Tsewang Norbu died like an old dog in a village called Nyemo.' Promise me that this is what you will answer if anyone should ask about me. Spread this message far and wide to all the lamas back in Kham."

Tsewang Norbu's personal copies of the *New Treasures*, his icons and his implements for empowerments were all kept at Tsikey until the Cultural Revolution.

Those who were present at his cremation were amazed to see a ray of rainbow-colored light extending from the funeral pyre to a point distant in the sky. I don't remember if there were any relic pills in his ashes, but I heard that some of his bones were filled with sindhura powder—I'm not sure anyone would call that "dying like an old dog."

9

My Precious Grandmother

My grandmother, Könchok Paldrön, was an unusually gifted person, very talented and wise. In our region, women were rarely educated as well as she was. It was hard to find anyone so accomplished in so many ways.

Grandmother knew all the chants and melodies as well as the correct use of ritual implements, having learned them directly from the tertön himself, who often received these melodies in his visions. If it weren't for her, the authentic tunes and procedures of our lineage would have been lost. She even knew the special ways of blowing the *gyaling* trumpets. Grandmother was extremely skilled at using the gyaling and everyone at Tsikey who was learning to play it would ask for her critique.

She also transmitted the complex mudras for each of the hundred peaceful and wrathful deities, and the rituals connected to them, which she had learned at Mindrolling monastery according to the thousand-year-old oral tradition. Her grasp of ritual tunes and the use of musical instruments remains the backbone of the *New Treasures* to this day.

Grandmother was also a respected herbal doctor who dispensed medicine to patients every day. She was an astrologer as well and an expert in several painting styles.[82] She was extraordinary.

Grandmother overcame any and all disadvantages of being a woman in our male-dominated Khampa culture. She was so impressive that there were no other women like her around where I grew up.

~

My first strong memories of my grandmother go back to when I was around seven years old, and she was staying at our family home, the Tsangsar mansion. I went to see her almost every day during those three years. My face must have had a darker, bluish tinge in those days for she nicknamed me Blue Face. She nicknamed my older half-brother Penjik, Pale Face, because of his light complexion.

Later, Grandmother moved to a small nearby chapel for a year and then farther away to lofty Fortress Peak, where she spent three years with her son Samten Gyatso. During that time, I wasn't able to see her much, since I had gone to stay with my father at his retreat place, Dechen Ling, which was two days' journey on horseback. She was very generous, always giving me gifts like dried apricots, small bags and other things. She also taught me proper table manners and how to behave in the company of others.

My father was the only son to produce grandchildren and, as I seemed to be her favorite, she lavished me with affection. She would regularly keep me with her to chat and would often share her tsampa with me—passing me small morsels that I would sit and wait for, then happily gobble up. She loved me as though I were her own child.

*

There was no one who knew the art of torma making as well as Grandmother did. It was really she who taught me how to make the tormas for the *New Treasures*. Because of her, I had so much experience with rituals that I later served as my father's shrine master for many years. Although I was still in my teens, he put me in charge of preparing all the necessary objects for the rituals.

The tormas were my particular responsibility; I can't count how many tormas I made as a teenager. I had first begun to learn the art of torma making from Penjik, who was quite deft with his hands. But there inevitably comes a point in the art of torma making when adjustments and refinements are necessary, so I would go to my uncle Sang-Ngak, who taught me many of the finer points. But when Samten Gyatso brought me along to Tsikey, he told me, "The ultimate arbiter of Chokgyur Lingpa's torma style is your grandmother."

One day, she gave me her stamp of approval. When my buddy Dudul and I showed her our tormas, she told me, "While Dudul's style leans more toward the Mindrolling tradition, yours follows purely the *New Treasures*. In the future, you can be the backbone of our ritual lineage."

When I was nineteen, I went to visit her at Tsikey. She would have been about seventy years old by then and was slightly ill. I stayed about two months and received the final teachings from her on how to make tormas. At the end of the two months, I had become quite adept at making all the different tormas used in the rituals for the *New Treasures* and received Könchok Paldrön's personal blessing. She told me, "You are actually the best torma maker in this terma tradition." Today I have no special qualities at all, except I really know how to make those tormas.

❧

My grandmother's way of correcting people was not by scolding or rebuke; instead she would give advice on "what a good person would do." It was then up to you to decide to act accordingly.

I never saw or heard of her striking anyone. I remember her saying to us children, "Using small lies as jokes to tease people is not a virtue, but hurtful and wrong. Don't tease in a mean way. Don't bicker."

She would make small suggestions like, "Don't talk with food in your mouth. Eat gently and quietly. When you talk, don't yawn or make other unnecessary sounds. Don't raise your voice without cause; you don't have to yell when you are talking to the person next to you. Speak like a gentleman: take the time to find the right words, then speak. By rushing you only end up sounding like a lunatic."

Such was the sort of advice she gave me as a small child. Every single time I went to see her, I got some such guidance.

❧

Despite her noble heritage, my grandmother—or Precious Mother, as we addressed her—was incredibly humble, always taking the lower seat. Various lamas and important disciples of her father came to pay her their respects. Invariably she would say, "There is no need for you to come and see this old lady. What has gotten into you lamas?"

The only way anyone could bow to her was by doing so outside her room, before entering. She would never remain seated as they greeted her with joined palms; if they bowed down she would get up and move away, saying, "What kind of lamas are you—bowing down to this old woman?"

While Grandmother was living at Fortress Peak, the lamas from Gebchak, the impressive nunnery nearby, would come to pay their respects to the daughter of the great tertön. Samten Gyatso would enter her room to announce which lama had come and she would say, "Why are they here? There's nothing they can get from me. Don't even bring it up again! They don't need to meet me."

Of course, Samten Gyatso couldn't tell an important lama to just go away, so he would arrange some seating for them in the meadow and then invite Grandmother to come outside and enjoy the weather. The lama was then told to approach slowly, from the other side, as if just strolling by, and then they could begin a conversation. Otherwise, there was no way to meet her; she was simply too humble.

Maybe her sincere humility was the reason the Chokling of Tsikey, who compiled Chokgyur Lingpa's biography, could find no way to approach her, let alone hear her stories. Whatever the reason, he didn't tap her memory when writing the official version of the tertön's life story.

❧

Despite all the great masters she met earlier in her life, Könchok Paldrön's root guru was her own son, Samten Gyatso. He was the one who gave her the essential meditation instructions. Of course she had received transmissions from other masters, including her brother Wangchok Dorje, who passed away at an early age. But it was Samten Gyatso who pointed out mind essence to her so that she recognized it unmistakenly—and that defines a root guru.

This is quite astounding if you think about it: her own son!

Samten Gyatso told me that he was amazed by his mother's level of meditation. When her life was drawing to a close, she had reached the level known as *collapse of delusion*, at which point there are no more dreams during sleep; the dream state is totally purified. Indeed, the tantric scriptures mention that at a certain point the stream of dreaming ceases, so that throughout day and night the continuity of luminous wakefulness is no longer interrupted.

She was truly amazing! People often said that their trivial thoughts and worries would immediately subside the moment they entered her room. One would feel very lucid and quiet. It was extraordinarily palpable.

This daughter of Chokgyur Lingpa was unusual in so many ways. For instance, she had three visions in which she met Tara as if in person—as though they were just having a conversation. This was not public knowledge, as she never mentioned a thing to anyone but my uncle Samten Gyatso. She didn't even tell me herself; I heard it from him.

The local people trusted her deeply. They would often ask for some grains of barley she had blessed, to carry in a small amulet bag on their body. They would also tie her protection amulets around the necks of their goats and sheep. Some people even tested whether her protection actually worked by shooting rifles at their goats.

"Each time I hit the goat," one of them told me, "after the impact it would cry out in pain, 'Baaaaah!' But on closer inspection, I couldn't

18. Tara— the female buddha of compassion

find a bullet wound anywhere. The amulet made my goat bulletproof—and I'm not lying!"

This test was perhaps not so bad; it made people trust in her protection.

❧

Könchok Paldrön also remembered once traveling with her mother to Old Khyentse's main residence in Derge, when Khyentse, Kongtrul and Chokling were all still alive.

The three masters performed an elaborate *drubchen* practice together—continuing for nine days and nights without interruption—probably using the terma known as *Embodiment of Realization*.[83] She and her brother Wangchok Dorje sat in. When it came time for the feast, the great Khyentse said, "As an auspicious coincidence, you two siblings must wear the tantric ornaments and bring the plates of feast offerings."

Grandmother remembered the two of them standing up and holding the plates in front of the three masters while they were singing the slow and melodious feast song. "My brother looked like a little god," she recalled, "and he had such a beautiful face—beyond belief!"

At the end, Old Khyentse joined his palms and said, "These children are certainly the offspring of a *vidyadhara* lineage."

❧

My grandmother also remembered meeting the great Paltrul.

Paltrul and her father, the tertön, met at Dzogchen monastery in the neighboring Derge kingdom. At the time, the tulku of Yongey Mingyur Dorje was the tertön's attendant, serving him tea and cooking his meals.

At dawn, Chokgyur Lingpa told him, "This morning the great master Paltrul Rinpoche is coming to see me. Please make special preparations."

A while later, when Yongey came out of the master's room after pouring him tea, he saw an old man at the door. Dressed in Golok style instead of lama's robes, he wore a simple sheepskin coat with the hairless side covered in red cloth. He had a large frame and a prominent nose.

"I must see Chokgyur Lingpa!" was all he said. Then he proceeded to walk in.

As the tertön's visitors never entered his quarters unannounced, Yongey blocked the door, saying, "Wait! Wait! It's not that easy. I must first announce you to the lama."

"Get out of my way!" the old man said and began to push Yongey aside.

Yongey grabbed the old man's sleeve and insisted, "You can't just barge in like this."

The old man pulled in the opposite direction and they began to tussle. Suddenly Yongey thought to himself, "Maybe this is not an ordinary old man from Golok. Perhaps I should go inside and ask."

What he had been told earlier about the day's visitor then dawned on him, but he had assumed that someone looking more like a great master would be coming.

When he turned around, he discovered Chokgyur Lingpa there on the floor prostrating to the old man—who then began bowing down in return. Yongey later said that "after they bowed to each other, they touched heads like two yaks."

❧

The Dzogchen monastery had invited Chokgyur Lingpa to be a guest of honor, the recipient of auspicious offerings. Since Paltrul was then the master in residence, he was asked to write the formal speech before the offerings.

You can find this talk in Chokgyur Lingpa's life story. Extremely elegant, the speech showers the tertön with praise, referring to him as the emissary of Padmasambhava.

During this visit, the tertön began to call Paltrul "Dzogchen Paltrul"—a name that stuck—and also gave him the empowerment for his terma containing teachings on the Great Perfection entitled *Heart Essence of Samantabhadra*. This transmission took place at the retreat center located high above the snow line overlooking the monastery's Shri Singha College.

Conversely, Chokgyur Lingpa placed Paltrul on a high throne and received the *Way of the Bodhisattva* from him. So the two masters were definitely connected.

My grandmother recalled that Tsewang Norbu wasn't there, but Wangchok Dorje was a witness, as was Chokgyur Lingpa's consort.

Paltrul practiced this particular teaching on the Great Perfection and later said, "I am usually the type of person who gets no visions, signs, nor any other indications of progress, but while practicing this terma something did happen, even for me. This teaching must be for real!"

My grandmother could imitate Paltrul's strong Golok accent as she recited what he said when giving mind teachings to an old man from that region: "When you don't follow the past and don't invite the future, there is nothing else to sustain but the uncontrived, unbridled and free state of your present, ordinary mind."

In that short statement, he had given the essential teaching of the Great Perfection.

But the old man from Golok then pleaded, "Give me a blessing to ensure that I won't end up in the hell realms!"

But Paltrul merely replied, "Unless you take care of it yourself, no one else can send you to the pure lands, as though they were just flinging a stone."

❦

My grandmother reached perfect realization before she passed away at eighty, quite an advanced age for someone in our region. One of my last memories is of her telling me, "I am leaving shortly. I want to leave my body at Tsikey, where my father's and brother's remains are kept."

Grandmother died at Tsikey a few years later.

I didn't visit her much while she was there, but from time to time I did receive presents from her—small delicate boxes in various colors and other things youngsters like.

Grandmother left her body while sitting up very straight. I remember her cremation, which was performed outside at a distance from Tsikey monastery itself. There was a large funeral pyre shaped like a stupa, in the traditional way. The head lama was Dzigar Kongtrul, a prominent lama in the region. During the cremation, five separate groups performed elaborate sadhanas, each based on different *mandalas*. Afterward, we discovered large quantities of sindhura powder in the ashes.

10

My Guru, Samten Gyatso

My grandmother's eldest son, Samten Gyatso, was my root guru and ultimate refuge. He was also, of course, my uncle. I feel a bit shy telling stories about him, because I don't want to sound as if I'm indirectly praising myself by lauding a family member. A disciple who emphasizes signs of accomplishment, clairvoyant abilities and miraculous powers in stories about his own guru, may—instead of honoring him—end up discrediting him. Yet though he was a relative, there is no way I can avoid praising him. I don't mean to be crude, but I'm related to him like excrement is related to fine cuisine.

I'm not just glorifying someone in my own family, like "the lower lip praising the upper," but, in all honesty, there was virtually no other master in Kham with such a high view and realization, with such commanding presence and majestic brilliance. I won't be able to tell you the inner or innermost versions of his life—as we customarily describe a person's spiritual experiences and realization—since I don't know them. But here is what I have heard or directly witnessed.

When Samten Gyatso transmitted the *New Treasures* to the great master Tentrul at Surmang monastery, I slept near the door in Samten Gyatso's room, so I often witnessed their evening discussions. Tentrul was extremely learned and very noble. One day, he told me, "Many years ago I met Samten Gyatso with your father, Chimey Dorje, in Derge, and even then I thought that due to his insight and lineage he would become a truly great scholar. I have studied many more philosophical works than Samten Gyatso, but when we get to the topic of the Great Perfection, I almost don't dare to continue speaking. When we discuss the *New Treasures*, somehow I am able to keep up, but he puts me to shame when we start talking about meditation."

Within the Barom Kagyu lineage, Samten Gyatso was regarded as an emanation of Four-Armed Mahakala, one of the more prominent guardians of the Dharma.[84]

Moreover, the second Chokling of Tsikey once had a vision of Samten Gyatso in which he saw him as an emanation of Vimalamitra.

From the time I was young, I respected my guru deeply. In his conduct, Samten Gyatso kept the monastic precepts quite purely and strictly. He never tasted alcohol nor ate any meat. In his attitude, he was always in tune with the bodhisattva trainings.

Some of us who were with him every day could be quite blind to his qualities, just like people in Lhasa who never go to see the Jowo statue of the Buddha, thinking there is plenty of time to get around to going. But if you paid attention to his personality, it was obvious that he was fully endowed with compassion, perseverance and devotion.

Samten Gyatso never flattered others by playing up to them or telling them how wonderful they were. He spoke straightforwardly. If something was true, he would say so; if not, he would say it was not, without adding or subtracting anything. He never talked around a sensitive topic.

My guru was completely reliable, conscientious in all matters. If you got his word on something, you would never hear him say later that he had forgotten. That's the kind of man he was, extremely dependable. He was almost never sick—or at least I never heard him complain, not even about having a headache or some other pain. Nor did he ever make plans for more than one day at a time and he always completed his tasks.

Samten Gyatso was scrupulously attentive to all his daily affairs, both spiritual and secular. For instance, when giving empowerments, he never skipped a word or phrase. He would perform the entire ritual, from the preparation to the concluding verses, in a state of meditative composure, so that upon entering the room you got the feeling that you were about to receive an empowerment for real. That's the kind of teacher he was.

Other people were intimidated by Samten Gyatso's meticulousness and, afraid of not living up to his standards, often felt unqualified to participate in rituals in his presence. You couldn't make a single mistake on a torma or leave out a single detail in a mandala arrangement on the shrine, because you somehow knew that he would not only detect it but find it unacceptable. You would be hard-pressed to find anyone more thorough—he was a true perfectionist! Novice lamas didn't dare put on airs when he presided over a ceremony.

Samten Gyatso was so learned and skilled, so trustworthy and matchless, that people compared him to Marpa, the master translator who brought the Kagyu teachings from India.

Yet my guru never postured nor put on the air of high realization, like those meditators who never lower their vacant, glaring gaze to the ground and who spout random "profound" statements such as "Everything in samsara and nirvana are equal!" What do you gain from such pretense?

Samten Gyatso would move about as if he were just an ordinary person. He kept to the hidden yogi style: he didn't flaunt his accomplishments and never behaved as if he were a grand lama. He would not bless people by placing his hand on their heads nor sit on a high seat. He didn't even let people bow to him—if anyone tried, he would jump up and move away. He avoided ostentatious displays like erecting impressive temples or commissioning fancy statues. He kept a low profile: he never dressed up or wore brocade, but just the robes of an ordinary monk.

If Samten Gyatso had any special understanding or powers, he was careful not to show them. Moreover, he would not tolerate anyone speaking to him about his good qualities—he wouldn't even give them an opening. For instance, if they started to say, "Rinpoche, you are very learned" or "You must be very realized," he would immediately scold them. He would never talk about himself as being special, not a single word. No one ever heard him say, "I have realized" such-and-such or "I have these special qualities." Not once!

❧

Samten Gyatso's daily practice consisted of the *Heart Essence of Samantabhadra* and the *Heart Essence of Chetsun*. You could say that these two teachings were his innermost personal practice. As he put it, "To meet with a practice like this just once guarantees you an end to samsara."

He also had a deep fondness for the masters Longchenpa and Jigmey Lingpa. He would often read aloud from Longchenpa's *Seven Treasuries*, not as a formal reading transmission but just for himself—slowly and in a gentle tone of voice. He always carried one of these seven volumes with him wherever he went, so that by the end of the year he would complete his reading of all seven. After some years, he knew exactly where to find every single detail mentioned anywhere in these *Treasuries*. He would sometimes comment, "How wonderful! What an amazing master Longchenpa must have been! How profound his words are!"

The *Lotus Essence Tantra* was a text my uncle Samten Gyatso considered of utmost importance. He transmitted it to people again and again and often taught it. This is probably why one of the first things I did when I came to Nepal was to have the blocks carved. Sometimes my uncle would prepare blessed substances by reciting this tantra along with two other tantras that give liberation through hearing, touching or tasting. One is the famous *Single Child of the Buddhas* and the other is known as the *Universal Panacea*. He would then ask people to put the substance into a large river to benefit all the beings who lived there and in the great ocean. Chokgyur Lingpa revealed several such tantras.

Samten Gyatso once told me, "I have two texts that can truly benefit others. One is the *Single Child of the Buddhas* and the other is the *Lotus Essence Tantra*. And there is absolutely no doubt about that!"

It was rare for him to make such a claim.

※

In terms of his tulku lineage, Samten Gyatso was the fourth incarnation of the highly accomplished master Ngawang Trinley of the Tsangsar clan.[85] At the age of five he was taken to Lachab monastery, where he stayed with my previous incarnation, Chöwang Tulku, who became his root guru. Samten Gyatso was then installed as the lord of Dharma of that monastery. In his youth, he stayed at Lachab and at Fortress Peak, while later he lived in one cave and hermitage after another.

Samten Gyatso received ordination as a monk from Karmey Khenpo. He may also have received the pointing-out instruction as well as the confirmation of insight from Karmey Khenpo, which might be why he had extraordinary faith in him—just like my father's trust in his root guru, Söntar Chönchok, and Uncle Tersey's devotion for his, Shakya Shri. Later on, Tsewang Norbu became Samten Gyatso's main guru, followed by many other great masters living in Kham.[86]

My uncle Sang-Ngak and, strangely enough, his own mother, Könchok Paldrön, both regarded Samten Gyatso as their root guru. My father too had profound faith in Samten Gyatso and every time we went to Fortress Peak, even before we came within sight of the hermitage, he would dismount and bow down twenty or thirty times.

※

I heard a wonderful story about one of Samten Gyatso's prior incarnations, Ngaktrin of Argong. He was recognized as a tulku while still a small child and brought

19. Fortress Peak—the lofty hermitage

to Lachab, his predecessor's monastery. One day, when he was just eight, he was having fun with his friends, as children do. An old *gönla*—the lama in charge of the chants for the protectors—was beating a drum and chanting while the kids were playing boisterously around him.

"You are an incarnation of a lama," the gönla suddenly berated the young Ngaktrin. "Don't behave like this. A tulku should be a noble boy, but you are a spoiled brat! Why are you doing this? What's the use? Listen: don't wander! Don't wander!"

"What does that mean?" the little tulku asked. "What does it mean not to wander?"

"Don't let your mind wander," replied the old lama. "That's what it means!"

"How does one not wander?"

"Look at yourself. Look at your own mind!"

When the boy heard these words—"Don't wander; look at your own mind!"—he recognized mind nature right then and there. Despite all the great masters he met later in his life, he always said his insight occurred when he was a young child.

❧

Later on, Ngaktrin went to Palpung monastery in Derge, where he went into the traditional three-year retreat. When he went through that retreat for a second time, he was installed as the retreat master. There he reached an incredibly high level of practice.

As it happened, the great master Situ Pema Nyinje was the head of the monastery. In the latter part of his life, Situ's eyebrows covered the upper part of his eyes, blocking his vision. When he had to read something, he needed to put his fingers to his eyebrows and lift them in order to see. Apart from this, his eyes were always covered or closed.

Only in the autumn would Situ open his eyes and look out the window, mainly to gaze at a rhododendron on the hill opposite Palpung, which blossomed then. "Ah! The rhododendron is in full bloom," he would exclaim. But as he got older, his eyes couldn't open at all.

One day, Chokgyur Lingpa came to Palpung for the first time. Someone announced to Situ, "A fellow who calls himself Chokgyur Lingpa is coming. He's that Kyasu tertön from Nangchen we've been hearing about."[87]

Situ didn't believe in just any tertön who happened to pass by. Indeed, Situ had been decidedly unimpressed by another recently visiting tertön, about whom he had remarked, "Well, well! That guy claims to be a treasure revealer, but his posturing seems to me merely an excuse to keep a woman. All he really succeeds in doing is defaming the Lotus-Born master."

But Situ had some confidence in Chokgyur Lingpa, and so was prepared to meet him. Nonetheless, he called for Lama Ngaktrin, saying to him, "I hear that you have clear dreams due to your practice of Naropa's Six Doctrines. This Kyasu Tertön claims to be an emissary of Padmasambhava and has declared himself a major revealer of treasures. But I don't trust just anyone who claims to be a tertön. Since our monastery has arranged to welcome him as a dignitary tomorrow, you should watch your dreams tonight for signs that might verify his claims. Report back to me any experiences or visions you have."

Ngaktrin was quite a remarkable practitioner and had accomplished much in his retreat. During his dreams that night, he received a prophecy confirming that Chokgyur Lingpa was indeed an authentic tertön. Upon hearing this dream, Situ was delighted and amused.

"Ha ha! Ha ha!" he joked, "Chokgyur Lingpa must be a true tertön—assuming of course that we can trust your dreams."

༄

When Chokgyur Lingpa arrived, he told Situ: "You are one of Padmasambhava's emissaries. The Lotus-Born master personally commanded me to give you a teaching called *Dagger of the Sevenfold Profundity* to protect against obstacles to your longevity."

"Is that so?" Situ replied. "I'm too old to do the recitations myself. While you do them, I will watch for the signs." Traditionally, on completion of a retreat, one looks for signs of blessings and success in practice.

Situ then put the tertön in strict retreat for a month to practice the *Dagger of the Sevenfold Profundity*. At the end of the month, Situ's servants prepared to fetch for him the blessed articles from Chokgyur Lingpa.

"No, the tertön has to come in person to give me the empowerment," Situ insisted. "It won't help me just to have the tertön send up shrine objects—the secret Vajrayana is not something you simply put on someone's head. Call for the tertön himself!"

So after he finished his retreat, this unknown tertön offered the empowerment for the *Dagger of the Sevenfold Profundity* to Situ, the most revered Karma Kagyu lama east of Lhasa.

༄

Here's another story I heard about Lama Ngaktrin, Samten Gyatso's previous birth.

The winters in eastern Tibet were so cold that the water from the snow melting under the sun's rays would freeze in its flow, creating broad barriers of icicles, some up to three stories high. These would sometimes block the steep mountain trails, making travel impossible. Yet no matter how cold it was or how much snow had fallen, there was never any snow on Lama Ngaktrin's roof: it would melt from his tummo, the yogic practice of inner heat.

One day, Ngaktrin received news that one of his major sponsors had passed away on the other side of the mountain pass. On the way there, a river had flooded and then frozen, so that huge ice curtains rose to a height of two or three stories. There was no way to get through.

A request arrived via a much longer trail for Lama Ngaktrin to come and do *phowa*, the ejection of consciousness, for the dead patron. Ngaktrin, without a moment's hesitation, replied, "I'm coming!"[88]

His attendants tried to dissuade him, protesting, "How can you go? Do you want to die in the icy water? And if you have to travel around the ice curtains, it will take you two or three days. How can you, an old lama, go there? There's no way—just forget about it."

But Ngaktrin said: "No, it would be very improper not to go. He has been a kind patron to me. If I fail to reach him, it would be a serious breach of samaya. I'm going tomorrow morning, no matter what!"

The servants could do nothing but obey, although unhappy that they would have to take the long treacherous way around. Ngaktrin however assured them that that wouldn't be necessary.

Bright and early the next morning, he told his attendants, "Last night I cleared the way."

Sure enough, all the ice on the whole mountain pass had melted. There was not a flake of snow anywhere; they could travel freely. When asked, "How can this be possible?" Ngaktrin simply responded, "Last night I practiced a little *tummo* and melted it."

⁂

Though he had been installed as the head of Lachab monastery, Samten Gyatso longed for the lifestyle of "a yogi of true simplicity." So one day he gave up responsibility for the monastery's upkeep, as well as all of his official duties and went to live in a cave.

His only wish was to meditate while leading the simple life of a renunciate, without any of the pomp and circumstance that surrounds an important lama nor the obligations of being at the disposal of benefactors. Since he was the main tulku of the monastery, no one felt they could object to his wishes; they had to let him do what he wanted. He would have been quite content to continue living like this, but it was not to be.

Eventually, Samten Gyatso journeyed to Tsikey monastery in order to study with Karmey Khenpo. As he grew older, Samten Gyatso became an invaluable upholder and advocate of Chokgyur Lingpa's termas. Of the four brothers—all tulkus—it was he who rendered the greatest service to the *New Treasures*, even more so than the tertön's two direct reincarnations.

❧

Here is how this vital Dharma activity unfolded. Being a direct descendant of the tertön himself, Samten Gyatso felt a deep appreciation for the *New Treasures*, and so he began a dedicated search for any of these texts he could find. In fact, this was the only project besides meditation that he put any effort into as a young man.

Even while living the life of a yogi in various caves, he always had four or five private scribes nearby whose task was to copy out all forty of the volumes. He would then proofread these handwritten texts to ensure their complete accuracy. I saw them—they were astounding![89]

Samten Gyatso's tenacious search for the full collection of the *New Treasures* also ensured that he received all their empowerments, reading transmissions and instructions. The majority of these he received from the tertön's son Tsewang Norbu—like one precious vase filled to the brim from another—but he also received every one of these teachings that Karmey Khenpo had.

Samten Gyatso's main interest—his innermost passion, you might say—was Dharma scriptures. He ardently collected each and every one that he considered of importance, not only the *New Treasures*. His library, very large by Nangchen standards, grew so big it would have filled the shrine hall at my current hermitage, Nagi Gompa. Even one hundred fully loaded yaks wouldn't have been enough to move his collection.

His willingness to undertake any necessary trouble in this pursuit of rare texts was famous; he sought them out wherever he could. If he was invited into someone's home for a ceremony, before he began he would scan every cloth-wrapped scripture kept on their shrine. He would take the time to explore their entire library, even if there were two hundred volumes. He would insist that each book be unwrapped from its cloth cover so he could inspect every single one of what often proved to be many texts within. He didn't care if this took an entire day.

Not only was my teacher extremely fond of books; they also had to be copied beautifully and precisely. Otherwise he would return the book to its scribe, saying, "You can keep this one—I don't need it. I only want true quality."

And he wasn't merely committed to collecting Dharma books. He also had a vast collection of the finest implements for rituals. Whatever was missing for a given ceremony he would commission an artisan to make, always to the highest standards.

If it weren't for the destruction wreaked by the communist invasion, these fine manuscripts and ritual implements would still exist today—but all of them have been lost.

~

Shortly before Samten Gyatso died, I spent many evenings with him. He would lie in his bed and I would sleep on the floor beside him. One night, as we were talking, Samten Gyatso began to speak, for the first time, about his innermost realization.

"I never had special experiences," he told me, "but as the years passed by, my trust in the authenticity of the Dharma has grown. I am now confident in the truth of the three kayas. At the age of eight, I recognized the nature of mind and since then I have never forsaken it. Of course my diligence varied and I got distracted at times, but mostly I kept to the practice of mind's natural state."

I heard him say this only once. Other than this, he never discussed such personal matters.

~

That same evening he also told me about his relationships with Khakyab Dorje and Tsewang Norbu, as well as with his other teachers. Here is one of those stories.

While Tsewang Norbu was giving the empowerments for the *Treasury of Precious Termas* at Riwoche monastery, all the major lamas and khenpos would gather in the evenings for supper and conversation. Usually this informal gathering took place in Tsewang Norbu's private room, which was otherwise the chamber of the head lama. The room would be packed each night and people would request all kinds of instructions, clearing up any doubts and uncertainties they might have had in their meditation practice.

One evening the three grand lamas of Riwoche were all there, as were both the Neten and Tsikey incarnations of Chokgyur Lingpa, as well as my youngest uncle, Tersey. Samten Gyatso was still quite young at the time and, among all these important masters and khenpo-teachers, kept a low profile, sitting close to the door.

He was dressed in ordinary, low-quality monk's robes, not in a brocade vest like some of the lamas.

One night, Tsewang Norbu scanned the room with his large eyes wide open, then pointed directly at Samten Gyatso all the way at the back of the room and boomed in his famously brazen manner, "By the Three Jewels! You see that humble monk sitting by the door? Lamas, take note, his name is Samten Gyatso! As you may well know, he is the son of Chokgyur Lingpa's daughter Könchok Paldrön."

He looked around the room, staring intensely at each person. Everyone stopped in their tracks.

"Right now you think highly of yourselves," Tsewang Norbu continued in his loud voice. "You there, you think you are one of Chokgyur Lingpa's incarnations and you over there think you're one too. And you," he was pointing at Uncle Tersey, "you consider yourself the tulku of Wangchok Dorje—don't you?!? Samten Gyatso back there by the door, he is not proud at all—but when it comes to continuing the lineage of the *New Treasures*, I swear by the Three Jewels, he will surpass all of you! Through him these *Treasures* will spread far and wide, like the renown of the Jowo statue in Lhasa. That humble monk will be the pillar upholding the teachings of Chokgyur Lingpa!"[90]

Remember, these were not unimportant lamas gathered around him; they were all tulkus and khenpos of high stature. The room went silent as they looked around at one another. Then they turned to look behind them at the little monk in ordinary robes.

For his part, Samten Gyatso felt ill at ease. He thought to himself, "Why does this great yogi have to say such things, even swearing, in front of great lamas?"

Although Tsewang Norbu was his uncle, even Samten Gyatso was a little afraid of him. And when he made a statement like this, it sounded like a prophecy—one Samten Gyatso never forgot.

After completing all the empowerments, Tsewang Norbu stopped at our Tsangsar family home on his way to Central Tibet. During his stay, he asked to camp in a big white tent, which was erected outside the nearby temple hall. One day, he sent for Samten Gyatso, who lived a day's horse ride away. In those days, Samten Gyatso was content to live the life of a simple yogi-monk.

"I received word that Tsewang Norbu has requested my presence," Samten Gyatso recalled. "On arriving I was led to his tent. When I entered the tent, I saw a large throne with some of his robes lying on it."

"We are going to have an enthronement—right now, in this very tent!" Tsewang Norbu announced. "You are going to take the position of a triple-vow vajra holder—do you hear me? And from now on, you are never to give up Chokgyur Lingpa's teachings!"

Then he forced Samten Gyatso to sit on the throne. While my guru sat there, Tsewang Norbu gave him one gift after another, beginning with his personal vajra and bell, as well as a full set of his own robes.

"From today on, I empower you to be a vajra master," Tsewang Norbu continued. "And now, by giving you a complete set of my robes, I appoint you as my representative. I entrust you with the lineage of the *New Treasures*. You must carry out the work of continuing Chokgyur Lingpa's teachings."

Though Samten Gyatso protested, he was still enthroned as a vajra master and invested with this weighty responsibility.

At the end of the ceremony, Tsewang Norbu said, "Nephew, tonight you and I will stay in this tent—we have lots to talk about."

That evening he told Samten Gyatso, "We won't meet again in these bodies. I place all my possessions in your hands."

Then he gave Samten Gyatso everything he owned—his clothing, brocade garments, ritual implements and all the rest.

"I say we won't see each other face-to-face again in this life, but even if we did, it wouldn't make any difference. All this is yours now."

The next morning, Tsewang Norbu set off on his journey and Samten Gyatso never saw him again.[91]

༄

After several years passed, Samten Gyatso received a letter from the Karmapa, Khakyab Dorje, asking him to travel to Tsurphu to give the empowerments for the *New Treasures*. After reading the letter, his only comment was, "There is nothing in terms of view, meditation, and conduct that I could possibly improve upon for Khakyab Dorje. But if this is his wish, then I will give him the transmission as if it were a mandala offering."

This was the other reason why Samten Gyatso accompanied Könchok Paldrön on the journey to Central Tibet.

Upon arriving in Central Tibet, Samten Gyatso went straight to the Karmapa's seat at Tsurphu. These are the first words Khakyab Dorje spoke to him:

"I tried to have Tsewang Norbu bestow the transmission of the *New Treasures*, since he was not only Chokgyur Lingpa's son but also an authentic vajra master endowed with the three levels of precepts.[92] I requested it from him because he was incomparable, possessing all the true characteristics of a master. Yet it appears he didn't see things as I did; otherwise how could he refuse me? I also made the same request of your brother, Tersey Tulku, who likewise refused. Now, Samten Gyatso, since you are the son of Chokgyur Lingpa's daughter and also in the divine bloodline of Tsangsar, you must confer the empowerments upon me."

This was the Karmapa's command.

Samten Gyatso stood up and bowed three times. "You are Avalokiteshvara in person. Honestly, I'm not qualified to bestow empowerments on such an exalted lama as you. To be a Vajrayana guru, one must possess the tenfold characteristics. Forget about all ten, I don't possess even a single one of them! If I had a choice between giving and not giving empowerments, I would rather not. That much is certain. On the other hand, I would never do anything to upset you."

"Whether you have all ten attributes, only one or none at all, you still have to give me this transmission." Since this was the Karmapa's order, Samten Gyatso had no choice but to concede.

"I guess I must," my guru said. "Chokgyur Lingpa's termas are like refined gold and as soon as this pure gold is in your hands, Wish-Fulfilling Jewel, it will definitely benefit both the Dharma and sentient beings."

He then proceeded to give the complete transmission of the *New Treasures* to the Karmapa. The lineage of this transmission went from Chokgyur Lingpa to Tsewang Norbu to Samten Gyatso, and this is how he passed it on to the fifteenth Karmapa.

Samten Gyatso received many teachings from the Karmapa as well—that's why Samten Gyatso regarded the Karmapa as one of his own teachers. My guru would tell me how the Karmapa was an inconceivably great master, about his clairvoyant powers and accomplishment, and how he could perceive the three times as clearly as something placed in the palm of his hand. Samten Gyatso's trust in Khakyab Dorje was so deep that merely mentioning this Karmapa's name would bring tears to his eyes.

※

Some time after Samten Gyatso arrived at Tsurphu, he was invited to the Karmapa's private chambers. As my guru walked in, he saw a throne set out, bedecked with brocade robes, crown and all the paraphernalia of a vajra master. Just as with Tsewang Norbu, the Karmapa told him to sit down on the throne. And again, at first there was much protesting back and forth.

"I command you to sit there," Khakyab Dorje finally said. "I am enthroning you as a vajra master. If you don't uphold the Dharma, then who will? On the outer level of the ethical precepts, you have not impaired them so much as a mustard seed's worth. On the inner level of a bodhisattva and on the innermost tantric level of a vidyadhara, there is no one who can match your realization of the view of the heart essence of the Great Perfection. You are truly a vajra holder of the threefold precepts."

The Karmapa continued, "It seems to be your wish to live as a simple renunciate in remote mountain dwellings and caves. You have done so until now—and isn't it true that you still prefer to do so? But now I tell you this: From this very day onward, you must renounce that idea!

"Today I enthrone you as a vajra master who guides sentient beings, as one who confers the ripening empowerments and who gives the liberating instructions with the supportive reading transmissions. I demand that you pledge to do so right here in front of me! From now on, this is your task."

He added, "Now it will be absolutely inappropriate for you to follow the example of the Kagyu forefathers by giving up everything. I want to hear you vow to give up such ways! I know full well that your intention has been to retreat to some secluded hermitage once you leave Central Tibet and return to Kham—but if you do so, you will be going directly against my command!"

Samten Gyatso stood up and went to the throne. But before sitting down, he made one last protest. "I do this with hesitation. I have lived in caves and wanted nothing more. I yearned to devote myself solely to meditation and I wish you wouldn't force me to do this."

"Listen here!" the Karmapa replied emphatically. "Do not sever our samaya link. Now sit down!"

This left Samten Gyatso quite cheerless. He would never say that the Karmapa had created an obstacle for his practice—but if he hadn't been given this direct command, you wouldn't have found him anywhere but in remote mountain retreats. There is no way he would have retaken charge of Lachab monastery.

Samten Gyatso often told me, "I had no wish whatsoever to be the head of a monastery. All I wanted was to stay isolated high above the tree line."

Before Samten Gyatso became enthroned as vajra master, he had very rarely placed his hand on someone's head in the gesture of bestowing blessings. If it ever did happen for some reason, the people of that area were overjoyed, telling each other, "How lucky I am! I received Samten Gyatso's blessing!" In the past, no one had received an empowerment or reading transmission from him either, let alone a blessing on their head.

"From that point on," he told me, "I really fell under the power of Mara," the demon of obstacles, "and began to give empowerments and teachings. That was when I fell down to my present low level. One distraction followed another, as now I had to perform rituals in a steady stream. But this was never my plan; I never aimed to live in splendor and admiration—only like a deer in the mountains."

※

Samten Gyatso was definitely the most self-assured of the four brothers and his confidence grew stronger as he aged. Because of his dignity and his dominating presence, people found it hard to approach him for small talk. In fact, I never saw him chat with anyone. His eyes burned with an astounding brilliance, like the flame of a butter lamp flaring up at its end—somewhat like the bright eyes of a kitten. Coming into his presence, you felt him penetrating your innermost core, laying bare your deepest secrets.

Everyone was afraid of him. It wasn't the way he dressed, for he wore the simple robes of a monk, yet even lamas were completely intimidated by him. Most lamas and monks would try to get out of his way if they saw him in the distance coming toward them. Whenever he entered a room people made way for him—even lofty dignitaries. It didn't matter who they were; everyone was completely terrified and would scramble to clear a path for him. Even my father would assume the role of servant the moment he was in Samten Gyatso's presence.

It was amusing to see how daunting that bald little old monk in ordinary robes could be. He even intimidated the sixteenth Karmapa, who, when he was already twenty, told me, "Now, take Samten Gyatso. There, finally, is someone I'm in awe of. I don't know why, but that old lama scares me! I even think twice about asking to be excused to go to the toilet!"

It was true for me, too. Every morning when I stood before the door to his quarters, I would hesitate before daring to open the door.

He possessed some remarkable quality, an intensely commanding presence. There was nothing really to be afraid of, but we were all definitely scared of him.

※

After Karmey Khenpo died, he was reborn as my cousin. We simply called him Khentrul, meaning the incarnation of Karmey Khenpo. The young Khentrul was quite courageous and remarkably eloquent. Once he said to me, "Why should we be scared of Samten Gyatso? He's just our uncle."[93] But whenever Khentrul came into Samten Gyatso's presence and saw his bald head, he would forget what he had been about to say. He would lower his gaze and start to tremble very slightly.

Khentrul explained, "Every time I go to meet Samten Gyatso—who after all is my own uncle—I try to remind myself that he is a human being just like me. Even though he is a very noble monk, there is absolutely no reason to feel intimidated. But the moment I'm in his presence, I find myself hesitant and trembling.

"I try to reason with myself: what are people so scared of? When I look at him, I see an elderly man wearing simple clothes. Maybe it's his bald head, I don't know, or maybe it's his eyes. They are kind of unusual and hard to look into. It's as if they see what's deep inside you. So I remind myself I don't have to be afraid; after all, he's my uncle. But none of that works!"

There's a saying, "True confidence overwhelms others." It's hard to put a finger on exactly what that quality might be—but you often see it in people who have profound meditative realization.

No matter where he was, Samten Gyatso had a certain influence on people. There was no small talk; he didn't leave any room for superficial conversation, just sincere questions about practice, for which he never lacked an answer. When he gave instructions, Samten Gyatso would foresee how his words would end up—whether they would be put to good use or not.

To laypeople, whose main aim was mundane success and raising families, he would give the mantra of Avalokiteshvara—OM MANI PEME HUNG—and teachings on trust and devotion. But he gave special attention to people who had dedicated their lives to deepening their experience and realization. With a sincere practitioner he would truly share his heart.

In either case, whenever someone left an interview with him, they were deeply inspired and full of admiration.

Many old ngakpas lived around Lachab monastery and whenever they heard that Samten Gyatso had come home, they would immediately flock to his room to receive teachings on the Dzogchen view. Sometimes they stayed throughout the night, not leaving until morning. These meditators, his closest disciples, marveled at the clarity of his teachings—and such seasoned meditators were very hard to impress.

These old ngakpas loved Samten Gyatso and felt that his mind was completely unimpeded. In fact, anyone who had a chance to discuss their meditation practice with him always came out amazed—no matter who, no matter how learned.

In any discussion Samten Gyatso had with knowledgeable scholars who had oceans of learning behind them, as the hours passed they all became humbled on the topic of meditation experience. Finally, their initial air of self-assurance would dissipate altogether and they couldn't help requesting teachings from him, asking one question after another.

As Samten Gyatso imparted the essential meditation practice, his majestic presence would shine through ever stronger, intimidating even the most learned khenpo. The more anyone talked with Samten Gyatso, the more clearly they discovered how invincible his self-confidence was. This unshakable assurance signifies profound practice and personal experience.

That's the kind of guru I had.

※

There were many other lamas and meditators who had deep devotion and trust in Samten Gyatso.

One day, a meditator who lived above Tsangsar came out of Samten Gyatso's room as I went in.

"Today I had the chance to help someone, just a tiny little bit," my guru remarked. "This guy is a first-class practitioner, truly industrious. But he believes he has been cultivating emptiness, while in fact he trains in imprisoning the awakened state. What's the use of keeping it locked up?

"I succeeded in making it clear to him that emptiness isn't anything you can possibly cultivate. How can you construct emptiness? After we talked, this meditator understood and was able to gain a little trust."

Later, I ran into this meditator, who told me, "In my life I have met many teachers and received numerous instructions. But if I hadn't met Samten Gyatso, I'm not sure I would have progressed along the true path. On that day he settled something in my mind with utmost clarity. Now I don't even have as much as a hair-tip of doubt."

This man had incredible devotion to Samten Gyatso. It was obvious to me that he had more than "a little trust."

※

Once at his monastery, my father arranged for a drubchen and asked Samten Gyatso to preside.[94] During the long hours of the drubchen, they and my two other uncles sat together.

"Something strange happened during this time," my father recalled. "I saw a shimmer of rainbow light surrounding Samten Gyatso. The next day, it happened again while he was sitting on his throne. On the third day, the colored light was so intense that I couldn't see his physical body.

20. Tsewang Dechen—the tulku of Samten Gyatso

"All three of us—his brothers—saw it, and we discussed what the reason might be. One of us had simple pure perception of the rainbow light. Another was unhappy, fearing it might be an ominous sign that he was nearing death.

"But none of us had the guts to mention it directly to Samten Gyatso. If we had done so, there is no doubt we would have been scolded. 'Why do you bring up such nonsense?' he would have said.

"But that doesn't change the fact that all three of us saw his body as though it were made of rainbow light."

Samten Gyatso passed away later that same year.

11

My Father,
the Performer of Miracles

When my father was very young, he was recognized as a tulku, the fourth incarnation of the master Sönam Yeshe of Tsangsar. One day, some lamas rode up to the Tsangsar family home; they were from the monastery where, in his previous incarnation, my father had been head lama. They demanded to see my grandmother and then asked her to hand the child over to them.

Their arrival happened to coincide with the passing away of my great-grandmother, Lady Degah.[95]

"This is a time of mourning," she told the monks. "My mother has just passed away and I'm very busy with her funeral arrangements. Please don't ask me about my son right now. I probably will have to hand him over to you—how can I ignore the Karmapa and his regents' command?—but this is not the time for me to accept a white scarf and to celebrate the tulku's return. Come back when the funeral ceremonies are complete. In the meantime, the tulku stays with me."

The emissary was very pushy and—let's not shy away from the word—*insensitive*.

"Heh, heh," he laughed condescendingly. "We are discussing a vajra command: there is only one thing for you to say and that is 'yes.' I will not accept any other answer from you. I cannot and I will not return to the monastery empty-handed," he added emphatically.

The lama's monastery was a two-day horse ride from the Tsangsar family estate. "This matter must be settled today," he continued. "I have come too far to return without the tulku. I won't accept any postponement."

"Dear lama," Grandmother cautioned, "don't be so brazen. I already told you I would give you my son—but this day is not right for an auspicious beginning. My mother's body is still lying there; only three days have gone by since her death."

She continued in a reasonable tone, "According to normal social conventions, people don't speak so rudely as you to someone they respect. You don't have to act like this. And remember, a mother always has the final say in the well-being of her own child."

"That doesn't make the slightest difference," the lama retorted.

My grandmother warned, "There's no need to talk like that! I'm only asking you to wait one week. Don't be so aggressive!"

But the lama persisted, saying he didn't have a week to wait. "I can't agree with you," he insisted. "This must be settled right now."

Grandmother was the kind of person who stuck to her word. She wouldn't budge.

"I told you no! I'm not going to hand my son over to you and I'm certainly not going to your monastery for a celebration. And one more thing: I am not afraid of you, nor should I be. You may be somebody important where you are from, but here I am somebody important. Why should I defer to you? You will gain nothing by being so aggressive!"

By then, the lama had already placed the white scarf before grandmother and she now handed it back to him. So he tossed it over to her again—and again she threw it back. The scarf went back and forth three times.

The lama made one more attempt to wrap the scarf around Grandmother's neck, as is the custom. She resisted, saying, "No one dresses up in their finest when their mother has passed away! Or maybe you want to strangle me!"

They got into quite a quarrel and it turned a bit nasty. Finally, Grandmother exclaimed, "Now I'm absolutely certain: I won't accept your white scarf! I shall never hand my son over to someone like you! As he is my child, he is in my care! You will never get him—so you might as well get out!"

The lama responded with spite, "Well, if that's the case, then we definitely don't want this tulku at all!"

Now there was no way to heal the rift and on that note, the lama marched away like an adversary leaving his enemy's camp.

But he didn't go far; the lama and his cohorts pitched camp in a juniper grove nearby. From that vantage point they kept an eye on our house.

It was very clear what they were up to. Chimey Dorje was kept inside and wasn't allowed to walk around outside unattended—otherwise they would have snatched him up and ridden off back to their monastery. I heard that three or four monks stayed in their little camp for several weeks, playing this waiting game. Finally, they all left.

I still have a hard time appreciating their brand of "devotion."

Not long after the funeral, Grandmother had to travel to Tsikey. As her party came out of a narrow pass, they suddenly confronted twenty-five monks on horseback. The monks blocked the trail; except for the absence of rifles, it was like facing a division of an opposing army ready for battle. They demanded Grandmother hand her son over to them right then and there.

Chimey Dorje, was only three, but he was clever. When the monks were about to grab him, he objected, "I'm not Sönam Yeshe's tulku. It's him!" and he pointed at his brother, my uncle Sang-Ngak, who was standing next to him.

Unfortunately, one of the monks in the "welcoming party" knew better and retorted, "It's not true. That's his brother."

During this confrontation, Grandmother's attendants had their hands on their knives. "We can at least kill a few of them," they whispered to her. "What do you want us to do?"

"No, today there is no need to shed blood," my grandmother cautioned. "Anyway, there are twenty-five of them; you would be lucky to overcome eight or ten. They have the upper hand, so they win this round. Rainbows don't appear every day—let's be patient. Our day will come."

You can see how obstinate some Khampas can be: Könchok Paldrön's small child was being abducted in front of her very eyes and there was nothing she could do.

In the meantime, a monk had grabbed Chimey Dorje, wrapping him up tightly in his shawl and the maroon-clad gang of monks carried him off.

❧

As soon as the locals around the Tsangsar family estate heard about the abduction, they prepared for battle and marched toward the monastery where my father had been taken. Fighting was just about to break out when the local *ponpo* chieftain intervened.

He prohibited them from fighting and instead offered to mediate the dispute. His proposal was that my grandparents would agree to give up their son and in return the monastery would offer an apology, with lavish gifts to appease my grandmother.

Her husband—my grandfather, Orgyen Chöpel—was a very influential person in the area and as a gentleman he was not interested in carrying on a dispute. His view was, "Of course we should give them the tulku. I don't blame the old lama for being assertive nor do I blame the child's mother for what she told him. The lama was at fault—but now he is happy to reconcile and see the case settled."

And so my grandfather accepted the settlement and my father remained in the monastery's care.

This was how my father was "invited" to his monastery as a reincarnated lama.

※

My grandmother was far from happy about this turn of events, and decided to leave her husband and his family estate.

"There is no way in the world I will remain here any longer," she proclaimed. "I will go and live near Tsikey Chokling." So she moved to the seat of her father and brothers.[96]

Meanwhile, my father's education began immediately, and at that early age he was forced to sit the entire day learning to read and write. He progressed in his studies and his monastery flourished. After two years, Chimey Dorje's reading skills were so impressive that word traveled around the countryside.

After five years had passed, he insisted on seeing his mother.

By now the manager at my father's monastery felt confident that since my father was eight it would be safe to escort him to see his mother for a short visit and then bring him back. Everyone at his monastery thought that the disagreement had been settled long ago, and now everything was just fine and dandy. So they allowed him to go see his mother at Tsikey, escorted by ten monks.

But after five or six days, Könchok Paldrön told them, "The ten of you can return now—but without my son."

And she kept Chimey Dorje there.

※

The ten monks were headed by a very nice lama, who put up no resistance. But they were heavy of heart as they rode back to their monastery without their tulku.

"When we reached the main gate," that same lama later told my father, "I yelled out, 'They kept our tulku!' And just then that brazen old lama who had started the whole affair fell out a window.

"It was all very inauspicious. Like a storm brewing, word spread quickly. All the monks and lamas gathered in the main hall, and the courtyard filled with local people. Everyone became quite agitated and incensed; tears fell and harsh words were spoken."

Messengers were sent back and forth to Tsikey. My father's monastery was relentless, but my grandmother remained adamant.

"We cannot possibly fight Tsikey Gompa," the lamas decided. "But we will definitely take this case to the highest authority." So my father's monastery brought a legal case against Tsikey and things began to get ugly.

As my father's monastery was Kagyu, they referred the case all the way up to Palpung, which was the major Kagyu seat in Derge. The monastery sent a representative to plead their case. Undaunted, the Chokling of Tsikey personally went to Palpung, pleading Grandmother's case with his well-known eloquence and ingenuity.

The head of Palpung was an incarnation of the great Situ Rinpoche, who was quite young at the time and very mild-mannered; he begged them not to fight. Tsikey Chokling and his entourage stayed in one room, and representatives of the plaintiff stayed in another. It was quite an elaborate dispute with many lamas involved and lasted about fifteen days.

In short, the plaintiffs argued that the Karmapa had recognized *their* tulku and according to tradition there was no doubt that the tulku should return to his monastery, where he rightfully belonged. Otherwise it would be like casting to the wind a letter bearing the Karmapa's seal.

Tsikey Chokling, on the other hand, argued that a child is born from its mother and there is no tradition that allows for taking a child without its mother's consent—and as Könchok Paldrön had sworn never to give up her child, he should stay with her.

In the end, it was decided that Chimey Dorje could stay in his mother's care.

☙

Looking back, I have to admit that as he grew up, my father became a bit of a rogue. In his younger days, despite being a tulku, his personality revealed an unusually gutsy side—a wild streak. By any standard, he didn't exactly seem a spiritual person, much less a descendant of great masters.

During this time, the younger brother of the Nangchen king had been given a large estate. This particular prince must have been greedy because he also usurped some land belonging to our family.

My father was not shy about confronting him. The dispute escalated into a physical confrontation and I believe several people ended up dead. But the Nangchen palace indirectly backed the prince and my father couldn't fight against the king.

Chimey Dorje now had to flee to Tsikey monastery. Since it was under the jurisdiction of Tsikey Chokling, the Nangchen royalty couldn't touch my father there. Instead of the quarrel continuing, messengers were sent back and forth until the dispute was settled.

Later, my father became a pönpo chieftain in Nangchen. Dressing up like a tough guy in the good old Khampa fashion, he carried a long knife and a rifle, and would go out shooting everywhere. He would frequently become involved in disputes and lead his band of followers into battle. He delighted not just in confrontations but in a good fight. Though incorrigible, he was brave and no one in the area could best him.

You could say he had a taste for heroics.

☙

But finally my father's previous karma caught up with him in the form of an old hermit, a close friend of Samten Gyatso's.

Being of serious mind, one day Samten Gyatso told my father, "I am going to meet a great yogi; why don't you come along?"

This master, Söntar Chönchok, was a meditator who had spent most of his life in mountain hermitages. He was regarded as an emanation of Namkhai Nyingpo, one of the twenty-five close disciples of the Lotus-Born master. He grew up in Nangchen at the Tsechu monastery adjacent to the royal palace. He then asked to be excused from the monk's life and lived as a yogi. The first Tsoknyi was one of his teachers among several others.

For years Chönchok traveled from one mountain retreat to another. Finally, he settled at a small hermitage above Neten monastery, where he remained until his death. He focused on nothing but meditation practice without being distracted by any mundane undertakings. As a result of his one-pointed practice, he became a Dzogchen master famous for his high level of realization.

21. Tsechu monastery in Nangchen

Chönchok was a special friend of Samten Gyatso; they were each other's guru and disciple. For instance, they were Dharma brothers because they received the *Treasury of Precious Termas* from Tsewang Norbu at Riwoche at the same time. When Samten Gyatso wanted to clear up any doubts about his experiences, he would consult Chönchok.

So my father went along as Samten Gyatso's attendant to the small hermitage in the mountains. When they arrived at the hermit's door, Chönchok came out to greet Samten Gyatso, "Welcome, Rinpoche!"

Then he noticed Chimey Dorje. "Who have you brought with you?" he asked.

"He's the reincarnation of Sönam Yeshe of Tsangsar," replied Samten Gyatso.

"Ah, so the Sönam Yeshe incarnation has arrived! I have waited *so* long to meet him," the yogi exclaimed as he began to bow down at my father's feet.

Chimey Dorje tried to sidestep him, but Chönchok kept bowing in his direction, an expression of deep respect.

"This is terrible!" my father thought to himself. "How can this lama have such pure perception of a sinner like me? Look at me—I'm dressed like a bandit ready for a fight. I'm covered in weapons; yet this old lama has such devotion to my former incarnation that none of this makes any difference. I have hurt so many people—how I have wasted my life!"

As these remorseful thoughts ran through my father's mind, the hermit kept bowing to him. Finally, the old yogi stopped.

"Standing there with him bowing to me was much harder than any fight I had been in," my father later admitted to me. "Somehow he had touched me deeply."

※

By the time my father went inside, Samten Gyatso was already sitting comfortably having a cup of tea.

My father was so moved that he vowed to Samten Gyatso, "Today, in front of this lama, I promise never to repeat any of the evil deeds that I have made my way of life."

"If you really mean it," replied Samten Gyatso, "then you should surely take that pledge. But if not, what's the use of making hollow promises you won't keep? It will only cause you grief."

"But wouldn't it be best if I became a Dharma practitioner and learned from this hermit?"

"That's up to you. If you have faith in him, then go ahead. If you don't, then I'm not going to force you to do anything. He's a close friend of mine and we have shared many teachings; he's also one of my gurus. Personally I have faith in him.

But you should follow your own heart. I never tell people they have to receive teachings nor do I ever discourage anyone."

"I have made up my mind," my father replied. "From this moment until I die, I will behave like a Dharma practitioner!"

So due to the skillful intervention of this old yogi, Chimey Dorje had a complete change of attitude.

❦

Determined to start right away Chimey Dorje told Samten Gyatso, "I must receive teachings and practice. Please make this request on my behalf."

"All right, all right, that much I *can* do," Samten Gyatso said. "Go and find the hermit," who was still outside.

Chimey Dorje went out and found Chönchok, and asked him to come in and sit with Samten Gyatso.

"I have something to ask of you," my guru addressed the old yogi. "Please instruct my brother in spiritual practice."

"No problem," Chönchok replied, "that I'll do." Turning to Chimey Dorje, he continued, "However, you will have to first swear an oath to me."

"Sure. What is it?"

"From this very day until you leave this life, whether you are a ngakpa or a monk, you have to wear the garb and shawl of a spiritual practitioner. There's no way around that! It is a sign of being a follower of the Buddha.

"We live in the age the Buddha described as 'adhering to mere appearances'. The three previous time periods have passed; in this fourth age, it is especially important to adhere to some sign that represents the teachings of the Awakened One. So right now promise me that you will wear the practitioner's skirt, the sleeveless shirt and the shawl."[97]

Then and there Chimey Dorje pledged, "From this moment until I die, I will shed these mundane garments and wear only lama's clothes. And I will live up to them as well!"

But having made the pledge, Chimey Dorje was puzzled, thinking, "What am I supposed to do now? I don't have any other clothes with me."

Samten Gyatso came to his rescue, saying, "It just so happens I have an extra set of robes with me. They're not of very high quality, but maybe they'll do. I would be happy to let you have them."

Chimey Dorje put on his new robes, bowed his head to Chönchok and said, "Please cut my hair."

Perhaps Chönchok saw that my father would soon take a consort and be a ngakpa rather than a monk.

"I don't dare cut your hair," he replied, "since you are without a doubt the reincarnation of Sönam Yeshe. Instead there should be a special ceremony to enthrone you as his successor."

My father was twenty-two years old at the time. He continued to request meditation instructions from Chönchok and regarded him as his root guru.

From that day onward, my father became more gentle.

❧

One day my father had a vision of his guru riding a lion in the sky. Within this vision, his teacher then imparted the oral instructions on meditation practice, including the pointing-out instruction to the awakened state of nondual awareness. From this vision it seems my father had received the blessing we call the transference of realization. People say he totally changed from then on; hardly anyone was as mild-mannered as he.[98]

As he put it, "I was no longer a rigid, relentless practitioner; it was like a clod of dirt had turned to dust. I felt totally free."

My father told me this personally, adding, "From that day on, my mind was like a sun shining from a cloudless sky."

And this is true—many people told me that from then my father was extremely gentle and treated everyone with respect and pure appreciation, no matter who they were. It would also appear that he had attained stability in nondual awareness. For this reason my father considered Chönchok his ultimate root guru, saying, "This master was the kindest to me!"

Shortly after this having this vision news arrived of Chönchok's passing.

❧

During the latter part of his life, Chönchok reached the stage called the *collapse of delusion*—the final of four levels in Dzogchen, which in Mahamudra terms corresponds to the stage of *nonmeditation*.[99] He had perfected his meditation training.

Samten Gyatso told me that the level of realization Chönchok achieved results in the rainbow body. Though he didn't show the rainbow body at the time of death, his body did shrink quite a bit after he died, a sign that he had definitely gone beyond delusion. When he passed away there were auspicious lights and sounds, *ringsel* pills, and some wondrous designs of rainbows in the sky—just as the Dzogchen tantras describe for someone with such a high level of realization. Even Samten Gyatso was amazed.[100]

I can still remember my father's respect and devotion at even the mere mention of Chönchok's name. If he had to say the name himself, he was barely able to speak, losing his voice for a while. His devotion was that deep.

And that is why to this day we include Söntar Chönchok in our daily chant to the lineage masters.

❧

Looking back, I see it was primarily thanks to Samten Gyatso and my father that I received the transmissions I have today. For instance, my father transmitted to me the entire corpus of the Buddha's words, which fills more than one hundred large volumes. He could read the whole *Kangyur* in three months, at a pace of about a thousand pages per day. His tongue was that agile.

My father was fond of pilgrimage and would often interrupt serious teachings and ceremonies to take the day off on an outing, including a joyous picnic. But there were no interruptions when he gave a reading transmission.

What's more, you could hear each word distinctly, so that at the end of a day of reading sutras aloud, most educated people could remember what the Buddha had said to whom and where, and were able to retell it to others. Three times he read the entire *Kangyur* aloud for others.

Because Chimey Dorje had such a beautiful voice, wherever he went people would gather from near and far to listen to him. Of his many fine qualities, one of the best known was his power of mantra—probably a result of his vast number of practices and recitations related to the Mahayoga tantras. And when he did the *Chö* ceremony, it was particularly impressive—important families from the entire area, all the way to faraway Ziling, would invite him to perform rituals to support their health, prosperity and longevity.

Perhaps his tongue had been blessed in some way, for it would be hard to find someone more articulate and with a voice that could project as far. When he chanted the Chö songs at his hermitage, they could be heard echoing across the entire valley.

After his body was cremated, they found his tongue lying intact in the ashes.

❧

I shouldn't be saying this about my own father, but nevertheless it is true: Chimey Dorje was the only one of the four brothers known for performing miracles. You could say it was part of his style. He had clairvoyant powers and also performed several miracles.

Chimey Dorje had many visions of past masters and yidam deities. But, unlike his brother Samten Gyatso, he didn't always keep his visions and premonitions to himself. I trusted in my father's clairvoyant abilities because I often heard statements from his own mouth about matters that he could not possibly have known otherwise and which were later verified. For instance, before someone of importance would unexpectedly show up at his hermitage, he frequently would tell me that so-and-so was on the way. When I would ask who had sent the message, he would reply it had just occurred to him—and sure enough, a short time later the person would arrive.

As for miracles, he did leave a set of footprints in a rock near our home at Tsangsar that I have seen myself and another set near Mount Gegyal—right beside a set left by Chokgyur Lingpa. And at his hermitage Dechen Ling, the Sanctuary of Great Bliss, there are imprints in solid rock of both his feet and his hands.

Often people would ask my father for a prediction of how long they would live. Once an old lady asked him, "Eh, Rinpoche, how long do I have left?"

"You have about three days," my father blurted out, without thinking.

Immediately she wailed, "I only have three days? Oh, no, what am I going to do?!"

Then my father softened the blow, saying, "No, no—I said three months, at least."

Again she wailed, "Do I really have no more than three months? Please, can't you do something?"

"Sorry, but I meant three years," father offered.

Two days later, Samten Gyatso asked my father to spend a few days with him and we went up to Fortress Peak. The next day we got a message that the old lady had died. That was how precise his predictions could be.

"It would be better not to give old people such bad news anymore," I advised my father.

He laughed and said, "So now I'm not allowed to give life predictions? This kid used to be *my* student—now I appear to be his."

I am sorry to say that one tends to have less appreciation and pure perception for a lama when he happens to be one's own father. Other people, however, regarded my father very highly, especially at Gebchak monastery, where they held a yearly drubchen of *Tukdrub Barchey Kunsel* for which he regularly gave the empowerment.

One time, a brother of one of the Gebchak nuns had gotten into a lethal fight with someone from a powerful family. Having received news about the fight and convinced that her brother was dead, the nun came to request my father do the name-burning, a ritual that guides the dead to a better rebirth.

"It's late now, so I'll do it in the morning," my father said. She left the room crying.

In the morning, I began to prepare the shrine for the ceremony. But Chimey Dorje hadn't said anything about the ritual, so after a while I asked, "Shouldn't you start the ceremony, father?"

He replied, "I'm not sure what has happened, but I am certain her brother didn't die."

"What do you mean?" I asked.

"If someone has died, their spirit always comes before me, but I don't feel any such thing today. So I'm convinced he's not dead."

After a while, the nun returned to make an offering for the ceremony; but I told her my father had said her brother wasn't dead.

My father interjected, "You will get clearer news in two or three days."

And sure enough, it wasn't more than a couple of days before she learned the whole story—and, of course, her brother hadn't been killed after all.

※

The innermost core of my father's practice was the *Heart Essence of Samantabhadra* and the *Heart Essence of Chetsun*, but the main framework for his practice was *Chö*. At one point the Chö tradition comprised over one hundred volumes.[101] Today probably only about eight survive, but they contain amazing teachings.

The heart of Chö is to benefit others by cutting through ego-clinging. One basic principle involves transforming your material body into ambrosia, a divine food that you first offer to enlightened beings and then give away to sentient beings. More advanced practitioners do this practice in a scary place, like a charnel ground and there imagine their body turning into ambrosia that they give away to appease negative forces, spirits and unhappy ghosts.

A goal of Chö is to reach perfection in the single nature of reality, which refers to the realization of Prajnaparamita, transcendent knowledge. This is also known as the samadhi of egolessness, the vajralike samadhi or ultimate truth. This realization is identical with the quintessence of the twelve thick volumes of the *Great Mother of Transcendent Knowledge,* one of the most famous sutras in Mahayana. "The main teacher of the Chö system in Tibet," my father explained, "was the female master Machik Labdrön, who attained realization by accomplishing the ultimate intent of transcendent knowledge. After that, for the benefit of others, she would daily recite all twelve volumes. She had achieved the 'sixfold tongue accomplishment,' whereby the capacity of one's speech is increased six times. People also saw her as having a third eye in her forehead."

He would sometimes say to me, "How can there be any difference between the view of Prajnaparamita, which is the very essence of Chö, and the view of the Great Perfection? They are completely identical! Mahamudra, Dzogchen and Chö ultimately converge in the same awakened state—the ultimate transcendent knowledge. There isn't the slightest difference, is there?"

❧

My father once explained, "The Chö system mentions four classes of demons: obstructive and unobstructive demons, demons of exuberance, and demons of indecision.[102] A practitioner has to cut through all four. The obstructive demon refers to incarnate demonic forces, like Mao Zedong, for instance. The unobstructive demon includes evil spirits of which there are thousands of kinds. The demon of exuberance means being seduced by success and followers, social status and recognition, which leads to fascination with the thought, 'I am truly special!' The fourth, the demon of indecision, is the source of all the others. The subtlest demon, this consists in clinging to a point of view; it is identical to cognitive obscuration, the most subtle veil that covers our buddha nature.

"The sequence of Chö," my father said, "follows the general principles of tantric practice. Then comes a particular retreat in which you perform the *Jewel Garland*, a long collection of Chö songs, once a day for one hundred days in a row. Alternatively, as the framework for the day's practice, you would use a shorter text, no more than six pages, known as the *Single Seat Session* or follow a similar text by Karma Chagmey. You would do that in the early morning and then throughout the day sing the various songs until one hundred days had passed. This was one way to measure a Chö practitioner's retreat.

"Later you would do another set of one hundred days on a mountain, then at a river and then at a major bridge. Only when you had accomplished all four sets of one hundred days would you deserve the title of Chö practitioner. It wasn't enough just to buy a large drum and a bone trumpet, and claim to be such.

"In the next phase, these Chö practices were done not only during the daytime; you would go to scary places in the dead of night. At some point, the practitioner might face tests known as 'eruptions' or 'challenges,' in which a local spirit would challenge your stability by creating magical apparitions of varying degrees of intensity."

When I was a small child, people would try to scare me by saying that many practitioners have met their end during Chö practice. These eruptions could be dangerous. Some practitioners might become seriously ill, others go crazy and in rare cases some have even been known to die.

"At one point in Chö practice," my father continued, "you would have to spend one hundred nights in a cemetery where corpses were buried or a charnel ground where they were lying around." In Kham we have places where up to ten thousand human bodies are buried, like some large cemeteries I've seen in Malaysia.

"You would go alone to the cemetery," my father continued, "sing the Chö songs in utter darkness and be willing to go through any eruptions, facing these tests until the break of dawn.

"Sometimes if a meditator's practice were in fact just a mere simulation of a high level of meditative stability, the local spirits would conjure up a spectacle in the practitioner's field of experience enticing him to get caught up in delusions of grandeur. Then, once the practitioner felt assured of his achievement, he could be caught off guard by a simple scary vision.

"True Chö practitioners, however, wouldn't take the bait but would simply carry on. Finally, they would be truly stable in all situations: cemeteries, remote valleys, marketplaces—anywhere.

"When practitioners reached the point where even the most terrifying eruption couldn't perturb them, they would do a final set of Chö practice lasting seven days. Six of the seven days would typically be utterly serene. But then, on the seventh night, terrifying visions would occur.

"At the least, meditators confronting an eruption should remind themselves that this is just a temporary experience, totally devoid of ultimate reality, and then remain composed in the continuity of the true view. Then, any such eruptions are nothing more than watching children play.

"The moment you give in to fear," my father told me, "you have already failed the test."

꙳

When I was small, I heard quite a few scary stories from my father. Here is one of them.

In eastern Tibet there was a cemetery where corpses were abandoned in a place between two cliffs. This spot was known to be extremely terrifying and strange things would often happen to practitioners who stayed there.

Precisely because of this terrifying reputation, my father went there one evening with two attendants. Since a Chö practitioner must be alone while doing his practice, his attendants had to remain at least eighty paces away.

"After night fell," Chimey Dorje told me, "I began my practice. All of a sudden, something fell down from the sky right before me. When I looked closely, I saw a human head staring at me with glaring eyes, its tongue waggling. Suddenly, another one fell down, then another and another. Each one made a loud 'Thump!' when it hit the ground.

"One of them even hit me right on top of my head and I felt a sharp pain. After that the downpour became violent, like a hailstorm of human heads. They all seemed to be alive. Finally, the whole place was full of human heads, complaining and making horrible noises. Some coughed and moaned, 'I died of rotting lungs.' Then they spat up globs of putrid phlegm."

Still my father didn't move. He continued his practice.

"Eventually, the heads shrank in size and diminished in number, until finally they all had vanished without a trace."

This exemplifies the kind of eruption we call "challenges from magical displays by gods and demons."

My father continued, "After a while, I stood up and walked over to see what had happened to my two attendants, who had been lying asleep in the middle of the hailstorm of human heads. They were still asleep and unperturbed; they hadn't noticed a thing."

At one infamous place in Tibet skeletons are said to dance—and so of course my father also went there to practice Chö. Skeletons, known as "bone demons," are greatly feared by Tibetans, as are "skin demons" and "hair demons."

While my father practiced Chö at that place, male and female skeletons arrived to dance together all around him. They even performed elaborate folk dances in their efforts to scare him.

"The dancing was not so hard to handle," he later said. "I simply continued my practice."

The other kinds of demons showed up, too. "The worst were the skin demons, big sheets of human skin that would slowly float toward me in grotesque shapes. When they got very close, I felt an intense pain in my gut, as though I had been struck. Once again, I simply remained in the nondual state of awareness, until the human skins shrank in size and finally vanished, just as the skeletons had.

"The hair demons were like big bundles of human hair that would swing back and forth in the sky in front of me, bouncing up and down. They staged all sorts of theatrics, until they too disappeared."

❧

Once Chime Dorje was practicing Chö at Drak Yerpa, a famous cave hermitage near Lhasa; he had been asked to perform a healing ceremony there for a government dignitary. Since he had decided to perform Chö, he went to a charnel ground at night with an attendant.

"When the attendant went to dispose of the effigy," my father recounted, "he vanished; he was nowhere to be found. I was left alone. Suddenly a huge army of monkeys appeared out of nowhere, all with grinning teeth and white beards. They threatened me, coming up to my face, touching and even biting me. As they grabbed for my hands, they felt solid and real. They were all dancing and baring their teeth viciously."

At first my father became frightened. But, on second thought, he reminded himself, "There are no monkeys anywhere around here in Central Tibet. This is just another eruption, so what is there to be afraid of?"

The monkeys jumped closer and closer, stomping him to the ground. Nevertheless, Chimey Dorje thought, "There are no monkeys here! This must be a test! This much is certain: these demons are pretty astounding! They're trying their best to put up a frightening spectacle—and yet they only offer an opportunity to display my power of samadhi."

My father never lost his confidence that "all this is merely a show; it is not real." He simply continued his Chö chant without interruption. Gradually the monkeys shrank until they were the size of rats. Then they vanished.

In the end, there was only one tiny little monkey left, looking feeble and forlorn. It looked up at him in such a pathetic way that he couldn't help feeling compassion for it.

"Just a few moments ago," he thought, "you appeared so huge and horrendous. What use are all your powers to conjure magical displays? Now look at you—you pitiful little thing!"

❧

Chimey Dorje was famous for curing people—more so than his older brother Samten Gyatso. Sometimes sick villagers were carried to him from as far away as two or three weeks' journey. Once every week he would do the Chö ritual and they would recover—or not—and return home.

During the ritual, the sick people had to lie down as if they had died, giving up all concerns. In his meditative state, Chimey Dorje would then open his "Chö eyes," with which he could see the karmic causes of their diseases and the remedies necessary for a swift cure. He would then announce his insights aloud for all to hear.

When people heard why and in what circumstances they had fallen ill, they were often astounded. This did not cure everyone, but the morning after the Chö ritual, it would always be clear whether they would recover or not.

My father cured a lot of people in this way and received plenty of gifts of gratitude as well as widespread respect. Ask any of the old people from my region—they all remember Chimey Dorje and his Chö practice.

Sometimes he was even able to cure people who had gone mad. Once at his hermitage a family carried in a woman bound with ropes and writhing angrily. I was there myself and witnessed the whole thing.

"Unless we keep her like this," her husband said, "she bites herself terribly. We can't talk sense to her or understand anything she says."

My father told the family to place her at a distance, all by herself. He then began the Chö ritual. After a while she stopped sneering, quieted down and became still. They untied her, but she just sat there.

My father let her sit there, in the same position, for five days. On the second day, she looked as if she had just awakened from sleep, and immediately urinated and defecated right were she sat. She was carried off, cleaned up and brought back to the spot. By the third day, some color returned to her cheeks and some life to her eyes.

On the seventh day, she walked home with the others on her own power.

※

The master Dabzang Rinpoche told me that an epidemic once broke out at his monastery, Dilyak Gompa; in just one year, eighteen young monks died. At the same time, the monastery inhabitants were being spooked by strange sounds at night, until no one dared venture outside after dusk. Finally, no one had the courage to visit the monastery and things became eerily quiet there.

At some point, a messenger came to Dabzang with a white scarf from the great Situ. The message read, "Chimey Dorje of Tsangsar must be called upon to help. If he performs a healing ritual, your problems will be over."

When the request was made to my father, as he had a close link to the Dharma protector Gyalpo Pehar, he had a tiny image of this guardian made. The monks of Dabzang's monastery carried the image in a procession and placed it in the small shrine room for the guardians of the Buddha's teachings. The procession was accompanied by the sound of trumpets, gongs, cymbals and drums. He then told the monks to chant a short petition to the guardian with their daily liturgy.

From then on, no further deaths occurred. All the nighttime sounds subsided as well.

For three years, everything was fine—until a thief made off with that small statue. Then the disturbances began again. So my father had the monastery build a tiny protector temple at the foot of a huge boulder nearby and put a similar image there. After that, all was well.

※

Once, the pönpo chiefs and their entourage from each of Derge's twenty-five districts were traveling north in a group of more than seven hundred. As they reached the other side of the small kingdom of Ling, their horses were stricken by a plague.

The epidemic became so severe that thirty of their horses died in a single day. The whole party was forced to stop. Everyone was deeply worried—they felt they could neither proceed nor turn back.

The chiefs sent a request for my father to come immediately. My brother Penjik journeyed with him.

"Yesterday, thirty of our horses perished. You are supposed to have some powers. What can be done?" they asked.

"Set up camp here," my father said. "Send people out to find firewood, a lot of it. I will need to conduct a lavish fire ritual."

He soon began. In the distance, Penjik could see the corpses of the dead horses and a great many others that were already sick. The healthy horses were off grazing separately.

Suddenly, Chimey Dorje ordered, "Gather all the horses together—every one of them, no matter their state of health—on the plain here before me, in front of the fire. Mix the sick horses together with the healthy ones! According to the Chö tradition, we should totally let go of hope and fear. Separating the healthy from the sick is nothing but hope and fear, so give it up!"

When they had done as he said, he began throwing special substances into the fire. At a certain point, he walked around the herd smearing each horse with what appeared to be grease from the fire.

Then he commanded, "Let all the horses loose. Free them to roam where they please, without any hobbles, halters, saddles or other riding gear."

My brother Penjik had incredible faith in our father; he had never once opposed or disobeyed him. He regarded our father as his guru and ultimate refuge. Yet, when he was lying in the tent together with Chimey Dorje that evening, trying to go to sleep, he was scared. "I knew that a number of horses were already sick," he later told me, "and I feared the moment when we would hear how many had died overnight."

In the middle of the night, unable to sleep, Penjik and a servant quietly snuck out to look around the camp. They soon saw a horse so sick it couldn't stand up and then another that had already died. They dreaded going further.

To their surprise as they proceeded they didn't find any other fatalities. My brother was then able to get some sleep, but was soon awakened by a cry, "Another horse is dead!"

"But that's the only one!" someone else yelled, "All the sick ones have begun to eat grass and drink water!"

All that day, Chimey Dorje just sat there chanting the Vajra Guru mantra, unconcerned. Not a single horse died after that.

He was quite the marvelous dad.

❧

Several years after he returned from Central Tibet, my father began retreat at his main hermitage, Dechen Ling, the Sanctuary of Great Bliss. In total I believe he spent around thirty years in retreat there. It was there he left his body, when he was sixty-three years old.

Before he died he told us, "If there is any need for me to serve Chokgyur Lingpa's treasures, I will return and do so. But I would definitely not be happy if someone were forced to be my tulku. So don't look for any after I die!"

That's why we never asked any masters to tell us where to find his next incarnation.

Like their uncle, Tsewang Norbu, none of the four brothers was at all interested in having his next life recognized and so we didn't look for Uncle Tersey or Sang-Ngak's tulkus, either.

12

Two Special Uncles and Their Teachers

Uncle Sang-Ngak

The Karmapa recognized Sang-Ngak, my third uncle, as a tulku.[103] The Karmapa told the tulku's monastery where he could be found and, as was the custom, the lamas there had to send a letter to my grandparents to inform them. This was just after my father's abduction and Könchok Paldrön was still deeply upset.

"One of my sons has just been abducted," she told the messenger. "And now you have come to do the same with his younger brother, Sang-Ngak?

"If this is true," she added with a tone of sarcasm, "please tell me now, so I can watch the spectacle! For you will never hear any word of consent crossing my lips—of that you can be sure! Already the eldest has been recognized as the reincarnation of Ngaktrin and carried off to Lachab. My second son has been ripped from my hands and taken off to another monastery. The great Khyentse predicted my youngest was the rebirth of my late brother, Wangchok Dorje, and he has been taken away to Tsikey, my father's seat.

"All I have left is Sang-Ngak and I need a son in the house to help me. Now you've come for him—are you going to act like brutes and take him by force?"

You could say that this was bad timing for that monastery because Grandmother got pretty angry. Still heavy with sadness over having lost Chimey Dorje, she never gave her permission for Sang-Ngak to be taken away and without her consent there was nothing the monastery could do. So Uncle Sang-Ngak remained with our Precious Mother and was of tremendous help to her, serving as cook and household manager for the first half of his life.

His greatest quality was perfect recall, so whatever Könchok Paldrön taught him he never forgot. In this way, it was through my grandmother that Sang-Ngak learned the entire tradition of Chokgyur Lingpa, especially the melodies for all the chants and the details of the various tormas. After his mother passed away, it was

Uncle Sang-Ngak who carried on the authentic knowledge of chants and tormas for the *New Treasures*.

Uncle Sang-Ngak became a monk while still young and he kept his vows with great integrity. He truly upheld the three levels of precepts: outwardly the ethical vows of individual liberation, inwardly the bodhisattva trainings and on the innermost level the sacred bonds of Vajrayana. He was honest, noble and learned—a first-class practitioner.

After my grandmother passed away, he spent most of his life in retreat. He only slept a little bit at night. To be honest, I haven't met anyone who was more persevering; he did nothing but meditate, primarily in retreat. Like Samten Gyatso and my father his main practices were the *Heart Essence of Samantabhadra* and the *Heart Essence of Chetsun*. He had extraordinary experience and realization.

Never famous like his brother Samten Gyatso, he had neither great sponsors nor obligations. He was a fine hidden yogi, kept a very low profile and had an easygoing personality. His was the simple life of a meditator, which was a very good life indeed.

That's the kind of lama he was.

❦

Uncle Sang-Ngak and I lived together for several years at Fortress Peak with Samten Gyatso. Uncle Sang-Ngak often acted as his older brother's assistant, serving him in many ways. Even though he too was a tulku, he never claimed to be Samten Gyatso's equal.

Uncle Sang-Ngak received the pointing-out instruction and all the pithy advice on meditation from Samten Gyatso, and he never went to any other teacher about such matters. He had such respect that he would never remain seated when his older brother entered the room—as if Samten Gyatso was the Karmapa in person. You rarely see that kind of respect among siblings.

Only after Samten Gyatso passed away could Uncle Sang-Ngak be forced to confer any empowerments from the *New Treasures*, something he adamantly refused to do before. There was just one exception.

Once at Fortress Peak Samten Gyatso forced him to give the empowerments for the *Three Sections of the Great Perfection* because Uncle Sang-Ngak alone held Karmey Khenpo's lineage. First Samten Gyatso made him give us the empowerments, which took almost a week. As soon as Uncle Sang-Ngak was done, Samten Gyatso very carefully gave the whole set of empowerments all over again to Uncle Sang-Ngak, my father and me.[104]

Later on, many people told me that whenever Uncle Sang-Ngak was the ritual helper for Samten Gyatso during empowerment ceremonies, he was like a cat. Unlike most, he was never clumsy while handling the objects on the elaborately complex shrine arrangements, never spilled a drop of anything, never stumbled over anyone no matter how busy he got. His footsteps never made a sound, a skill in which he had obviously trained, nor did he make undue noise in any other activity.

Uncle Sang-Ngak didn't have many students, and he never gave meditation instructions—unlike his brothers, who were known everywhere, like the moon and stars. In his later years, though, his renown grew and people from all around showed more devotion to him; they had started to appreciate that through his mother he held the direct lineage from Chokgyur Lingpa. In this way, the transmission of the *New Treasures* came to rest on him, since there was no one else with such purity of lineage.

Later in my life, while in retreat at a hermitage above Tsurphu, I received the news that he had passed away.[105]

Tersey Tulku

My uncle Tersey, the youngest of the four brothers, had originally gone to Central Tibet on pilgrimage, but even after several years passed had not returned home to Kham. This eventually prompted my grandmother's search to bring him back home.

Uncle Tersey had traveled far and wide, even visiting India and Bhutan, making pilgrimage after pilgrimage. In this way, he had stayed in Central Tibet for approximately eight years in the first part of his adult life.

Tersey had quite a powerful personality. He once led a large group of people to safety when they were threatened by bandits on their pilgrimage around Mount Kailash. Because of such exploits, Tersey became famous for his deftness.

He was known as "the bearded Tersey Rinpoche," where *Tersey* signifies being the tulku of Chokgyur Lingpa's son, the handsome, long-haired Wangchok Dorje, who died at twenty-four after cutting his hair.

Uncle Tersey's root guru was the master Shakya Shri. During his long absence from home, my uncle lived at Shakya Shri's encampment when he wasn't on his occasional pilgrimage journeys.

Back in Kham, Uncle Tersey's status had been equal to that of the two reincarnations of Chokgyur Lingpa and their thrones were of the same height during ceremonies at the great tertön's main seats.[106] Tersey was an elegant writer who arranged many manuals for the procedure of giving the empowerments in the *New Treasures*. He also wrote an explanation of all the deities in the *Tukdrub* practice—all this in spite of never having had any serious education. Someone with deep insight can often teach as well as a learned khenpo.

At some point, the need arose for Tersey to carry on the *New Treasures,* and fulfill his main duties at Tsikey and the other monasteries. That was why his mother and three brothers all went off to Central Tibet to find him, and bring him back to Nangchen.

Still, it took them five years to get Uncle Tersey back to Kham. At the end of his life, Uncle Tersey took up residence at the retreat center above Tsikey. By then he was suffering from an illness that forced him to walk with two canes. I heard that this might have been a punishment from the dakinis, carried over from his previous life, due to his taking monastic ordination rather than being a tantric practitioner.[107]

୬

Uncle Tersey's main practices were the *Heart Essence of Chetsun* and the *Heart Essence of Samantabhadra*. In addition, he was really fond of a particular practice of the Lotus-Born master known as *Guru Mahasukha*, a mind treasure of Shakya Shri that he had received personally from that tertön himself.

I heard that Uncle Tersey displayed miracles and had clear foreknowledge on several occasions, but he refused to confirm such things himself. In this way, he showed true integrity.[108]

Once Samten Gyatso remarked to Uncle Tersey, "It seems that even high meditators, for some reason, have to lose consciousness for a moment or two while in the state between waking and falling asleep—even though, of course, our basic awakened state doesn't lose its cognizant quality. If the rest of the time confusion has vanished, not only in the waking state but also at night, that signifies achieving the level of a great bodhisattva."

"But even below that level," Uncle Tersey replied, "I'm not sure a bodhisattva won't fall back into samsara or even into hell."

Uncle Tersey sometimes made such outlandish remarks.[109]

୬

You may remember that the fifteenth Karmapa had wanted to receive the transmission of the *New Treasures* from Chokgyur Lingpa's son Tsewang Norbu. Since that proved impossible, as his next choice the Karmapa sent for Tersey.

Uncle Tersey was extremely learned and paid great attention to details, so he was highly qualified to give the *New Treasures* in a very precise way. After Tersey arrived in Central Tibet, the Karmapa sent him a message.

To make this request—as he had before with the tertön's son Tsewang Norbu—the Karmapa once again sent Jampal Tsultrim, his most trusted servant.

"The Karmapa requests that you come to Tsurphu and give him Chokgyur Lingpa's *New Treasures*," Jampal Tsultrim told my uncle.

Like his brother Samten Gyatso, Uncle Tersey was a hidden yogi type, who always tried to avoid the spotlight. So he responded, "This is utterly ridiculous! Why are you making this demand?"[110]

"It's not I who am asking you to do this," replied Jampal Tsultrim. "It's the Karmapa giving you his command."

Then they got into a heated argument. Finally, Jampal Tsultrim gave in to his Golok temperament and slapped Uncle Tersey across the face, yelling, "You lowlife!" and burst out of the room. He then walked off.

On returning to the Karmapa, he said, "This Tersey Tulku is impossible—the lowest of the low! I argued with him, but he utterly refuses to come."

The fifteenth Karmapa merely replied, "That's all right. We'll see."

The Karmapa was right not to be upset. He then invited Samten Gyatso to come to Tsurphu, without telling him exactly what the purpose of the visit was.

❧

Uncle Tersey was known to be very meticulous. Once at Tana monastery, half a day's ride on horseback from my own place, Uncle Tersey was asked to confer the empowerment for Padmasattva, the wisdom-body of Chokgyur Lingpa.

He began his preparations at the break of day, performing the sadhana alone down to the recitation—which then went on and on, not finishing the preparation before the sun had set!

Tersey was the kind of lama who would retain the meditative states of development and completion during the entire empowerment ceremony. His painstaking way of doing these things was quite unusual, since other masters could easily give fifteen to twenty empowerments in a single day. But not our Tersey. When he finally began conferring the empowerment, he would teach in thorough detail on the six types of liberation and then go on to guide the disciples through personal experience.[111]

In this way, Tersey's empowerment lasted the whole night. If he hadn't been a lama, people would have gotten really annoyed at him.

At one point, he almost gave up giving empowerments entirely.

"I can't give them anymore," he told me.

"Why not, Rinpoche?"

"The empowerment preparation should be stable and authentic," he replied. "Otherwise I just don't feel satisfied. And the minimum number of recitations during the preparation should exceed many thousands for each mantra. But when I do this, it takes all day."

In our region, we still use the saying, "giving empowerments like Tersey Tulku" for someone being meticulous in the extreme.

❧

One prominent trait of masters with a sense of integrity is that they never boast about or make any public display of their inner spiritual qualities. My uncle Tersey was like that.

"It was the great Khyentse," Uncle Tersey once said to me, "who proclaimed me a tulku of Chokgyur Lingpa's son and there is nothing that escapes the reach of his knowledge, since he sees the three times as clear as day. Wangchok Dorje, Chokgyur Lingpa's son, was an emanation of King Jah, who received the eighteen Mahayoga tantras on the roof of his palace.

"So if I am supposed to be the emanation of such masters, I should feel a little special somehow. Shouldn't an emanation of King Jah at the very least have some mental clarity? But when I look into my own mind, I see only the complete darkness of ignorance and confusion. So I can't be sure that I am such an emanation.

"Luckily, the great master Shakya Shri introduced me to the awakened state with these words: 'Listen to me carefully. The awakened state cannot possibly change. Do you hear me? Once you notice this empty, awakened state, in which there is no thing that can change, then there is no need to create it by meditating nor is it something that can truly slip away. Do you understand? Once you have recognized that which cannot change, that's the awakened state. Now keep it in mind, always. Trust me, this is very important! The awakened state is *the* most important thing.'

"Those were Shakya Shri's last words to me and, even though my meditation state is still one of utter darkness, they contain the only thing I feel certain of."

When he made remarks like that, we would usually break out laughing, but Uncle Tersey would continue with a deadpan expression on his face.

"If I say that I'm not an emanation, it would be the same as calling the great Khyentse a liar—and I wouldn't dare do that! But every once in a while, I carefully scrutinize myself to see if I can find any perfect qualities and I can't find a single one. I draw a complete blank."

Again we would laugh. He was that kind of lama.

In spite of what he said about himself, Uncle Tersey was not only a close disciple of Shakya Shri but an extraordinary master in his own right.

※

When both Karmey Khenpo and Tsewang Norbu had left this world, my uncle Tersey was the most learned in Chokgyur Lingpa's *New Treasures*, as well as a capable writer. As long as he was alive, you didn't need to rely on any other master for writing any needed manual.

After his return from his extended pilgrimage Uncle Tersey stayed for a year or two at Tsangsar and then for a couple of years at Fortress Peak, the lofty hermitage linked to my monastery. Being the most learned and competent writer of the four brothers, he passed this time codifying the many texts for rituals and meditation practices needed in his grandfather's lineage. Although no one seems to have compiled Uncle Tersey's writings after he died, there must have been enough to fill more than five volumes. He did a lot to develop the practices found in the *New Treasures*.[112]

When Uncle Tersey was near the end of his days, he announced, "Death will come soon. I am leaving this year."

Then he personally supervised the distribution of every single thing he owned, specifying which item should go to which lama or monastery. He managed to clear everything out and be totally free of possessions, except for one item: a terma treasure in the form of a tiny little statue of the Lotus-Born.

At an earlier point in his life, he had vowed to recite ten million VAJRA GURU mantras and during this recitation retreat he kept this statue concealed in a pure gold amulet box inside a small brocade bag. He treated it with tremendous respect and would say, "I regard this little statue as being Padmasambhava in person. I didn't have the good fortune to meet him otherwise. But the Lotus-Born made this statue out of sand from Lake Manasarovar at Kailash and has infused it with his wisdom-being."[113]

I was told that after Tersey had finished giving everything away, it was no more than three days before he fell ill and died. The last thing he did before passing on was to insert the tiny statue inside the heart center of a newly completed Buddha statue, the size of a fully grown man.

He then said, "Now I'm done, come what may."

Later the communists destroyed everything at Tsikey monastery—including that Buddha statue.

13

Shakya Shri, the Lord of Siddhas

During his stay in Central Tibet, Uncle Tersey frequented the encampment of his root guru Shakya Shri, the great siddha-master. Shakya Shri was also known as the Lord of Siddhas and as Precious Realized Master. His main guru was Old Khyentse.[114]

"Shakya Shri lived with about seven hundred disciples in Kyipuk," Uncle Tersey told me. "His disciples had dug caves all around the two surrounding slopes, while others stayed in tiny tents made of either canvas or yak-felt. Shakya Shri himself lived on a meadow in the only house around, which was a simple structure of stamped mud with one large window."

People revered Shakya Shri immensely. But he had not always been so widely respected, as a story I heard shows—one that may or may not be included in his official biography.

Shakya Shri's first teacher was the great master Khamtrul. Shakya Shri started out caring for his master's horses and doing other manual labor. On one occasion, the yogi Tsoknyi was invited to Khamtrul's camp to bestow the empowerment of his own mind treasure.[115] As the ceremony began, Shakya Shri took the opportunity to slip in and sit by the door. At this time, no one regarded him as special in any way.

"What do you think you are doing here? Get out!" some of the monks turned around and whispered. "This is not for someone like you, only for lamas and Dharma teachers.

22. Shakya Shri—the Lord of Siddhas

Didn't you hear the announcement? This isn't for everyone!"

The monks were about to throw him out, when they suddenly felt Tsoknyi's gaze.

"Let him stay!" he thundered, "You all sit down. A day will come when you won't even be given the chance to drink his pee!"

Tsoknyi made sure that Shakya Shri stayed to receive the empowerment and eventually Shakya Shri became an accomplished master.

Even though so many disciples had gathered around him, Shakya Shri didn't teach year round but only at particular times during summer and winter. These rare occasions were known as the summer teachings and the winter teachings.

Shakya Shri told some of his disciples, "You belong to the Mahamudra side of the valley," while to others he said, "You belong to the Dzogchen side." And so he divided them up in two groups and gave instructions in Mahamudra and Dzogchen in accordance with each follower's individual disposition. My uncle Tersey belonged to the Dzogchen group.[116]

Uncle Tersey explained, "The rules were quite strict: stay put on your meditation seat. The meditators were allowed to walk about only at mealtimes. In the morning, a bell would sound, signaling that the practitioners could light their fires to heat water for tea. All seven hundred monks and nuns would come out of their tents and caves.

"If you were to look around the mountainside then, for a short while people would be milling about with smoke rising from the fire pits. Then the gong would sound again and the whole area became completely still and deserted, as everyone returned to their meditation. The total quiet would last until lunchtime, since no one was allowed to walk outside or cook until then. Around noon the bell would sound again for everyone to begin preparing their meals. At two in the afternoon, the bell rang, after which not a single soul was permitted outside. Again it would be utterly still."

This was the amazing Dharma encampment Shakya Shri maintained.

23. Druk Kharag Yongdzin Rinpoche

Being a siddha, Shakya Shri would remain detached and indifferent no matter who came, with two exceptions. One was Drukpa Yongdzin, the rebirth of one of Shakya Shri's gurus; when he arrived, the master would show particular respect, saying, "Be on your toes! Yongdzin Rinpoche has come!" The only other exception was the highly renowned reincarnation of Chokgyur Lingpa's son—who happened to be my uncle Tersey. Everyone else was treated with equal detachment, no matter who they were.[117]

In those days, Uncle Tersey and Yongdzin must have been young. But they were the only ones who were allowed to do as they pleased; everyone else was supposed to begin and end their meditation sessions at exactly the same times.

One day, when the two of them had been playing around, Shakya Shri called them into his house.

"You two!" the old yogi master rumbled. "Don't disturb other people's meditation! Your own practice may be undisturbed, but don't make obstacles for others!"

That was the only time they got a scolding.

༄

In the afternoon, Shakya Shri usually went outside to relieve himself. He would walk out back in the large yard and squat. Then he would come back in and sit down on his mat, simply remaining there in utter stillness.

But sometimes dusk would fall and it would get dark, and he still hadn't returned. Then Shakya Shri's servants would say to one another, "Rinpoche is absorbed in samadhi again!"

Then one of the attendants would walk out back, find him and whisper, "Rinpoche, you better come in now."

Shakya Shri would then boom in his deep voice, "Ah! The stars are already sparkling!" and walk back to the house.

༄

Once the king of Bhutan sent yaks packed with loads of rice escorted by thirty men, up through the perilous paths in the district of Lhodrak, as an offering to the siddha master. In an accompanying letter, the king explained that he had included an expensive bowl of Chinese porcelain in one of the sacks of rice.

The carriers were supposed to present the master with the china bowl immediately. On their arrival, they began a frantic search for the bowl, poking through one rice sack after another, right there in front of Shakya Shri.

After a while, Shakya Shri pointed his finger and boomed, "The bowl is in that sack over there!"

Sure enough they looked inside and found it. He had that kind of clairvoyant power, although he would never admit it if you asked him.

❧

Three times in his life Shakya Shri got rid of all his possessions, sending them to Lhasa to be given away as offerings. There is a well-known tradition for doing this: you keep only the clothes you are wearing, a cup, a bowl and a spoon, and a few other basic utensils. Everything else is packed up to be dispersed, without even a needle and thread left behind.

The people who witnessed this saw that for a very long time afterward he remained totally free of any possessions. For a while he even refused to accept offerings of any kind.

During one of these periods, my uncle Tersey was in possession of a beautiful gilded statue that he sincerely wished to offer to his guru. However he knew that there was no chance that Shakya Shri would accept it if he presented it under normal circumstances. So he simply showed it to the master.

"What do you think of the proportions?" my uncle inquired. "Are they correct?" After a series of such questions, he finally asked, "What kind of merit would result from offering something like this?"

In the end, the statue became one of the only objects that Shakya Shri accepted during those years.

Uncle Tersey later said, "This was one of the times in my life I was truly able to put illusory wealth to good use."

❧

My uncle Tersey told me the following story when I was a kid. He was one of my teachers and never lied. If he hadn't personally witnessed it with his own eyes, I certainly wouldn't have believed it. But he assured me that this did happen.

Many strange people visited the encampment of Shakya Shri. Once there was a big commotion and crowds began to gather. Tersey went out to see what all the fuss was about.

An old lama from the distant Golok province had just entered camp. After a while, his attendant arrived carrying his baggage. The attendant caught up with him in the center of the camp.

Then the lama shouted "Phey!" and the attendant just fell flat on the ground. Much to everyone's amazement, the lama nonchalantly took the luggage off the attendant's body and set about cooking dinner for himself under the open sky.

24. Cool Grove charnel ground in India

"Don't get too close. Just leave that body alone!" the lama shouted to the crowd.

Uncle Tersey was present when the lama later explained to Shakya Shri what was going on. "I have come from Golok on foot, and that body is my benefactor's corpse. After death he became a *rolang*"—a walking dead—"and now I'm taking his corpse to one of the big charnel grounds in India to dispose of it there. Since the zombie can walk, I thought it might as well carry my bundle. Don't let anyone near it. Tell them to leave the corpse alone and not make a commotion."

But of course no one could be kept away. Everyone wanted to see the corpse that carried luggage. It was as dry as a stick, its eyes were closed, and all the skin and flesh on the soles of its bare feet had worn down to the bone. No one could quite believe it.

The next morning, the lama woke up and made some breakfast. When he was done eating, he performed the ritual of burnt food, probably to "feed" the zombie on the fumes, as it didn't eat or drink anything. Then he packed his bags on the back of the corpse and shouted "phey!"

The corpse immediately stood straight up and, unable to keep its balance when standing still, started to stagger slowly, one foot after the other. The lama headed off with the zombie trailing behind him, the bones of its feet creaking and clacking and making scraping noises against the pebbles and hard ground.

"It always walks at the same slow pace," he had told Shakya Shri. "I have to keep within view, otherwise it loses its way. When I climb to the top of a mountain pass,

I have to wait there until the zombie slowly climbs up after me. Then, I continue on down the other side and wait below until it catches up. I'll come visit again on my way back from India."

The old lama didn't ask for any teachings nor did Shakya Shri ask him any questions. He simply had his morning meal and left.

After he had disappeared from sight, Shakya Shri exclaimed, "Wow! Now that's incredible!" This was one of the amazing feats that someone can perform after attaining stability in the awakened state.

After a year passed, the lama came back through the encampment.

"My kind benefactor's body carried my provisions all the way to India," he said. "I left his remains there at the Cool Grove charnel ground and walked back by myself. On the way down, I had to be careful to keep the zombie in sight all the time because I noticed that people fall unconscious if they touch it; some even become paralyzed or go mad for a while. So how could I have let him walk about in Tibet? The gravest danger with a zombie is that you too will become a zombie if it has the opportunity to touch you on your head. That's why people shouldn't touch him."

Uncle Tersey later told me, "I was never really sure if this lama wasn't just playing a joke. Who knows? Maybe there wasn't a mind in that dead body. Someone who has reached a certain degree of stability in the awakened state can move material objects around at will. Nevertheless, if the lama was playing a big joke on everyone, it was quite a remarkable joke!"

He must have been an accomplished yogi—not because he was able to animate a corpse but because he didn't need to ask Shakya Shri any questions. That's what has stuck in my mind all these years.

14

The Master-Scholar Katok Situ

The author of Shakya Shri's biography was Katok Situ, a great scholar from Katok monastery. Once when Katok Situ visited Central Tibet, he also came to the seat of the Drukchen Jamgön—one of the most prominent lamas in the Drukpa Kagyu school—and was then invited up to Kyipuk, Shakya Shri's mountain hermitage higher up the valley.

He arrived at Kyipuk just after Shakya Shri had passed away; though my uncle Tersey was still there. Shakya Shri's lama disciples discussed who would be the best person to write the master's biography, and they decided upon the learned and eloquent Katok Situ. It fell to Uncle Tersey to make the request.

"Our master was very remarkable," my uncle said. "Please write the story of his life."

"Very well," replied Katok Situ. "Do you have the record of his deeds? Bring me his records!"

Traditionally, lamas write notes in a calendar listing the empowerments and reading transmissions they have received and given, the practices done, as well as other important events and deeds. Katok Situ read Shakya Shri's diary of short notes late into that same night.

During the following days he would give teachings and in the evenings he wrote by the light of a lamp. In less than a week—before he left the camp—Katok Situ had completed a wonderful biography.[118]

❧

"I studied the many topics of philosophical scriptures and traditional sciences," the learned Mipham once told Katok Situ. "In that way, I have been carried away by distractions in the name of the Dharma.

"Shakya Shri, on the other hand, has exclusively practiced Mahamudra and Dzogchen while remaining in the mountains. Shakya Shri raised the victory banner of realization in a single lifetime. If we were to compare our realization, his would be greater!

"The reason for this is simple: he didn't distract himself with a lot of studies of philosophy and the five sciences, but focused simply on the key points of the paths of Mahamudra and Dzogchen. This lord of siddhas practiced day and night."

༄

Let me explain why Katok Situ had come all the way from Kham on this trip to Central Tibet.

Almost a thousand years ago, many tantras and sadhanas were brought from India and translated into Tibetan, primarily by Padmasambhava, Vimalamitra and Vairotsana and their disciples.[119] Some of the explanatory texts that clarify the tantras were lost over the millennium.

One scripture in particular, the renowned *Armor Against Darkness*, was a clarification of Anu Yoga practice according to an original tantra known as the *Scripture of the Great Assemblage*. This commentary, written by Sangye Yeshe of Nub, one of the Lotus-Born's twenty-five disciples, had vanished centuries ago.

For some reason, Katok Situ took it upon himself to find the lost text, leaving no stone unturned in order to include it in the collection of important scriptures. So wherever he would go, he stopped at various monasteries, searching through every library all along his way.

During his stay in Lhasa, Katok Situ asked my uncle Tersey to assist him. Tersey, of course, couldn't pass up this special opportunity to accompany the learned master through the regions of U and Tsang.

Prior to their arrival in Shigatse, they had sent a letter ahead asking permission to visit Tashi Lhunpo monastery, the seat of the Panchen Lama, and look through its vast libraries. The reply came: "You can have permission, but it will be very costly. The chief librarian, the bursar of the monastery and the chief disciplinarian, plus other monastery staff must all be present. You will not be allowed to look through a single book on your own. Taking all the necessary people into account, the fees for research in our library will include food and wages for forty people. And we can only set aside seven days for you. If you can cover the expenses, then you can have access."

Katok Situ was a lama of means and he readily accepted these demands, replying, "Very well, I will spend seven days searching through your library."

The master-scholar from Katok began the search, but after seven days, the book had still not been found. Katok Situ was quite disheartened.

"What an awful shame!" he exclaimed. "I was fairly sure we'd find this book at Tashi Lhunpo. But now there is little chance of ever recovering it anywhere." By this point he had looked through the libraries of most major Nyingma and Kagyu monasteries. My uncle said he looked very sad indeed.

Katok Situ wasn't staying in the monastery but with a family nearby. It then happened that a girl in her late teens from a common family came to see Katok Situ. She asked him to bless her by placing his hand on her head.

At the moment he touched her, she seemed to change. Just as the scriptures describe how the dakinis communicate in gestures and symbolic words, the girl began to move her hands in unusual ways, as though indicating something to Katok Situ.

Then she performed an elaborate dance, singing in Sanskrit and ending the verses with "Ah la la ho!" Finally, she repeated one line, "The *Armor Against Darkness* clarifies the Anu Yoga scripture. Ah la la ho!"

No one present had the least idea what she was talking about. "It's so embarrassing," one person remarked, "that some patrons let a crazy girl in to visit such a great master. What an arrogant kid! Let's drag her out!"

They were about to grab hold of her when Katok Situ told them to leave her alone. Having repeated the line about the book again, she bowed her head to receive a blessing from his hand. Then she stood up and walked out as if nothing had happened.

As soon as she had left the room, Katok Situ said to Tersey and his other attendants, "Well, now! It seems we have to go back and take another look. I think there might still be a chance that we will find it. You must go back up to Tashi Lhunpo and ask permission to continue the search. I will start over, beginning with the libraries on the upper floor and working my way down. I don't care if they charge as much as last time—I would be happy to pay it! Let's hear what they have to say."

My uncle said he hiked back up the stairs and made the request. The administrator he dealt with replied, "You have already looked and found nothing, didn't you? And now you want to do it all again! It looks to me like you want to throw your money away—but if that's what you want to do, go right ahead!"

When my uncle relayed the news of the approval, despite the price Katok Situ was overjoyed and immediately sent him back up with the money. They commenced the search that same day. The text was found five days later.

Katok Situ was really lucky that time because it was Sangye Yeshe of Nub's own commentary, the very master who had brought the Anu Yoga teachings to Tibet.

Afterward, he told my uncle that a dakini had come to him in the form of that girl. That is why the *Armor Against Darkness* is still available to us today.

⁂

Word had spread that Katok Situ was a great scholar. So, during his stay in Lhasa, as soon as dusk fell over the city, groups of a half dozen or so of the most learned *geshe* scholars from Sera, Drepung and Ganden monasteries would come to debate with him.

"If all these people keep coming," my uncle thought, "it will be a burden for the old master. Maybe I should go and lock the door."

When he went to the door, he peeked through the crack. He saw that the scholars were already engaged in a discussion with Katok Situ, taking turns in directing an attack on the master's philosophical position, slapping their hands as they went, in typical Tibetan-style debate. In the beginning, their voices were so loud it almost made your ears ring. Slowly the volume diminished. After a while, the main voice he could hear was that of Katok Situ. In the wee hours of the night, the geshes took leave one by one, touching heads with Katok Situ and thanking him for his time.

As they went out the door, Uncle Tersey heard one of them remark, "Amazing that there is such a learned master alive! I wonder if any debater could beat him. He appears invincible."

This scene played out over and over during their stay in Lhasa, and Katok Situ's fame spread even wider.

Upon his return to Kham, Katok Situ built a most exquisite replica of Padmasambhava's celestial mansion—the Palace of Lotus Light on the Glorious Copper-Colored Mountain—with many bronze statues unequaled in Tibet.

Later, he was sent to China as an emissary to attend an important political meeting. But on his way, having reached an advanced age, he departed for the buddhafields.[120]

And as for that glorious mansion he built? The Chinese invaders leveled it to the ground.

⁂

It was after Uncle Tersey had studied with Shakya Shri and traveled with Katok Situ—and after spending so many years away from home in faraway Central Tibet—that my grandmother decided to go searching for him.

Part Two

Early Years

15

My Childhood

Let me explain a little about my immediate family. My father Chimey Dorje had five children with my mother. First was my sister Tsagah. I was next, and then came my brother Tenga. He was one year younger than I and had been recognized by the Drukchen as a rebirth of a fine master named Lama Arjam. He died when he was thirty-seven years old. After him came my sister Mingyur Chödrön who died in 1989. Both sisters had children, some of whom are still living in Kham. My youngest brother was Kunzang Dorje.

Kunzang Dorje was an astonishing human being and was supposedly an incarnation of Neten Chokling.[121] While still young he had shown many miraculous signs. Early on, he gave clear predictions about the coming destruction of Buddhism in Tibet, which were recorded by a monk at Gebchak Gompa. Once he said that one of our relatives had died while on a pilgrimage around Mount Kailash—just at the time that it happened. He also knew that his own life would be very short. One day, when he was only fourteen years old, he told my mother, "Poor mother, I am very sorry that you will be so sad when my corpse is cremated." He died later that year.

My father had two children with another woman, the eldest being Penjik. In addition he had a daughter and a son by two other women. The son, Kungo Kalsang, was born from a practitioner in Shakya Shri's camp. My father had been living at this encampment for a while when they got together.[122]

~

My birth took place at Drakda, a small place on the way from Lhasa to Samye, situated near the Life-Lake of Yeshe Tsogyal.[123]

As a newborn infant, I became severely ill with some unknown disease, and was at the brink of death. My parents took me to Samye monastery. At the Castle of Samye was one of five sacred statues of Padmasambhava, which the Lotus-Born had said looked exactly like him.[124] The statue was placed inside a vase from which people could receive water as a blessing. By then I had actually stopped breathing, so there was little my parents could do but place me in front of the statue and pray to the Lotus-Born.

My parents prayed that their newborn baby would not die—and later they said that it was because of Padmasambhava's blessings that I didn't. As they prayed, I opened my eyes for the first time and started breathing again. After that, they brought me along to all the other pilgrimage places around Samye. Of course, I don't remember any of this, but my father told me the whole story.

My father was very close to the eminent master Drukchen, so we went to his main seat by way of the Yarlung valley.[125] In the upper part of the valley was the practice center known as Joyful Cave where the accomplished master Shakya Shri resided, having been invited from Kham by the Drukchen.

My parents told me that the eminent Drukchen was very kind to us. He also asked my father to perform rituals to support his health and long life. We stayed there for four or five months. So it was that I spent the first part of my life at the encampment of Shakya Shri. The Drukchen had special brocade garments made for me and my siblings; some of this brocade was made into a jacket that I wore until I left for Kham.

꿏

My uncle and the Karmapa had a mutual teacher-disciple relationship, and at the time of my birth, my uncle Samten Gyatso was at Tsurphu, giving the *New Treasures* to the fifteenth Karmapa and receiving some transmissions as well. Since Samten Gyatso was the eldest of his brothers, my father sent him this message, "A boy child has been born to me. Please ask the Karmapa, Khakyab Dorje, to give him a name."

So the Karmapa wrote my name—Karma Orgyen Tsewang Chokdrub Palbar—in his own hand, mounted it on a piece of fine brocade, stamped it with his seal, and sent it to my parents accompanied by a white scarf and five yards of red Chinese brocade embroidered with golden thread. "Give this brocade to the boy; it is my present to him," the Karmapa said. Strangely enough, we never managed to make anything useful from that brocade. Since it was from the Karmapa, people regarded it as so special they didn't dare cut it up.

It might seem improper for me to repeat this, but anyway, the Karmapa also said, "The boy is a genuine tulku." At the time, however, he didn't mention of whom I was a reincarnation.

Over the years, I lost the small scroll with my name on it several times, but I always found it again. The first time I lost it I was quite young. It appeared that a mouse had stolen it, because later when I was looking inside a mouse hole I found the scroll there. I lost it again while I was staying at my mother's house. Her family was so wealthy that the pile of used tea leaves from all the people passing through was big enough for us kids to play around in. One day, I noticed the scroll sitting on the heap of tea leaves. It was a bit discolored after sitting in the old tea but otherwise fine. I assume a mouse had carried it there, too. Now I keep it safely in my reliquary box.

My parents and I stayed on in Central Tibet for a few years, where I picked up some of the Central Tibetan dialect and some of their songs as well. Then we began our slow return to Kham. My father had gone ahead to Drong Gompa—the monastery of Lama Tendzin Dorje, my son Chökyi Nyima's previous life—which is situated several days' journey north of Lhasa on the route to Kham.

My family was gathering at Drong monastery before we began our journey home. Samten Gyatso had been there to confer empowerments for a whole month.[126] Lama Tendzin Dorje was a very close friend of Uncle Tersey; they had a brotherly affection for each other and were both close disciples of the great master Shakya Shri. That was another reason Uncle Tersey hadn't returned to Kham yet: he had been held up there at Drong for a year and now his mother, Könchok Paldrön, also resided there, with Uncle Sang-Ngak as her attendant. My father had just arrived, and now—finally—everyone was supposed to journey together back to Kham.

*

But before we left Central Tibet, the fifteenth Karmapa passed away. I had been taken to see the Karmapa when I was three years old, and I remember the area around Tsurphu, the temple hall and meeting many lamas, but being just a small child at the time, I don't remember the Karmapa's face. At the time of his death, I recall that an hour's walk from Tsurphu, there were some sand dunes, and people were weeping on both sides of the road.

Right after this, we began our trip back to Kham. For a three-year old, the journey was a very long horse ride indeed; I rode along sitting in a basket hanging from the side of a horse. I remember once falling out of the basket and getting hurt.

Back home in Nangchen, I stayed with my mother and was united with my older sister. I spent the rest of the year there with them. Soon after that, my brother and I began learning the alphabet, tutored by a kind old lama. When I was finally able to read, I was taken to Gebchak monastery and continued my studies with my maternal uncle as tutor.

About this time, we heard that my grandmother wanted to move to Tsikey. She said, "I want to drop my body at the monastery of my father and brothers. I refuse to die anywhere else." And, true to form, she wouldn't listen to anyone who tried to dissuade her.

You know how a child can keep raising questions? I was like that as well—extremely curious, always asking impossible questions and twisting people's remarks around for no reason whatsoever. No matter who came, I would attack them with queries, interrogating them until they lost their power of speech. I was inquisitive to an exacting degree, just like my grandson Phakchok, our present Tsikey Chokling's oldest son.

Wangdor, an old lama, was very affectionate toward me and I barraged him too with one question after another: What is mind? What is its nature? How does one meditate? And I was particularly fond of bugging the old ladies in my mother's house. I would start out by asking, "Where do earth and water come from? Who made them that way? How did the first water begin and in what direction did it flow? Why is the sky blue? How long has it been this way? Was it always blue? If not, how did it change?"

They would become dumbfounded and say, "What an annoying child!" Finally, someone would ask, exasperated, "Can't someone else take care of this kid?"

25. On the road from Lachab to Dechen Ling

As a child I remember studying with a personal tutor and spending lots of time with my mother. She came from a wealthy family and had her own house connected to the main manor in Tsangsar Dranang. But when I was around nine, I was handed over to my father at his hermitage, a day's ride away. When I was eighteen, I went to Lachab Gompa, where Samten Gyatso took over my education.

I had many homes. My family home was the Tsangsar estate—my father's original house, which was now run by my older brother Penjik—but my father's hermitage was home, too. I also had Lachab Gompa with Samten Gyatso. In addition, I also regarded the hermitage Fortress Peak that belonged to Lachab as a home.

My father's cousin, a sweet old lama, once teasingly said, "Maybe you are lucky that you can freely roam among your many homes, never staying long enough to be controlled by anyone—but maybe you'll turn into a spoiled brat. Watch out; you know the saying that an orphaned yak calf often starves to death, spending all its time going from teat to teat but never staying long enough to get any milk."

I was pretty free to go to any of my places every few months or so and was pampered whenever I arrived. But that all ended when Samten Gyatso got hold of me.

*

One of my first tutors, who taught me reading and writing, was Gargey Lama. My brother Tenga and I both studied with him. He was a tulku and quite extraordinary. When he was sweet, he was very sweet—but when he got angry, he would beat us. Nevertheless, he was very kind.

Sometimes he seemed to have glimpses of clairvoyance; he made many predictions. I remember him occasionally telling us small boys, "When I die, it won't be from disease but from a gunshot."

Later, during the communist invasion, he went up the mountain and stayed in a cave. But sure enough, the Red Army found him, brought him down and shot him.

*

Before continuing with my tale, I want to emphasize that the Dharma was remarkably widespread throughout the snowy land of Tibet. It so permeated our society that even small children didn't have to deliberately study prayers such as the supplication to the Lotus-Born master. They would learn how to chant it just by growing up in this Buddhist environment and hearing it over and over.

Children's games reflected this atmosphere and we often played at building monasteries. Groups of us kids would pile up mud and stones, under my supervision, and we managed to make some small "temples" in which we would play "lama." Sometimes these games went on from early morning until sunset.

Aside from the hermits and vast assemblage of monks and nuns living in the big monasteries, practitioners often stayed together in large encampments, such as the group surrounding Shakya Shri. For instance, the seventh Karmapa never stayed long in one place but moved from one camp to another throughout Tibet.[127] Any offerings he received he would pass along on the spot to the local monasteries.

The seventh Karmapa's close entourage consisted of at least one thousand monks, who followed along wherever the Karmapa went. The monks and attendants with their horses and yaks were so numerous that not everybody could fit in one place. So they staggered their movements in groups of one hundred, camping at seven or more different places a day's travel apart, staying a day in each place.

People camped in tiny meditation tents with a single pole, just big enough to sit in. The whole monastic community would stay in such tents, though the master's tent was typically larger. They were all required to keep the Kagyu tradition of four practice sessions a day, even while traveling. At a designated time, a bell would be rung and they would eat their meal together.

As soon as the meal was completed, according to the tradition, they would recite the *Kangyur*, the Buddhist canon in one hundred large volumes. As they traveled along, walking in a line across a vast plain, younger monks would distribute separate pages to each of the hundred monks, collecting the pages as they finished. All together they could easily complete all one hundred volumes by the time they reached the next mountain range, each monk reciting just two or three pages from each volume. The whole encampment was so large that, when everyone was together, the monks could recite the whole *Kangyur* in just an hour. The heap of their used tea leaves was often as tall as a man.

The Karmapa's caravan was known as "the great encampment that adorns the world," one of countless examples illustrating how deeply the Dharma was woven into our very existence.

❧

Nangchen, where I am from, was not known for its many learned masters. However, we had so many lamas and tokdens—full-time meditators who never cut their braided hair—that there was a tradition among laypeople to ask whichever of these they met for teachings on the nature of mind, and then train in and realize it. Previously, the famous master Tsoknyi and his disciple Tsang-Yang Gyamtso had given teachings on the nature of mind quite extensively throughout the land, and so this tradition had become ingrained in the culture.

This tradition was particularly strong at the many nunneries in Nangchen. The nuns were perhaps not very learned as scholars, but they focused wholeheartedly on pith instructions. They would request teachings on the nature of mind from every single lama who visited the region. Whenever a young tulku arrived at a hermitage or nunnery, he would immediately be surrounded by twenty or thirty nuns and pressured into giving "mind teachings," often for the first time in his life. This caused many a young tulku to break out in a sweat, as these nuns were known for asking very subtle questions. As soon as the lama was finished talking about the nature of mind, a barrage of questions would come, each more difficult than the last.

One such tulku told me that he was in dire trouble finding the right answers. He soon found his back against the wall. But it wasn't just him; the nuns would do the same with everyone—that was their style. The solution was simple: you needed to have the authentic lineage of instruction, not just be a tulku or professor of philosophy in name only. It often happened that if someone had been given the title of "tulku" at an early age, people would automatically assume that he could give mind teachings. This particular tulku said that he felt it was improper to refuse the nuns—but he probably would have done so had he known that their understanding was better than his theory.

This didn't happen only at the small practice centers; the largest of these nunneries, Gebchak Gompa, was filled with female meditators, and whenever a lama visited they would ask for teachings. And if you took a walk around the countryside near a nunnery, you would often see nuns sitting on big rocks or under trees, usually in groups of two or three, meditating.

In Nangchen being a nun was synonymous with being a meditator.

꩜

It was often the case that the sons in my mother's family were affirmed to be incarnations of lamas. The family's young incarnate lamas would sit in on ceremonies done for the benefit of the living and the dead, and would receive gifts from the faithful.

Even as a child I used to preside over such ceremonies, being regarded as both a tulku and the descendant of this important family. In addition, they brought me along when rituals were to be performed at people's houses so that extra donations could be collected. I believe that for a summer and a winter I was forced to sit in quite a number of rituals involving the peaceful and wrathful deities to secure a privileged rebirth for the recently deceased. I'm sorry to say I received my fair share of undeserved earnings this way.[128]

But these activities were brought to a halt when Samten Gyatso performed my enthronement ceremony and thereby established that I was a rebirth of the previous Chöwang Tulku.

꩜

When I was around nine years old, I was placed in my father's care. He was residing at the mountain hermitage Dechen Ling, a small nunnery surrounded by

26. Dechen Ling

retreat huts. I was very fond of my father's hermitage; the scenery and views were beautiful, and its history went back to our early forefathers.

Darma Wangchuk, one of the forefathers of our Barom Kagyu lineage, had established two monastic seats, one in Central Tibet and one in Kham. These were referred to as the upper and lower seats. The lower was on the mountain known as Jewel Heap of Countless AH Syllables.[129] The name comes from a small mountain decorated with self-appeared AH syllables in untold numbers.[130] Self-appeared syllables are quite wondrous. You could see the syllable AH in almost one hundred different places on the rock. I personally saw at least forty or fifty of them on the cliff face.

This was an immensely blessed place where many past masters of the Barom lineage had lived and displayed their miraculous powers. When Darma Wangchuk was living in a cave there, many disciples gathered around him and later they became renowned as the "thirteen with super-knowledge, the thirteen who could run like horses, the thirteen who could fly like birds" and many other feats of accomplishment. They all had lived on the mountain where Dechen Ling was situated.

Dechen Ling stands out in my memory. Most of the people I remember in Kham are from the area around that mountain. I probably spent eight years there, interspersed with short visits to Fortress Peak to be with Samten Gyatso. I eventually served as my father's *nyerpa* for a whole year until I graduated to shrine master and became responsible for making all the tormas.[131] I was able to serve my father well in this capacity as Könchok Paldrön had taught me how to make the tormas for the *New Treasures*.

Sometimes I went to Lachab to see Uncle Sang-Ngak. Later, when I was about fifteen years old, he came to stay at Dechen Ling. Uncle Sang-Ngak taught me how to do the rituals for the *New Treasures*, including the tunes, the mudras, what texts to insert where, how to jump from place to place in certain liturgies and the like.

Life at Dechen Ling was idyllic. The hillside was covered with huge juniper trees, and I remember it having mainly clear blue skies and lots of sunshine. But later, during the Cultural Revolution, all the trees were cut down.[132]

At the top of the mountain, within walking distance, there was an image of the Buddha of Boundless Light about three stories tall. The first Tsoknyi's guru, Chögyal Dorje, who was a contemporary of Chokgyur Lingpa, left distinct footprints in the four directions of the mountain.

Over the centuries, Dechen Ling had fallen into disrepair, and was restored by one of the lamas from Gebchak. My father settled down at this hermitage and spent many years in retreat until he left his body there approximately twenty years later. He lived there continuously, with one major interruption: when he went to Tsikey for the cremation ceremonies of his mother, Könchok Paldrön. He made a few small visits on the way back, but otherwise he spent all his time there. It was while he was living there that the hermitage became known as Dechen Ling, which means the Sanctuary of Great Bliss.

Directly below my father's retreat house was a small nunnery belonging to Gebchak. During the twenty years that my father stayed at the hermitage, the number of nuns grew from half a dozen to around one hundred. When my father lived there, the nuns were poor but highly motivated. After my father's passing, the nuns all worked together to build a fine temple hall to replace the previous substandard one. Despite how nicely the temple was made, it was still leveled to the ground by the communists. My youngest son tells me that the temple has been rebuilt and there are again between eighty and ninety nuns.[133]

⁂

I remember some outstanding meditators living around Dechen Ling. They did nothing but train in the natural state of mind, wearing only a simple sheepskin coat and eating little more than tsampa flour and the occasional piece of dried meat. Beneath them they had a few planks covered with a sheepskin, in front of them a small table, and below it one cup beside their bag of tsampa. People who make up their mind only to practice don't seem to need much.

Among them was a nun living in a small shack; she had no possessions. This nun originally had been a disciple of my father's. While still quite young, she had walked all the way to Mount Kailash and back. I knew her personally and found her simplicity truly inspiring. She was the type of person you almost wouldn't notice in a shrine hall, typically sitting near the door on the lowest seat and keeping her head down.

27. Tsangsar County—on the road to Dechen Ling

She was pretty unusual. She would do five hundred prostrations every day. At one point, she asked to have her door sealed up with mud and stones, something in Nangchen we call "sealed retreat". Only a small opening was left, just big enough to pass meals and provisions through. She stayed like that for one year and then unsealed the door. She would alternate like that from one year to the next.

Normally, she didn't talk to anyone, and all you could hear was the soft murmur of her clear and melodious chants. Once, while passing through the area, the Chokling of Neten stopped at her shack and stuck his head in the door. He wanted to check whether she was just a tenacious but stupid meditator.

He called in to her, "What are you doing in there? Are you hibernating like a little marmot? Trying to sit still for a long time, resting in a state of stale quietude?"

"No," she calmly replied, "I am sustaining the state of original mind, just letting be in uncontrived naturalness. This mind is empty and an emptiness that is empty by itself doesn't require me to do anything."

Once she had explained her practice to him, he felt there was nothing he needed to teach her.

He later told me this story, remarking, "That was the most impressive old nun I have ever seen. She had nothing more than the bare essentials and darn fine practice!"

She spent her life there, supported by various people. She was quite old by the time the communists came and she refused to leave, saying, "I am sure they will give me a hard time, but so what? I can take it."

She was still a nun when she passed away. This old lady exemplifies one of the more resolute meditators—but most of the nuns there had an outstanding perseverance.

⁂

I remember three main aspects of my childhood: a strong desire to live in caves, practicing meditation and being a bit of a charlatan.

When I was quite young, I had deep trust in two masters: Milarepa and Longchenpa. At times my devotion to them overwhelmed any other emotion. Sometimes when local people came to me in their traditional way to ask for blessings, I would say, "May Milarepa watch over you" or "May Longchenpa protect you." I would even say this to my parents and Samten Gyatso when I wished them goodnight.

As these two famous masters had spent a good part of their lives in caves, when I was six or seven I got the urge to be a serious cave dweller. I asked everyone I met if they knew where a cave might be found and searched them out. In this way, I became familiar with all the caves in the area. My main wish was to move into one of them and devote myself to spiritual practice.

I was also very fond of pitching small tents in the countryside with whomever was looking after me; we would spend whole days camping in the hills. Using our camp as a base, we would take long hikes to search out every cave in the area. Every time we found a cave, we would sit there very happily, expounding upon the virtues of cave dwelling. In particular, I remember a small but very interesting cave on the cliff rising above our house at Tsangsar. Every so often, I went up there and pretended to meditate, imitating the posture of a meditating hermit. I also practiced the meditation instructions I had heard from various lamas.

Later on, another cave above my father's hermitage caught my attention. Interestingly enough, there was no access to it from below. The only way to enter was to lower yourself down the cliff by rope, which looked like a very difficult undertaking. On an outcrop on the steep cliff was a big tree I used to climb out on to scout for access. Despite my keen anticipation, I never got into that cave.

There was also a cave at Fortress Peak, right on the brink of the abyss. Generations before, people had hammered iron rings and carved footholds into the solid rock; the rings were then connected with ropes. It was said that there were many representations of enlightened body, speech and mind inside the cave. To top it off, I was told that a local protector had gotten into the cave and was sometimes seen in the form of an enormous snake, preventing thieves from running off with the valuables. So through the centuries not one item had ever gone missing.

Hearing all this, of course I had to get to that cave. I could see from across the valley that it was pretty large, but none of the images were visible. The shrine appeared to have been walled up with stones and mud, so I imagined all the amazing stuff that would be found if we were able to excavate.

One day, I asked Samten Gyatso if I could attempt to climb down to it. "Absolutely not!" he said. "No one can possibly reach that cave. It was once accessible long ago, but not nowadays—unless you can fly like a bird!"

Nonetheless, having heard that the proper way to mountain climb was for the main person to have a rope tied around his waist, I gathered a group of young helpers to carry ropes that we would tie to a large juniper tree on the top of the cliff. I think my cousin, the young incarnation of Karmey Khenpo, was there along with eight or nine others. Our plan was to excavate the treasures—serpent be damned—and then share the goods with my parents and Samten Gyatso.

Each of us had a strong rope around our waist, and off we marched. We hadn't gotten far before a voice rang out behind us, "Hey, you! Young lamas! Where are you going?" It was my aunt Tashi Chimey.

"We're just walking over there," I said.

"So, why do you need so many people to do that?" she inquired.

"It's no big deal, we're just taking a walk," I said.

She must have gotten worried, though, because she went and got Samten Gyatso, who came out after us. All he had to do was show his face and ask us what we were up to for us to abandon our plans and scatter.

That cave lingered for quite a while in my hopes as a place I could hide away and practice; the objects inside weren't that important. But I never got in there. Last I heard, not even the Chinese invaders could overcome the formidable challenge of the sheer cliff and so the sacred images inside remain undisturbed.

❧

Toward the top of Fortress Peak was a place purported to be a cave where the Lotus-Born master had stayed. It looked more like an indentation with a rock overhang and barely had room for one person. Next to it was a VAJRA GURU mantra[134] that had self-appeared on the cliff face. With the idea of making a cave I put a lot of effort into piling up rocks to build a wall around the indentation. Another tulku from Lachab had heard about something called "cement" and said he knew how to make it and offered to help. Over lunch at Fortress Peak, we had a very serious discussion about how to go about making it, but that plan never amounted to anything either.

So in the end, unfortunately, I never did get to live in a cave, as all my time was taken up by my studies.

28. View of Fortress Peak from the road to Lachab

I was so obsessed with cave dwelling that I fear my next life will be as a bug in a cave!

❧

Apart from my longing for caves, I was also fond of playing "meditator." My father and Samten Gyatso often taught the grown-ups how to meditate, and I had many chances to sit in and listen. Well, at least my ears were present; as I was a child at the time, I won't pretend to have understood all that they were saying. However, being young and inquisitive, I had heard something about a "mind nature" that could be recognized and trained in, as well as something about sitting quietly without doing anything. So I tried to imitate it, "meditating" on the mountainside around Dechen Ling.

I also caught hold of the word *semtri*, which means "guidance in understanding and experiencing the nature of mind." I used that word with great enthusiasm and, being of a talkative nature, pestered every single lama who came, forcing them to give me "semtri." I don't remember what they said in those early years, but as I got older I started to pay attention to their words and meaning.

Apparently, there is always a need to have the nature of mind pointed out; even tulkus don't seem to know it on their own. Some people think that the Karmapas have no need for the pointing-out instruction and can recognize mind nature by themselves. But with a sense of deep respect, the sixteenth Karmapa told me about the time he was given the mind transmission by the great Situ of Palpung, his devotion for this master was very deep. So the transmission of mind nature is definitely important; someone must always demonstrate it.

In the life stories of masters, you often find that when they first received the pointing-out instruction and recognized mind essence, they experienced awareness stripped bare of the veils of conceptual thoughts, revealing a state that is wide open like the sky. However, being an ordinary person, I didn't experience anything like that at all. Rather than an amazing or extraordinary experience, it was more a sense of being very simple and uncomplicated. I never had any spectacular experiences such as swallowing the sky in one gulp.

It is not only extraordinary meditation experiences that I have missed out on; I have also never had any unique visions or received any earth-shattering prophecies about the future. Maybe it is my insensitivity—like a stone. As a matter of fact, I have never had any amazing experiences. However, from an early age, I was fond of acting like I was a meditator and, as I mentioned, I had a natural faith in Longchenpa and Milarepa.

As I grew up, Samten Gyatso became my main meditation instructor. Though he was well aware that I was a small child and hence likely unable to comprehend all the teachings, he didn't hold anything back. I was about eleven when he clarified the details of the principal teachings.

Until then, my meditation was guided mainly by what felt right. As a child, I would go to nearby caves and "meditate," but what I experienced then as the meditation state and my practice right now seem to be exactly the same—don't ask me why. I must have had some habit of letting be in the natural state carried over from former lives. Yet in those early days, I wasn't that clear about what it was until Samten Gyatso instilled in me a certainty about the natural state. Up to that point, meditation experience had been more spontaneous, but with Samten

Gyatso I could ask one question after another and I discovered that what he was explaining was the same as what I had experienced as a child.

I don't have much to brag about in terms of realization, so the clarity I am talking about has more to do with demonstrating personal confidence. The faith and devotion I had as a kid were quite natural and not imposed on me by anyone. Along with my devotion, I also had an acute feeling that mundane aims were futile. The only thing that made sense was to be a tough guy—tough like my heroes Milarepa and Longchenpa.

When I look back on my life, it seems I haven't been very diligent; I have only been distracted day and night, letting life run out.

*

When I was twelve I broke my right arm falling down a staircase, and a year or so later, I fell off a horse and broke the left one. The first time there was a problem with the bone and an old doctor was summoned all the way from Lachab. The problem was that the arm needed to be set and he was too soft-hearted to cause a child such intense pain. He just couldn't bring himself to do it. I started to scold him for not respecting my gutsiness, regarding me as a mere child.

"I'm the one who has to spend the rest of my life with a crooked arm!" I argued. "So, give it a yank and be done with it!" He finally gave it the yank it needed and then bound it, Khampa style, with a splint.

This still wasn't as bad as the following year, when the bone stuck out of my flesh. The accident happened way up on the mountain and it took me half a day to get back. Once again a doctor had to be sent for. There was a choice between a man who used to help repair the broken legs of cattle and an old geezer, a doctor who had been a disciple of the fifteenth Karmapa. The old one was sent for, but as he approached our place, his horse was startled and threw him. He was hurt quite badly and people thought he was dead. Around dusk, just as I managed to reach home, I ran into two guys carrying the injured doctor.

The old healer tried to direct his two assistants in setting my arm, but they weren't that brave. Again I had to take charge. "Wait a minute," I told them. "Neither of you will feel the pain! And if you don't do it, I'm the one who'll be walking around with a crippled arm. So just do it!"

"Pull it! Pull it!" the old doctor yelled.

Then I said, "You think you're being kind by protecting me from the pain? I think you're being cruel! You two are useless!"

I began pulling my own arm into place. But I wasn't doing it right and the bone was sticking out at a funny angle. Finally, out of pity, they took over and aligned the bone. They dressed the wound, but not that well—I was bedridden for two months with incredible pain. Lying there in bed, I could see the birds flying past my window. I often thought how happy they must have been to be able to fly and wished I had been born a bird. Seeing the lambs and kid goats, I thought how lucky they were to be healthy and not sick like me. The pain was continuous day and night, and so intense I couldn't sleep. For a long time I couldn't even lift that arm, but slowly it healed.

At least in my early years I had some courage.

※

Now for my short-lived stint as a charlatan. The first time I went to Gebchak, I was around five years old. In those days, just after dusk, I could "see" things, as if in a dream. Sometimes I even believed I was having a vision of Buddha Shakyamuni. It was probably just a trick of the light, but I happily used these occurrences to my advantage.

The nuns would treat this little pretender with great respect. Sometimes they would ask, "What practice are we doing?" And because of my "visions" I was able to tell them the name of their particular *yidam* and Dharma protector. When it turned out to be true, they were flabbergasted and prostrated before me.

So the nuns began to treat me like a precious object. I even succeeded in fooling the head nuns who lived near the abbot's quarters. When someone takes advantage of people simply because of a bit of clairvoyance or a few clear dreams, but doesn't yet have the substance to guide others—would you call that person anything other than a charlatan?

I took delight in the nuns' wide-eyed amazement and devotion. As I grew older, this clairvoyant ability slowly faded. Though my career as a charlatan didn't last long, it was quite successful.

So, when people talk about clairvoyant and miraculous powers I'm not that impressed. In fact I actually feel a certain distrust.

※

I did have another stint as a charlatan again when I was a bit older. After I had gone to Dechen Ling to live with my father, he kindly taught me and I began to understand the scriptures. My father would sit outside under a huge tree on top of a large boulder and often teach me using the songs of Milarepa, half an hour at a time. He taught me many of the tunes and I grew very fond of them. My father had two distinct ways of singing those songs and I can still remember them clearly.

Once when I made a trip back to Gebchak, the nuns there didn't know I had learned the songs by heart. One time, I remember sitting in a small cave, wrapped in a white flag to look like Milarepa, singing for forty or fifty nuns. You should have seen them—they were really impressed! I basked in their devotion. I was still a young kid, and when I went to pee, they would sometimes collect it and drink a handful, thinking I was Milarepa in person.

16

The Nunnery of Yoginis

Tsang-Yang Gyamtso, the founder of Gebchak Gompa, had passed away long before my stay there as a child. Tsang-Yang Gyamtso had been born into an important local family and was rich, powerful and quite arrogant. As a young man he had enjoyed hunting. In those days rifles could shoot only one bullet at a time. One day he saw a herd of deer in a valley. Taking aim he hit a fawn. Its mother turned toward him and, letting out a pleading cry, continued to guard the rest of the herd.

As she stood there looking straight at him, Tsang-Yang began to have second thoughts, "Oh no! She knows I am going to kill her and yet she lingers there to save her fawn. I am a true murderer!"

As he reflected on this a deep sense of self-loathing welled up within him. He flung down his rifle and smashed it with a large stone. Next he threw away his knives and daggers; unleashing his horse and yak, he set them free. At a villager's house along the way, Tsang-Yang told the owner where he had left his horse and that the man could have it.

Then he set off on foot with only one thought in mind, "I must meet Lama Tsoknyi!"

At this time the first Tsoknyi was the lama at Nangchen palace's main temple. That morning Tsoknyi had told his attendant, "A man will probably come to meet me today, a stranger. Let me know the moment he arrives!"

At mealtime, Tsoknyi asked, "Has anyone come yet?"

The attendant replied, "No one special, just this frazzled, tired-out guy. I gave him some food and a place to rest. No one important has come, only him."

"That's the one!" exclaimed Tsoknyi. "I told you to notify me right away. Bring him up here immediately."

29. Gebchak Gompa—the nunnery of meditators

As soon as they met, Tsang-Yang Gyamtso said, "I have completely given up the aims of this life. Now my only goal is to practice the sacred Dharma from the core of my heart. Please accept me as your disciple."

"Very well," Tsoknyi replied. "If that's what you really want, you must start from the beginning. I will teach you only if you follow my instructions while you stay in retreat."

Tsang-Yang Gyamtso was then given a small hut on the hillside. It's still there; I've seen it myself. After a while Tsoknyi told him to stay in that hut and not come back for three years. Tsang-Yang readily accepted. Noble beings make faster progress than others during a three-year retreat. The story goes that after those three years, he had attained a very high level of realization.[135]

Tsoknyi himself was an incarnation of Ratna Lingpa, one of the major revealers of terma treasures.[136] I was recognized as an incarnation of Chöwang Tulku, who was also one of the first Tsoknyi's disciples.

Under Tsoknyi's guidance, Tsang-Yang Gyamtso became an eminent practitioner. He was also very bold and intrepid. For example, once he traveled to the lower part of Kham to visit both Khyentse and Kongtrul. Upon meeting Kongtrul, he insisted on being given a complete set of the wonderful new collection of sacred scriptures that he heard Kongtrul was about to publish. Because of his audacious tenacity, Tsang-Yang was the first lama to receive a printed version of the *Treasury of Precious Termas* from Old Kongtrul himself.

Tsang-Yang Gyamtso became an outstanding master, and had between five and six hundred disciples who showed signs of accomplishment. These disciples themselves had innumerable disciples who were able to benefit beings in countless ways—I personally met many of them.

*

One day, Tsoknyi told Tsang-Yang, "Your forte in benefiting beings lies in building nunneries. Female practitioners are often not valued, and so they have a harder time finding proper guidance and instruction. Therefore, rather than keeping a congregation of monks, you should take care of nuns. That is your mission."

Tsang-Yang followed Tsoknyi's command and built two major nunneries, one of which had thirteen retreat centers. His benefit for beings became broader than his master's. Most of the nuns practiced the revealed treasures of Ratna Lingpa, which include Hayagriva as well as the peaceful and wrathful deities. Each retreat center focused on a different cycle of these treasures.

Tsang-Yang Gyamtso had his own opinion about how his large community of nuns should live. "Of course it would be wonderful to have a well-off monastery, but I pity monks and nuns who get so fat from donations given out of faith that after their death they plummet straight down and have no chance to rise back up from the lower realms. Honestly, what good does that do? Practicing meditation, on the other hand, doesn't require eating tasty dishes. It is much better if their families provide for each nun individually and they live on that fare, simple as it may be.

"Donations given directly to the nunnery we will keep for the community as a whole to be used at the annual drubchen ceremonies, when tulkus and lamas are invited to participate. Otherwise, people who dine on donations to a monastery ensure their own imprisonment in the lower realms. If one starts out building monasteries and nunneries with the aim of freedom and enlightenment, but ends up eating offerings to the Three Jewels, I feel it would be pointless."

Tsang-Yang stuck by his view and spent all the donations to the nunneries at the annual ceremonies. The rest of the year, the nuns had to get by on what they got from their families and seasonal begging tours. This actually worked out well; it was quite easy to obtain enough provisions in this way. At each retreat center, the fuel for the fire was provided by the main monastery, while the nuns could always get hot water from the big copper cauldron in each retreat center. But the nuns cooked their own dinner soup for themselves in small groups.

*

Gebchak's main abbey had thirty-six connected nunneries. Some of these had as many as four or five hundred nuns each, while even the smallest had about seventy. On the other side of the valley was a *gompa* for male tokden meditators, literally, "realized ones," with their hair tied up on the top of their heads—many of whom actually were quite realized. But I noticed some of them covered up their lack of realization by putting on pretentious airs.

Looking down through the valley, you could see at least twenty large stupas. This entire valley was unique, but you only realized how unique when a great master was passing through. Then, as far as the eye could see, the landscape became a sea of red robes. Another time it became visible was once a year when the nuns would put up prayer flags by the thousands. When they were done and the wind blew, the entire mountain seemed to come alive.

The main abbey was divided into two areas: the upper for full-time retreat, where visitors were prohibited, and a lower one where the rules weren't as strict. The nuns here would go for alms during harvest, then carry their provisions back to share with the others. Near the main monastery were thirteen retreat centers, each named after the particular mandala of deities those nuns practiced. Twenty or thirty nuns lived in each center.

The nuns' quarters had a few holes in the roof to let in some light, but no actual windows. It is remarkable how little light it takes to see quite clearly, even when there are clouds in the sky. When it rained, the rough planks on the roof were laid over the openings, but still a few drops leaked through. I wouldn't say it was the most comfortable of places.

Under the table inside each meditation box, the nuns would keep their bags of tsampa flour and pieces of dried meat to supplement the tea and soup. One of the younger nuns would serve the others. The nuns didn't need much, just supplies of tsampa, butter, and some dried meat and dried cheese—simple food, but enough to survive on.

The head lama had made a rule that there should be no loud talking outside. The nuns could talk to one another in a low voice. But if they wanted to call someone, they couldn't yell. They had to clap their hands and beckon the person with a wave. Even with so many nuns living on that mountainside, I always felt it was totally quiet.

Each nun would sit in a little box about one square meter—only slightly larger than her. The boxes lined the walls, with a space in the middle, so that about sixteen nuns could reside in an average room. The program was to practice throughout day and night. Upon entering a practice center, a nun would take her seat in a box containing a stuffed mat. After that there was no more lying down—not even to sleep!

I visited these rooms, which were on average the size of my small living quarters here at Nagi. Each room would have an altar with the representations of body, speech and mind. One or two of the senior nuns would keep the schedule. In the early hours before dawn, a gong would be rung. In the center of the room was a small hearth for keeping the teapot warm and, sometimes, the soup. There was no fixed duration for this kind of retreat, but many nuns would stay for life.

30. Gebchak nuns sitting in their meditation box

The nuns' simple way of practice deeply impressed me. I felt it would be a meaningful way to spend one's life.

~

While the nuns' retreat approach is known as *drubdra*, sadhana retreat—focusing on yidam practice and mantra recitation—there is another style of intensive group practice called *gomdra*, meditation retreat.[137] In meditation retreat, people often sit outside, not in one continuous stretch from morning to evening but with the day divided into sessions. Once, the Chokling of Tsikey was invited to the famous Dzogchen monastery near Derge, where there was such a meditation retreat. My father, Chimey Dorje, went with Tsikey Chokling as his attendant.

In that gomdra there were about sixty meditators, all practicing outside, sitting in rows of five or six with their backs straight. Both behind and in front of their heads, at a level just below their necks, were strands of thin thread suspended between two poles. During the actual sessions, their bodies were not to move even one inch. Their minds were supposed to remain in the state of nondual awareness. If the meditators fell asleep and their heads moved either forward or backward, the thread would break. At that point, the retreat disciplinarian would come and reprimand them, "Hey, you broke the thread!"

The meditators were also not supposed to move their eyes. For beginners, it was difficult not to blink, but eventually they could remain without moving their eyelids. To ensure that the meditators were actually doing this, the disciplinarian would sometimes put red sindhura powder below their eyelids. If anyone blinked, then some red powder would stick on their eyelashes—evidence that they had blinked.

~

When I was a bit older, I returned with my father to Gebchak when he was invited to teach a group of two hundred nuns who were quite adept at yoga. Whenever he taught there, in the evenings his room was always packed with fifty or more nuns asking additional questions.

Many of these nuns displayed signs of accomplishment, such as the inner heat of tummo. Once a year, on the night of the full moon of the twelfth month of the Tibetan calendar, there was a special occasion to show their mastery in the tummo practice of inner heat called "the wet sheet." In the eight directions around the practice center, nuns lit fires to melt snow where the sheets would be soaked. At this time of year it was so cold the wet sheets would instantly freeze upon being pulled from the cauldron. Despite the bitter cold, many local people would come to witness the ceremony, often bringing their children along as well.

The nuns were naked underneath the large sheets, except for short pants. I forget if they were wearing boots or not; they may have been barefoot. Those without any tummo experience found the cold almost unbearable; they would get stiff legs and frozen toes as the night wore on. For ordinary people it was virtually impossible to take even a few steps wearing only shorts, let alone a wet sheet.

The nuns began at midnight by singing the beautiful melody of supplication while walking one full circumambulation of the monastery complex covering the hillside, which was quite a long distance. The nuns wearing the sheets would walk slowly during the song. They were singing and asking for the blessings of Tsoknyi, Tsang-Yang and the other masters of the lineage, as they continued to circumambulate until dawn. They begin at midnight, at first the sheets are not soaked; the nuns merely walk while practicing tummo.

Halfway through the night, their sheets are lightly moistened from the water in the cauldrons and you begin to see a wisp of vapor from the heat of their tummo. Then the time would come to completely soak their sheets, immersing them for longer in the cauldrons. Sometimes the vapor from the line of nuns would be like a bank of mist drifting down the mountain. You could see beads of sweat on their bodies while the rest of us were standing there shivering. I saw this with my own eyes several times. There were about eight hundred nuns participating. Of these, around two hundred had some degree of mastery in tummo; only these nuns would soak their sheets in the water cauldrons.[138]

It is incredibly inspiring and moving to watch such a procession and I haven't heard of this happening on such a scale anywhere else in Tibet or Kham. Those nuns were quite impressive. Upon passing away, a great many of them remained in samadhi and some even left relics in their ashes.

I feel that this is one story people should definitely hear.

17

Receiving My First Teachings

I remember receiving my first formal teaching while still a child. It was the cycle on peaceful and wrathful deities revealed by Karma Lingpa, a teaching I had had a deep yearning to receive. I pushed very hard for this teaching and finally obtained it from my father when an old lama from Gebchak requested it.

When the empowerment was postponed for just one day, I was very upset and, someone told me later, I looked extremely displeased. When the ceremony finally began, I joined in enthusiastically, even to the point of pushing and shoving in the traditional Tibetan manner when people stand up to be blessed with the implements.[139]

Following that, I often listened in when my father gave empowerments and instructions. But it was only from the age of fifteen that I began to take serious note of what I had received. I began the curriculum of large collections of scripture beginning with the reading my father gave at Dechen Ling of the *Kangyur*—the recorded teachings of Buddha Shakyamuni, which we respectfully call *The Great Translated Words of the Victorious One*.

Soon after, my brother Tenga invited the master Kyungtrul Rinpoche to the temple at our family home to give the *Treasury of Oral Instructions*. This was no small gathering, and many tulkus and lamas attended the transmission, which lasted for three straight months. In between, another master gave the reading of the collected works of the first Kongtrul as well as the *Treasury of Knowledge*.[140]

During the yearly rituals of Kilaya at Dechen Ling, I learned to chant the *Secret Essence Kilaya* by heart; I still remember it to this day. At Dechen Ling, I participated in the yearly rituals of exorcism based on Vajra Kilaya.[141]

My older brother Penjik had a small kilaya dagger that was reputedly not forged by human hands and regarded as so special it was placed on the shrine during these ceremonies. A ritual dagger is placed vertically on a stand and decorated with a scarf. Once, the scarf somehow got stuck to the torma tray that was to be hurled out at the end of the exorcism. My friend who threw the torma obviously hadn't noticed this and the tray was thrown down the hill.

When we tried to find the dagger, we were too late—a large raven had just flown off with the scarf in its beak. We knew how precious that dagger was and at first we were too scared even to mention it. We kept looking for it over the next several days before finally telling Penjik. But he was a true gentleman and said, "It'll be all right. Let's just keep looking for it."

Under my father's supervision, I began the traditional preliminary practices of the four times one hundred thousand, which I completed as best a child can. The text I used is part of the *Tukdrub* cycle of terma revelations. I probably didn't do the practices very correctly, since I was only about eleven years old at the time.

As a teenager, I also went through the pretense of going into strict retreat several times. For two months I did the *Secret Essence Kilaya*, in which I had great trust, professing that it was to prolong my father's life. I believed it, too, and made the elaborate tormas that dispel hindrances to longevity—but this was just the play of a child.

❦

During my early years at Dechen Ling, there lived an old lady who was a healer in the ancient tradition of herbal medicine. She possessed knowledge of some rare and secret concoctions that I should probably have learned. But I never did—and it was actually her fault. She was a seasoned meditator but would often blame the art of healing for all the clients who came to see her.

"There is nothing worse than healing. I am an old woman, almost on the verge of death, and these sick people never leave me alone," she would lament. "It's all the fault of being a doctor. If I refuse, everybody will hate me. Of course no one but me is to blame, for when I had the chance to choose, I thought it would be useful to learn the art of healing. But now it is too late—there is no greater obstacle for a practitioner than being a doctor."

Since I was young, I didn't realize she was just feigning the inability to be both a meditator and healer, and I believed all that she said. So I didn't take advantage of this opportunity to learn medicine. I may not be very bright, but I felt that I could have learned at least a little about medicine.

This old lady was extremely skilled and cured one person after another. I knew of only one other person who held the same lineage as the old lady—a famous doctor in Nangchen. He later died at the hands of the communists and now it appears that this lineage has died out. I hear that the text still exists, but that is not enough. The recipes and the hands-on experience of preparing the medicines must be passed on from one person to the next.

The special recipes of their lineage originated from a healer named Tendzin Rabgye, an accomplished master from one of the old temples of the Barom Kagyu. These recipes were connected with one of the twenty-one *genyen*—guardian spirits of the Dharma who, when Padmasambhava was in Tibet, were bound under oath to protect the Buddha's teachings.

This particular guardian resided in the Kechu River and came before the healer to tell him about eighteen new diseases that would afflict future generations. The guardian gave the master the instructions on how to cure them, saying, "You must keep them as a secret lineage taught to only one person at a time. Don't squander them."

Tendzin Rabgye wrote the recipes down and taught them to his most important disciples. It was unfortunate that Kongtrul didn't receive these recipes because he would have made sure that their use spread. Instead they perished in the remote valleys of my homeland.

The old lady told me the particular locations where the different medicines grew, as well as the specific time of year they should be picked. It was all very precise and complicated. For instance, she knew a mixture of nine flowers that could cure a particular fatal disease that involved swelling from water retention and, most likely, kidney failure. Another medicine had twenty-five ingredients, the exact combination of which was very effective for healing boils and sores within a few days. Some of her methods involved touching a particular spot on the body with a warm piece of metal.

I wouldn't be surprised if one of the eighteen maladies these medicines treated was cancer—in fact, I am pretty sure this is so, as it is one of the newer illnesses of our times. Although the text still survives in the hands of one person from Nangchen, the oral lineage is vital.

Isn't it a shame that such a lineage has been broken?

18

An Extraordinary Speech

My half-brother Penjik was supposed to be a tulku, but he didn't want to be recognized as such. He was incredibly bright. Personally, I haven't met anyone as sharp as he was. For example, in a single day he memorized the entire text of *Chanting the Names of Manjushri*.[142] Think about that! Isn't it astounding? That's the kind of person he was. I certainly was in awe of him.

If he had gone to Derge to pursue Buddhist studies, there is no doubt that he would have become a great scholar. Everything he heard, he understood. It's a shame he didn't stick to a spiritual path.

Penjik was very brave and intelligent; no one could outdo him or dominate him in anyway. If you heard his full story, you would be in awe. Let's begin with his mundane qualities: He was extremely eloquent—so much so that he could be mistaken for a demon.[143]

Penjik was known throughout Nangchen for his bravery; he was completely fearless and not intimidated by anyone. He was also tall and broad-shouldered. You should have seen him race his horse or shoot his rifle while riding! He was an excellent marksman. I felt that he had all the important qualities of a hero.

31. The Derge royal family

According to tradition when a Nangchen king takes a queen, the suitable match is a princess from a neighboring kingdom, often Derge. When the current king married, guests were invited from all over the two countries. As was the custom someone from each side must stand up during the ceremony and give an impressive speech mentioning the royal ancestors, the history of the kingdoms and so forth. A very fine monk was chosen, who spent three months trying to memorize the names of all the past kings.

For his part Penjik was appointed the task of giving a particular speech comparing the new queen's beauty with divine turquoise and the arrow of longevity.

It was no coincidence that Penjik was chosen for this occasion. Many years earlier, at a wedding in Nangchen, he had given the traditional toast so impressively that the name Tsangsar Penjik spread far and wide as an orator of renown. He was only in his late teens at that time; by this time he was in his late twenties.

Yet when he received the request Penjik rode a full day to come and tell my father he wouldn't give the speech. But my father told him, "You can't refuse. You have the intelligence and knowledge, so you must speak. You should respect why they chose you. When people have placed their hopes in you, it's not right to disappoint them."

At this time the Derge king had four gurus to bestow empowerments on him.[144] The holders of these four roles have changed over the course of history, but there were always supposed to be four gurus for the king of Derge. These four were prominent among those assembled at the Derge royal palace, including the nobility of the kingdom, their families and the eighty district governors.

For the first ceremony, in which an official request for marriage is made for the princess, a group of sixty officials were sent as delegates from the Nangchen court, with Penjik at their head. I won't burden you with all their names, but one of them said to Penjik, "Tomorrow, you need to give the speech. Wouldn't it be better if you did a rehearsal now?"

"If I prepare what I am going to say," Penjik replied, "I wouldn't be a real Nangchen man. There is no way I am going to embarrass myself with such artificial preparation."

He did, however, have a little notebook containing some notes written by Chokgyur Lingpa's private secretary, Pema Yeshe, which someone had by chance handed to him on the way to Derge. Since his friend continued to pester him, Penjik did read through it once or twice on the road. That was all it took for him to know the whole thing by heart.

The next morning, the party went before the king. Penjik was ready to praise the princess, and his friend, after three months of preparation, was ready to praise the king, the royal ancestors, the virtues of the kingdom, and the skill and ingenuity of the citizens. At least that was what was supposed to happen.

At this gathering, with everyone in their finest brocade, Penjik himself had on four or five brocade robes, one on top of another to look his finest, Khampa style.

Inside the huge assembly hall, everyone was asked to take a seat on the elevated platforms, tea was served and then Penjik was signaled: it was time for the "turquoise and arrow" speech to begin. An ornate arrow with silken streamers was brought before Penjik and planted in a large vessel of rice.

32. The Situ of Palpung

The people of Nangchen are a bit simple-minded and as no one was in charge of the delegates, none of them knew where to sit. Many of his companions were still lingering by the door and Penjik was left to his own devices. But a Chinese delegate gestured to Penjik to begin even before all the Nangchen officials had been seated, so he stood up on his seat and began giving his speech.

Penjik noticed the great Situ looking down at him from a lofty throne and felt his heart freeze. Penjik later said, "Now, that was a lama with majestic presence! But the spell only lasted a second. Next I composed myself by thinking, 'Huh! The great Situ of Palpung or not, he's still only a human being made of flesh and blood. And I am also a human being—so why should I be afraid of him?' As I felt courage welling up inside me, I got annoyed at myself for having lost my nerve for a moment and began the speech."

Other people who were there later told me that his speech was more far-reaching than any they had heard before. It was precise and unbroken. Penjik started with how the world was formed and how the first sentient beings took birth in samsara, covering in great detail how the world had come to its present state. He followed that with a long comparison of historical links between Nangchen and Derge and how the kings were like brothers, and the entire background for the Derge king's lineage. Then he gave a similar explanation of the Nangchen kings, leading to the present occasion of joining the two families in matrimony—the reason everyone was there—comparing it with the union of means and knowledge to benefit the Buddha's teachings and all sentient beings.

As if that weren't enough, he went on to explain the difference between ordinary worldly rulers and Dharma kings, emphasizing that the monarchs of both countries were *dharmaraja*, religious rulers, which made this an extraordinary occasion. He then went straight into the "turquoise and arrow" speech, but not only did he employ the metaphors of the turquoise and arrow, but he expanded to include the entire setting of the Derge temple hall in Lhundrub Teng, known as the Palace of Spontaneous Perfection, bringing in the thousand-spoked golden wheel on the ceiling above and the eight auspicious emblems in the various directions, while pointing to them with the arrow and making the silken streamers flutter dramatically in the air.

At some point, everyone started to smile and then began to laugh, because he had already poured out everyone else's speech. They were all pretty happy though, which was of prime importance because in the past physical fights or even diplomatic incidents would break out if one side hadn't been praised sufficiently by the other. To tell the truth, instead of a happy marriage party, the danger always loomed that a one-sided speech could be the cause for a real fight to begin. But Penjik had covered all the bases.

The four gurus each gave him a big white scarf and chanted their good wishes. Penjik looked up at the great Situ again and this time he was smiling.

That afternoon there was a private meeting between the organizers. Someone stood up and said, "Tomorrow we are supposed to continue with the speech about the royal lineages."

Then the great Situ of Palpung said, "But this guy has already said everything there is to say! None of us can give a better or more detailed speech. Unless it is better than the speech he gave this morning, we can't outdo him. So, let's just skip the royal lineage speeches tomorrow." The others agreed.

That's why Penjik ended up being the only speaker. He was that kind of man.

Afterward people were heard saying things like, "That was such a lengthy speech I wouldn't have been able to learn it by heart."

"I wanted to see the cue cards that Penjik must have hidden up his sleeve," someone else mentioned. "I went over to check, but there weren't any."

It seemed there was another side to the whole story.

Later, I heard our father say, "From early that morning and through the entire day, I sat alone under that tree over there continuously visualizing myself as Four-Armed Mahakala. Upon the curved knife I had brought, I had attached a small plaque with Penjik's name on it as a way to increase his majestic presence."

*

True to the Khampa spirit, Penjik was always ready to ride into battle if need be. "Everyone has to die; it's just a matter of time—there's no doubt," he would say. "A good son must be a brave warrior. And a warrior must fight his enemies to protect his friends and family. If one dies doing this, so be it! It has to happen anyway. I am not afraid and I have no regrets." Just the same, fearless though he was, when the communists came, Penjik was caught by the Red Army and killed in prison.

19

My Previous Life

I must have been around thirteen years old when I heard that Shakya Shri's son, Sey Phakchok,[145] was living at a particular hermitage. Sey Phakchok was also one of my father's own teachers and I had often heard him mentioned with a lot of respect. He was a great master, similar to his father.

At one point, my yearning to go there was so strong that I almost couldn't sit still. I began forming plans to run away from home. I came up with all kinds of subterfuges, but finally decided there was no way I could avoid telling my father. My only problem was choosing a trustworthy confidant. I was still living at Dechen Ling at the time, but I finally chose a monk from a nearby monastery who was two years older.

He said, "It will be hard for us to leave and your father will be very displeased."

"We'll tell him just as we're about to leave," I replied.

The day came when we were all packed and ready to go, and I went to my father and told him I was leaving. He asked me where I was planning to go.

"You have told me so often of the greatness of Shakya Shri and his amazing son, Sey Phakchok, that I want to go and stay with him!"

My father replied, "Sure, he is a great teacher, but you're too young to go. If you insist, I'll arrange a proper escort for you with supplies and pack animals—but not this year. Absolutely not."

This took the wind out of my sails. "Anyway," my father continued, "you just need to make sure that Samten Gyatso knows beforehand. He is my older brother and has the final say."

However, the next year passed and I never ended up going, for Samten Gyatso took over my education soon after. By then I had been recognized as a rebirth of Chöwang Tulku, an old lama from Samten Gyatso's monastery.

Here is how it happened. The sixteenth Karmapa, Rigpey Dorje, had confirmed in writing that my present rebirth was the continuation of the mind-stream of Chöwang Tulku. I don't know how great a lama Chöwang Tulku was, but he had spent many years up at Fortress Peak performing longevity rituals for the Nangchen king, a duty he shared with his brother, who was Samten Gyatso's previous incarnation. At some point, I was sent to stay with Samten Gyatso, who then gave me the title Chöwang Tulku, and I became a follower of my uncle.

This meant sharing responsibility for the same monastery and retreat centers. I guess I was around seventeen or eighteen at the time. After I got locked into that situation, it was very hard to get away, for Samten Gyatso was not as lenient as my father. On the contrary, he was firm and steadfast, and whatever he said had to be obeyed.

Once Samten Gyatso's former incarnation saw that his brother was an incarnation of Guru Chöwang, one of the five most important tertöns. According to Chöwang Tulku's own visions, he was also an emanation of Sangye Yeshe of Nub, one of Padmasambhava's twenty-five disciples. As Chöwang Tulku said, "It's vividly clear in my memory—so clear that I can never forget my former life as the Nubchen master."

Chöwang Tulku apparently began practice at an early age, and they say that he was a meditator with a profound level of practice.[146] During the latter part of his life at Fortress Peak, he used his time wisely, proceeding into a phase of unelaborate practice where he simply sat and didn't do much other than meditation training. I heard from people who had met him that he was quite corpulent and had a long braid tied around his big head.

The *Treasury of Precious Termas* was being assembled during Chöwang Tulku's life, and upon hearing of this treasury of teachings, he had the deep yearning to receive it. Eventually he received it from Lama Latsey, who was one of Karmey Khenpo's disciples and a very important holder of the monastic precepts in Kham. It was an unusual transmission because there were only the two of them present—master and recipient—for the entire *Treasury of Precious Termas,* which took six months. Only two attendants were permitted, to help with the shrine affairs. It took place at a remote hermitage where they locked the gate so that no one could visit.

It sounds as if Chöwang Tulku was a bit eccentric. He ardently collected the *Five Treasuries* of Kongtrul, paying to have them transferred into his custody.[147] Apart from this expenditure, he would hoard all his many donations, which included precious coral, turquoise and other valuables. Then once a year, he would have them all packed up and shipped off with one sentence, "Give these to my guru, he knows how to use this stuff to promote the Dharma. Me, I can't do anything with it."

In this way, his storeroom was completely emptied once a year, with nothing left behind. His own attendant told me this with a mixture of admiration and regret, adding, "As a matter of fact, for half of his life, he didn't do anything at all."

❧

Chöwang simply led the life of a hidden yogi. But apparently he had clairvoyant powers, and now and then he let a prediction slip out. Once his attendant, Kalpa, wanted to demolish part of the hermitage and build an expansive new structure. But Chöwang Tulku said, "Don't build anything!" Then, as if reading from a page, he added, "In the future, a lama will come who will expand this place and if we build anything now, he will demolish it anyway. So don't trouble yourself."

This same old servant also told me the following story.

One day, Chöwang saw that his attendant was about to build a little workshop for *tsa-tsa* clay statuettes on a certain spot and told him, "Don't build it there, because one day you will have to move it."

His attendant asked him, "Why, Rinpoche? There's lots of space around here."

"No, no," Chöwang replied, "later on Lama Tulku will build a large house here." Chöwang always referred to his brother, the third Ngaktrin Tulku, as Lama Tulku and never used his real name.

This turned out to be true: Many years later, his brother's reincarnation, Samten Gyatso, built his hermitage, Sanctuary of Lotus Light, on that very spot.

❧

Kalpa, Chöwang's attendant, was quite old when I met him. He had continued his meditation practice, and it seemed to me that he had reached a solid level of experience and realization. Kalpa told me many other interesting stories about Chöwang. They must be true because that old monk never lied.

Tsang-Yang Gyamtso once went up to meet Chöwang Tulku and when Kalpa went in to announce his arrival, Chöwang simply said, "He doesn't need to see me. There's nothing he can get from meeting me." So, the visitor did several circumambulations and left.

Another time, a guest who had traveled quite far came with an offering he had been given to present to Chöwang Tulku—a large brick of expensive Chinese

33. Pages from the writings of Chöwang Tulku

tea. Halfway to Fortress Peak this guest stopped at a river to have a meal and, as he looked at the fine tea, decided to steal half of it.

So he took out his knife and cut it in two. He wrapped one part back up in the white scarf and the rest he hid in his bag, thinking to himself, "The lama doesn't need more than half, so I'll just keep the rest."

When he approached Chöwang Tulku, the guest of course didn't mention anything about taking some of the tea. As he handed over his offering of tea, he simply said, "This is for you."

Then he noticed that his knife, which he was especially fond of, was missing. So he said, "Hey, Rinpoche! Could you perform a divination to see if I will find my favorite knife? I lost it somewhere on the way here."

Without a moment's hesitation, Chöwang Tulku replied, "Don't you remember where we divided up the tea, half for you and half for me? Go back and you will find your knife lying right there."

Hearing this, the man was petrified and began to cry. He apologized, confessing the whole story. Weeping, he prostrated and took out the tea he had stolen.

Chöwang Tulku said, "Don't take it so hard! I don't need that much tea. It's fine if you take some home. Take it back there and make yourself some delicious tea. Enjoy it—and tell your family that I gave it to you."

※

In the kingdom of Nangchen lived Yönga, a realized master and close disciple of Old Khyentse. You could even say he was a siddha. One day he decided to go pay Chöwang a visit at Fortress Peak. Chöwang's bed, where he sat day and night, was a meditation box, a wooden frame with sides about one foot high all around. Chöwang usually never stood up when visitors came, but this time he did.

He told Kalpa, "Put the yak skin over there," and to Yönga he said, "Sit."

Yönga later recounted, "He did come outside to greet me, which was a marvelous feat in itself; but that was it. After we sat down, he didn't say a single word to me. He just sat there, upright and still."

Yönga must have dozed off while sitting there, because when he was leaving he said to Kalpa, "I got what I came for, so I'm going home now. I came all the way from Nangchen Gar because I wanted to meet Chöwang. I had a good nap. It's been a very pleasant visit."

Then he headed off.

※

In the latter part of his life, Chöwang Tulku stopped talking almost completely. One day, it appeared that he was having some trouble walking, but when asked he would say, "I'm fine! I'm not sick at all."

That evening, he and Kalpa took a short stroll to a small crest where an ancient stupa containing the sacred remains of one of the forefathers of the Sakya lineage is located. The siddha who had established Fortress Peak had been a disciple of this Sakya master and when his teacher passed away, the siddha flew through the sky carrying some of the remains back to Kham. He built the stupa in order to protect against obstacles.[148]

After Chöwang Tulku had walked around it four or five times, he had a hard time walking back inside. Kalpa thought, "If the master is having trouble walking, why did he go to the trouble of going around the stupa?"

Early the next morning, Chöwang Tulku said, "Don't forget to arrange the shrine. It must be done before the first rays of the sun light up the sky from behind the eastern mountains."

"I can already see the first rays of dawn," Kalpa told his master. At that, Chöwang Tulku did the yogic practice of exhaling the breath three times. His third long exhalation was his last.

"I was suddenly panic-stricken," Kalpa later told me, "and began to run around, confused. Until then, only the two of us had resided at Fortress Peak; now there was

34. Lachab monastery

only me, and I didn't know what do! I ran down to the mountainside toward the nearest village and yelled at the top of my voice so that the people could hear me. Some of the locals came running up, and I yelled, 'Our guru's dead! Our guru's dead!'

"Before the master left his body," Kalpa continued, "he gave written instructions to leave it untouched for a week. The document read, 'Send a message to Lama Latsey, from whom I received the *Treasury of Precious Termas*, and invite him here.'

"With the long braid still coiled around his head, his body continued to sit, much as Chöwang had done for most of his life. We sent for Lama Latsey. As he lived three days' journey away, about six days later he was seen riding up the trail in the early morning. Telling him about the letter, I assured him I had kept the room locked until he had gotten there, so no one had disturbed the body.

"When he entered Chöwang Tulku's room, he saw the body sitting up straight, just as if nothing at all had happened. He counted the days and he said, 'According to the letter, we must leave the body as it is for one more day.'

"So we left the room and the door was again locked. Lama Latsey then said, 'Well, there are some things we need to get done. First, arrange for someone to begin building the funeral stupa, and send someone to invite fifty or sixty lamas and monks from Lachab Gompa.'

"On the morning of the eighth day, we went back into the master's room and discovered that the body had shrunk quite a bit. By the time it was placed inside the funeral stupa, it was barely eighteen inches tall, but it still retained human proportions. It fit in a copper pot and was easy to put inside the stupa. The braid, however, didn't shrink and practically covered the remains. We then cremated this small body."[149]

So that's the type of lama they say I'm the rebirth of. Whether it is true or not, I don't know. But it was Samten Gyatso who settled that it was so, and then he took charge of my life and education. For a while I moved back and forth between Lachab and my father's hermitage in order to spend time with him. Before this, I don't remember having stayed a full year in any one place.

In those days, I did some short retreats lasting a couple of months here and a couple of months there, but none of any significant length, except for a six-month stay at Fortress Peak in something resembling a retreat. It was only when I went to Tsurphu that I got the chance and freedom to dedicate myself to a strict three-year retreat.

It seems I have spent my entire life moving from place to place.

20

My Monastery and Enthronement

Samten Gyatso and I shared the same monastic household at Lachab; my aunt Tashi Chimey acted as the manager. Many of the important shrine objects would be with me today if it hadn't been for her refusing to let me take them with me when I later went to Central Tibet. She said that they belonged to the monastery and to Samten Gyatso's future tulku.

My aunt somehow sensed that I had no desire to take responsibility for the monastery—and, to be honest, in my heart I had already given up any concern for it. Lachab was situated in a large valley, with many fields, and I had no desire to take care of them even though a normal person would have been more than happy to own them. Taking care of a monastery in Kham was a heavy burden. Frankly, it's a big headache. You are constantly dependent upon others and have many obligations.

"What is the use of going through all that?" I thought. It was better to give up running a monastery altogether.

To tell the truth, I never had the wish to live in Kham and longed to journey through Central Tibet from one new place to another, with no fixed schedule or direction, but it would only be after Samten Gyatso's passing that I could do so.

The temple at Fortress Peak wouldn't qualify as a monastery but fits what we call a *gönchung*—a small gompa. Actually, many, many centuries ago, Fortress Peak was the residence of Bönpo meditators and many of them attained accomplishment there; I've heard amazing stories about them. Later this sacred place came into Buddhists' hands. Padmasambhava went there while he was in Tibet and, after he blessed it, many VAJRA GURU mantras naturally appeared on the face of the cliffs.

Several centuries later (in the early twelfth century), it was the practice place of Ga Lotsawa, or Galo for short, one of the first Karmapa's gurus and a translator of the Dharma who had been to India. Galo was a great master, comparable to the deity Chakrasamvara in human form. In his writings we find an eloquent tribute describing the qualities of Fortress Peak.

The story goes that in the early morning, Galo and one of his chief disciples flew across the valley to fetch water, then flew back. There are numerous footprints in the solid rock where they landed. Both the guru and his disciple were siddhas; you can still see the stupa built at Fortress Peak to hold his remains.

Later on, an accomplished master from near the Chinese border took up residence at Fortress Peak. Later still, in the sixteenth century, the ninth Karmapa, Wangchuk Dorje, sent a message that the king of Nangchen's longevity would be assured if long-life practices were performed for him on the summit of Fortress Peak. Throughout the following centuries, masters would come once a month to practice there at the request of the current king. In more recent times, Samten Gyatso and Chöwang Tulku took turns.[150]

On the day I was enthroned, an extremely vicious gale blew up—call that an auspicious sign! It was so strong that some people couldn't stand up and it almost carried off the canopy. It seemed to be relentless, and the wind kept swirling around the gompa. I asked Samten Gyatso what it might mean.

"I wonder," he replied. "Maybe it's bad, maybe it's good. Maybe it's the guardians, the protectors of the Dharma, showing off their powers."

35. View from Lachab monastery

36. On the road from Fortress Peak to Lachab

I asked him again and he said, "Who knows, perhaps this gompa will stay, perhaps it will perish. For the remaining years of my life, it will stay, but during your time it will disappear. Who knows, during your lifetime perhaps Lachab will crumble and be destroyed by war."

It seems he saw something, because he continued, "But it will be restored again sometime after that.[151] There is a link between your health and this gompa. As long as it stands, you will be free of sickness, but when it crumbles, you too will fall ill. Some of the vital energy for your present life is anchored in Lachab. But then again, who knows? As long as the two of us are together, the gompa will be fine. I, of course, will stay here for the rest of my life, but I wonder if you will ever live here after I pass away.

"After I am gone," he continued, "I am not sure what will happen. I have the feeling that bad times are coming, severely bad times—the evil influence will come from the east." At the time, I wondered what he meant. He looked at me with clear, wide eyes.

"If it happens that you are forced to leave, you must go to Nubri," Samten Gyatso added.

"Where is Nubri?" I asked.

"Right now it belongs to the Gorkha king in Nepal and so is no longer under the Tibetan government. A descendant of King Trisong Deutsen still lives there, as well as a couple of my disciples with deep faith in the Dharma. When you leave here, you will first go to Central Tibet, but after a while there you will be unable to remain. At that time, go to Nubri. The Nubri people are humble and simple. They are not rich, but they have deep appreciation for the Buddhist teachings. The one you must contact is the descendant of the Dharma king Trisong Deutsen."[152]

Around that time, the rulers of Ziling province, who were Muslims, did not favor us. Quite the contrary, the governor of Ziling beyond the northern border of Nangchen had already begun imposing increasingly heavy taxes on everyone in our region, including the monasteries. For example, a huge number of yak hides had to be handed over once a year.[153]

Earlier, we had learned that Japan and China were at war, and Japan was inflicting heavy casualties and oppression in parts of China. Since we were under Chinese rule, upon hearing such rumors we anxiously wondered what would happen to China.[154]

This conversation took place long before the communist invasion—in fact, we hadn't even heard the word *communist*—and I wondered why he was telling me this—it seemed so out of context. But, in the end, it wasn't the governor of Ziling who destroyed us, but the communists.

This is one of the few times Samten Gyatso revealed any of his clairvoyant powers; otherwise he was a hidden yogi. He wouldn't even mention any special dreams.

༄

People may or may not believe in the power of the Dharma protectors, but let me tell this story anyway.

Four monks from Lachab had gone on a pilgrimage to Mount Kailash. On the way back, they had to cross a great river that, because it was summer, had swollen far beyond normal. They walked along the bank trying to find a crossing, which in those days was not easy in Tibet.

They had run out of food and were starving. For a while they sustained themselves on a rotting sheep carcass they had found. With the help of a fire, they were able to salvage enough cooked meat to carry on for another four or five days. As one monk later said, "We survived thanks to that sheep."

Finally, they sat down on the bank, and one of them said, "This is it! We're going to die anyway, so what's the use of walking further?"

"If one of us were to die first, the others could eat his flesh. If it turns out to be me, don't hesitate," said another. They carried on like this for a while.

Finally, the youngest one lamented tearfully, "I'm not sure I can eat meat from your body. Oh, what to do!"

Their only hope, they all agreed, was to do the petition to Dusölma and Four-Armed Mahakala, both guardian protectors of Lachab. They must have put all their heart into it, supplicating from the depths of their being.

"Look there!" one of them shouted.

The others turned around and saw that the river had parted!

Later one of them told me, "It was wide enough to walk through; I figure it was about two arm spans. We have no idea why, but two walls of water were somehow held apart. This was no narrow river, I tell you! None of us could believe it, though, and we discussed among ourselves whether this could really be happening—having such doubt was almost harder than starving."

Finally, one of them said, "Let's run for it!" and they dropped everything and ran across.

"The walls were quivering as we made a dash for it," the monk continued, "and the moment we reached the other side, there was a loud SWOOSH! We turned around and saw that the gap had closed. This is no lie. I'm telling you, I've nothing to gain from making up such a story."

This monk was quite old when he told me the story. Independently, I went to the three others, who gave the exact same account. I made all of them swear on the name of their guru that they weren't lying. They were not great masters but merely ordinary monks. Their only asset was pure faith in their Dharma protectors.

Hard to believe, isn't it?

⁂

When I was around twenty, Samten Gyatso told me, "You appear to be someone who can give mind teachings. You are the kind of person who finds it all quite easy, not seeing how anyone could have problems understanding the nature of mind. You could end up too blasé; then again, maybe you simply will be very confident.

"Sometimes I think you assume too much. I must caution you that there is one thing you should watch out for: on the one hand, you could assume it is all so simple that everyone would understand. But then, on the other hand, that's not the way things are. People will often comprehend something totally different from what you mean, concluding that there is nothing to gain, so that they become careless and give up.

"You feel that realizing the nature of mind is simply a matter of course," he continued, "but I want you to understand: some people do not know the nature of mind, and there definitely *is* a reason for that. There are many people whose practice of 'mind essence' is nothing more than remaining absentminded and unaware in the state of the all-ground.[155]

"Nevertheless, for the time being, you should go ahead and test your confidence on a few old men and women. You might be able to benefit one or two, so it's fine for you to teach them."

In this way, he gave me the go-ahead to begin teaching.

I started giving people advice on understanding the nature of mind because I was very talkative. I couldn't help it; it would just slip out! When I spent time with Samten Gyatso, I listened in on whatever instructions he gave. Often it would be the pointing-out instruction and advice on how to truly meditate in the simplest way.

Afterward, there might be some people outside his room who couldn't quite understand what he had said. They would ask me, "How can it be that easy?"

And I would say, "Why do you think it has to be difficult? It really *is* so easy."
Then they would reply, "But I don't get it."
And I'd tell them, "What do you mean, you don't get it? Just let be!" I had that attitude because I'd heard what my uncle had said and I'd just parrot it.

My uncle would then call me in and repeat, "It seems you are the talkative type, as well as someone who thinks that recognizing mind nature is totally easy. I think that in the future you will be like this as well—you will be both talkative and somebody who acts like it is really simple!" And he was right.

On one hand, maybe with my teaching style I'm just fooling everybody, making it too simple. But on the other hand, this *is* really how it is! It is the truth. What is the use of trying to sit and push and struggle, when we can allow the three kayas of buddhahood to be naturally present? Why do we have to strain and contort ourselves into an uncomfortable posture and an uptight meditative state with some hope that in the future, after lots of effort, we may get there? We don't need to go through all that trouble and tension. All we need to do is totally let be and recognize our nature right now.

However, my style was mainly to just spin the heads of uneducated people, something for which I seem to have a knack.

As I said, I started to talk about mind nature after having heard Samten Gyatso give instructions on it many times and understanding somewhat. So I would sometimes repeat what he had said to others, like "a parrot giving a Dharma talk," which means trying to teach others a truth about which one has no personal experience or an instruction one has not personally practiced.

So in those days I guess I acted the charlatan once more.

※

The Buddha realized that different beings have various capacities. So out of great compassion and skillful means, he gave an assortment of teachings, each right for different individuals. Although the essence of all teachings of all enlightened ones is to simply let be in recognition of one's own nature, the Buddha taught a wide variety of complex instructions in order to satisfy people at their own level. Another reason the Buddha and the great masters taught the nine vehicles is not just that they couldn't leave well enough alone, but to make everybody happy. It seems to be human nature to love complication, to want to build up a lot of concepts. Later on, of course, we must allow them to fall to pieces again.

The great variety of teachings that exist doesn't change the fact that the very essence of the Dharma, the nature of mind, is extremely simple and easy. In fact, it's so simple and easy that sometimes it's hard to believe!

The general tradition for giving the pointing-out instruction to the nature of mind holds that we need to go step by step. First, we complete the reflections of the four mind-changings. Next, we go through the preliminary practices, and after that the yidam practice of deity, mantra and samadhi. And indeed, these are all still necessary, even if we have already received teachings on mind essence. Don't get the idea that suddenly all the practices taught by the enlightened ones are unimportant. On the contrary, they are incredibly important.

Since it's not so easy nor very common for someone to ever have the opportunity to receive mind teachings, I felt that I should speak up and give it. Please remember that we can easily receive the other important teachings from various masters, so don't ignore them. Please be diligent in practice. In truth, perseverance makes the difference between buddhas and ordinary beings.

There is a story from Kham in which an old guy says to a lama, "When you talk about the benefits of recognizing mind essence, it's certain that *you* have no problem; in fact, even this old sinner will probably be safe from rebirth in hell. But when you talk about the consequences of our actions, there's no doubt I will end up in hell. In fact, I wonder if even you might not be in trouble, my lama!"

A phony meditator might be able to fool others while alive, but there's no doubt he'll be caught unprepared when facing the bardo. I am quite certain that, in the long run, the greatest benefit comes from simply trusting in the Three Jewels. Of course, if one also has authentic experience of mind essence, then, as the Kagyu saying tells us, "Though death is regarded with so much dread, a yogi's death is a small awakening."

I also feel that even if one still hasn't reached the splendid heights of experience and realization, some simple, sound comprehension is extremely beneficial. An understanding, even intellectually, of emptiness—the empty and awake quality of mind—will surely help you cross over to the other side in the bardo. When sentient beings pass on, it is their own mind that becomes bewildered—and it is their own mind that needs to come to their rescue, since no one else is going to do it at that time.[156]

Therefore, a sound understanding of mind essence could become the reminder that liberates in the bardo. The most essential benefit, however, comes from *actually* training in mind essence while you are alive; this is the only thing that will ensure true success. First, liberate your own stream of being through realization, then liberate others through your compassionate activity. Proceeding in this way makes a human life meaningful.

When I taught, some understood and others didn't, but I kept at it just the same. This bold attitude has stuck with me and is now my style. I don't know if it helps others much. The teachings on mind essence may be the most precious and secret. They may also be "liberation through hearing," so that whoever hears them will be benefited. So I feel it's acceptable to give them from time to time.

I don't claim that everyone to whom I explain the essence of mind recognizes and trains in the genuine experience. There are many different types of students. Those who don't recognize are inevitably preoccupied by fleeting phenomena and will get distracted. But even if they have not recognized the natural state of mind, anyone who has heard the essential teaching, even once, will slowly grow closer to realization—so long as they don't abandon the attempt entirely but continue to practice. Those who *have* recognized, and so have some trust in mind essence, cannot give up the Dharma, even if someone tells them to. This springs from confidence in their personal experience.

At one point, Samten Gyatso went on a pilgrimage around the mountain above Palpung monastery in Derge, walking all the way accompanied by Dudul, his attendant and my close friend. An old lama who Dudul ran into turned out to have been a personal disciple of the first Kongtrul.

"Where are you from?" he asked Dudul.

"I'm from Nangchen," Dudul replied.

"Ah, then maybe you know this Nangchen lama who I hear is visiting somewhere around here," inquired the old lama. "His name is Samten Gyatso, and he has been both the teacher and disciple of the great Karmapa. I know of him since he is often mentioned in his collected writings. Do you happen to know where he is staying?"

"Yeah, I do know," Dudul replied, "since I'm his attendant."

"I'll be damned! Please tell me," begged the old lama. After getting directions, he then declared, "Thank you *so* much. Early tomorrow I will surely pay him a visit."

The next morning, the old lama came to visit Samten Gyatso, and they had a long, profound exchange. When the old lama came outside, he sat down with a cup of tea and asked my friend, "So tell me, how many disciples has this lama?"

"Not that many close disciples," said Dudul. "He gives a lot of empowerments, but not that many meditating hermits call themselves his personal disciples."

"Alas! What a shame," exclaimed the old lama. "It's obviously true what they say about those spineless folk from Nangchen. Why are they so damn ignorant? Here they have a fine meditation master with such a high view—he totally amazed me with his answers to my questions—and you say he doesn't have many disciples?! Are the people of Nangchen no better than cattle? I really pity you guys."

That old lama was speaking the truth: not that many people gave up everything to follow Samten Gyatso, certainly not compared to the vast numbers who became disciples of the first Khyentse and Kongtrul. In fact, only four or five come to mind—but they were some very fine meditators indeed. If a lama was to be judged by the number of his followers, then Samten Gyatso was nothing special at all.

Yet he was regarded as a lineage guru by the fifteenth Karmapa, Drukchen Jamgön and Taklung Tsetrul, who were some of the most prominent lamas in Central Tibet. In Nangchen, he also transmitted teachings to the masters Adeu and the second Tsoknyi and became one of their root gurus. As for lamas in Derge, you can include Dzongsar Khyentse, who received the restricted section of the *New Treasures* at Fortress Peak. And Karsey Kongtrul came to Tsikey to receive the *New Treasures* from Samten Gyatso.

The old lama did touch upon a vital characteristic of my country: scholastic education was not the main emphasis. Not that I'm proud of that. On the other hand, in such an environment, only realization would qualify someone to be a lama—not just talk. Impostors had a hard time gaining a foothold where I came from.

※

Samten Gyatso occupied a very prominent position in Nangchen and was busy with his many responsibilities. But since we shared the same monastery, I had no problem spending time with him. Sharing a monastic household is much like living as a family under the same roof. So I had plenty of opportunity to ask questions and receive guidance.

I remember well one particular instruction that Samten Gyatso gave me at an early age. It had to do with a teaching on the profound topic of *essence, nature and capacity*. He said, "The word *capacity* refers to the unconfined basis for experience, as in the moment just before something takes place. Once the arising has occurred, it usually has already turned into a thought. Capacity means the basis for that to happen, an unimpeded quality of awareness.

"This unimpeded quality is extremely subtle and significant. Once you acknowledge this unimpededness, nothing more needs to be done. In this unimpededness, it is impossible to find any subject or object. The analogy for this is a bright mirror, a readiness for experience to unfold without any preconception whatsoever. So please understand very well the third of these three: essence, nature and capacity."

This is an example of how Samten Gyatso would teach. I feel very fortunate to have been instructed by such a master when I was young, because there are many people who misidentify capacity as being not the basis—like the mirror—but the manifestation, like the reflection in the mirror. But the reflection means that the mind and sense object have already linked up, and the attention has already been caught up in distraction.

"One should not identify the capacity with being caught up in subject, object and the act of perceiving," he said. "An unconfined basis for experience means the readiness, being able to experience—just ready to be, but not yet involved in dualistic experience. If your training is in this readiness, rather than in conceptual thinking, you won't be caught up in duality during daily activities. This capacity, in essence, is the unimpeded omniscience of all buddhas, which is totally unlike the attention that focuses on one thing while eliminating everything else."[157]

Like others, tulku's obviously have emotions too. Just look at Marpa, the translator, with his incredibly strong emotions, blazing like flames. But the moment an experienced meditator looks into the nature of mind every thought and emotion vanishes like snow flakes falling on a hot plate. At that moment a meditator is truly free of any attachment. Marpa may have treated Milarepa with a lot of abuse, harsh words and beatings—but that was totally unlike the anger of an ordinary person in that there wasn't even a shred of selfishness involved. You can't only judge people by their behavior.

Even though his kindness was boundless, Samten Gyatso could be quite wrathful at times. Once in a while, I saw him slap one of his attendants. Sometimes I even had to bring him the cane and that scared me too, because even one whack would hurt—it was big! Occasionally, he gave more than a little tap. He could give a real thrashing, especially to Dudul, who often had it coming.

"With this guy, there is no other way," Samten Gyatso once said. "He's too dense, and a slap of the stick gets through to him; it's effective for at least five or six days." Afterward, Dudul would act like a real human being, bright and gentle—at least at first. Then he would start to be argumentative again, finding fault and loudly complaining about every little thing.

"Why don't you just let it drop?" I often told him, "Nothing is that bad. Don't you remember what happened to you last time?"

But the story would always end with Samten Gyatso sending me to fetch the cane one more time. Oh my! Once, Samten Gyatso smacked him so many times I thought he wouldn't be able to walk the next morning, but when I met Dudul afterward, he was carrying on with his duties as if nothing had happened.

The story often repeated itself, but he just wouldn't listen. Once, I asked him about it and he said, "That was nothing. I don't care that much. It hurts for a moment and then passes."

He too had a lot of devotion for Samten Gyatso.

21

The Young Karmapa

Another major influence early in my life was the sixteenth Karmapa, Rigpey Dorje. I first met him in east Tibet at Tana Gompa.[158] I was young at the time, and Samten Gyatso brought me along as his attendant. I didn't become that close to the Karmapa then—he just knew me as "the tulku who was with Samten Gyatso."

When the Karmapa was young, he was pretty strong-headed; you couldn't force him to study, and he was very playful. Only Samten Gyatso could intimidate him enough to get him to pursue his studies. For that reason, the Karmapa received quite a few teachings from Samten Gyatso. They later became very close.

Thanks to the communist forces, the Karmapa later came to Nangchen.[159] He was supposed to travel directly to Derge, his intended destination, but was unable to do so because of a border upheaval between Kham and China.

This is when we first heard about "the communists." We knew them by their Chinese name, *gungtreng,* which soon took on an ominous connotation. We also heard of someone called Mao Tse-tung, and that the gungtreng had arrived at the old border town, Dartsedo and begun a march on Derge.

This was around the time when the Chinese forces were at war with the Japanese. Those in power in China were coming under increased pressure from two sides, since the communists were becoming ever more powerful and raising an army of their own. If the Chinese forces had been able to overpower the Japanese army, they would have been able to suppress the communists, but they were stretched too thin.

It seems to be an old story, often repeated: the powers that be in the capital are distracted by good times and enjoying the status quo, while their opponents and neighboring countries begin to eat away at their power base. While China's upper class was indolent and careless, the communists were busy day and night preparing to take over the country.

The next thing we heard was that one of the governors of Derge had been captured. But then the communists were defeated and disappeared for a while. I was around sixteen at the time.

After the governor of Derge was released by the communists and returned to power, the feeling was that it was now safe for the Karmapa to visit there. He visited many places along the way, including various monasteries in Nangchen that were under royal patronage. He was invited to Lachab as well. And before he proceeded to the famous Dilyak Gompa, my Tsangsar relatives also hosted him and his party.

On this trip, the Karmapa had been given some small white *abra*s, a local type of mouse-hare. Sometimes people would keep an abra as a pet, but only in a box, otherwise they would run off. When I was young, I had two or three of them, but they all ran away. They are not easy to hold on to either, and it was almost certain that if you took them out of the box you would lose them. But our Wish-Fulfilling Jewel, the Karmapa, refused to imprison his pets in a box, so he had five or six abras running free in his tent.

I tried to warn him. "Wish-Fulfilling Jewel, you have to keep them caged. Mine took off as fast as they could."

37. The Sixteenth Karmapa— a willful incarnation

"Doesn't matter, doesn't matter," he said. "Let them all out."

The abras darted around the tent. It looked to me as though they were circumambulating him, and they didn't even seem to mind when he picked them up. Though the tent was open, they would stay near him; not a single one ever seemed to want to escape.

One day, the Karmapa decided to dye his abras yellow and red. They seemed entranced by him, and so when he decided to change their coat to a different color, they just sat still and let him do it. Abras usually have light colored fur, and I was worried that if the ones the Karmapa had dyed were set free again, the other abras might attack them. But that never happened. Not one of them minded when he dipped them in water to wash the dye off.

I must say, the way the young Karmapa handled the abras impressed me deeply.

※

It was during this journey that Samten Gyatso became the Karmapa's tutor. Back at Tsurphu, the Karmapa was taught by a very level-headed but strict lama. I heard that he would sometimes bolt the door from inside, prostrate to the young Karmapa three times—and that was often enough of a warning for our Wish-Fulfilling Jewel to snap back into line and concentrate on his studies. A certain mixture of fear and respect ensured that he made good progress in his education.

However, there was a relative of the Karmapa who was a bit fainthearted and couldn't bear the thought of the precious incarnation being physically disciplined on occasion. So he scolded the tutor, "You treat the Karmapa, a buddha incarnate, like an ordinary person. Your behavior is criminal!"

At that time, the young Karmapa had many visions and prophecies, and he would share these revelations—including which buddha he had just seen and what they told him about the future—with this tutor, who would write them down. Some of these predictions were mixed up with the Karmapa's remarks about such-and-such relative being a "demon," and eventually the fellow who had complained found out that this had been written about him.

He took this personally and decided that although the tutor had good intentions, he obviously wasn't up to the task of educating such an eminent incarnation. So the relatives took the opportunity to relieve the tutor of his duties. This was a shame in a way, as the Karmapa had learned to read very well under this tutor.

The official statement was, "Our Wish-Fulfilling Jewel has no need for a tutor. The Karmapa is a buddha whose qualities spontaneously manifest. He is not someone who should be treated as an ordinary person, beaten and pinched. So during a meeting it was decided to tell the tutor that his services are no longer required."

The young Karmapa was sad and defended his tutor, saying, "Yes, he does occasionally pinch and strike me, but he does so out of a good heart. He only wants me to advance in my studies."

The Karmapa insisted that the tutor be given nice presents, including a fine set of monk's robes. Then for a while the Karmapa went without a teacher.

But when the Karmapa arrived at Dilyak, the lamas of Nangchen insisted that another tutor be appointed. This is when Samten Gyatso's name came up. Since he already had been one of the gurus of the Karmapa's previous incarnation, he seemed the obvious choice. And so Samten Gyatso was asked to assume the role of tutor. He replied, "I'm getting old, but I will serve at Palpung. It is a great monastery." So Samten Gyatso became the Karmapa's tutor during the journey from Dilyak.

Samten Gyatso's teaching style was never to beat the teenage Karmapa but instead to punish his own attendant Dudul right before the Karmapa's eyes, which had the desired effect. "I never had to hit him," Samten Gyatso told me. "Striking Dudul was enough to get the Karmapa to stay in his seat and continue his studies."

◈

But upon their arrival at Palpung, Samten Gyatso asked the great Situ if he could be excused from his teaching duties. Situ replied, "I realize that you are old and have gone to a lot of trouble. You were one of the teachers of the previous Karmapa, so I can't force you to be a tutor now. So I'll ask the Khyentse of Palpung to take over."

Palpung Khyentse was a disciple of the fifteenth Karmapa and had wonderful qualities, but he was such a stern presence that the Karmapa almost didn't dare move when he was around. Even though Palpung Khyentse was a perfect candidate, after he slapped the Karmapa a couple of times, influential members of the Karmapa's family again found reason to object and wanted him dismissed.

"Even a lama is human; even the illusory body is flesh and blood, so unless it gets hurt a bit, the Karmapa won't study," Palpung Khyentse said in his defense. "A Karmapa is supposed to be a teacher for the world as a whole, so the more educated he is, the better."

He must have struck the Karmapa a few more times, because finally the Karmapa's father went before the great Situ and said, "Even though he is the Karmapa, he is also my child; being my son, he belongs to me. My wife and I cannot bear to witness him being physically punished. You decide how to implement it, but we want Khyentse of Palpung dismissed."

Personally, I think this was a mistake. The Karmapa was moving in a very good direction in his education. But his father, an important and influential official, was unyielding and difficult. He had the haughty attitude of a Khampa aristocrat and had no qualms about placing his opinion above that of most lamas.

The great Situ replied, "Khyentse of Palpung is no ordinary man. Not only is he the reincarnation of the great Khyentse, he is also one of the four main lamas of Palpung.[160] How can I tell one of the great lamas of Palpung to resign?"

"But you must!" the Karmapa's father insisted. "Otherwise we will take care of our little tulku ourselves."

"You don't know how to take care of a Karmapa," Situ replied. "He is being educated, and he will turn out well."

Yet no matter what Situ said, the father wouldn't listen. And in the end, Palpung Khyentse was relieved of his duties. After that it was impossible to find anyone of the same caliber in terms of wisdom and erudition to be his teacher.

After one khenpo was let go, the Tentrul of Surmang was appointed; he proved to be a boon, transmitting the *Treasury of Knowledge*, the famous work by the great Kongtrul, from cover to cover over the course of three years. But he fell ill and passed away soon after.

By then, the Karmapa had grown into a man who made his own decisions and was receiving transmissions from Situ and Karsey Kongtrul.

☙

During the Karmapa's journey through Nangchen, his mother fell ill. Since my father was renowned for successful healing rituals, he was called upon to travel with our Wish-Fulfilling Jewel, and I got to go along. But at Dilyak my father asked to be excused from traveling any farther.

"Does this mean that my mother is going to be okay now?" the Karmapa asked.

My father said, "I've done what I could do," implying that she would die soon. "I have done the Chö ritual every evening, and it appears there is nothing further to be done."

"Tell me my mother is not dying," the Karmapa repeated.

"Sorry, I can't tell you that," my father replied.

The next morning, Chimey Dorje and I left. We later heard that the Karmapa's mother died a week later. The Karmapa had her remains cremated on the vast plain north of Dilyak.

Chimey Dorje insisted on leaving before she died, although he had been asked to stay longer.

"There always comes a point when supportive rituals are no longer of any benefit," Chimey Dorje told me.

"What do you mean?" I inquired.

"Near the end, whenever I looked at her with a Chö eye, she had no head," he explained. "To me that means death is inevitable. That is why I asked to be excused."

⁂

The next time I met the Karmapa was at Surmang monastery, where I had gone to greet my father on his return from Ziling after a long journey. Fortunately, this coincided with the Karmapa's visit to that monastery. In those days, I alternated between being my father's and Samten Gyatso's attendant, depending on which of them was in the Karmapa's entourage.

At Surmang I had a chance to see the Karmapa's horse. This horse was quite unusual, known to give blessings by placing one of its hooves on people's heads. People would stand in line and as the horse touched their head it made a sound that—with a bit of imagination—sounded like HUNG HUNG HUNG. Most people got touched very lightly, but once in a while someone got whacked.

I thought to myself, "Who knows what that horse will do to me? Maybe it will split my skull open!" So no one was going to make me get a "blessing." I preferred to stand and watch the others.

Word went around that the Karmapa's horse was giving blessings. There was a long line of people who, each in turn, gave white scarves and offerings of money to the horse. In Khampa style, they would not make such a request empty-handed.

Of course, the horse didn't speak. But it did make a sound each time it touched a person's head and many people heard the sound as OM MANI PADME HUNG. I was waiting for someone to receive one of its "dynamic" blessings, but it didn't happen that day; the horse was quite gentle with everyone.

Many years later, I heard that one day the horse just sat down on its hindquarters and passed away, then continued sitting there. Pretty amazing, wouldn't you agree?

⁂

Once in a while, the Karmapa would reveal his clear perception of the death and rebirth of beings. One time, on a journey north, some villagers offered the Karmapa a horse. After receiving the horse, the Karmapa turned to his general secretary and said, "This horse is the rebirth of your father."

The secretary was very upset and asked the Karmapa if he could do something. The Karmapa replied, "What do you want me to do? He's a horse! He's already taken rebirth and there he is."

"Then, please, give the horse to me and I will take care of it myself," the secretary pleaded. "No one will ride it."

For two years the secretary kept the horse, fed and groomed it, and took the very best care of it, until the horse passed away.

※

On another journey, the Karmapa was passing through a valley with a following of about ninety horsemen, when all of a sudden a kid goat broke away from its flock. It ran after the Karmapa as best it could, bleating and trying to keep up. Our Wish-Fulfilling Jewel turned to look and then said to his servant, "Take the kid back to the village we just came through, find its owner and ask him to give it to me."

The servant took the kid, which had a colored string around its neck, under his arm and rode back to the village. The colored string made it easy to identify the goat and the servant was quickly able to find its owner, who readily agreed to offer it to the Karmapa.

The goat in tow, he caught up with the Karmapa's traveling party by nightfall. He brought the kid to the Karmapa and asked, "Wish-Fulfilling Jewel, why are you so interested in this goat?"

"Do you remember that orphan who was given to me some years ago and recently died?" the Karmapa replied. "That's him, poor guy! Somehow he must have recognized me and, unable to bear to be separated again, he ran after me bleating at the top of his voice. I'll keep him for a while."

For the rest of the journey back to Tsurphu, the Karmapa kept the small goat as a pet.

22

Grandmother's Death

Spontaneous devotion is often due to aspirations and karmic links created in former lifetimes, and my grandmother felt such devotion for Old Kongtrul. When she fell seriously ill, she heard that his reincarnation, Karsey Kongtrul, was currently residing at Karma Gön south of Nangchen. She sent a messenger to invite him. As this happened to coincide with the annual drubchen of *Tukdrub Barchey Kunsel*—the most famous of the great tertön's treasures—performed at Tsikey, Karsey Kongtrul was asked to preside over the ceremonies.[161]

While at Tsikey, Karsey Kongtrul stayed in a very special chapel. This little temple, adjacent to the assembly hall, was called Kutsab Lhakhang because it contained the statue regarded as the representative (*kutsab*) of the Lotus-Born master in the form of Guru Mahasukha. Even though it is quite small, it is a rather famous statue connected with a cycle of terma teachings known as the *Spontaneous Fulfillment of Wishes*, which had been revealed nearby. After its revelation, the great Khyentse saw a vision in which this statue grew to the size of a mountain.

Let me tell you a little bit about Karsey Kongtrul. He mostly resided at Palpung. Later, at Tsurphu, I received the *Treasury of Precious Termas* from him. You may remember I mentioned the great scholar Tashi Özer, a learned and accomplished master and a disciple of both Khyentse and Old Kongtrul. Years before, Tashi Özer had been invited to Tsurphu to give the fifteenth Karmapa the reading transmission for the *Kangyur*, the translated words of the Buddha.

38.
The terma site above Tsikey and the present tulku

When Tashi Özer had finished reading this voluminous collection of the Buddha's words, the Karmapa said with gratitude, "Whatever wish you have, I will fulfill."

Tashi Özer replied, "I have only one request: as you know, we both have the same root guru, and as he has been born as your son, please let me take him back to Palpung monastery."

"Very well. I will not break my word," the Karmapa said. But since the tulku was only three years old, Tashi Özer knew that he couldn't have the child right away. Still, he is credited with eventually returning the Kongtrul incarnation to Palpung.

39. Karsey Kongtrul—the son of the fifteenth Karmapa

Much later, Karsey Kongtrul requested Samten Gyatso to confer the complete empowerments of *Tukdrub Barchey Kunsel* and so had come to Tsikey to receive them. The empowerments were given in Könchok Paldrön's private room; I was one of the assistants for the empowerments, alternating with Dudul every other day.

Karsey Kongtrul was the son of the fifteenth Karmapa and also a reincarnation of the great Kongtrul. When Samten Gyatso was ready to give the empowerments, often Karsey Kongtrul didn't seem to be in any rush to come in. Sometimes he would be out strolling, relaxing or discussing various topics.

One day, Samten Gyatso had finished the preparation for the next empowerment and said to me, "Well, now! Isn't Rinpoche coming? Go look for him."

I went to Karsey Kongtrul's quarters and said, "The empowerment is ready to be given."

He replied, "Very well." But being a person of high social status, he felt no pressure to hurry; he took his own sweet time, slowly ambling toward the empowerment room. When he finally arrived, Samten Gyatso, as usual, came out of the inner chamber to welcome him as a sign of respect.

I've mentioned that Samten Gyatso could sometimes be a bit stern. As he stood waiting there, we could see he had a pretty wrathful demeanor, and what he said next to Kongtrul scared even me.

"We all know you're the son of the Karmapa and the rebirth of the great Kongtrul. But it is you who have ordered me to give these empowerments and that is why I'm doing it. Isn't it true that I didn't insist on offering them to you? Therefore, if *you* want to receive the empowerments, come when they are ready to be given. If you don't want to come when they are ready, all you have to do is tell me. Then I won't go to all this trouble for nothing."

Seeing Samten Gyatso's fierce expression put a scare into Karsey Kongtrul. From then on, he was afraid to come late and his cook was always waiting next to me for the signal to go fetch his teacher, asking, "Is it time? Is it time?"

Once, his cook leaned over and whispered to me, "I shouldn't be saying this because he is also the guru of the Karmapa, but isn't Samten Gyatso pretty wrathful?"

Nevertheless, Samten Gyatso gave Karsey Kongtrul more than one hundred empowerments.

During these empowerments, Karsey Kongtrul asked Uncle Tersey if he would be so kind as to give him the reading transmission for the first volume of the

New Treasures known as *Essence Manual of Oral Instruction.* Of course Karsey Kongtrul wanted Uncle Tersey to sit on a throne—to which Uncle Tersey responded by immediately sitting down on the floor.

"Don't force this heavy burden upon me," Uncle Tersey implored, "making me the teacher instead of the disciple! The only way I could give you this transmission is by presenting it in the form of a mandala offering."

Uncle Tersey was an extremely simple person that way and sincerely humble, so they argued back and forth. Karsey Kongtrul even sent for several cushions, but Uncle Tersey refused to sit on those as well. Finally, he agreed to sit just a bit higher—one thin cushion more than normal—and gave the reading transmission.

Uncle Tersey's utter humility was one of the reasons I never received more than a couple of empowerments from him. Instead I received most of the *New Treasures* from Samten Gyatso. As was his style—so meticulous and exacting—he would neither omit nor mispronounce even a single syllable. Although the *Essence Manual of Oral Instruction* is only a single volume in length, it still took him two days to read it aloud for Karsey Kongtrul.

Karsey Kongtrul once told me that he had performed a drubchen three times using the treasure *Tukdrub Barchey Kunsel*, and each time, without fail, there were special signs. "Please tell me what they were," I asked.

"Once a profuse amount of nectar poured forth, very sweet and slightly sour like excellent *chang*; it flowed from the torma on the shrine all the way to the entrance of the temple. Another time, the liquid in the *amrita* and *rakta* vessels on the shrine began to boil, sounding like roiling water, and rays of rainbow light surrounded the shrine inside the assembly hall, extending to the farthest walls, for all two or three hundred participants to see. The third time we also prepared sacred medicine and its sweet fragrance could be smelled seven days' walk away. In my whole life I have never witnessed signs as amazing as during those three times.

"If you want to ensure having extraordinary indications and signs, then the *Tukdrub* is outstanding," Karsey Kongtrul said.

All this could also have been due to the combination of the profound terma teaching and such an extremely great master. "Wouldn't these signs also have something to do with you being present?" I asked.

"How special am I compared to the Lotus-Born? *Tukdrub* is the method for realizing his mind. I am quite happy to have seen only a few tiny signs of his greatness."

༄

Karsey Kongtrul was a fully ordained monk as well as a master who could ordain others. So, at the drubchen ceremony he presided over, many people took the opportunity to take monk's vows. As it happened, my uncle Sang-Ngak said to me, using the affectionate title for the master, "Why don't you ask our Noble Protector to become a monk too? It is much better to be fully ordained if you want to uphold the Buddha's teachings. Look at your father and all the hassle he has with his wives and children—it's so much trouble to be a householder. Then look at me and how easy it is living the life of a simple monk.

"The only way to keep your freedom is to become a monk—if I want to stay or go, it's my decision and mine only. Once you hook up with a woman, I tell you, sooner or later you will be under her control. Once you have children you have to look after them as well as their mother—and sometimes her family too! Look around you: how many people are their own master? Compared to Samten Gyatso and me, don't you think it is much more difficult for your father and for Uncle Tersey, who is a ngakpa? Do yourself a favor and think this over really well. Why don't you just go ahead and become a monk?"

Samten Gyatso was also in the room, but he didn't say a word.

I replied, "I can't make up my mind."

"What's so hard in deciding about this? Right now we are graced by the visit of the reincarnation of the great Kongtrul, who is truly Vairotsana returned in human form. You have a perfect opportunity. Don't think about it—just do it!"

Again I answered, "I'll have to think about it. Give me time."

That afternoon, he brought it up again and yet again the next morning. Uncle Sang-Ngak was not considered a penniless lama, since he had no monastery to look after and now he said, "I'll give you all I own down to the smallest item, if you will take the monk ordination."

Finally I broke the news to him, "I have honestly questioned myself about this but have failed to find any wish to become a monk. Of course I want to realize the Dharma—that goes without saying—but I have no inclination to be fully ordained. What is the use of being a monk if one's heart isn't in it? Shouldn't it come from oneself? Honestly, Rinpoche, there is no use in being forced rather than being inspired by true renunciation. Please don't push me so hard."

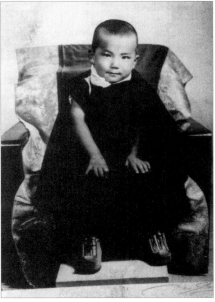

40.
The tulku of Karsey Kongtrul

Yet he didn't give up; he came back again and again to see if I had had a change of heart. On the other hand, though himself a monk of outstanding integrity, Samten Gyatso never said a thing to me about becoming a monk.

In the end, I told Uncle Sang-Ngak, "It is very kind of you to entice me with all your wealth as a present, but I have made up my mind. Even if someone were to offer me a yak-load of pure gold, I would not take ordination at this time."

"Well, well," he responded. "I see you have indeed made up your mind!" And that was the end of that.

That is why I am still a layperson, a common householder. Out of fondness, I wear some of the Buddha's robes, like the shawl, but actually I am a worldly man.

The reason I didn't take the ordination then or any time after was simply that I didn't trust that I could keep the vows. Not only did Samten Gyatso never touch women, he never even touched meat or liquor. Uncle Sang-Ngak was no different.

If you take monk's vows, you should keep them pure, like my uncles or like Karmey Khenpo. I have great respect for anyone who does so, but not for the half-hearted renunciate so common nowadays. Maybe it was my lack of pure perception, but I didn't see that many pure monks even then.

I had a strong feeling that it wouldn't do to merely put on robes and be a monk in name only. Instead, I decided to be honest about who I really was and to dress accordingly. I thought why should I hide my shortcomings? It's like the saying, "What's the use of wrapping shit in brocade?"

❧

I attended the drubchen at Tsikey, as did Samten Gyatso, Uncle Tersey and my father, who all sat up front near Karsey Kongtrul as he presided. During the tea breaks, they would all go up to their rooms for a bit, and one afternoon after a break none of them returned. I began to fear that my grandmother had left her body—and sure enough, someone came to tell me that Könchok Paldrön had passed on.

Apparently, just before she died, she told Karsey Kongtrul, "I have now reached the final point between birth and death."

Karsey Kongtrul remained with her for a bit and gave the instruction called "the reminder for samadhi." He then went down to his own quarters. I joined my father, my uncles and Penjik in the main room upstairs.[162]

Uncle Tersey was the first to say anything. He was in the habit of acting as if he had absolutely no self-confidence, and said, "Here we are, her four sons. Among us, I am the one who usually stayed with our mother; I am the one who was closest to her. You all would come and go, but I stayed by her side. Now she is gone—gone! And it feels as if my heart has been torn out."

Tears were streaming down his cheeks as he continued, "I am deeply worried now when I think of the subtle workings of the law of karma. What will happen to our Precious Mother?"

The others sat there and said nothing as Uncle Tersey wept. Finally, Samten Gyatso said, "Stop it now! What use are tears?"

"Whether of use or not, when someone is deeply sad, tears come—I can't help it," Uncle Tersey explained.

"You are not the only sad one—we all are. Aren't we all children of the same mother?" asked Samten Gyatso.

"But where is she going to go now?" Uncle Tersey lamented. "Don't you remember the story about Smritijnana, who went all the way from India to eastern Tibet to rescue his own mother, who had taken rebirth inside a stone in the hearth of a house there?"

Uncle Tersey was referring to the story of the Indian pandita who came to Tibet but, not knowing the language, had to work as a shepherd for three years. In the end, he pretended he wanted to leave, and the landlord asked him what he wanted as a farewell present. The master pointed to a large stone in the fireplace. It was an unusual request, but he was given the stone. When he split it open, a large insect was found in a crevice, where it was being tortured each day by the heat.

The master then entered samadhi and, in front of everyone's eyes, the insect was enveloped in rainbow light. The light rose into the sky. Then the master picked up the insect's carcass and tossed it into the fire.

With tears still welling up, Uncle Tersey continued. "Even though he was such a great master, his mother still didn't fare well. The law of karma is so subtle. Think about it! Our mother might be in trouble. Oh, where will she go now?

"And don't you remember the story of Old Khyentse's mother, who was a mundane type of *dakini*? When she passed away, he had to practice intensively, directing his power of samadhi into purifying her obscurations. Isn't it true that it's hard to find a master greater than he, in this day and age? Even so, his mother was in trouble after she died.

"Of course, our mother was Chokgyur Lingpa's daughter, but after he passed away, she had one child after another and lived as a daughter-in-law in someone else's home. She went through great suffering. Of course, she practiced more, later in her life, but I still worry about her. That's why I am so sad."

Since Uncle Tersey was known for making scenes like this, Samten Gyatso broke in: "Don't talk like that! Pull yourself together and think! We are all close family here, so we can speak freely. Listen to me! First of all, Chokgyur Lingpa was no ordinary person, but rather the personal emissary of the Lotus-Born. As you well know, all of the great tertön's main followers, headed by the ten primary Dharma holders, were predicted by Padmasambhava.

"And you must be aware of this line of prophecy: '*Three sons will appear as emanations of the three chief bodhisattvas.*' One of these three, no doubt was Tsewang Norbu, another was Wangchok Dorje—and the third was our mother. This is not something you can say in public; in this day and age, people would get the wrong impression if they heard this. Nevertheless, mother is an emanation of Vajrapani, the Lord of Secrets. I don't have even a shred of doubt about this. You wouldn't call Chokgyur Lingpa a charlatan, would you? And would you call the Lotus-Born a liar? So pull yourself together!

"Would Vajrapani be forced to take rebirth in hell? Think about it!" Samten Gyatso continued, "It's not possible; it goes against the very nature of things as well as against the Dharma. I'm not at all worried about our mother—I know she is faring better than well. I have a totally pure perception of her; not even for a moment do I entertain the thought that she could go to the lower realms.

"I am only saying this in private to family, but she is one of the three emanations that were predicted. The causes and circumstances for her to be born as one of Chokgyur Lingpa's three sons were fully present, but people say that some pollution of samaya caused a change in gender. They claim that one moment of obstinacy on the part of Chokgyur Lingpa's consort caused her son to be born a daughter. But, on the other hand, because she was born as a woman, our mother was able to give birth to the four of us, who now apparently are the tertön's lineage. Do we have any cause to complain about our lot in life? This is all thanks to our mother. I feel one hundred percent certain that she was an emanation of Vajrapani, without a flicker of doubt."

Then, turning to Uncle Tersey, my father joined in: "In your opinion, would it be possible to fall into the hell realms after you have had three visions of Tara? If you do, then it would mean that noble Tara has no blessings. Also, many times I put grains of barley that my mother had blessed into small bags and gave them to people for protection. When these were hung around the necks of goats and sheep, the animals were immune to bullets. This happened more than once! Could anyone with such blessings be reborn in hell? Or are you saying that our mother has no power of blessing?

"Of course, what you say about the extreme subtlety of the law of karma is true, but, just between us, don't include our mother among ordinary beings."

From the side, a deep voice was heard saying, "That's true—those are my thoughts exactly." It was Uncle Sang-Ngak. "I don't feel mother will be in any trouble. The workings of karma are subtle, to be sure, so what do I really know? Nevertheless,

I was her main attendant and what I saw of her in these last few years may not be the mother you think you remember. I swear she had gone totally beyond the state of delusion. I know this from my own experience: she had become quite spontaneous and uncontrived; she stopped discriminating between different qualities of food. No matter what happened, she didn't have a single objection—everything was fine. I am certain that she was no longer like an ordinary human being."

Again Samten Gyatso spoke, "I'm the one who gave her mind teachings. She was the daughter of the great tertön, and true enough when she grew up, she got married to a young man of the Tsangsar family and was caught up in worldly responsibilities. Then the four of us were born, with all the distractions that entails.

"Later, it fell to me to do my best to point out the nature of mind to her. But, unlike an ordinary person, she recognized it before I had even finished. She made steady progress every year, every month, every single day. Four or five years ago, she changed completely: she transcended any moment of delusion, whether day or night. She explained this to me very clearly. As you know, our mother was no liar. She told me, 'I no longer get distracted during the day or night. I do, however, get a short period of uncertainty between falling asleep and beginning to dream.'

"What you call 'the subtle working of karma' is dependent upon conceptual thinking; someone like her, whose awareness is undistracted, is no longer caught up in thoughts. Isn't samsara the magical play of the thinking mind? Isn't it an illusion? How can I think for even a moment that someone beyond distraction could fall into the lower realms?

"Moreover, you could say that our mother had attained perfect recall. Think about it: she didn't forget a single word, no matter what you told her. Couldn't she retell every single event she had witnessed, down to the finest detail? It's quite difficult to give an eyewitness account with that kind of detail.

"Wasn't she also the one who had the final say in the tradition of torma making, as well as the fine art of ritual trumpet playing? Compare her style to that of monks nowadays—she carried on the authentic art. Who around here has a better calligraphic hand than she mastered while at Mindrolling with her father? Wasn't she also a healer with medicinal herbs? And didn't she know astrology? Wasn't it our mother whom we turned to for advice on all matters? No matter how much I think about her, I find no need to worry.

"You are worried about the law of karma, but isn't samadhi the remedy against it? When these two cross swords, we all know that one is relative and the other ultimate. When has it ever been the case that relative phenomena win out over the ultimate nature? Can the clouds conquer the sky? Think about it, Tersey!"

As always, Samten Gyatso spoke very convincingly.

"It is so," Uncle Sang-Ngak added. "Over the last couple of years, I too have noticed that she didn't hold any selfish notions. This must be what they call the collapse of delusion. She accepted everything as it was."

I was sitting there quietly and heard it all with my own ears. When telling you this today, I haven't added or distorted anything they said.[163]

Extensive ceremonies for grandmother were performed for the traditional forty-nine days, and at their completion a cremation stupa was built on the large meadow in front of Tsikey Gompa. Karsey Kongtrul was asked to preside over the funeral ceremony, but his health was not very good at that time and for a while it was uncertain whether he would be able to. When Karsey Kongtrul finally arrived, I was appointed his private attendant. Sometimes I snuck into his room in the evening and sat with him in silence. Even though other people were present, the atmosphere wasn't one in which you could just blabber in needless conversation.

At the ceremony many lamas, including the previous Dzigar Kongtrul, were seated in the four cardinal directions. There were also a great number of monks and lay practitioners—so many, in fact, that the area around the funeral stupa resembled a crowded marketplace. Karsey Kongtrul himself oversaw the central funeral ritual.

There was an auspiciously clear blue sky and many extraordinary signs such as streams of rainbow light. When we opened the cremation stupa, many of the bones were filled with crimson-colored sindhura powder. Karsey Kongtrul kept one of the bones. On another was a small self-appeared image of the dakini Sangwa Yeshe. Dzongsar Khyentse and other masters considered this image very precious. This bone was kept by Dzigar Kongtrul in a special reliquary made of fine sandalwood.

According to Tibetan custom, each of Könchok Paldrön's descendants was given one of her most prized possessions as a sacred heirloom. Penjik received the personal rosary of the second Karmapa, made of the finest jade. I inherited a small piece of yellow parchment containing dakini script that was about the width of four fingers, which Chokgyur Lingpa had found as a terma. I'm not very good at keeping track of my belongings though. After a while, afraid that I might lose it, I felt that this yellow parchment would be safer in Uncle Tersey's hands.

༄

Once, Dzongsar Khyentse was traveling through Neten, on his way to Central Tibet. My aunt Tashi Chimey, who had great faith in him, found a chance for them to talk in private. I heard about this from Dzongsar Khyentse's attendant, who followed him for many years and later died in Sikkim.

My aunt offered Dzongsar Khyentse some hair and a rosary that had belonged to Könchok Paldrön. Dzongsar Khyentse placed them on the top of his head for a moment. He told his attendant he had just received something extremely precious that he would place in his special chest of relics.

After she left, the master said to his attendants, "Tashi Chimey, Könchok Paldrön's daughter, came to present her understanding to me today and it was quite impressive. She has a remarkable level of experience and realization. She told me, 'I am just the caretaker. I have many daily tasks and my meditation state is neither lofty nor placid. I don't dwell in a state of quietude. My state is one of being totally lucid and awake without clinging to anything whatsoever.

"'When you look at me,' she added, 'you see this old woman going about her business, just being a servant—don't you? But I'm not like that at all. I was introduced to the awakened state a long time ago. I don't have to try to keep still as if afraid my cup might spill. I'm not afraid of that at all.'

"She continued, 'My awareness is one of being totally present and awake. I am not like others: busy keeping a serene countenance with a vacant state of mind. As a matter of fact, I don't see any need for that. My mind is wide open. I see other meditators so anxious and worried that their equanimity may be disturbed. How can fear maintain the true state of samadhi? Isn't meditation meant for transcending the three realms of samsara? How can one be free while still afraid of losing emptiness? How can emptiness be lost, anyway?'"

That's the sort of thing she would say. Later that day, Dzongsar Khyentse remarked, "Of course, Tashi Chimey's mother was a realized meditator, but it appears that the daughter made quite good progress herself—don't you think?"

23

The Colorful Chokling of Tsikey

Tsikey Chokling was not only incredibly bright and ingenious but also famous and influential, as well as quite savvy politically. He was well known for his ability to settle disputes, though if he were your opponent in one, you wouldn't stand a chance. He was incredibly self-confident and had an impressive, dignified bearing, as if there were no one above him. His was a very dominating presence.

Tsikey Chokling's eyes were like those of no one else I have ever met—very bright and clear. Most people couldn't bear his gaze for more than a short while. He was also very handsome and I felt that as a young man he must have looked almost like a god.

I found him simply astounding!

Once there was a political dispute between the Tibetan government and the Chinese province to the east of Kham, and he acted as the mediator. Both sides gave him a specific high political rank with the accompanying brocade robes and insignia. The problem was serious enough that it could have led to a major conflict; but thanks to his discriminating intelligence and self-assurance, he managed to resolve the dispute and avoid a war.[164]

The great Khyentse and Kongtrul had already passed away while Tsikey Chokling was still a youth and, of the old generation of masters, only Karmey Khenpo remained. Due to differences in their personalities, I'm not sure how much Tsikey Chokling and Karmey Khenpo connected. In the end, it was Samten Gyatso who pointed out self-existing awareness in its naked state so that Tsikey Chokling recognized it in actuality. Therefore, in the last part of his life, he regarded Samten Gyatso as his one and only root guru, and trusted him with unwavering faith. Samten Gyatso was the younger of the two, but that didn't seem to matter—he still asked Samten Gyatso for teachings.

Tsikey Chokling was not in the habit of placing himself below other masters. "I don't bow to just any lama who happens by," he would say, "except for the

Karmapa." The rare occasion when he could be seen prostrating was when Samten Gyatso was around.

At that time, Tsikey Chokling had almost the same rank and position as the Karmapa, and he never asked other lamas to put their hand on his head to give him a blessing. Whenever other masters—no matter how revered—arrived, he would treat them as his equal. But despite his own high spiritual rank, he refused to sit higher than Samten Gyatso. The sole exception was on visits to his teacher's monastery, where he was forced to sit on the main throne. Samten Gyatso, for his part, showed Tsikey Chokling immense respect.

Unlike Chokgyur Lingpa himself, it wasn't Tsikey Chokling's style to give teachings and empowerments, although he did give me a few short instructions on the nature of mind.

Near the end of his life, Tsikey Chokling didn't act like a normal person but instead would behave with complete childlike innocence. He almost never said a single word unless asked. He never initiated anything except as a response, but once he did, he did so beautifully. For instance, he would sit motionless and never lift his cup to his lips unless you said, "Rinpoche, please have some tea," and then he would take a sip. Or if a visitor came, he would simply sit there until I said, "Rinpoche, there is a visitor—please talk to him." Then he would say, "Oh yeah" and start to talk.

No one was quite sure whether he was in a state of samadhi, had transcended delusion, or had had a stroke—and the master himself surely didn't comment on it. But even when he was ill, he didn't seem to be suffering any pain. As a matter of fact, it is difficult to find an adequate description for him.

Since he was quite old and not that well, he had asked my father if Penjik or I could come to Tsikey to look after him. Penjik was already a pönpo, a local lord, but since Tsikey Chokling insisted, Samten Gyatso finally gave permission for me to go. "The lama is really old," Samten Gyatso told my father, "so let's let him have his way."

I stayed with Tsikey Chokling for about six months as his attendant and nurse. We got along quite well; we were very fond of each other and I gladly did whatever he asked me to. I had some good times with him over those months.

One of my jobs was to entertain him and to keep him from falling asleep. Since I was good at modeling tsampa dough, I sometimes made sculptures of his head. He had a particularly striking profile and seeing his own big nose caused him to burst out laughing in a deep, loud voice.

I was pretty good at keeping people awake.

Tsikey Chokling told me many stories in his own down-to-earth style—no exaggerations, just the plain facts.

Apparently, he had many visions as he told me several stories from his visit to Padmasambhava's pure land where he even met the Lotus-Born master in person![165]

Once when we went for a picnic by the river, he told me, "They say Samten Gyatso is an emanation of Four-Armed Mahakala and I think that is quite apt."

"Why do you say that?" I asked.

Then he told me about a vision in which he visited the Glorious Copper-Colored Mountain, the pure land of Padmasambhava; he even described the layout of the outer and inner walls.[166] In each of the four directions of the central palace, there was a stupa and one of them contained an amazing stone with a naturally formed mandala depicting the forty-two peaceful deities carved on its surface. Anyone entering the Glorious Copper-Colored Mountain had to walk through the base of this stupa, hence purifying their cognitive obscurations.

As Tsikey Chokling approached the stupa, he came to the boulder with the imprints of Padmasambhava's hands and feet. As he was leaving, he noticed that to the right of the stupa there was a cave in the face of the mountain and he asked the gatekeeper whose cave it was.

"This is the cave of Four-Armed Mahakala," the gatekeeper replied.

"I must meet him," Tsikey Chokling said, but he was told that Mahakala wasn't there, though his consort Dusölma was. In the cave he saw Dusölma, the female guardian of the teachings; beside her was a vacant lotus seat.

When Tsikey Chokling looked down at the lotus seat, he saw Samten Gyatso's knife lying there. Throughout his life, Samten Gyatso carried this particular knife. Since he was a vegetarian, it wasn't the normal dagger Khampas wear to cut up meat, but a small knife he always kept on his belt.

"Hey!" Tsikey Chokling exclaimed. "What's Samten Gyatso's knife doing here?"

"Why don't you just look down and see?" Dusölma replied.

As Tsikey Chokling turned around and looked down upon our world—which he could do since this was a vision—he zoomed in on Kham and saw Samten Gyatso's shining bald head there in his monastery.

"The Four-Armed Mahakala is right down there," Dusölma continued. "Can't you see him? Don't you know who he is?"

Tsikey Chokling scanned throughout the entire region of Tsikey and the rest of eastern Tibet. Finally he said, "I don't see any Mahakala, only Samten Gyatso, Chokgyur Lingpa's grandnephew."

"That's him," Dusölma said. "Don't you know that knife is Mahakala's curved cleaver?"

Tsikey Chokling thought to himself, "Now I know why he always carries that little knife."

⁂

In another vision, Tsikey Chokling saw that Samten Gyatso was also an emanation of Vimalamitra, the Indian master of unparalleled importance in the Dzogchen lineage.[167] From this vision, he wrote down a mind treasure, a small volume of texts including a sadhana revealing the magical nature of Samten Gyatso's present incarnation, the story of his spiritual realization, pith instructions and other details. He kept this book hidden in his coat, never parting from it and using it in his daily practice.

Now it happens that the great Khyentse had told Chokgyur Lingpa to establish his seat at the place where the Tsichu and Kechu rivers join—hence the name Tsikey, where the monastery was built. It was also prophesied to be a sacred place containing the extraordinary terma treasure *Spontaneous Fulfillment of Wishes*. Up the river are some naturally formed hot springs, and often people would trek there and spend a week recuperating in the warm water.

On one occasion, Tsikey Chokling, along with my precious grandmother, Samten Gyatso, Uncle Tersey and some officials from Tsikey headed up to the hot

41.
Tsikey monastery

springs. They pitched tents along the riverbank and the lamas went to bathe in the hot pools. As Tsikey Chokling was taking his clothes off, he carefully wrapped up his book inside his robes. Wearing only his yogi shorts he entered the hot pool. As Tsikey Chokling was getting out of the water, Samten Gyatso walked over to get him his clothes and when he picked them up, the book fell out.

One of Samten Gyatso's traits was that he couldn't leave a Buddhist scripture alone without scanning its contents.[168] As soon as he saw the book, he began to unwrap it.

"If he sees the text, he might destroy it," Tsikey Chokling thought. "I must keep it from him!"

So he yelled, "Give that to me! Hand it over! You don't need to unwrap it!"

This triggered Samten Gyatso's suspicion. "Sure I'll give it to you," he replied. "Just let me take a glance first."

Samten Gyatso read the title, flipped the page and continued to read how he himself was supposed to be an emanation of Vimalamitra; there was even an accompanying guru sadhana, complete with the subtle tantric stages of development and completion.

Instead of getting his book back, Tsikey Chokling got a severe scolding. "You are supposed to be a reincarnation of Chokgyur Lingpa—at least according to the great Khyentse—and until today I had absolute faith that this was true. I was counting on you to uphold the *New Treasures* for the benefit of the Dharma and all sentient beings. But now, when I look at these scribbles of yours, I see that you are a charlatan through and through, a deceiver of other people, an outright liar! What a disgrace to the Dharma! Swear to me that from this day on you will never again succumb to writing down such pretentious nonsense!"

Samten Gyatso immediately marched to the broad and turbulent Kechu River and flung the book out into the churning waters.

Samten Gyatso wasn't done berating Tsikey Chokling however and continued, "You're making this old monk, who is completely devoid of any qualities, into something he's not! What a preposterous fraud! If you are going to act like this, there is no benefit in your being the tulku of Chokgyur Lingpa. From now on, don't do anything that will damage our sacred bond."

After that, Samten Gyatso never mentioned a single word about it.

As you can see, Samten Gyatso was committed to the lifestyle of a hidden yogi. Vajrayana in general should be kept private—doing so increases rather than decreases virtues. The same holds true for the personal qualities of a yogi. The moment a special ability is announced, worldly people will see it as nothing but an attempt to aggrandize oneself. If we truly care about the well-being of others, we should not give them the least pretext to think such negative thoughts about Vajrayana and its practitioners.

Even though someone like me can't see these things, I have simple-minded faith that Samten Gyatso's sentiment still doesn't change the facts: Tsikey Chokling *did* reveal a mind treasure showing that Samten Gyatso *was* Vimalamitra in person.

In a very matter-of-fact manner, Tsikey Chokling later told me, "There was much more detail in that mind treasure I could have written down. Samten Gyatso really was Vimalamitra in human form, but he forbade me ever to speak another word about that."

※

Uncle Tersey and Tsikey Chokling shared the same monastery. At times—acting as though his pure perception had slipped for a moment—my uncle commented with his usual tongue-in-cheek humor on how "cunning" this tulku of Chokgyur Lingpa was. He would say, "Tsikey Chokling is very clever and audacious in presenting a legal case—but he's also a skilled liar. When we are together, he makes up fantastic stories; he exaggerates and embellishes the facts. Sometimes I wonder how an incarnation of Chokgyur Lingpa could be so involved in worldly affairs. But on the other hand, the great Khyentse couldn't be wrong."

Tsikey Chokling had in fact been given a letter of recognition in the great Khyentse's own hand and bearing Khyentse's personal seal, a sign he truly was an incarnation of Chokgyur Lingpa.

Uncle Tersey would often speak in a playful, even outrageous manner. He would continue, "Since I have spent so many years with him, I know his level of experience and meditation. As he grows older, his realization becomes obvious—such depth surprises me. Often he reveals his clairvoyant powers. This is why I have great trust in him.

"As a noble incarnation, he ought to be replete with perfect qualities. But every now and then he appears to be so full of political scheming. His sharp tongue ensures that he always comes out on top in any situation. Sometimes, I wonder who he really is—he's so bold and daring that I think he might be better off as a general in the army. Or maybe he's simply the incarnation of a demon."

Uncle Tersey would burst out laughing.

Then he'd start up again: "Our Rinpoche's so tall and handsome and has such a commanding presence that when he walks into a group, no one has the least doubt about which one is Chokgyur Lingpa's tulku. He's a great bodhisattva, endowed with all the qualities, free of all faults. But then, at second glance, doesn't he delight in fighting court cases to help friends and subdue enemies? And he's so good at it no ordinary person can outdo him. Spiritual and secular aims are supposed to be contradictory—even the Buddha gave one up for the other!"

Again we had to laugh with my uncle.

"Of course, I have no doubt in him," Uncle Tersey would finish. "It's simply that every now and again these thoughts slip into my mind."

The truth is that these two lamas were very close, sharing everything. Uncle Tersey had deep trust in Tsikey Chokling, which made his remarks so much funnier.

※

One time Tsikey Chokling told me an odd story about what it means to have confidence in the view.

There was an old lama, the bursar in a small monastery, who had only spent the last few months of his life in retreat. He was lying on his deathbed and called on Tsikey Chokling, who was often asked to give a final instruction or empowerment when someone was about to die.

"You are the reincarnation of Chokgyur Lingpa," the old man began, "so I have something special to ask you. It's not the normal type of request; you have to make me a promise."

Tsikey Choking thought, "Poor old guy! People get so afraid on the verge of death, and they think that in the final moment there is still time to change their entire life. Here's another one, scared out of his wits, afraid of going to the lower realms. But how can I promise him that his evil deeds won't drag him down into the lower realms? Perhaps he should have begun his recitations and meditation much earlier in life."

But to the monk he just said, "Tell me what you want."

"Before I tell you, you must promise to say yes. Only then will I tell you!"

Tsikey Chokling replied, "You tell me first, then I'll decide!"

The dying lama continued to argue his point until Tsikey Chokling finally had to agree.

"I have no other wish than this. We all know that the three lower realms are horrifying, especially the eighteen regions of hell.[169] Isn't the lowest of these the Hell of Incessant Torment? And below that isn't there the dreaded Vajra Hell? That's where I want to go. Please lama, send me straight there the moment I die. That's what you must promise me you will do!"

"Why in the world would you want to go there?" asked Tsikey Chokling, "Why do you need my help to go there?"

"Without your help and blessing, I cannot possibly end up there by myself," the old lama replied. "Unless I am sent there by someone with special powers, it's not possible. By myself I have already visited the eighteen hell realms from time to time. But I just can't seem to get all the way down to Vajra Hell. So you, the tulku of Chokgyur Lingpa, must help me!"

Tsikey Chokling later told me, "That old guy really had confidence in the view; he was completely without fear. He died soon after, and I have yet to meet anyone with that level of courage. Every other dying person I have visited asked me for blessings to escape this and be free from that. One person even asked me to make sure he attained complete enlightenment, but no one else has ever asked to be sent to hell, least of all Vajra Hell.

"I was very impressed with that old lama," he added. "As a matter of fact, I gained some faith in him. Of my own accord, I returned to attend his cremation. I saw with my own eyes that his ashes were unusually full of relic pills. During the cremation, we all saw lots of rainbows from the funeral pyre."

What this all means is that the old lama had totally transcended both hope and fear. Once someone has realized the original wakefulness of dharmakaya, the lower realms are no longer a threat, and the prospect of enlightenment in some other place is no longer seen as a promise, since he or she is already awakened within the inner space of primordial purity.[170] Such a person stands on the verge of attaining complete enlightenment at the moment of death. So is there anything to be afraid of then?

Someone who has attained the fourfold confidence mentioned in the Dzogchen teachings[171] has also attained stability in the awakened state. So there is no yearning for liberation in some other place and no dread of a low rebirth in samsara. That is the meaning of transcending hope and fear. At that point, even if you try, you can't be reborn anywhere near the hell realms through the force of negative karma. So when someone attains mastery in nondual awareness, there is no way he can fall into Vajra Hell—and I doubt Tsikey Chokling had any luck in sending him there either.[172]

Near the end of his life, it was obvious that Tsikey Chokling was clairvoyant. He even told me where he would be reborn: in the Yarlung valley in Central Tibet.[173]

He said, "Despite all my roaming about, I never managed to visit Yarlung. Now my mind is attached to that place, so I am bound to take rebirth there. But I do so happily; I have wished so many times to be in Yarlung.

"For a while," he added, "I have imagined that my surroundings here are Yarlung. I even find myself believing that this Kechu River is the river in Yarlung. As a young man, I had the habit of living in tents and I enjoy that, so now I will camp by the river in my little Yarlung. I imagine it to be Yarlung; I meditate on it as Yarlung. That is where I want to stay."

The Kechu isn't a small river; neither horses nor yaks can cross it, only large boats. Tsikey Chokling held a very high position; he owned a tremendous amount of land, equal to that of the Karmapa—and so when he moved to the tent, about fifty officials and attendants had to accompany him.

Later I heard that he actually moved into his tent and stayed by the river for two or three months.

※

One day I got a message that Tentrul, one of the important lamas at Surmang monastery, had invited Samten Gyatso there to give the transmission of Chokgyur Lingpa's *New Treasures,* and my presence was required. I wanted to remain with Tsikey Chokling, especially when he told me, "If you leave now, we won't meet again," adding, "but neither of us has a choice in the matter. You must go and receive the *New Treasures.*"

I was well down the road when I suddenly heard his voice booming behind me, "Tulku!" So I went back to him and asked, "Yes, Rinpoche?" He just sat there with his big eyes wide open, not saying a word. So I slowly backed out of his presence and again began my journey to Surmang. I was almost out of earshot when a second time I heard his voice calling, "Hey, tulku!"

How could I dare just keep walking? So I walked all the way back to him and again asked, "Yes, Rinpoche what is it?"

But he just sat there silently with open eyes. This scene was played out about six times.

I got a strong sense that this was not the right time to leave and that he was not really giving me permission to go. Yet on the other hand, my father and Samten Gyatso were waiting down at Surmang and had sent for me to come as soon as possible.

I remember that each time I was able to get farther and farther away before he called me back, until I finally vanished from sight.

I never saw him again.

※

Tsikey Chokling's next rebirth was recognized by the Karmapa in a piece of poetry beginning with these words:

"In the upper end of the Yarlung valley, near the Tramdruk Temple,[174] he is born in a noble family of moderate income. His father is Powerful Merit, while his mother is Bountiful Longevity. He is the youngest of three siblings."

The poetry concluded with the year and month of his birth, as well as which constellation would be in the sky at the time. Never has it been so easy to find a tulku. To top it off, the first thing the child said upon the arrival of the search party was, "You must have come to fetch me." There was absolutely no doubt that this was the tulku. This tulku was beautiful, like a child of the gods.

The young Tsikey tulku was enthroned at Tsurphu by the Karmapa, and then also by Reding, the Tibetan regent, with whom he had a special connection from the past. The regent gave the tulku a famous image of the Lotus-Born known as Guru Mahasukha and the helmet of Machen Pomra, one of the most important guardian spirits of Tibet. He very affectionately kept the tulku on his lap, and let him play with some of his sets of vajras and bells, one of which had belonged to the great Khyentse. There were several sets and he asked the little tulku if he recognized any of them.

"I recognize this," the little boy said pointing to one. "That's the one!" And sure enough, it had been his. He was invited to Kham when he was but a teenager. One time he stayed for six months in the monastic college at Dzongsar. During this short time, he would teach Shantideva's *Way of a Bodhisattva* from memory. He was bright and very well-spoken. He also learned a rare form of calligraphy, and in his spare time he copied out eight or nine large volumes of scriptures in a beautiful hand.

After arriving in Kham, he received a request from the family of an old lama who was near death. The lama was from an influential family who would give hundreds of cattle and horses to the monasteries of the region each year.[175] This lama was regarded as the most important disciple of the past Tsikey Chokling.

When the bursar told the tulku of the request, he refused outright. "I definitely will not go," he protested. "That's all there is to it. It's not going to happen."

But some people don't know when to stop—the lama's family was adamant. In addition, the tulku's monastic household also insisted, "This lama was so close to your previous life that you are obligated."

Before departing, the tulku went into Uncle Tersey's quarters, as was the tradition before taking leave. Here again he said, "I really don't want to go."

Uncle Tersey replied, "If everyone in the monastery has formed an opinion, what good is my word? I'm not telling you that you should go, but it also appears that I cannot prevent it."

"I'm not going! I'm not going!" The tulku again repeated; he even started to cry. But everyone else was set to leave, and they came to fetch him.

His parting words to Uncle Tersey were, "If I take this journey, we won't meet again!" The boy was just a teenager, but somehow he knew—more so than Uncle Tersey, who always said that he could only see dense darkness rather than clairvoyance.

The real problem here was entangled with the responsibilities of running a large monastery, where many people need to be fed on a daily basis. Connections with wealthy households must be maintained. So sometimes concerns for prominence and material gain take precedence. These were actually the compelling reasons.

The journey to the lama's family as well as the cremation ceremonies all went well. The offerings given to the monastery and to Tsikey were indeed lavish. It was on the return journey that disaster struck.

As they were passing through a valley, they received news that a dignitary residing there had suddenly died. He was known as a diehard liar and perpetrator of many a crime. Upon hearing that Tsikey Chokling and his entourage were passing through, the family came to beseech them to preside over yet another cremation.

"I will neither go there nor perform any ceremony for that man!" the tulku responded.

"But Rinpoche," they begged, "it is so close, it's not even out of your way!"

Again a major argument ensued and again the managers of the monastery got their way. The tulku performed the purification for the departed spirit and the funeral pyre was lit.

The first time the smoke blew in the tulku's direction, he suddenly cried out in pain. Those seated closest to him could see a boil forming on his throat. The tulku appeared in constant agony from then on. The boil opened soon after and by the next morning you could see the vertebrae in his neck. He passed away soon after.

When the party arrived back at Tsikey, his horse was carrying his corpse, leaving everyone in shock. Uncle Tersey in particular was extremely saddened, not only by the tulku's death but especially because he was so young and it seemed like such a waste.

24

Transmission at Surmang

Within the Karma Kagyu lineage, there are two additional branches known as Surmang and Nendo, both of which had major monastic centers. Tentrul was one of the great masters of Surmang; he was also counted among the ten major Dharma heirs of Chokgyur Lingpa. He was an extremely important master, learned in both Sutra and Tantra.

The current Tentrul had invited Samten Gyatso to one of the Surmang branch monasteries, where he personally sponsored the transmission of the *New Treasures*. Many learned masters had gathered at Surmang for this event, including eighteen major lamas and tulkus from Kham.

Honestly, it's hard to find a match for the quality of the lamas at Surmang among the Kagyu lineages. There were around nine hundred fully ordained monks, plus three hundred more in the monastic college. Many were quite learned. Twice a month, on the tenth and twenty-fifth of the lunar calendar, Samten Gyatso would give a talk for all of them. Several of the khenpos would also give impressive speeches, one after the other.

Also present was Dzigar Kongtrul, the former incarnation of the Dzigar Kongtrul that you know today. He was renowned throughout Derge for having a tongue "as sharp as a knife cutting water"—his eloquence was unimpeded. When his turn came to give a speech, it was remarkable. He would insert verbatim quotes from all the scriptures without a moment's hesitation, astounding everyone.

For three straight months, my father and uncle worked in tandem: in the mornings, Samten Gyatso performed the empowerment preparations, while my father gave the reading transmission. In the afternoons, Samten Gyatso would give the empowerments in the large assembly hall.

In the beginning, Samten Gyatso made me a shrine attendant, together with Dudul and another monk. But after a while, my father said, "If you run around like that between the lama and the shrine, you are going to miss some of the transmissions. I'll try to find a way to ask Samten Gyatso if you can be excused."

I knew that even my father was intimidated by Samten Gyatso, and so I told him, "I feel I am getting the empowerments in this way. Better not to say anything—I'm fine."

But my father did bring it up, and Samten Gyatso agreed. I was excused from my duties. For the rest of the *New Treasures* I could simply sit and receive the teachings in the company of the outstanding masters assembled at Surmang.

❧

Near the end of the three months Samten Gyatso said to Tentrul, "The learned lamas among you understand and appreciate the nature of the *New Treasures*. Starting tomorrow morning, I will begin giving the restricted empowerments.[176] I am not here to promote myself, nor will I give the secret empowerments indiscriminately. I've noticed that some self-important officials and arrogant benefactors have joined the gathering, but from tomorrow their presence will not be welcome. Tentrul, it is your duty to decide who will be allowed to attend and who will not."

That day, at the end of the gathering, Tentrul announced that from then on not a single layperson would be allowed, only lamas and ordained monks.

The next morning, however, there was a curtain hanging at the back of one of the lamas' thrones; behind it sat various local dignitaries and officials. They pretended not to be there; such people from Surmang were known for their brazenness.

Usually, at the end of an empowerment, the lamas would come to the front and receive the blessings with ritual implements from Samten Gyatso in person, after which the blessed objects would be carried around the gathering. That day, however, Samten Gyatso simply remained seated on the throne, motionless.

After a heavy silence, he proclaimed, "I have heard that the ruling class around Surmang is very brave. Isn't that what you tell me? But the great bravery of the Surmang upper class is no reason for me to throw Chokgyur Lingpa's termas to the wind. This old monk doesn't have to obey any local VIPs; the only people I must obey are my root gurus. I said I would pass on the transmission to lamas and ordained monks, but not to worldly people. This is what I told Tentrul yesterday and that is what he announced to all of you. But tell me—isn't it true that behind that curtain over there, fifty worldly people have crept in? So today is the last day. I am leaving, so the empowerments end here."

This scolding shocked everyone, and the assembly hall went dead quiet. Samten Gyatso told his shrine assistants to start packing up, and everyone filed out except for me, my father and my cousin Karmey Khentrul.

Tentrul also remained behind and called my father over to the throne where he sat. "You're his brother. You have to tell Samten Gyatso that if I allow this to happen and don't correct it before the day is out, I will become a samaya violator. I sincerely appreciate the close lineage of the *New Treasures*." As a matter of fact, centuries before, the Lotus-Born master had prophesied that this very Surmang Tentrul would one day be one of the ten major lineage holders.

"I have arranged for this event out of concern for the Buddha's teachings and sentient beings, and out of pure aspirations," Tentrul continued. "I deeply regret the present turn of events. It appears I have broken the guru's command. Please ask him to reconsider and, after a three-day break, to bestow the rest of the transmissions upon us. At that time I will personally enforce his wish strictly."

When Chimey Dorje delivered the message, Samten Gyatso was adamant. "Absolutely not! How can I freely hand out the profound terma teachings from which the warm breath of the dakinis has still not disappeared?"[177]

Since he had great respect for Tentrul, yet was also quite mild-mannered, my father was in a tough spot. Luckily, Karmey Khentrul had more guts, and so he was asked to break the bad news to Tentrul. Heartbroken, Tentrul began to weep.

Samten Gyatso heard him and asked, "What is he doing?" I told him that Tentrul was crying and asked what we should do.

"He delegated what he should have done himself," Samten Gyatso said. "He neglected to keep out those pushy dignitaries. How can I give the precious terma teachings to such self-important people? Anyway, it doesn't matter what he says now, I'm packing up!"

Undaunted, Karmey Khentrul again approached, asking, "Uncle, what's the use of interrupting the empowerments? You need to finish what you started. You can't leave a great master like Tentrul stranded."

"Nonsense," was all Samten Gyatso replied, dismissively. Then my father began to mediate, going back and forth between his brother and Tentrul. All the while, Dudul and the other shrine attendant were standing outside the door, preventing anyone from entering.

"He must forgive me today," Tentrul implored. "Otherwise I refuse to eat or sleep."

"Why is he still sitting here?" Samten Gyatso snapped. I told him what Tentrul had said, since my father didn't dare repeat it. "He says he won't sleep at night or eat during the day unless you forgive him."

"How's that going to help?" my uncle replied. "All he'd be doing is making his own life miserable. Blackmail like that shouldn't occur between master and disciple."

This went on until Samten Gyatso finally yielded, saying, "Fine! Tell him it's all right, he can leave now."

That was one tough day! And for five days afterward, the monks and lamas performed a feast offering with thousands and thousands of tormas as part of a formal ceremony to heal the rift. The empowerments then continued, but in a very somber atmosphere.

As you can see, Samten Gyatso could be quite stern.

25

The Master in the Hollow Tree

Let me tell you about the extraordinary scripture the *Light of Wisdom*. This fundamental text by Padmasambhava reads like a poetic song. As a guidance manual for practice, it is strikingly clear all by itself. The *Light of Wisdom* is immense in its scope, including virtually every aspect of the Buddhist path to enlightenment. Old Khyentse described it in these words, "This single volume, the size of my forearm, is worth more than one hundred yak-loads of scriptures."

Accompanying this root text is an extensive commentary by the great Kongtrul. This document is truly a mind treasure, a revelation in its own right, written in incredible depth and detail—studded with abbreviations that require copious cross-referencing to numerous other scriptures.

In my youth, the eccentric master Jamdrak was regarded as *the* person to go to for an explanation of the *Light of Wisdom*. At the end of the root text several paragraphs prophesied individuals who in the future would work for the benefit of the Dharma and all living beings, and exactly how they would do so. The great Khyentse even said that Jamdrak was among those predicted eight hundred years before by the Lotus-Born master in the scripture itself.

The specific activity of those prophesied was also given in the text. "Your activity," Old Khyentse told Jamdrak, "is to propagate this scripture as widely as you can." And so throughout his life Jamdrak gave the reading transmission of this text to every single person who came to see him—whether they requested it or not.

Once, a man came simply to pay his respects by offering a white scarf, in the traditional Tibetan fashion. Jamdrak asked him to sit down, then promptly began reading aloud the thirty-three large sheets of scripture. This dragged on for quite a while, and the man became restless and complained, "But I only came to offer you a scarf!"

"If you didn't want the transmission, you shouldn't have come," Jamdrak snapped. "Now sit down and be quiet."[178]

❦

Having studied with the renowned masters Khyentse and Kongtrul, Jamdrak was extremely learned. He helped Kongtrul compile the *Treasury of Precious Termas*, a collection of the finest revelations from Padmasambhava. Later, some of the greatest lamas of the twentieth century studied with him, including the later reincarnations of both Khyentse and Kongtrul.

Before Jamdrak passed away, Samten Gyatso and my uncle Tersey sent a gifted khenpo to receive instructions from the old lama. Uncle Tersey had given him a letter with this request, "Please give your particular lineage of explanation on the *Light of Wisdom* to this learned monk so that it will not disappear."

This khenpo, known as Jokyab, was renowned for his literary skills. He later told me that this was due to having studied the extensive biography of the Lotus-Born master, the *Golden Garland Chronicles*, when he was quite young. "I walked everywhere with that volume slung over my shoulder, and I asked every lama I came across for teachings on different passages." In this way, he became well-versed in the Buddhist teachings.[179]

By the time Jokyab had set off to see him, Jamdrak was eighty-three years old. He lived contentedly in the hollow formed by the roots of a huge tree at a remote hermitage way up in the mountains. The old master couldn't sit up straight, as his spine had curved with age. Jamdrak was not only extremely old by Tibetan standards, but he was quite peculiar in his ways. He wore a large cotton bib around his neck because he tended to drool, and he never blew his nose but let it run freely. He couldn't care less what people thought about how he looked. He was a real yogi.

He didn't wear the shirt and shawl of an ordained practitioner—just a coat fashioned out of scraps of old sheepskin, the outside patched together with different kinds of cloth. One of these was a large piece of exquisite brocade with a golden dragon design. Apparently, he had stitched this fine swatch of silk on his tattered robe after someone offered it to him, though it cost him a few bitter remarks from the manager of the nearby monastery, who hated to see such good brocade go to waste like that.

Jokyab made the arduous journey—several weeks on foot and horseback—to Jamdrak's hermitage accompanied by a friend who was an incarnate lama. But once they finally arrived, Jamdrak's first words to them were, "Three years ago I started life-retreat." By that he meant he'd made a commitment to remain in retreat until death. "I don't teach anymore," he continued. "I'm far too old for that. Please don't be angry."

Jokyab and his friend weren't angry, but they *were* extremely upset. To be turned down this way, especially after traveling such a long distance, was a huge disappointment. So they kept insisting. "Come back tomorrow morning," was Jamdrak's only reply.

The next morning, the old lama said, "My body is not as strong as it used to be. What can I do about that? Please don't be angry. But come again tomorrow morning." Jokyab and his friend were at a loss as to what to do, but there wasn't really anything they *could* do.

The following morning, Jamdrak took out Uncle Tersey's letter and touched it to the crown of his head in a gesture of respect. He spoke in a feeble voice, "Oh dear! I'm too old to teach, but this is a letter from the incarnation of the great tertön's son. I never met the tertön in person, but I was a disciple of his son Wangchok Dorje. This is a command from one of Chokgyur Lingpa's sons, so I must fulfill it. If I don't, I would be breaking the sacred commitment to my master."

Then he shook his head weakly and added, "But it's too much for me today. Come back tomorrow."

The next morning—this was day four—old Jamdrak took the letter out again, read it once more, put it on the crown of his head as before and repeated what he had said previously. Then he added, "Oh dear! Anyone who breaks his guru's command is sure to go to Vajra Hell. I must by all means give you this teaching, but honestly, it's too much for me today." And that was it for that day.

Jokyab returned the following morning, this time armed with the traditional mandala plate for requesting teachings. While he was chanting his request, the old master gently pulled out the letter, read it, raised it to his head and again said, "I must obey my guru's command, but it's too much for me today. Come back tomorrow."

This went on every morning like clockwork. After about a month of this, Jokyab's companion had had enough. "I know we came here on the command of Samten Gyatso and Tersey Tulku, but this old geezer can barely talk. On top of that, I'm not sure he isn't senile. His vital energies are so depleted that his body is caving in on itself. How is he ever going to be able to teach us? Look how he eats his food—half of it spills down his chest! You can see what he's eaten the last several days all over his shirt. He's turned into a child! I don't see the point in staying here any longer."

Even so, the young Jokyab convinced his friend to persevere—and the days went by, with no change. Sometimes, right after mumbling, "It's too much for me today," the old lama would simply doze off.

When three months had passed in this way, the companion's patience ran out. "That's it! It's totally absurd to stick around here any longer. That old lama will never be able to teach us anything. He can barely talk! Frankly, I doubt he has long to live. I don't feel that we'd go against our teacher's wishes if we left now. After all, we've tried hard for three solid months."

"Do as you like, but I'm not leaving," Jokyab replied. "Even if it takes a year, I'm going to stay. How can I disobey masters like Samten Gyatso and Tersey Tulku?"

Together they went back to Jamdrak one last time, but it was the same old story. Finally, Jokyab's companion asked to be excused.

"Oh dear!" the old lama said. He didn't say to go nor did he say not to. He simply repeated "Oh dear!" a few more times. So the tulku offered him a white scarf as a formal gesture of farewell and began his journey home.

⁂

After that, although Jamdrak still did not give the *Light of Wisdom* teachings, the situation actually did improve. Jokyab knew another text by heart, as did Jamdrak: the *Guhyagarbha*, the *Tantra on the Essence of Secrets*, which is the most vital of all the tantras in the Old School of Tibetan Buddhism. In a casual way, the two of them discussed it in detail over the course of the next three months. Jokyab was able to clear up many difficult points and thus became quite learned on that tantra. "Looking back over those months," Jokyab told me, "it seemed we were just having a simple conversation, but I actually received an enormous number of detailed instructions on this precious tantra."

So they settled into a regular routine. Around nine each morning, the master would say, "It's time to take a leak. Why don't you come along? I'll walk ahead, but bring my cushion to put in the sun."

Jokyab would take along the large cushion—on which Jamdrak both sat and slept—and place it in a small meadow nearby. The old master would come back from relieving himself, flop down on the cushion and simply lie there for the next several hours.

"Now he's definitely not going back to the tree until lunch," Jokyab would think. The old yogi would lie there on his back, eyes wide open, gazing into the sky until it was time to eat. At noon a small monk would announce that lunch was ready. That's the way it went, day in and day out.

⁂

Every day at dusk, without fail, Jamdrak would perform a short subjugation ritual and throw a torma—an offering cake, which symbolized a weapon—toward the east.

"Rinpoche, why do you do this every day?" Jokyab asked him.

"Oh dear!" the master explained. "From a country in the east, an evil force will rise up. It will utterly and completely destroy the Buddha's teachings in this snowy land of Tibet and leave the country in pitch-black darkness. This force cannot be stopped, but merely trying to stop it brings more benefit than if I were to chant the ritual for the peaceful and wrathful deities one hundred times and light ten thousand butter lamps. When I throw this torma, I imagine hitting the demon square in the head. It won't help, though; no one can repel this demon. Nevertheless, simply by trying, I will accumulate great merit and purify obscurations on the path to enlightenment."

Still being young when I heard the story from Jokyab, I thought this part was quite strange—for in those days, I hadn't heard of Mao Tse-tung.

By now six months had gone by, three with nothing and three with some conversation and questions.

Then Jamdrak finally began teaching on the *Light of Wisdom*, spending several days on the title alone. He continued teaching, without skipping a single day over the next six months, covering every single detail in the text. Wherever the great Kongtrul had written "and so forth" in his commentary, Jamdrak would specify which book to pull out of the monastery's library and on which page the information could be found. Without fail he was right.

Once the teachings on the *Light of Wisdom* had begun, Jokyab would occasionally suggest, "Why don't you move over to the monastery? It would be much easier for us to complete all the work we must do. It's quite difficult for me to carry books back and forth from the library all the time."

Jamdrak replied, "My whole life I've never lived in a building. I am very comfortable in this hollow tree. If you and other lamas want to live in a monastery, go right ahead."

During his time with Jamdrak, Jokyab saw many people come to visit, including important lamas and wealthy benefactors. They often gave Jamdrak presents including quite expensive objects and money. Yet the old master was completely free of pretense with regard to these offerings. If an object happened to be beautiful, he would hold it up and say, "Wow, what a lovely little gift! Thank you so much!"

Then, after the person left, regardless of what he had been given, he would simply turn around and toss it into a box behind his seat. Huge hunks of dried meat, chunks of turquoise, sacks of dried cheese, bags of tsampa, priceless pieces of coral—all of it got mixed together. He never looked at an offering twice.

Jokyab noticed that one of the visitors didn't dare to come in. He was a beggar, and it sounded like this wasn't the first time he had come. Instead, he stuck his head in the window. "Eh, Rinpoche! Give me some alms, won't you?"

Each time this beggar came, Jamdrak would reach back, put his hand in the box of offerings and, without looking, grab something and hand it out the window with a loud, "Here you are—enjoy!"

One day, an official from the monastery came by and saw that the beggar had just walked off with an exquisite golden statue. He rushed into the hollow tree and started to complain.

"Rinpoche, you can't just give away things like this. Everything should be counted and priced first; *then* you can give what is appropriate to someone like that guy."

"Oh dear!" Jamdrak replied, "You want to put a price on the priceless Buddha. I am not able to do that." To which the manager had no reply.

Jamdrak turned to Jokyab and said, "Poor fellows. They are actually very kind to me. I can't hold it against them—they have to cover the monastery's needs. First, the manager came and said he wanted half of all my offerings. He told me that they were expanding the buildings and have many expenses, and that I don't need so much because all I do is practice. I agreed and let them have half. Apparently it has turned out to be quite a lot. Now it looks as though they have grown to feel they own my offerings and want to count them to make sure they get their share.

"They've offered me a room in the monastery, but I always tell them that I am simply an old geezer living in a tree. I'm happy here," he added with a chuckle, "but if they want to live in a monastery surrounded by fancy statues and lots of glitter, let them—if that makes them happy."

❦

Jokyab spent an entire year with Jamdrak in pursuit of these teachings, returning with an enormous sheaf of notes. Because he had run out of paper during his stay there, he had resorted to writing his notes on birch bark. When Jokyab came back from his mission, it looked as if he were carrying a load of wood shavings! When he untied his load, we saw that each scrap of bark had a little number. Samten Gyatso ordered him to copy them all out in the right order, which took several months.

Jokyab's notes expanded on the abbreviations and cross-references found in the text and clarified the difficult points. Eventually he compiled them into one remarkable volume, which is now widely used under the name *Side Ornament to the Light of Wisdom*.

Jokyab sometimes joked, "These notes are the real repository for keeping the *Light of Wisdom* teachings clear and alive in my mind. Without them, I would not be able to give a thorough explanation. This is all thanks to Jamdrak." There was a slightly rueful tone to his voice, for he had not had an easy time getting these teachings.

Jokyab later gave me an extensive series of teachings on the *Light of Wisdom* over a six-month period.[180] Samten Gyatso thought these teachings were so important that even he attended them. Jokyab taught by first going through the root verses from beginning to end and then teaching it one more time including the commentary. The second time through, he added every note that he had received, each in its proper place. Without them, even the most educated teacher would have had a hard time finding all the references.

26

An Eccentric King

Samten Gyatso had become exceedingly famous in Nangchen. Because of his renown as well as his high level of realization, toward the end of his life he had become the guru to the Nangchen king. Let me tell you a bit about how this came about and the ramifications it would have.

To give a bit of context, Nangchen was a country in its own right. The government had twenty-five ministers of external affairs and eighteen of internal affairs, while the king ruled over them all. My forefathers of the Tsangsar clan fell under the control of the Nangchen kings centuries ago, and this continued until an invasion by Muslim warlords from Ziling in the 1930s.[181] The invaders weren't as strong as an organized army—they were more like a gang of bandits. Still, they reached deep into Kham, plundering as they went; in the process both palaces were demolished.

In those days Queen Yudrön, whose name means Turquoise Lamp, was a Derge princess. She bore several children—three boys and three girls—but the children all died, one after the other. Many rituals were performed to remedy this recurring calamity, which in Kham was regarded as a specific obstacle, a demonic force called *tsiu*. But it was all to no avail.

One of these rituals seeks to "re-summon" the victim's life force and it requires a master of high caliber.[182] A message was sent to the Karmapa, saying, "Our princes and princesses have died, one after the other. Nangchen now has no male heir to the throne. Please recommend a master capable of solving this problem."

By this time, the fifteenth Karmapa had passed away, and Rigpey Dorje, the sixteenth Karmapa,

42.
The king of
Nangchen

was residing at Tsurphu. He sent back this reply, "At present in the kingdom of Nangchen, there is no lama better than Samten Gyatso. Invite him to your palace and request his protective rituals." Simultaneously, a message—also pointing to Samten Gyatso—had arrived from the great Situ of Palpung. So my guru was forced to leave his hermitage at Fortress Peak.

43. Prince Achen of Nangchen

During the three years he spent at the royal palace, next to the Tsechu monastery, the queen gave birth to a son, Prince Achen. In the first years of his life, the young prince was under Samten Gyatso's constant protection and, unlike his less fortunate siblings, didn't die. After that, the king had five more children—three sons and two daughters—many of whom, I believe, are still alive.

People believed that Samten Gyatso had used his remarkable abilities to save the royal lineage. Of course, the king of Nangchen was overjoyed and gave Samten Gyatso vast parcels of fertile land, as was the custom of kings in former times.

So in his old age my teacher became the most important lama for the royal family—the one to whom they were extremely grateful and from whom they asked advice in all matters.

Since the king of Nangchen regarded Samten Gyatso as one of his gurus, I often visited the palace as my uncle's attendant. Otherwise, no ordinary lama, and definitely no mere common subject, could enter the king's inner chamber—only the highest-ranking religious dignitaries were allowed an audience.[183]

The king was much more interested in supporting Dharma activities than in secular affairs. He even refused to meet an important chieftain, calling him "an enemy of the Dharma."

This king was a lama in his own right. He only slept a few hours each night and the rest of the time he practiced with great perseverance. He spent his entire day reciting the Kilaya mantra at top speed, yet clearly enunciated. He never skipped a syllable nor interrupted his recitation. I heard he chanted 130 million Kilaya mantras during his life.

Eventually, the king turned over his rule to the prince and remained in strict meditation retreat.

Here's another story that gives a sense of what kind of a king he was.

Flocks of migrating wild geese and cranes would land inside the palace gardens. As it happened, one crane flew into his compound with a broken leg, lingering for a time.

The king took this very seriously; he sent out emissaries to discover who was responsible for the injury. They managed to find a kid who confessed to having flung a stone at the bird. On hearing this, the king had the boy kept under arrest while the bird was treated. Only when the bird had finally recovered was the boy released.

Later, there was a similar incident with a wild goose, and another teenager was arrested. Word then spread that all birds in the kingdom were protected by royal decree, so no child dared raise a stone against one.

*

Samten Gyatso stayed in the old palace, while the king and his family resided in a new mansion nearby. In the new palace was an assembly room called the Square Hall, where the big chieftains, ministers and dignitaries sat in meetings, with their haughty airs and their fine, long-sleeved brocade *chuba* coats. They strutted about with their noses in the air, ignoring ordinary people.

The king, who as you might have noticed was a bit eccentric, refused to allow any upholstered seating in the Square Hall—only hard wooden benches. No matter how special the ministers might think they were, they had to sit on bare wooden planks!

Those officials with access to the king for secular affairs were of the elite *behu* rank. There were four of them and they all wore long garments of the finest brocade. They too held their heads high, signifying their dignity and lofty status—they almost couldn't see the ground they were walking on. They were supposed to be "noblemen," but my friends and I found their self-importance amusing and enjoyed imitating them.

Anyway, Samten Gyatso was often summoned to the palace, where he presided over religious ceremonies. When he arrived, he had to pass through the Square Hall and he would usually cough slightly before entering. When the dignitaries heard the cough, they would stiffen and all try to stand up at once. Once they tried to stand up by leaning on the shoulder of the person next to them. Then, like dominoes, they tumbled here and there, making a mess of themselves.

When he finally entered the royal chambers the scene wasn't that much different—the queen, princes and princesses immediately leapt to their feet, abandoning whatever they were doing. It seems everyone was afraid of him—even the king.

Queen Yudrön was fond of inviting important people to the palace. But other than Samten Gyatso, I believe, the king allowed only the Karmapa and the great Situ into his private quarters.

Once, the king invited the Karmapa into this inner sanctum to perform the celebrated Black Crown ceremony with a small entourage of a shrine master, two trumpet players and a bursar.

On such occasions, another great tulku might be included—but not as a matter of course. Once, it happened that Surmang Tentrul, who was one of the major lamas in Nangchen, had arrived at the palace along with the Karmapa.

"Wish-Fulfilling Jewel," Tentrul requested, "please bring me in with you. The Nangchen king is said to be exceptional, an emanation of Avalokiteshvara. I have often wished to see his face at least once. But as yet he has never given me the opportunity. Please be so kind as to include me among your attendants."

"Certainly," the Karmapa replied. "You are one of my chief lamas, so why not?" So now there was one more in his retinue.

After the ceremony was completed, the king turned to the Karmapa and asked who the extra lama was. Karmapa replied he was Surmang Tentrul.

"Ah! So that's Surmang Tentrul. Well, well! So now we've met." And that was all the king said until the Karmapa had taken leave. But then the king called the Karmapa's bursar back into his room.

"Isn't Tentrul one of my subjects?" asked the king. "Isn't he a citizen of Nangchen, like a pebble beneath my feet? And yet he wants to be placed above me? Under the pretext of being one of the Karmapa's attendants, he forced his way into my private quarters without asking my permission. Is this not so?

"Now go ask that Tentrul if this is not the case—and ask him the reason for such subterfuge. Is his plan to allow the king's subjects free passage at their own whim—like a stone thrown in my face? Ask him if that is his intent."

The bursar was usually quite bold and overbearing, but when he returned, he couldn't bring himself to repeat the king's words to the Karmapa. So he tried to skirt the issue by first conferring with Samten Gyatso, who in turn called my father in to help.

"How do we break this news to Surmang Tentrul?" they wondered.

One of them pointed out, "Since the king invited the Karmapa back for a dinner banquet, we *have* to tell Tentrul beforehand."

Another asked, "What can we say?"

Finally, they decided it would be best if the Karmapa himself were the one to explain.

But when they beseeched the Karmapa, he replied, "I can't say anything to Surmang Tentrul. He is not only one of my chosen representative lamas, he also holds a very high rank, having received the seal of the Chinese emperor. In addition, he is also one of my gurus. So if anyone should apologize to the king, it should be me!"

For his part, Tentrul didn't feel he had broken any law, since he had asked permission from the Karmapa and was sincere in his wish to meet the king. The real problem was the king's quirky nature. The outcome of their discussions was that the Karmapa would sort it out himself. "If any crime has been committed, I express my regrets," he would tell the king.

After the Karmapa had apologized, the king replied, "There is absolutely no way I can accept an apology from the Karmapa—*that* is not the issue! The issue is that one of my subjects brazenly made his way into the king's inner chamber."

Such was our king's peculiar character. Whatever his reasons—either that he was in strict retreat much of the time or that people shouldn't be allowed free access to the royal palace—he wouldn't budge an inch.

In all matters, he was very uncompromising, to say the least.

In those days, technological innovations began to arrive in Kham from China. These became known as "foreign inventions," and at one point the king issued a decree, "Not a single one of these foreign items will be allowed inside my palace walls." As a matter of fact, even his windows were devoid of glass, the holes being covered with only cloth or paper, as in olden times. He reasoned that as our forefathers did not have them, neither should we.. So while he was alive, you couldn't find a trace of glass anywhere in the palace.

Next the king declared that he also didn't want foreign weaponry in his palace. So the soldiers had only a few single-shot muskets that, when fired, enveloped the marksman in a cloud of smoke. He included modern weapons within the *duruka* category, which he explained this way, "The old prophecies mention three kinds of duruka: invading armies, infectious diseases, and material substances. Though warfare, famine, and disease are predicted to spread in our time, I will do everything possible to delay their arrival. I know that foreign goods are becoming ever more popular in my country, but I forbid a single one of these accoutrements of duruka to be carried through my gates."

The king stuck by that attitude his entire life. You might say that he was truly old-fashioned.

27

My Last Days with Samten Gyatso

Well before my time, Samten Gyatso had offered the complete transmission of the *New Treasures* to the fifteenth Karmapa, Khakyab Dorje. The Karmapa's consort later told me that the two lamas often sat together and talked late into the night. After Samten Gyatso left one evening, the Karmapa joined his palms together in respect and told his consort, "At this time and during this age, there is probably no one who has as great and authentic a realization of the innermost essence of the Great Perfection as Samten Gyatso." Such was the sincere appreciation the Karmapa had for my guru.

Years later, Samten Gyatso invited the new incarnation, the sixteenth Karmapa, to the Fortress Peak hermitage, where they exchanged transmissions of spiritual teachings that each needed from the other. The young Karmapa held my guru in great esteem, since Samten Gyatso had taught both the Karmapa and his previous incarnation as well. When they were finished, the Karmapa was invited to another monastery and Samten Gyatso accompanied him.

At the end of that visit, Samten Gyatso said to the Karmapa, "You and I will not meet again. I will not return to Central Tibet, and you are going west from here and won't be back for a long time. I'm an old man now and death is not far off. Today is our last meeting."

The Karmapa did not say a single word in reply. He only looked sad and remained silent, and then Samten Gyatso departed. My father and I, who were there, stayed on for a few more days. This was also the last time my father saw the sixteenth Karmapa.

※

I want to tell you more about my teacher, Samten Gyatso, but all I can relate are a few fragments of his outer life story; I cannot adequately express his inner stability in meditative awareness. He was an extraordinary practitioner. He himself never bragged about his level of achievement and in fact very seldom gave even the least hint of it. Rather, he kept to the hidden path, practicing without making a display of his realization. Rarely, something would slip out.

During the year preceding his death, he visited a small monastery, and I went along as his attendant—I may have been in my mid-twenties. "Why don't you stay in retreat here?" I asked. "I will serve you."

"Better I go back to my hermitage," Samten Gyatso replied. "One can't stay in strict retreat in a monastery."

That evening, I packed for our departure. We lay down to sleep but instead began talking. I asked him one question after another and he told story after story in reply.

At one point he told me, "I received the pointing-out instruction to the unexcelled view of the Great Perfection at the age of eight. I recognized the nature of mind then and I have continued training in it steadily ever since. Because of my firm disposition—so typical of the 'earth element type'—I have made steady progress.[184] My development hasn't come in leaps and bounds, but I didn't backslide either—just slow and steady. In fact, I only notice the change when I look back, comparing my present development with that of previous years.

"You sometimes hear of yogis who advance tremendously within a few months and reach realization very quickly. I must admit that this never happened to me. Yet since I have practiced continuously from the age of eight, you might say that my level of practice is now fairly good.

"I still have one problem, though: maintaining awareness in the brief period between falling asleep and actually sleeping. There are a few moments in which I still lose presence of mind and the awakened state is briefly lost. But once sleep begins, the awakened state is recognized and remains stable throughout the whole night. The only challenge left now is that one small gap just as I fall asleep.

"You are the only person I've told this to," he added. "No one else has ever asked me about this—and even if someone did, I wouldn't say a word."

At some point, I noticed that dawn had come; the birds were already singing outside. My first thought was that we hadn't gotten a wink of sleep. But Samten Gyatso said, "It doesn't matter, just get up! Losing a night's sleep every once in a while really doesn't make much of a difference."

This was one of the few times he shared his innermost experience. Otherwise he virtually never talked about his own realization.

But during that winter before his passing, I talked with Samten Gyatso quite a lot, and on occasion he revealed some extraordinary secrets about his own practice.

One day he told me, "I really have no great qualities, nothing marvelous to boast of, except that my distraction has vanished. The tendency to forget mind essence now seems to have vanished completely from my experience.

"No matter how much work piles up, no matter who comes in to see me, no matter how many people crowd into my room, the lucid quality only grows. I find that when I stay alone and uninvolved, with no task at hand, the clarity of awareness subsides somewhat, although I am not distracted. But the more people, the more busyness and the more turmoil I am involved in, the more the strength of the awareness grows.

"Just between you and me, I am sure that I will not end up in hell."

Then Samten Gyatso added, "After I die, there is no doubt that people will ask the Karmapa to find my tulku. But please understand, I honestly don't have the slightest ambition to have my name pinned onto someone as though he were my reincarnation. Maybe they will name one anyway, but as a matter of fact, I have already discussed this with the Karmapa.

"I told him during his last visit to Kham, when you and I were both there with him, 'I am an old man who will soon die and people will come asking you to identify my reincarnation. But truly there will be no reincarnation. My real tulku will be Tulku Urgyen and he will look after my monastery. Therefore, please don't recognize anybody as my reincarnation.' The Karmapa didn't answer—he neither agreed nor disagreed."

I know this was my guru's wish because I heard it with my own ears.

For my part I wasn't very happy to hear any of this. Back in the privacy of his room I told him, "You are the lord of the teachings,[185] and your reincarnation *must* be found to continue this lineage. I, on the other hand, probably will roam about from one unknown place to another. I definitely won't remain at Lachab. I'm quite unhappy to hear about what you said to the Karmapa, because I won't stay in Kham, absolutely not. It's one hundred percent certain that I will go somewhere else! I want to go where no one has heard of me."

"Who knows? The compassion and skillful means of our Wish-Fulfilling Jewel are extraordinary," Samten Gyatso responded, referring to Karmapa. "But one thing is for sure: there will still not be any direct reincarnation. For that I have no wish. On the other hand, someone will probably come along capable of benefiting the Dharma and sentient beings, who will be given the title 'Samten Gyatso's tulku.'"

28

My Guru's Passing

In those final days I had a vague and troubling sense that my time with Samten Gyatso was running out. So whenever the opportunity arose I didn't waste it but asked for clarification on many points.

During this time I also grew bold enough to ask about his innermost aim in life. Here is what he said, "In my youth, I longed for nothing but to stay in the mountains, in one cave after another. I never desired the title and status of a high lama. In fact, I wanted to remain incognito and tried my best to do so."

He told me of another goal, adding, "I had a heartfelt yearning to assemble a complete set of Chokgyur Lingpa's termas."[186] This he managed to accomplish, collecting not only the scriptures but also the accompanying icons and mandalas, as well as every other necessary accoutrement—all of impeccable quality.

Samten Gyatso always considered being a vajra master or guru for others a personal obstacle, even though he was very successful at it and became very famous. Because his chief aim had actually been to spend his life practicing alone in caves, he lamented to me, "I have the feeling that my whole life has gone in the wrong direction—that I fell under the sway of obstacles."

In the past, the tradition was that one obeyed the command of one's guru, who would say, "Go to such-and-such a place and raise the victory banner of realization. When you have reached accomplishment, then you can truly benefit beings."

The disciple would go to that spot and practice one-pointedly until reaching realization. Afterward, he or she would venture out into the world to benefit beings. That is the way it should be. Without receiving permission or the command from one's guru, one does not start to work for the welfare of others as a vajra master. But after receiving the command or permission, one should definitely undertake the task.

When Samten Gyatso grew older, he often thought, "I should have stayed in caves, but instead I fell under the power of hindrances."

This wasn't just talk: he actually felt that way. He had no ambition to become a vajra master or sit above anyone else. He once explained, "Being successful is actually called the pleasant obstacle. Whereas any unpleasant obstacle is easily recognized by all, success is rarely acknowledged to be a barrier on the path. Unpleasant obstacles include, for example, being defamed or implicated in scandal, falling sick or otherwise meeting with failure and misfortune. Able practitioners can deal with these. They recognize these situations as obstacles and use them as part of the path.

"But with pleasant obstacles—such as becoming renowned, having disciples gather around you and working for the welfare of others—one starts to think, 'Well, now! I'm becoming really special. I'm benefiting many beings. Everything is fine! I'm so successful'—without recognizing that the infatuation with success is a major hindrance to progress."

When this happens, Samten Gyatso warned that people only think, "My altruistic capacity to benefit others is expanding!" This is what they tell themselves, all the while failing to notice that they have actually fallen prey to an obstacle.

～

Samten Gyatso once mentioned, with his usual understatement, that he expected his family would render at least a small service to the continuity of the *New Treasures*.

My cousin Khentrul, who was the reincarnation of Karmey Khenpo, was exceedingly sharp-minded and well-versed in the Buddhist scriptures. I took it for granted that he would be the main lineage holder. But that was not in Samten Gyatso's plans. Khentrul and I often lived in the same gompa, and yet I was closer to Samten Gyatso. I often wondered why our master never treated Khentrul as a lineage holder, "If not him, then who could possibly hold the lineage? Why doesn't Samten Gyatso give him more special treatment?"

This young man was already quite learned as well as very gutsy, with a commanding presence. But at some point he went to Central Tibet to receive more teachings and empowerments, and we got the news that he had passed away there.

We were all very sad when Khentrul passed away—and before he was able to transmit the lineage. Otherwise I have no doubt he would have been a competent master. But looking back, I think Samten Gyatso most likely had realized that Khentrul's life force wouldn't hold and that he would die young.

After Khentrul's passing, Samten Gyatso said, "You are my second hope for the continuation of this lineage." It was very unusual for him to talk like this. He would never flatter anyone, least of all members of his own family; he wouldn't even compliment the Karmapa to his face.

On the other hand he never criticized anyone. If anyone was at fault, he would simply overlook it, saying nothing. I heard him praise only Khyentse, Kongtrul and Chokling—no one else. He was very dignified and reserved, a no-nonsense kind of guy. Unless you knew him very well, you would have absolutely no clue as to what his opinion really was.

But I looked at myself frankly and thought, "I'm nothing special. I'm not well educated. My only advantage is that I've lived with Samten Gyatso." In those days, I had no particular ambition except just to stay by his side.

He told me several times, "Whether the lineage of the *New Treasures* will be broken one day is in your hands. So I hope my being a little firm with you will pay off."

When Adeu Rinpoche came from Nangchen some years back, he said that back home they regard me as the main holder of the *New Treasures*. This isn't because I have been especially diligent; it is entirely due to Samten Gyatso.

Since we shared the same monastery and I stayed with Samten Gyatso all the time, asking to be excused when he gave an empowerment was simply out of the question.

"I am expecting that you will uphold this lineage later on," he would say. In this way, I received every single empowerment and teaching he gave. This was not always by my own choice—I just didn't dare be absent since he could be very intimidating.

⁂

Near the end of his life, Samten Gyatso gave me a special entrustment to the guardians of the *New Treasures*,[187] a transmission he had never given to anyone else. Chokgyur Lingpa had given this particular practice to the great Kongtrul only, who had then given it only to Karmey Khenpo, from whom Samten Gyatso received it. He was now the only person who knew the particulars and practiced it regularly at Fortress Peak. One of its special functions was to protect crops against frost.

Unfortunately, one of my personality traits seems to be a lack of perseverance. If a transmission required any kind of serious attention on a daily basis, it went against my nature. That's why I didn't pursue the special applications of that practice.[188] So today I have the reading transmission and empowerment and can pass them on, but not the know-how necessary for practical application. Apparently no one else does either.

In Gangtok, Dzongsar Khyentse asked if I had brought some of the charmed substance produced during that practice, and I gave him whatever I had. Now I have none left and, even though Dzongsar Khyentse attested to its immense effectiveness, there is no one left who can make it.

※

Before my father and uncles each passed away, their faces seemed to change in a remarkable way, as if they were becoming younger. Their gray hairs did not turn black, but their skin definitely became younger-looking and shiny. Some say that this youthful skin tone and radiance is a sign of realization. And, in fact, the tantric scriptures mention that at a certain level of experience and realization, the skin becomes soft and supple.

I first noticed the change with Samten Gyatso. The year he left his body, his skin became noticeably vibrant. His facial features seemed like those of a young man, so that you totally forgot that he was indeed quite old. His skin had become a light, lustrous color, as if something unusual were happening from inside.

Before that he had looked old and tired, but then he suddenly took on this youthful appearance. People would ask, "How old are you really, Samten Gyatso? You look so young! What happened? Are they feeding you something magical or are you doing some special practice?"

This shift in appearance began about a year before he died. But honestly, if you thought about it, it wasn't a good sign—somewhere in the back of your mind, you felt that it couldn't last.

It was the same with my father. His skin glowed with a bronze hue; you could call it a majestic brilliance, as though there were embers behind the skin. His face too took on a very fresh, youthful appearance. He died three months later.

When Uncle Sang-Ngak passed away, I was at Tsurphu, but I heard that the same thing happened with him. All the local people noticed that his wrinkles had disappeared and wondered why. They said among themselves, "What has happened to Sang-Ngak Rinpoche to make him look so young? We can't see his wrinkles anymore. We've seen this twice before with his older brothers—could this be a sign that he may die this year?" And such was indeed the case, for he died later that year.

Uncle Tersey once remarked to me, "Ordinarily one ought to be happy when close family members like my brothers seem so young and radiant at their age. But I am not. I feel it's a bad sign; it means that death is near." As for Uncle Tersey himself, not long before he passed on, although his hair was gray, his face was like that of a young man.

That was how one could foresee that these brothers would soon die. I'm not making this up, nor is it just one or two people's impression—every single person who met them remarked on it.

※

Near the end of his life, Samten Gyatso entered retreat, intending to remain there for the rest of his life. But instead of announcing this directly, he simply made it known that he was going to stay in loose retreat for two weeks at Fortress Peak, a day's journey away from Lachab. During that time he would perform protective rituals for the people of the country. Then, once he settled in, he sent the message that now was the time for him to stay in strict retreat for a while.

But after only a short time had passed, the prince of Nangchen fell ill and two important ministers were sent to summon Samten Gyatso.

"Our prince is gravely ill and may soon pass away," they announced. "You must come back with us to the palace. We've been directed by His Majesty not to return without you, so we're not going to!"

As these two dignitaries waited in the guest room, those of us close to Samten Gyatso debated what to do. Uncle Sang-Ngak was around at that time, as well as his sister Tashi Chimey, who served as the steward of his monastery and retreat center.

Even though I was only a youngster, I wasn't intimidated by the ruling family. I argued that Samten Gyatso should not leave retreat at *anyone's* request, no matter how important they were.

Someone else made the counter-argument, "Earlier, the master stayed at the royal palace for three years and often performed ceremonies to support the king. Everything has been auspicious so far. The king donated a huge piece of land with many fertile fields to our monastery. He has been a very generous benefactor. So there is really no choice—Samten Gyatso *must* break retreat and go there."

"Our teacher should ignore the message and refuse to go," I insisted with all sincerity, though perhaps a bit naïvely.

Someone again countered, "Our king has given a command—don't subjects usually obey?"

"Even though it's difficult to refuse such a command," I continued, "if you agree this time, you will always have to acquiesce. Since our guru is so highly treasured, I'm afraid that everyone may ask him to do one thing after another. The requests will be endless!"

A sense of foreboding weighed heavily on my mind. One of my less admirable traits is that I can't keep such feelings to myself. Therefore, with my whole heart, I tried to dissuade everyone in the room.

At one point during the discussion, the decision was actually made not to go. We informed the two waiting ministers of this.

But one of them replied, "If that is the case, we will not return to the royal palace. We'll just spend the rest of our days here! I'll sleep right there in front of Samten Gyatso's door!"

He said this in the adamant manner so typical of the hardheaded and tenacious Khampas. He added, "Even if I have to wait for Samten Gyatso at Fortress Peak for nine years, I am not returning without him!"

At that point another important lama said, "If Samten Gyatso refuses and the young prince dies what will happen? Really, he has no choice but to go."

Eventually, a consensus emerged that Samten Gyatso had to go. I gave it one last try, raising my voice to say, "If he breaks retreat now to go to the royal palace, there will be no end—he will never be able to get back into retreat. If you obey the king's wish this time, you cannot disobey in the future—you will always have to comply. Therefore ask to be excused and stay firm."

But it seemed I was the only one in the entire group who held this opinion and, as I was still regarded as a youngster, how much power did I have to persuade anyone? The others had the final say and in the end Samten Gyatso decided to go.

I was asked to go along but refused, "I definitely won't go, especially not under these circumstances. To tell you the truth, I am deeply unhappy about this turn of events. Please excuse me; I am going back to Lachab."

※

Just before Samten Gyatso left, his small knife was nowhere to be found. He had never parted with this knife; the sheath was still there, but the knife was missing and he had to leave without it.

On arriving at the royal palace, Samten Gyatso began an elaborate nine-day longevity ritual.[189] By the time the ceremony concluded, young prince Achen had recovered. No trace of disease or any evil influence remained—such was the powerful effect of that ritual.

Then, just as I feared, there was another request. Since the queen of Nangchen belonged to the royal family of Derge, Samten Gyatso was invited to perform ceremonies at the Derge court as well. A long procession was formed to welcome him there and they treated him with the deep respect that all who are hosted by the royal court receive. Finally, after several weeks, he completed his responsibilities and set off back home.

Everything seemed to have gone well until he reached the foothill below Fortress Peak, where he fell off his horse and injured his leg. His attendants helped him back up on the horse for what would be his last ride up to the hermitage. I'm not sure what went wrong, but he wasn't able to walk after that.

※

The morning after Samten Gyatso arrived, he sent for me at Lachab. It took the messenger a full day to reach our monastery. It was late afternoon by the time a monk walked in. "Samgya Rinpoche has fallen ill," he said, referring to my guru. "It appears to be quite serious and he is asking for you."

Hearing this filled me with overwhelming sadness and I was overcome by the gripping intuition that Samten Gyatso was about to leave us. It certainly was inauspicious for him to leave retreat—and the missing knife couldn't have been a good omen either. I hadn't had a moment of joy since he left; in fact that very morning I'd had a deeply ominous dream in which I saw that Samten Gyatso was about to leave Fortress Peak. I was there as his attendant. Looking up toward the western mountains, I saw that the sun was low in the sky.

"Hey, Rinpoche!" I urged, "Don't leave now! The sun is about to set behind the mountains! Don't travel in the dark; please turn around and come back in."

I reached for him with my hand to guide him back in, but he said in response, "No, no! My time has come; I have no choice but to leave."

In the dream I pleaded, "Please don't say that!"

But he replied, "Isn't it true that the power of karma is unstoppable?" He slipped from my grasp and rode off. A moment later, the sun set and he vanished into the darkness.

The next moment, I woke up and thought, "What an awful dream!" That morning, I told my cook, "I had a disturbing dream about Samten Gyatso. It makes me think he has arrived back at Fortress Peak."

"Don't say such things!" the old cook protested.

So when the messenger arrived later that day to summon me to Fortress Peak, it came as no surprise—the only thought in my mind had been that our guru was close to death, a thought as painful as a knife in the heart. It was very hard to sleep that night and long before daybreak I was up preparing for the ride to Fortress Peak.

After more than twelve hours on the trail, still out of breath, I walked directly into Samten Gyatso's room and asked him about his health. Clearly he was in bad shape, suffering from relentless pain. He wasn't able to speak more than a few words.

Two doctors were consulted, but, to be frank, they were completely useless. One of them diagnosed the dreaded illness known as "thirtyfold blackness" and saw signs that Samten Gyatso's intestines had ruptured.

"He needs to be treated with fire," the other said, "but that should have been done long ago. It's too late now and I'm not sure I can do it."

The doctor was speaking of *metsa*, a traditional medical treatment reserved for serious illnesses.[190] I prepared the tool for the fire treatment, then lightly touched his skin with the red-hot iron. This alleviated the pain somewhat and he was able to say a few words. But what good was temporary relief when the disease was eating away at his bowels?

"Rinpoche, it doesn't look good!" I said. "What is going to happen?"

"Who knows?" he replied. "Chokgyur Lingpa and most of his descendants didn't live long. His son Wangchok Dorje died young. His daughter, our precious mother, did better, living to well over seventy. His other son Tsewang Norbu died in his sixties. On the other side of the family, our Tsangsar lineage also doesn't seem to be long-lived. Nearly everyone in this lineage, including my own father, has died in their fifties. I am now sixty-five.

"On the other hand," he continued, "It's fine for me to die now. It really makes no difference. It's fine if I live a little longer, but if I pass on it's also fine. I've had enough time."

"Rinpoche," I then asked, "is there anything I can do to help you recover?"

"Don't talk about this any longer," he replied.

This made me extremely sad. Later that day my last hopes for his recovery faded. Clearly he was on the verge of leaving his body.

※

At one point, my guru said, "Manifestations of mind defy the reach of words. There is no point in attempting to express them for the descriptions would be endless. I see this now. There is nothing left unseen, nothing left unheard. All phenomena of samsara and nirvana can manifest from this mind—don't you agree?"

"Yes, Rinpoche," I replied.

The situation seemed to demand that I play along, even though this profound perspective surely wasn't part of my immediate experience. I had never had any doubt as to Samten Gyatso's extremely high level of realization and clairvoyance, but it was becoming even more apparent as he reached the end of this incarnation. He seemed to speak from a state of unimpeded mind.

After a period of silence, he continued, "Ah! Jamyang Khyentse Wangpo has come! Now the great tertön Chokgyur Lingpa has arrived! And here comes Jamgön Kongtrul!"

Among all the masters, it was in Kongtrul that he had the greatest trust, an incredible faith. He marveled at Kongtrul's writings and often described him in these terms, "The incarnation of the translator Vairotsana, Buddha Vairochana in human form, who was proclaimed with the glorious conch—the unambiguous and fearless voice of Shakyamuni—with the name Infinite Wisdom."[191] This was a reference to Kongtrul having been prophesied by the Buddha.

And now Samten Gyatso said that he too had arrived. It made me even sadder to hear this, because now I felt that there wasn't much time left.

His attendant Dudul and I didn't sleep that night but stayed up to take care of him. We tried to give him something to eat, but he was only able to drink a little water and was so weak he couldn't say more than a word or two. Dudul was fond of sleeping and soon I found myself alone with my ailing guru. Throughout the night, the only words Samten Gyatso uttered were to request a drink of water.

We all started to feel the end was close. I asked him but he would neither confirm nor deny his departure. All he said was, "I can't say. Let's wait and see. Tomorrow morning it will be clear. Either way, there's no need to worry."

The next morning his fever began to rise even higher.

☙

Right around this time, my brother Penjik was involved in a land dispute. He had a very assertive, even confrontational personality. Later we found out that on this very day—the nineteenth day of the fourth month—a gang of rivals had caught up with him. At that moment, Samten Gyatso exclaimed from his bed, "Oh no!"

"What is it, Rinpoche?" I asked.

Once more he said, "Oh no!" adding, "Penjik is in big trouble!"

"What's wrong with him, Rinpoche?" I asked.

Samten Gyatso replied, "Oh no! Now Penjik's in dire peril! He's about to be stabbed!"

From time to time, Khampas in our region would have gang fights, and occasionally one or two would enter the bardo rather than returning home. As a matter of fact, a few months earlier, Penjik's attendant had been among the unfortunate ones killed in a fight.

Referring to him now, Samten Gyatso continued, "Penjik's late attendant now tells me that he owned a horse. After his death, when his possessions were given away in his name to increase his merit, his family for some reason forgot to include that horse. Now he asks me to please tell his family to sell the horse and make offerings. He is in the bardo and needs help."

After a while Samten Gyatso added, "Well, well, there's no end to what one could say—so what's the use of talking endlessly." Then he smiled, chuckling as he looked at me.

I spent that entire night in his room. Early in the morning, I asked how he felt. Instead of answering me directly, he addressed me affectionately and asked, "Kargah, has morning broken yet?"[192]

"Yes, it's about dawn."

"Well then, ask Ngakdi Lama to come in," Samten Gyatso whispered, using Uncle Sang-Ngak's nickname. I told Dudul to fetch him.

Uncle Sang-Ngak arrived and bowed down three times.

Samten Gyatso invited him to sit on a small throne. Then he said, "Well, well! Since the lama is here, why don't we all chant Jamgön Kongtrul's *Calling the Guru from Afar?*"

This is a very famous text intended to open one's heart with devotion, a state in which it is much easier to merge our minds with the guru's.

We began to chant together, Uncle Sang-Ngak leading with the lines:

> Lama, hear me.
> Kind root lama, hear me.
> Essence of the buddhas of the three times,
> Source of the sublime Dharma, realization and the statements,
> Sovereign of Sangha, assembly of noble ones,
> Root lama, hear me.

As we chanted, Samten Gyatso sang along with us in a surprisingly strong voice. He was now sitting up with his legs loosely crossed, the palms of his hands covering his knees in the meditation posture known as "resting in the nature of mind." He wore a cloth cap with earflaps to protect his bald head from the cold and there was a remarkable glow to his skin.

We never reached the end of that prayer, because at some point Samten Gyatso interrupted by repeating this one sentence from the text:

> Bless me to sincerely be aware of death.

We all stopped chanting and a few moments later he sang the line again:

> Bless me to sincerely be aware of death.

As the sun began to rise, he sang it a third time and then his body sagged slightly. You could see the looseness that comes over the body at the moment of death.

As I looked at my guru, I was convinced that he had passed away, even though his face had a beautiful smile, and his eyes were clear and wide open, looking very much alive. His skin was glowing, almost luminous.

He was still sitting in the same meditation posture seen in depictions of the renowned master Longchenpa. He looked perfectly confident and composed but showed no signs of either pulse or breath.

According to Dzogchen tradition, at a particular moment in the death process, one can remind a practitioner of the ultimate nature of mind by repeating the syllable AH twenty-one times into his ear. I now knelt close to him and began repeating, "AH, AH, AH, AH, AH . . ."

But I ran out of breath and felt I had to start over again. As I was drawing my breath for a second time, he nodded his head quite clearly, as if to indicate that he had already gotten the point.

I still recited the sequence a second time and he nodded again, but only slightly.

Since I wasn't sure that this was enough, I continued with a third repetition. As I ended, his body drew even more upright. He sat there with brilliant, wide-open eyes and a lucid smile.

It truly seemed as if he hadn't died at all.[193]

Only Dudul, Uncle Sang-Ngak, and I were present. If Uncle Tersey had been there, no doubt he would have had the audacity to request precise information as to where Samten Gyatso's reincarnation could be found. He was able to ask such highly personal questions. I hadn't dared to ask, remembering what Samten Gyatso had said to the Karmapa earlier about not wanting a tulku to be found after he died. And, anyway, I was overcome with sadness.

Our guru had departed from this world and there was simply nothing we could do about it.

❧

After a while, we wrapped his body in brocade. Later that afternoon, it was carried down and placed on a throne in the main shrine hall. A great master's body is usually placed inside a huge copper tray to prevent liquid from seeping out and covered with bags of salt to absorb the moisture; robes are then wrapped over all this.

On the table in front of him we placed his vajra and bell, as well as other ritual implements. When people looked at his face they simply refused to believe that he had passed away. He still looked alive, smiling peacefully with brilliant clear eyes, and he remained like that for three days. Then the body started to sag a little and we covered his face.

A messenger had been sent off to Uncle Tersey, who was residing at Riwoche monastery, and another to inform my father. My father arrived on the third day, but Riwoche was a five-day journey each way, so Uncle Tersey didn't reach Fortress

Peak until the following week. Once everyone had gathered, we began a drubchen in the presence of the kudung—the sacred remains.

A monk from Lachab, who was later killed during the Chinese invasion, was overheard exclaiming, "How can someone like Samten Gyatso die? I don't believe it. It's simply not possible! It never crossed my mind that he could die. But if it is true, then there's absolutely nothing to rely on in this world."

I asked him, "Why would you think that?"

"Because he was perfectly reliable in every way," he replied. "Because of his firmness and sense of precision. He had unchanging integrity—not a speck of deceit. How could someone like that die?"

After the cremation, we discovered something remarkable among the ashes: the skull was still intact.[194] And one of his garments was undamaged by the fire, though all the rest burned up; for some reason this cloth had all the five colors of the rainbow on it. His ashes contained numerous relics, both those known as *dung* and ringsel.

During the cremation, everyone present witnessed an incredible display of rainbow patterns in the sky. It was amazing, since the sky was a deep blue, so clear you couldn't see a single cloud anywhere. As you may know, this is considered the best sign.

Such were the signs that accompanied my guru's passing into the unmanifest space of all phenomena. With my ordinary eyes, this is what I was able to witness; beyond this there is not much more I can say concerning his general life story.

All three of Samten Gyatso's brothers had gathered for his cremation. In Kham it was customary to perform two rituals after someone's death; one was Chö and the other *dur*. The dur pertains to certain classes of spirits connected to each and every person's corporeal existence. In the main part of the ritual, the presiding master disengages nine devouring spirits from the vital energy of the deceased. The understanding is that unless these nine spirits are disconnected when a person dies, they can slow down or create obstacles to liberation in the bardo.

My father, of course, performed the Chö. Though superstition held that the dur shouldn't be performed by the son or father or other close male relative, I volunteered to carry out the ritual and nothing untoward happened.

Often I have heard of families in Nepal complaining that the ghost of the deceased relative has returned home to haunt the premises—sometimes even stories of a husband trying to get back into bed with his wife after he's dead and cremated.

The wife doesn't see anything but might, for example, hear his voice or the sound of snoring. In Kham though I never heard of this happening—perhaps because there we always pacified these nine spirits by means of Chö and dur as soon as someone died.

The dur rituals have both a peaceful and a subjugating aspect. Sometimes they involve ritual name-burning, a pacifying activity that summons the deceased's consciousness, purifies it, and sends it to a buddhafield. The subjugating aspect exorcises evil influences that may have taken possession of the deceased. These devouring spirits are demon ghosts, a type of sentient being. You hear a lot of HUNG and PHAT during the part of the ritual where the nine spirits are being chased from their various hiding places.

This ceremony is necessary even for a great being like Samten Gyatso because such a master's splendor attracts many mundane spirits. The same holds true for most great vajra holders, because there is a certain interrelationship between these nine spirits and the master dissolving into the invisible sphere that is the basic space of all things.

Because Chimey Dorje was such a powerful master and an adept Chö practitioner, he probably succeeded in "divorcing" these nine spirits.

❧

When all these rituals were completed, I made the journey to Central Tibet to make the customary offerings in connection with Samten Gyatso's passing. In Lhasa I ran into one of Samten Gyatso's disciples from Derge, who was a very devoted but headstrong lama. Even though he had heard about Samten Gyatso's explicit wish that the Karmapa not be asked to find a tulku, this lama joined forces with the bursar of our monastery and went off to Central Tibet to ask the Karmapa anyway.

We exchanged a few words. "Didn't your guru tell you not to look for his tulku?" I asked him. "And yet against his will you travel all the way to see the Karmapa."

But that did no good as Khampas can be quite obstinate, as it is said: "Khampas are headstrong like yaks—either bandits or great meditators."

So the disciple went ahead and asked the Karmapa despite all my objections. That's why today someone is known as Samten Gyatso's tulku.

29

Meetings with a Remarkable Teacher

While in Central Tibet I had the opportunity to meet the Karmapa once again. I went to Tsurphu and stayed for two weeks. Then, after a few days in Lhasa, I headed straight back to Kham.

After arriving in Nangchen I assumed responsibility for Lachab Gompa. In spite of that obligation I tried to cut all involvements and go into a strict retreat for three years. My father looked after the monastery and during my seclusion he passed away. The time in retreat added up to three years though it was interrupted by the instability of the time.[195]

During this period, I invited Kyungtrul Kargyam, a precious master whom I regard as one of my more important teachers and root gurus. Kyungtrul had big, bloodshot eyes and dark skin. He was also extremely gentle and kind. He was amazing and I feel grateful to have known such an accomplished master—anyone who met him would be impressed.

He had come by his education as if it were second nature and was extremely learned, especially in the philosophical scriptures. I felt that there was no question I could ask about practice for which he would lack a profound reply. No one knows how he became so learned so quickly, but at the age of thirteen he had already given the reading transmission and an explanation of the entire *Kangyur* to a large gathering. Everyone was amazed at how this kid could explain the Buddha's words so clearly.

Even then it was expected he would turn out to be an outstanding master and the overseers of his monastery treated him specially—that is, until, under the cover of night, he fled to Derge, where he stayed with Barwey Dorje, a master who had been a disciple of the great tertön.[196] He was just sixteen at the time.

Barwey Dorje received him warmly, giving him guidance as well as the pointing-out instruction. "You are truly a sublime being," the master told his young student. "Just travel around Derge—you don't need to go anywhere else."

Then Barwey Dorje gave him a list of the most important masters to visit. Kyungtrul made the journey on foot, dressed as a beggar and carrying only a staff and a knapsack. He first went to Palpung where he met the great scholar Tashi Özer and received many teachings. Tashi Özer asked him where he came from and he replied that he came from the Kyungpo region. When he left, Tashi Özer said, "He must be a tulku, let's call him Kyungtrul—the tulku from Kyungpo," and the name stuck.

Later, Kyungtrul went on to the four main Nyingma monasteries in Kham—Shechen, Dzogchen, Katok, and Palyul—and managed to meet every single great master, including the famed Khenpo Ngakchung. On the way back, he again visited Palpung, where the great Situ was so impressed that he made Kyungtrul the master at the retreat center for nine years.

During this time, Kyungtrul had many visions and extraordinary dreams, as well as signs indicating he was a tertön. Though he was effortlessly able to write down one practice after the other, he held these termas back and refused to put them in writing until he had received the Karmapa's stamp of approval. Finally, he asked Situ for permission to leave and return to his homeland, Nangchen. He didn't rest there, though, as he felt a strong need to meet the Karmapa.

Years later, Kyungtrul told me, "The Karmapa was the one who could decide whether my mind treasures were authentic. Only he can verify a tertön and whether the termas will turn out to be beneficial. I could have written down so much more—there is no end to what can surge forth from the expanse of the all-ground."

The only terma Kyungtrul had written down at the time was a sadhana for the Three Roots, which was astoundingly beautiful. But before he could reach Tsurphu, the great Karmapa left his body—and therefore he never received the authorization.[197]

※

At Tsurphu, Kyungtrul met Samten Gyatso, who was saddened that, for some karmic reason, he had been unable to offer the Karmapa the transmission of the *Three Sections of the Great Perfection*—Mind, Space and Instruction. And now Jampal Tsultrim, one of the Karmapa's chief disciples, repeatedly requested these very empowerments.

Kyungtrul too wanted to receive this transmission, so Samten Gyatso told him, "Well, if you are also participating in the transmission of the *Three Sections*, you must use your skill and erudition to compose an empowerment manual." Kyungtrul consented to help and succeeded in arranging the empowerments for the Mind Section.[198]

Samten Gyatso gave the empowerments at Lotus Garuda Fortress, the famous retreat center above Tsurphu. As he did so, Kyungtrul wrote the liturgical arrangement and during this process they were able to discuss many fine points. Due to Kyungtrul's broad knowledge, the manual for the first section filled an entire volume by itself. Sometimes when the scope of a master's learning is extremely vast, he can write endlessly.

Shortly after the empowerments began the young Dudjom arrived, unencumbered by servants, a following or possessions. Being from the Pemakö province he was becoming famous under the name Pekö Dudjom. He was a ngakpa with long hair and a white skirt. He too requested some of the empowerments and joined the others. The young Dudjom put up a small tent in a meadow and stayed there for nineteen days.[199]

Dudjom also offered to help Kyungtrul with the empowerment manual by writing notes for the sequence. Dudjom wrote in an abbreviated style and had caught up by the end of each empowerment. Kyungtrul was then asked how long it would take him to finish the manual.

"If I make it short, it will take four months; otherwise it looks like it will take me about one year," he replied. Hearing this, Dudjom expressed surprise. But Kyungtrul made the empowerment manual so detailed and elaborate that it didn't get finished. In the end, as time passed, their combined effort was never completed. Kyungtrul said he didn't feel like staying around until the writing was done, so he left, bringing the copy of his empowerment text back to Fortress Peak.[200]

With this story in mind, when I later met with Kyungtrul, I asked him if he would please lend me what he had written so that I could read it. It was a small and beautifully composed volume, but I am sorry to say that he seemed to have gotten carried away by elaborate details—he was so extremely learned and had added in all the lines of transmission to the Mind Section. It was also amazingly profound, but if they had continued like this, the Mind Section alone would have been a large volume unto itself.

Kyungtrul admitted that Samten Gyatso had told him, "It's wonderful that you can write like this, but if I have to give the empowerment with such precise detail, it will take a year each time. I don't have time to stay at Tsurphu for a whole year!"[201]

Reading this text deepened my faith in Kyungtrul. His opening lecture in the empowerment manual was so elaborate and brilliant it surpassed anything I had ever read. It wasn't that Samten Gyatso was displeased at this—on the contrary.

At this point, Kyungtrul himself had said, "I very much doubt that my efforts in this will come to anything." And he was right—he never wrote the manuals for the Space and Instruction Sections.

❧

Back in Kham, Kyungtrul became known as a tertön and, being from a long line of ngakpas, took a consort. He was also requested to give teachings and empowerments more and more frequently. He transmitted the entire *Treasury of Precious Termas* twice.[202] While receiving the *One Hundred Chö* empowerments from Kyungtrul, my father became good friends with him. Samten Gyatso also treated him with deep respect.

As noted earlier, I invited Kyungtrul to Tsangsar monastery to give the transmissions for the Great Perfection entitled *Realization Directly Revealed*—teachings for which he showed the deepest respect—and to Lachab for the *Collected Nyingma Tantras* in a special annotated edition.[203]

In this way, he spent three months with us, and we often relaxed together and had interesting conversations. Occasionally he would say, "I must leave; I want to go to Pemakö."

But I asked him to delay his departure for the sake of the Buddha's teachings and sentient beings, and each time he replied, "All right, that's fine by me. In the end, it doesn't make any difference."

Then he would stay a while longer. One day, he suddenly left his body.

When I look back on those times and what followed in the next few years right after his passing, it appears that he had a clear foreknowledge of what would befall Tibet and Kham, though he didn't mention anything in detail.

❧

I was fortunate enough to receive three months of instructions on the *Light of Wisdom* from Kyungtrul. He was staying in a cave that was connected to a small shrine room. In the mornings he would sit outside in the sun and enjoy one of his favorite meals: pea soup. He would lick his bowl at the end and set it aside, looking fresh and content.

One morning, I mustered the courage to say, "Please teach me the *Treasury of Dharmadhatu*."

"Well, well," he replied. "Do you want me to read it to you?"

"Not just read it, I want you to explain it."

"Well, well, these days it appears that nothing is impossible," he answered, then made a joke about an ordinary lama who was teaching a laywoman the profound realization of Longchenpa, speaking as if the lama was a serene vajra master pouring forth the nectarlike Dharma for a qualified dakini at the Mansion of Lotus Light—until he burst out laughing.[204]

You see, the woman in question was actually my aunt, who had recently requested the same teaching from a disciple of Dzongsar Khyentse at Fortress Peak, which for some reason Kyungtrul found incredibly funny. He played on the word for samsara, which means "realm of possibilities," by saying, "This only goes to show that nothing is impossible."

All of which was simply Kyungtrul's way of making the point that teaching the profound *Treasury of Dharmadhatu* is no simple task. I asked again the next morning to which he replied with the same story and once again burst out laughing.

᪄

While Kyungtrul was staying with us, people would often come to him for instructions on knowing the nature of mind. One young meditator came and, as is traditional, related his experience.

At some point Kyungtrul said, "It seems to me that you should simply allow basic space and awareness to be intermingled."

"Very well, Rinpoche," the young man replied. "But how large should the space be?"

Kyungtrul kept a straight face as he replied, "Oh yes, oh yes! Mingle it with any size that makes you comfortable; that would be fine."[205]

The young fellow was persistent, however, since he continued, "Please, Rinpoche, give me the true meditation instruction on mind essence!"

"Oh yes, oh yes," he replied, still keeping a straight face. "It appears that I myself haven't received the true instruction."

One could, however, see the mirth sparkle in his eyes.

᪄

Several years before, on his way home from the *New Treasures* empowerments at Surmang, Dzigar Kongtrul stopped at Neten monastery while Kyungtrul was giving the *Treasury of Precious Termas*. They had became very close friends. Later I had the opportunity to ask Dzigar Kongtrul questions and our conversation often gravitated to the life of great masters. At times we just relaxed, talking until we heard the birds begin to sing in the early morning and realized we had totally forgotten to sleep.

One of the things Dzigar Kongtrul confided to me was that "nowadays, in all of Tibet and Kham, Kyungtrul is probably the greatest master. I have studied many of the scriptures with many a good master, but when Kyungtrul and I discussed any topic, be it philosophy or any of the sciences, I knew some points better than he did, except for one thing: he seemed to know the details of the lives of every single master in this Land of Snow.

"But, strangely enough, when we met two years later, although I had the feeling that by then I knew as much as he, once again he knew many more precise details of their lives. Then again a year later he seemed to know even more than before.[206]

"I have no idea where he learned all of these details. If they were just from the usual life stories of the masters, then I would have known them as well. Finally, I had to ask him, 'How do you know this in so much more detail than last year?'

"Kyungtrul just chuckled, telling me, 'All their lives come marching straight out of the expanse of the all-ground, like endless ripples on the surface of a great lake.' That was all he said."

Dzigar Kongtrul continued, "As far as I'm concerned, there isn't so much as a hair tip's worth of difference between Kyungtrul and the great Marpa of the Kagyu lineage—except of course that Marpa was an expert in Sanskrit. When I read about Marpa the translator, his vast insight and accomplishment is fully matched by that of my teacher, Kyungtrul. But when it comes to insight into the tantras and pith instructions, I don't feel that I would get a superior teaching even if Marpa were to arrive in person. There is no difference between them—not even as much as a mustard seed's worth.

"We know that Marpa is supposed to have attained accomplishment, but there is no doubt that this guy is realized too. Kyungtrul is a true hidden yogi—but the fact that he goes around hiding it doesn't change a thing. His clairvoyant powers are clear and precise. As far as I am concerned there is no master superior to him in this part of the world."

These were no small words coming from a teacher of Dzigar Kongtrul's caliber and sharpness, since his power of speech was incredible. Every sentence he spoke was like a sword cutting through the water, totally unimpeded. In that region of Kham, when it came to debate, whether on Sutra or Tantra, no one could keep up with him. He was also an expert in proverbs and colloquial sayings, and when he combined them with philosophical arguments, every opponent would go mute. It was hard to find a master as erudite as him. Yet he shared these words of high praise with me after Kyungtrul passed away.

There was a special weight to his words because Kyungtrul was from Nangchen, not from Derge, which was known for its learned masters. If you look back through its entire history, Nangchen had very few great scholars. In fact, Old Khyentse once said after a visit to Nangchen, "The monks over there don't even know how to wear their robes properly. They toss them on and wind up looking like they have a load on their back."

So considering where he came from, Dzigar Kongtrul's praise puts Kyungtrul even higher. And yet, even this great master passed away.

※

During our times together Kyungtrul told me quite a few stories, many from Tashi Özer of Palpung, who himself had been a student of the three great masters—Khyentse, Kongtrul and Paltrul. These three masters were classmates at Shechen monastery.[207] Paltrul was from the Golok district, a land of virtuous highland nomads. His family was either poor or too far away to offer him any support, so he would often run out of provisions.

Khyentse, however, was rather well-off due to his rich father, an aristocrat from a wealthy and powerful family. Kongtrul's family lived nearby and was fairly well-off too. So Paltrul often ate the leftover tsampa balls from his friends' plates.

After his meals Paltrul would lie down, covering his head with his monk's shawl. When Khyentse and Kongtrul would tell him he should study instead of lying down, Paltrul replied, "Why study? Isn't a human being just someone who can listen and speak? All I have to do is repeat what the teacher said. So why should I worry?"

If Paltrul were called upon to explain the topic from the previous day, he would repeat it almost verbatim and nearly better than the teacher himself. Though Kongtrul was the most diligent student and Khyentse seemed more intelligent, Paltrul was totally unimpeded.

※

Paltrul once told Tashi Özer, "Now, my son, you should be a renunciate. Live like a child of the mountains: wear the mist as your robes, keeping just a simple sheepskin coat; walk on foot with only a walking stick and forsake riding horseback. Give up all involvements and live like Milarepa!"

Tashi Özer agreed and gave away all his possessions to live as a wandering mendicant. This is how he arrived at Dzongsar, where the great Khyentse resided.

"The famous scholar Tashi Özer has arrived," the attendant announced, "and it looks like he is now a disciple of Paltrul."

"Put him up in the monks' quarters," Khyentse replied.

A whole week went by and nothing happened, so Tashi Özer thought perhaps he should take the initiative and go see the master; but the attendant told him just to stay in his room.

"I wonder what happened," he thought. "Whenever I saw Khyentse Wangpo before, he treated me with special honor. Have I done anything to displease him? He couldn't be jealous of me; that's impossible. He must be doing this to purify my bad karma and obscurations."

Although he was a great lama in his own right, these doubts disturbed Tashi Özer deeply. After a while he felt so miserable he began to cry.

But soon after he was told to come into Khyentse's room. When he entered he saw that there was a throne next to Khyentse's and on the table was a complete monk's outfit: shawl, skirt, everything.

"Hey, you!" Khyentse proclaimed. "At Palpung monastery you were awarded the rank of *khenchen*—great scholar—a great honor. What were you thinking when you threw that away to wear a stinky sheepskin? Take it off immediately and put on these robes!"

"Please don't force me," Tashi Özer tried to object.

"If you hesitate one second longer, I'll use my stick on you!" Khyentse threatened.

That was the last day he wore the old sheepskin coat.

❦

Once Paltrul said, "I hear that Shabkar lives in the lower part of Golok.[208] I am going to go meet him," and he headed off. Along the way Paltrul met a man who asked where he was going.

"I am on my way to see Lama Shabkar," said Paltrul.

"Well, you are wasting your time. I have just come from there and even if you go, you will not be able to meet him for he has recently passed on." Immediately Paltrul made one hundred full prostrations while chanting in sorrowful tones.

Some time later, he remarked, "I wanted to meet Lama Shabkar not because there was any teaching I needed to receive—I have nothing to ask of him, and he would have nothing to ask of me—but in the world today he was the one with the most authentic bodhisattva spirit. I felt what great merit it would be if I could see his face just once!

"Well then, there's nothing to be done. Let's turn around and go back. I have made a mandala offering by bowing one hundred times. That will have to suffice."

❦

One time, while Paltrul was living at Dzogchen monastery in Derge, Do Khyentse, another great master, came from the lower part of Kham to visit him. On his arrival Do Khyentse mentioned that he had set out that very same morning, which was quite impossible since the journey typically took fifteen days on horseback.

On the other hand, who knows—since Do Khyentse was capable of reviving the dead, like the great siddhas of India, and had done so on many occasions. For example, I've heard that he had a following in the form of a huge pack of wild meat-loving dogs. Sometimes, as a feast, he would carve the flesh off the bones of a deer and feed it to the dogs.

Then he would tell his human disciples to pile the bones on the deer's skin, and as soon as he struck the skin with his staff, the deer would stand up and dart off. This happened many times, and hunters began to routinely offer a few antelope or deer to the master and his disciples. They would eat the meat, and though Khampas enjoy taking the bones and sucking on the marrow, Do Khyentse forbade them to. Instead they would collect the bones and pile them on each skin, and when Do Khyentse hit the skin with his staff, the deer would jump up and run off.

But once, not realizing he wasn't supposed to, a new disciple cracked open a bone. Do Khyentse tried to stop him, but was too late. When they collected all the bones, they included the pieces from the new disciple and wrapped them up with the others in the hide. When Do Khyentse tapped the bundle with his staff, the deer staggered to its feet and hobbled off on a broken leg.

☙

Anyway, this was the Do Khyentse who had come to Derge to make sure Paltrul became his disciple. Upon his arrival, he promptly began circumambulating the main temple counterclockwise, the opposite direction taken by everyone else, including Paltrul. Two people are bound to meet when circling in opposite directions.

But the moment the two crossed paths, Do Khyentse yelled at Paltrul, "You old dog! Charlatan! Fraud!" Not only did he hurl abuse on Paltrul, but he also slapped him and when Paltrul tried to get up Do Khyentse knocked him back down.

It suddenly dawned on Paltrul that this stranger might be Do Khyentse. His next thought was, "This master is a *heruka* in person. Why is he abusing me?"

Then, all of a sudden, his usual way of perceiving reality was brought to a complete halt.

"That's it, Old Dog!" Do Khyentse yelled. "From now on, for you, that's it!"

Paltrul later told Tashi Özer, "That was when I recognized the nature of mind in its naked state, without the least clinging or concept. At that moment, I was brought face to face with the authentic awakened state. That's why I now use 'Old Dog' as my secret initiation name, since it was bestowed upon me by the great master Do Khyentse."

You could call that a *very* direct pointing-out instruction.

❧

Once, a yogi from Nangchen named Angi Tendar—who was not just an ordinary practitioner but quite realized—went to see Paltrul.

"Where are you from?" asked Paltrul.

"I am a disciple of Tsoknyi in Nangchen."

"Well, well. I have heard mention of this Tsoknyi of Nangchen who is supposed to have realized the view of the Great Perfection. Isn't he the one who is so fond of teaching in a way that, as Milarepa said, 'If you practice in the morning, you are a buddha in the morning, and if you practice at night, you are a buddha at night—and the destined person of karmic fortune becomes a buddha even without meditating'?

"If this is your teacher, tell me: How many of his disciples have attained the rainbow body?" Paltrul teased.

"There was one who *would* have attained the rainbow body," Tendar replied, "if he hadn't passed away from badly infected boils."

Now there is no way in the world *any* illness can prevent an advanced practitioner from attaining the rainbow body, so for a moment Paltrul was left speechless.

Then they both burst out laughing.

❧

The quote Paltrul used came from Milarepa's life story. Before Milarepa met Marpa, he had requested instructions from a Dzogchen master.

"You seem to be a formidable practitioner," the master told Milarepa. "Therefore, I will give you my Dzogchen teachings, which brings liberation through seeing, hearing and remembering." And he told him the very words Paltrul had repeated, about becoming a buddha in the morning or the night.

The real meaning of this instruction is that whenever one remembers to recognize the awakened state, that moment is in essence identical with that of the Buddha, be it morning or night. What's more, recognition of the natural state is not an act of meditating; anyone capable of training in this is therefore said to become "a buddha without meditating." This is true for someone who not only recognizes the awakened state *authentically*, but also trains in it continuously. That is what is meant by "destined person of karmic fortune." (In the past, Shechen

Kongtrul also gave me the instruction, "Hey, you, don't meditate, don't meditate!" meaning that the awakened state is not an act of meditating.)

Unfortunately, what Milarepa understood from the Dzogchen teacher was that he was such a special person that there was no need for him to even train in the nature of mind. He misunderstood the meaning of *simplicity* and spent a week just taking it easy.

On the eighth day the Dzogchen master called him back in and asked, "Explain to me your present experience and understanding."

"What experience and understanding?" replied Milarepa. "I don't have any. You said that someone like me doesn't need to practice, so I didn't."

"Oh my!" the master exclaimed. "It seems I gave away the highest teachings too soon! I don't think I can help you now. But in the Drowo valley to the south of here lives the great translator Marpa, a yogi of the new transmission of Vajrayana. You and he have a karmic link, so go see him."

The very moment Milarepa heard Marpa's name, he was thrilled to the bone, so that every hair on his body tingled and his eyes filled with tears. That was a sure sign of a karmic connection. Immediately Milarepa asked to be excused and set off to find Marpa.

One day, a dead man was brought before Paltrul for the necessary rituals. But after the bereaved family had left with the corpse, Paltrul burst out laughing. Surprised at this, one of his disciples asked why he was so amused.

"When I first saw the family I felt like crying. Just yesterday this man had come to see me, alive and well. Then today his poor family brings in his lifeless body, dull and bloated. How sad it was to see his wretched face.

"But when I looked from the state of meditation to see where his spirit had gone, I saw that he had already taken rebirth in a god realm.[209] He is a joyful little child with a beautiful face, sitting on his mother's lap. Samsara is truly strange! His relatives are still crying and yet he is full of joy—what a strange world!"

Another day a disciple asked him, "Rinpoche, how many past lives do you remember?"

"I can't see as clearly as the great bodhisattvas nor am I able to see countless lives like the Buddha could. But I could give you details of at least five hundred. Also, if I really had to, I could tell you what will happen in my next five hundred."

When a master of Paltrul's caliber gave teachings on the nature of samsara and reality, it wasn't merely dry words.

Every afternoon Paltrul was in the habit of chanting the famous aspiration for rebirth in the realm of Buddha Amitabha. He usually sang it outside at a gentle pace, while prostrating in the direction of the setting sun.

One day, upon returning, he told a disciple, "I just heard some very bad news."

"What was it, Rinpoche?"

"I met an ant who told me 'Paltrul is about to die.' Do you know how to chant the ejection of consciousness according to *Longchen Nyingtig*?"

"Of course," replied the disciple.

"Please sing it for me, then."

At the end of the chant, the disciple uttered PHAT three times and on the third one, Paltrul left his body.

༄

Near the end of his life, tiny white pearls, or ringsel, occasionally fell from Kyungtrul's face. Sometimes people mentioned this to him, but they would soon regret it because his only response was, "What an evil sign—you can also find such ringsel in pigs. It's surely bad luck when someone who is still alive leaves relics. Who ever heard of that? Get rid of them immediately! Just throw them outside. And don't ever bring this up again!"

That's what he said, but think about it—isn't it a bit strange? So people would collect the ringsel without him knowing, filtering his urine and the water he used to wash his face in order to find them. They even found that his feces were full of ringsel.

Kyungtrul appeared to have totally transcended the state of delusion. He was always calm and smiling—he never even let on when he was seriously ill. He passed away at a monastery near Lachab.

The day before leaving his body, he told his disciples to perform a particular ritual for the guardians of the Dharma, saying, "The wisdom protectors will guide you in this life, in the bardo and in the next life. So now, please perform the *Mending of the Sacred Link* on my behalf.

"The most impressive way to die," Kyungtrul continued, "is like the Chokling of Neten. He was on his way back from a visit to Riwoche and on the road he saw a tiny hermitage up on the hillside. He asked to be taken there. The next day, he quietly let his mind dissolve into the basic space of all phenomena. There was not a single sound of wailing or crying around him, and nobody pestered him to remain. He passed on in an atmosphere of complete tranquility. When one dies, that's how it should be done. And you, my disciples, try to leave this life in the same way."

The next morning they found that their master had passed away.

~

I didn't know it then but those days with Kyungtrul would mark my last extended stay in Nangchen. Right after, I returned to Central Tibet to receive the *Treasury of Precious Termas,* and began serving the Karmapa more and more. And, as I came to realize, Tibet as I knew it was soon going to be changed forever.

Part Three
Central Tibet

30

At Tsurphu with the Karmapa

When Karsey Kongtrul visited Lachab, I requested a letter from him telling me to attend the empowerments of the *Treasury of Precious Termas* that he was going to give at Tsurphu. As he was the greatest among all the Kagyu masters of the time, my monastery had no choice but to let me go.

When I appeared at Tsurphu, he showed great delight in seeing me again and said that although he had no ambition to be someone who gave the extraordinary *Treasury of Precious Termas*, nevertheless he felt obligated to do so as the Karmapa had asked him to.

Then he added, "Since you are here, I feel more enthusiastic; there seems to be a purpose to it now." He frequently spoke to me with such affection. I stayed there for the seven months it took to complete all the empowerments.

Kongtrul had extremely high realization, and one got the impression that he was definitely someone who had reached the level known as the collapse of delusion. Every afternoon following the empowerments, he would take a stroll, circumambulating the main temples. It seemed to me that his body was moving while his mind never left the state of samadhi.

When he spoke, it was mostly about practice and how to develop further.

I'm not sure what his experience was, but sometimes he would leave his shawl and most of his robes behind while walking to his chamber and arrive in only his undergarments.

"Rinpoche! What happened? What are you doing?" one of his attendants would ask.

"What do mean?"

44.
The young Karmapa

45. Mural of Tsurphu monastery

"You took off your clothes on the way in."

"I thought I was already home," Karsey Kongtrul would reply.

Don't get me wrong here; he wasn't just eccentric—he was extremely realized. This odd behavior was just a peculiarity of the collapse of delusion, which he reached a few years before he passed away.

❧

At the end of the empowerments I asked Karsey Kongtrul for permission to remain at Tsurphu in retreat for three years, and he happily agreed to write another letter to my monastery to make this possible.

In those days I was quite shy and didn't feel I should impose myself on such a great master, so I only saw him when he specifically asked for me. However, on our last walk together, he confided in me what his experience was. This was something he would never state in public, but for some reason he trusted me.

"What I am about to say is straight and honest talk," he began. "The fifteenth Karmapa, Khakyab Dorje, was the one who pointed out the nature of my mind. He told me to refrain from extensive study; he said that although there are many important streams of teachings kept alive in eastern Tibet, as he put it, 'You have to uphold the teachings of the ultimate transmission.'[210] Therefore, as your main practice, simply sustain the continuity of the natural state that I have shown you—don't try to be a great scholar.' That is the command my father, the Karmapa, gave me. So except for grammar and spelling I haven't studied much.

"Nevertheless, from training in the natural state, I have reached a level where the entire valley of Tsurphu appears as the mandala of Chakrasamvara and with each passing day conceptual thoughts are fewer and farther between. Now there is only one problem left: I still lose presence of mind in the moment of falling asleep. It lasts no more than a couple of seconds, but I am sorry to admit I do become unaware.

"Apart from that, this mind no longer gets distracted at any time, day or night. The view is wide open and continuous, and there is no parting from it. I'm telling you this in private; until today I haven't mentioned it to anyone else. I am now confident that I can die at any moment and not be in trouble."

That's how he spoke. Later it turned out that these were also his parting remarks to me, because I didn't see him again before my return to Kham. And it also seems an indication that he knew his death was imminent.

After the empowerments, I went into retreat high up the mountain above Tsurphu monastery, at a beautiful cave known as Lotus Garuda Fortress. The hermitage had an impressive view and had been the hermitage of many past incarnations of the Kagyu lineage masters.[211] The Karmapa gave me his permission to stay there, as well as providing a servant. He also very kindly sent builders up to construct some extra rooms for my retreat.

While I was in retreat at Tsurphu, as it happened, my oldest son, Chökyi Nyima, was born. At the time Chökyi Nyima's mother, Kunsang Dechen, was staying near the monastery of his previous incarnation.[212]

Actually, ever since I was a young boy, I had felt quite bashful and shy in general. For instance, in the countryside, people usually go a little distance from the house to relieve themselves. But if a house was surrounded by open fields, I found it very difficult to do so with people watching. So I would wander off looking for someplace more private. Sometimes a benefactor would think I was leaving or going for a stroll and would chase after me to find out where I was going—how I wished they would go away! But of course they had no idea, so they would just trot along until finally I would have to return to their house with a full bladder. Then I'd wait for my next chance to sneak out, this time without an escort. That kind of bashfulness can be very inconvenient.

46. Lotus Garuda Fortress above Tsurphu monastery

In the early part of my life, I also had been very shy around people of the opposite sex—I almost didn't dare to look at women except from a distance. I think I was in my early twenties before I had my first girlfriend. It never entered my mind to get married, but neither was I interested in being a monk.

Anyway, I met Kunsang Dechen while in Central Tibet and she returned with me to Kham, slowly becoming known as my consort. This was several years before Chokyi Nyima was born. She was quite a practitioner and had already completed the preliminary practices thirteen times. People were very impressed by her perseverance. Imagine doing one million three hundred thousand prostrations! Her family had a lot of cattle, and she would take all the excess butter and send it to Lhasa to offer butter lamps in sets of one hundred thousand, one after the other.

Now that the truth was out that I was not a monk, I lost some of my shyness. I even slowly overcame my reluctance to look women in the eye.

❧

Near the end of my retreat, I received a letter from Karsey Kongtrul telling me to return to Lachab. The people at my monastery must have pressed him to send this letter, because he mentioned that they were in desperate need of funds. It seems Samten Gyatso's tulku was still too young to take responsibility, some of the buildings needed repairs and the main lama—me—was off in Central Tibet.

Karsey Kongtrul's letter said, "Your monastery is pushing very hard. It appears there is no way you can avoid visiting Kham one more time. So please go back there as soon as your three-year retreat is over."

I did not want to disobey Karsey Kongtrul. Besides, the political situation in Tibet was steadily deteriorating and I felt a pressing need to visit Kham anyway. So when my retreat was over, I asked the Karmapa for permission to return to Lachab and began to prepare for the long journey back to Kham. Yet it turned out there was something else I had to do before going.

Years earlier, as I mentioned, Samten Gyatso had given the *New Treasures* at Surmang monastery in Nangchen. On that occasion, many of the extremely realized masters of the Kagyu lineage had come to receive these transmissions from him. As was usual, however, Samten Gyatso had kept some of the important empowerments secret—including the *Three Sections of the Great Perfection*—and hadn't transmitted them.

Later on, Surmang Tentrul and Karsey Kongtrul transmitted much of what they had received to the young Karmapa. Yet there were still six volumes missing—those that Samten Gyatso had withheld at Surmang—and the Karmapa was very determined to possess the complete lineage of the *New Treasures*. Apparently, he had singled me out to offer him the rest. Once when we had met in Nangchen, the Karmapa had asked me to bring those books along to Tsurphu on my next visit, hinting, "It is possible that someday you may need to give me the empowerments for the *Three Sections*."

"That is completely out of the question," I replied. "I couldn't possibly do that!"

"Why?" the Karmapa responded. "This lineage is still unbroken."

I tried to put up an argument, "It has two lines, one through Tsewang Norbu to the two incarnations of Chokgyur Lingpa and my uncles Samten Gyatso and Tersey. The other lineage comes through Tsewang Norbu to the great master Katok Situ and Dzongsar Khyentse. These lineages are still alive. Even though Samten Gyatso passed it on to my father and me, the lamas who received it through Katok Situ are still alive.

"So there is no reason you should depend on someone like me," I continued. "I neither understand it nor know how to pass it on. But next time I return from Kham, I will make sure to bring a copy of the scripture, as well as the necessary icons, as an offering to you."

Years later, on my way to Central Tibet, I mentioned the Karmapa's remarks to my uncle Tersey. Later, Uncle Tersey wrote me, "My mother, the tertön's daughter Könchok Paldrön, said that after three generations, the seal of secrecy would be naturally lifted. At that time there will no longer be any fault in propagating the *Three Sections* more widely. These were the words of the great tertön himself. The three generations are to be counted as first Tsewang Norbu, second Samten Gyatso, and the third one appears to be you. So you must fulfill the Karmapa's command!"

If it weren't for this letter, I would not have had the courage to pass these teachings on, but instead would have insisted on waiting for Uncle Tersey to come.[213]

Anyway, one day at Tsurphu I had received the message that the Karmapa wanted to see me right away. When I arrived at his quarters, the Karmapa told me that I had to give him the empowerments for the *Three Sections*. I was astonished and objected, "How can I do that? I'm nothing special. Don't ask me to do such a thing."

I noticed that a small stack of thick cushions covered with a huge tiger skin had been set up beside his seat. I also noted that the copy of the *Three Sections* that I had brought was already lying open on a decorated table in front of the cushions.

Then the Karmapa commanded, "Sit down! Begin with the reading transmission right now. Then start with the first empowerment tomorrow. I need to go to Sky Lake soon, so make sure you finish everything by then."

The shrine had been arranged and the mandala laid out, and the shrine master was already holding the plate with the mandala offering. Before I knew what was happening, they had begun the offering chant and the Karmapa had placed a large gold coin in the middle of the mandala plate.

"It is my custom always to offer gold when I request an important Dzogchen empowerment or make a new Dharma connection," he said. Then he signaled me to start.

"You can't force me to create the negative karma of placing myself above the Karmapa," I protested. "There is no tradition that allows an ordinary person like myself to confer an empowerment upon a Buddha such as yourself." I pleaded over and over again to be excused.

The Karmapa took on a wrathful air, "I have never met anyone as stubborn as you! I don't know anyone who refuses my wishes; everyone always listens! I'm asking you to give an empowerment—isn't that a sign of my respect? But all I get in return is your refusal. How can anyone be like this?" He looked quite displeased.

In spite of this, I bowed down once more and said, "Please, don't force me! The line of transmission need not be broken just because *I* don't give it; there are greater lamas in Kham who can offer this empowerment, like Dzongsar Khyentse.[214] In this present age you won't find any master in these parts greater than him! You only need to send a letter and there's no doubt he would come. I'll be happy to carry the letter; when I get back to Kham, I'll go straight to Derge to deliver it." Again I bowed down.

The Karmapa then said, "I've had great hopes that you would give me this transmission. Don't refuse me. This is not just some whim. Not only are you a descendant of Chokgyur Lingpa, you are also a tulku. I chose you only after careful consideration. When I ask someone to give me a transmission, they are not supposed to refuse. You are the first ever to do so!"

He stamped on the floor furiously, red-faced.

The Karmapa's attendant, the Tsurphu vajra master, with whom I got along really well, had been frantically signaling to me to come over to him, out of earshot. Obviously he knew the Karmapa was quite displeased and didn't dare to approach.

"Can't you see that our Wish-Fulfilling Jewel has become quite displeased?" the attendant whispered. "Yet you still refuse to relent? Don't you understand that going against him will cause a rift in your relationship and damage your samaya with him? Unless you offer to give him the empowerment, how can you still claim to have pure samaya with the Karmapa? This will make it difficult for you to come back here—please reconsider! Please begin the transmission right now!

"Apart from you, who in Chokgyur Lingpa's lineage is still alive to offer it to our Wish-Fulfilling Jewel? If you don't give it, that particular lineage will be broken. The Karmapa specifically wants this lineage, which goes through Chokgyur Lingpa's family. There is no reason for you to displease the Karmapa by being so stubborn. Just yield and give it!"

Now the Karmapa turned around and said sternly, "Well then, what's it going to be? Will you start now?"

Somehow, "Certainly, Rinpoche!" just slipped out. I took a seat below his throne and prepared to begin.²¹⁵

47.
Shri Singha—the early master of Dzogchen

"Do you really think you can give the precious Great Perfection from the floor," the Karmapa objected, "as if water could flow uphill?"

So I was finally forced to sit on a throne. The shrine master began to chant the mandala offering a second time and I began the reading transmission, which took two days.

When I finished it, the Karmapa said, "It's now time to begin the empowerment! Today is a good day, let's start this evening."

"Oh dread!" I thought. The Karmapa had already called in the shrine masters and ordered them to begin preparing the tormas. We began with the empowerment for Shri Singha, the Indian master who is central to the Dzogchen lineage.

⁂

Only five days were left until our Wish-Fulfilling Jewel had to leave for Sky Lake in northern Tibet. Since I had no shrine master experienced in this transmission—just an old monk from Lachab—every night I had to piece together the empowerment manuals for the next day. By the end, I was so exhausted from lack of sleep that my urine turned red with blood.

When it was over I needed a good rest. But the Karmapa had other plans, "You must accompany me on the journey to Sky Lake, so that every morning and evening you can continue giving me the remaining empowerments from the *New Treasures*."

He also wanted me to give the entrustment to the life force of Tseringma, the female guardian of Chokgyur Lingpa's treasures. I took the bursar aside and asked if it would be all right to offer them at a later date and begin my journey back to Kham. Every morning and evening droves of people would flock to see the Karmapa, and there would be absolutely no opportunity for me to offer him the transmissions.

⁂

Many extraordinary things happened in the company of the Karmapa. For example, he kept hundreds of birds. Karsey Kongtrul had given him a bird with an extremely melodious voice, which was very dear to him. When this bird got sick, he kept it alone in a special room. One day he was told that the bird was dying and he asked that it be brought to him.

The bird was placed on the table before him.

"This bird needs a special blessing," he said. So he took a small vessel with mustard seeds and made his usual chant for dispelling obstacles as he threw some of the grains on the bird. Suddenly he said, "There's nothing more to do—it is dying. No blessing can prevent it."

Then he turned to me, saying, "Pick it up and hold it in your hand."

The bird was still alive and it sat there in my palm with one eye half-open. But soon I saw its head slump, then its wings. But, strangely enough, the bird then straightened back up and simply sat there. An attendant whispered, "It's in samadhi!"

I didn't want to disturb it, so I asked him to put it on the table. The attendant seemed used to handling birds in this state, because he didn't disturb it as he put the bird down.

Somewhat astonished, I commented to the attendant, "How remarkable! A bird that sits up straight right after death!?!"

"That's nothing special. They all do it," he replied matter-of-factly.

A second attendant chimed in, "Every single bird from the Karmapa's aviary that dies sits up for a while after death. But we're so used to this, it has ceased to amaze us."

"When birds die," I objected, "they keel over and fall off their branch to the ground—they don't keep sitting!"

"Well, when the Karmapa is around, this is what they do," replied the attendant. "But you're right—when he's away, they die the normal way."

At this point everyone had arrived for dinner and I had to sit down, however I couldn't help keeping my eye on the bird while we ate. Halfway through dinner its right wing slumped and soon after the left followed.

An attendant whispered, "Wish-Fulfilling Jewel, it seems the samadhi is about to finish."

The Karmapa paid no attention and kept eating, even when the bird finally keeled over. I looked at my watch—approximately three hours had gone by. No matter what the attendants said, I was still pretty amazed because I saw it die in my hands. Most people probably wouldn't believe this unless they saw it with their own eyes.

The Karmapa was very fond of dogs as well and he had several Pekingese that, I was told, also died sitting up with their forelegs parallel.

In short, the Karmapa was an incredible human being.

~

The Karmapa was so busy those days that I never was able to continue the empowerments. Then a well-timed letter from Uncle Tersey asking me to return to Nangchen offered me a graceful excuse to leave. And so I was temporarily excused.

After leaving Tsurphu I took the northern route that went by Drong monastery. Kunsang Dechen was staying near there with my first son. Chökyi Nyima was the reincarnation of the head lama, Tendzin Dorje, who had been a close disciple of the great master Shakya Shri and a dear friend of my uncle Tersey. He was also a disciple of Samten Gyatso, having spent at least four months with him.[216]

Tendzin Dorje once told me about the time he went to see Tsewang Norbu in Lhasa.

"Knowing that this master was the son and close disciple of Chokgyur Lingpa, I had sincerely looked forward to meeting him. I sat down with others in the waiting room when all of a sudden a tall, naked man comes out of Tsewang Norbu's room and stomps across the wooden floor headed directly for the toilet, his testicles swaying with each step. You should have seen the Lhasa women and their young daughters scampering to get out of the way!"

The others ran out of the room, but Tendzin Dorje—who was very open-minded and not an ardent admirer of superficial etiquette—just kept sitting. A few minutes later the naked man stomped back through the room. A short time later Tendzin Dorje was shown into the master's room only to discover that the naked man was no other than Tsewang Norbu himself.

In his area, Tendzin Dorje was known as the Black Jambhala, the god of wealth, and it was said that whoever had the fortune to invite him to their home would become rich. Tendzin Dorje was someone with a "lucky hand," meaning that old and precious things always seemed to end up in his possession. His monastic household was considered extremely well-to-do. Tendzin Dorje himself was the owner of at least one thousand fine horses; at the time of the communist takeover, there were still five hundred horses left.

While Tendzin Dorje was the head lama, Drong monastery was known to possess some of the finest dance costumes west of Kham; they were used in extensive rituals and sacred dances.[217]

When the communists took over they confiscated all the costumes of fine brocade and all the yellow hats used in ceremonies, as well as the other ritual implements and burned them all in one big pile.

~

I had been at Drong monastery for a just a few months when a messenger arrived saying that the Karmapa was ordering me to return to Tsurphu. It was "time to give the remaining empowerments." So I headed back to finish the task.

Meanwhile Karsey Kongtrul had begun a three-year retreat when he received the news that his close friend and disciple had passed away in Nangchen.[218] He tried to be excused from attending the funeral ceremonies, but the messengers wouldn't accept his refusal. When he finally consented to leave retreat and go to Kham, he warned, "All right, if I must then I shall. But I won't return to Central Tibet."

While Karsey Kongtrul was in Kham, I was with the Karmapa back at Tsurphu. One day the Karmapa suddenly exclaimed, "Tulku! I just had a very bad dream. I can't possibly pretend that it's good."

"What was it?" I asked.

"I saw that a stupa made of pure crystal descended from the vast reaches of space. Inside the sphere of the stupa I could clearly see a statue of Buddha Shakyamuni made of pure gold. In my dream I stood up with the intention of taking hold of the statue. But, just as it was about to land, it rose again. There was no chance; it was already out of reach and soon vanished into the depths of space.

48.
The young
Dalai Lama

"In this life, I regard two masters as my root gurus. One is the Situ of Palpung and when he passed away I had a similar, inauspicious dream. This morning's dream made me wonder if my other root guru hasn't passed on as well," he remarked, referring to Karsey Kongtrul.

Of course I tried to reassure him that this probably wasn't the case, but he replied, "No, my heart is uneasy. It definitely wasn't a good dream. I fear that my loving protector is gone."

Several weeks later, the Karmapa went to Lhasa to visit the Dalai Lama at the Potala and to receive several empowerments from the old Kadam tradition from him. The Karmapa also sponsored the grand empowerment of Kalachakra at Norbu Lingka Park and I accompanied him as his assistant. While preparing to leave Tsurphu, the Karmapa told his personal attendant, "Make sure you bring the guru sadhana of Marpa, Milarepa, and Gampopa," the three forefathers of the Kagyu lineage.

But sometimes the monks at Tsurphu were quite the independent thinkers. When the attendant left the anteroom, he wondered, "What's the use of bringing that text to Lhasa? He's about to receive the Kalachakra from the Dalai Lama. I don't know of any custom allowing private rituals while partaking in a grand empowerment."

I pointed out that if our Wish-Fulfilling Jewel told him to do something, he simply had to do it. But he balked, objecting, "What possible reason could there be for taking that text?" Later that day, the Karmapa asked him once again if he had packed the text. The attendant lied, saying he had. In an aside to me, he repeated, "There's no way he'll need that text."

Again I had to tell him, "Don't talk like that! If he asks you to do something, just do it!"

The next morning, just as we were about to leave, the Karmapa asked yet again, "Now, you *have* brought that text—haven't you?"

The attendant replied, "Of course I have." Then he went outside and said to me, "That's the third time he's mentioned it!"

I warned him he better bring the text or he would get into a lot of trouble in Lhasa. He said, "Okay, I can carry it! What's the big deal?" Then he went off and brought the text.

Down in Lhasa, grand arrangements were under way for the Kalachakra empowerment. All the dignitaries of Central Tibet had assembled for this important occasion. The ceremonies would take five or six days.

We arrived a few days early. The Karmapa was one of the few masters in Tibet invested by the government with the special honor of traveling under the "parasol of the Dharma," a dignified procession accompanied by great fanfare, as he did on his visit to the Jokhang. Besides the Karmapa, only the Dalai Lama, the head of the Sakya School, the throne holder of Ganden, and a very few select others could be shown this honor inside the city of Lhasa. Otherwise, there was a prohibition against honoring one's lama with such lavish signs of respect.

The Karmapa visited the Jowo statue, where he made copious offerings of butter lamps. On his way back, he was invited to dine at the family home of Karsey Kongtrul's mother, the respected consort of the fifteenth Karmapa.

The bursar and chief steward of Tsurphu were all seated for a meal when—against all the mores and etiquette of Central Tibet—a red-faced and exhausted

Khampa burst into the house. He could be heard saying he had just ridden in from Thrangu Gompa and had an urgent message.

"Hey!" he exclaimed. "Karsey Kongtrul has died! I and two others were immediately dispatched to tell you. I have here his seal, stamped on this scarf, to prove it. I used it to switch horses along the way, so it only took us twenty days to get here.[219] We arrived in Lhasa this morning and were told this is his family's house. We also heard that the Karmapa is here, so let us in to see him right away!"

One of the Tsurphu officials tried to hush him. "Could you please lower your voice and be quiet?" They immediately ushered the messengers into another room under the pretext of serving them a meal.

Apparently Karsey Kongtrul had begun the ceremonies upon arrival at Thrangu Gompa. Then one day he went to spend a few days at the nearby cave of the famous Mipham and it was there that he had passed away.

The bursar reasoned, "We can't tell the Karmapa this bad news just now. This is surely not the time or place. It's the Jamgön's family home," he said referring to Karsey Kongtrul. "I suggest we wait until after the Karmapa has met with the Dalai Lama—otherwise their meeting will be very inauspicious. I know that our Wish-Fulfilling Jewel will be deeply upset; I saw that when the Situ of Palpung passed away. We *cannot* tell him now!"

So, the two officials prevented the sad news from being conveyed. They decided that the messengers should go somewhere else for a time, and then tell the Karmapa after he had met with the Dalai Lama.

The next day, after the meeting, I advised them, "You can't delay this any longer, or our Wish-Fulfilling Jewel will give you a severe reprimand. It would be best to tell him tonight, or tomorrow morning at the latest."

Dudjom Rinpoche was in China at this time, and so we stayed at his house that night, where the Karmapa was shown great hospitality. But the next day I discovered that the officials still hadn't broken the news.

"If you don't tell him now," I scolded them, "I'm not going to stick around and be party to your timidity."

"Please don't go!" they pleaded. "If you do, we'll be sent to look for you."

When the officials finally told the Karmapa, they got a well-deserved tongue-lashing for their presumptuousness.

One of them implored, "Wish-Fulfilling Jewel, please don't be so upset!"

"You are going to tell me what to be upset about?" the Karmapa retorted. "I'm not upset like a worldly person. I'm upset for the beings of this time who don't have the merit to keep such a great master! Karsey Kongtrul was truly a master who had transcended delusion—a rare master indeed! During his final years, he fully matched the example for realization set by the masters of the Kagyu lineage."

Then he began to weep for quite some time.

Meanwhile, just outside his room, many government officials had taken seats, awaiting an audience. Foremost among them was the regent of Tibet, who holds the highest political office. When he prostrates, even the Dalai Lama and the Karmapa have to stand as a sign of respect.

Government officials in Lhasa can be quite arrogant and pushy, but the Karmapa's attendants didn't dare bring them in just then, thinking it would be inappropriate for them to see the Karmapa's tears.

But at my request he wiped his eyes before receiving the first dignitary, so as not to be misunderstood by worldly people.

The Karmapa's first response to the sad news was to send a gift of condolence to Karsey Kongtrul's elderly mother and the rest of his family. Then he said to his attendant, "I told you to bring a guru sadhana of Marpa, Milarepa, and Gampopa—do you have it?"

"Of course, Wish-Fulfilling Jewel!" the attendant was able to reply, honestly this time.

"Set up a shrine and perform it every third day from now on," the Karmapa ordered.

That was a good lesson in why one should always do whatever the Karmapa asks, no matter what.

After the Kalachakra was over I asked to be excused for my journey back to Kham. Once again the Karmapa revealed his clairvoyant abilities when he asked me where I intended to stay upon my return there.

Now, the Karmapa wasn't just an ordinary person, so I figured his question must have some special significance.

"Wish-Fulfilling Jewel, I'm going to stay at Fortress Peak. You remember the place; you stayed there for a week when you visited Kham."

"You won't stay there," the Karmapa replied. "Just you wait and see. I swear you won't!"

The Karmapa spoke in plain language and used Khampa slang for swearing, "If I'm wrong, I'll take on all of your bad karma." What he meant was that he was one hundred percent certain.

Being rather obstinate I still had no doubt that I would stay there, since I could see nothing to prevent it. But the Karmapa insisted, "I'm telling you, you won't be able to stay there. Listen to me, you have to come back to Central Tibet as soon as you can! You must not stay in Kham!"

The next day, when I asked to be excused, the Karmapa insisted, "Don't go to Kham this year. But if you feel you really must go, then don't stay for long—just long enough to pack your belongings and return here."

Again I extolled the virtues of my retreat place at Fortress Peak, "My plan is to stay in retreat there for the rest of my life."

"I know," the Karmapa warned, "but you'll never get the chance to do it. It will never happen."

"There is one way to make it possible," I replied. "Fortress Peak is the special place for performing the longevity rituals for the king of Nangchen, and he always sponsors either Samten Gyatso or me, with a few attendants. He covers all expenses for food and ceremonies. Right now I secretly have another lama in my place covering for me. The royal court of Nangchen doesn't know that I'm in Central Tibet, and they would be very upset if they found out. The king would be angry and make my life difficult.

"But once I return I will be head of the monastery, and so I will be in charge of my life. That's why I know that I'll be able to stay in retreat."

"That's what you think," the Karmapa persisted, "but you won't be able to!"

The next day the Karmapa asked me, "Where do you plan on staying when you return to Kham?"

I blurted out that I was intent on staying at Fortress Peak.

"By the Three Jewels! You'll see—it will never happen!"

"Why not? I am a Nangchen lama and no lama can live there without following the king's wishes. Samten Gyatso's tulku is still very young, so there is only me to perform the rituals. I cannot possibly abandon Fortress Peak until he is older."

"Just the same, you won't stay there."

When I started to object yet again, he simply said, "Well, well! Then we'll just have to wait and see who is right!"

On the eve of my departure, the Karmapa told me, "Let's be careful about parting tomorrow. Twice in the past when I bid my teachers farewell, things didn't turn out so well. First it was with the precious Situ. I followed him along the way in an elaborate parting ceremony, but I never met him again. Then I did the same with Karsey Kongtrul and I never saw him again either. Therefore I think it would be better if we said good-bye this evening. So don't come to see me in the morning."

As a farewell present he gave me twelve yaks of the small but sturdy Central Tibetan type. Then he repeated, "Make sure you come back to Central Tibet as soon as possible. You may think that you can practice in Kham, but I'm telling you it would be better for you to do retreat at Tsurphu! I'll be sending you a letter—make sure you come as soon as you get it!"

The next morning I started off for Kham, still firm in my belief that I was going to end my days in retreat at my beautiful hermitage Fortress Peak.

☙

Immediately upon arriving in Kham, I began making arrangements for my retreat. Fortress Peak was about a day's journey from Lachab where Samten Gyatso's young tulku was staying at the time.[220] His father was an influential governor in Kham, a good-hearted man, but also attached to the belief that his family and position were of immense importance. Not long after I had begun retreat, he began to meddle. He felt that there was much work to be done at the monastery and didn't want to burden his son with all these managerial responsibilities.

"The young tulku should be the one to stay at Fortress Peak," he wrote me. "Being the older lama, you should reside at Lachab so that you can take better care of monastery affairs, rather than just staying carefree in the mountains, having yourself a good old time."

I gave the excuse that I had to do the ceremonies for the king of Nangchen. "It's better for me to be in a mountain retreat and fine for the tulku to live in the monastery. I'll take care of business from here."

The governor sent back the message implying that it was impossible for me to take care of affairs from Fortress Peak and that he would not allow me to do as I wanted.

"Why not?" I countered. "How can the tulku perform ceremonies for the king? I'm the only one who can do them properly. Do you want me to go against our king? That won't be good for either of us."

"No," he replied, "the tulku should stay at Fortress Peak. I'll send up a lama to do the longevity practice. I want the tulku to stay there and you are welcome to come back down to the monastery."

To back-up his argument, he now started to quote other lamas including his brother, "I have just been to Dilyak monastery and discussed this with Sabchu Rinpoche, and he completely agrees with me!"

His attitude was starting to annoy me. I retorted, "Isn't it the case that someone who is about to stay in long retreat is allowed to mind his own business?"

"No, it's not!" the tulku's father replied. He was quite obstinate, the kind of person who only becomes more inflexible the more you oppose him. At this point I remembered what Sabchu had once told me about being skillful in discussing things with his brother and not opposing him directly.

I thought to myself, "He won't be persuaded if I remain so firm. I should try a gentle approach. Since he is the father of the Ngaktrin tulku, there is no benefit in starting an argument."

So I agreed to move my retreat to Lachab and the governor moved his son up to Fortress Peak. Lachab was a large monastery, so I didn't feel that it really mattered that much. I entrusted the young tulku to my aunt's care at the hermitage, closed off my quarters and didn't allow any visits, not even from benefactors. In this way, I avoided a fight with the governor. So my retreat proceeded in peace and quiet—but also with a more acute sense of trust in the clairvoyant abilities of the Karmapa.[221]

One could call the tulku's father strong-willed and steadfast, but one could also say he was rigid and inflexible. It was like trying to move a boulder with a silk string. This opposition to my wish to go into retreat in the mountains contributed to a weariness that welled up within me. These feelings, combined with the Karmapa's command to return to Central Tibet and the impending threat from the communists in the East, led me to make up my mind that my time in Kham in this life was drawing to a close.

49.
The inner retreat room at Lachab

Earlier on, I had wished to remain in retreat at Fortress Peak for my entire life; but everything, both external and in my own heart, began to conspire against it.

During my retreat, the Dalai Lama, Panchen Lama, Chung Rinpoche of Mindrolling and the Karmapa all went to Beijing at the request of Mao Tsetung. They traveled separately, visiting a variety of places along the way. The pretext of the invitation was to honor these masters and show off the wonders of Communism, but the real reason was to force the Dalai Lama to publicly acknowledge that Tibet was an integral part of China.[222] Upon their return, I went to Chamdo to meet the Karmapa.

"In the eighth month of this year"—it was now 1955—"you must come to Central Tibet," the Karmapa declared. This was not merely a wish; it was a direct order.

"You have to put that in writing. Otherwise, my monastery will never let me go. The people back home are very simple-minded and they will prevent me from leaving."

Not only did he give me a letter with his explicit wish, but, as I wasn't very wealthy, from his herd in a nearby valley he gave me two horses and four yaks to carry my supplies and belongings. This gift was not usual for the Karmapa but a sign of his affection for me. In this way, he made sure that I would come to Tsurphu.

50. Dudjom Rinpoche—flanked by Dordrak Rigdzin and Minling Chung

I hadn't seen Uncle Tersey for quite some time. As I had developed a physical weakness that prevented me from traveling during the winter, I wanted to visit him during the summer. So I asked the Karmapa how long Uncle Tersey had to live.

After a while, the Karmapa said, "Well, well. I can't say for sure. But let's make him stick around for another year." He said it as if we had control over such things.

"Wish-Fulfilling Jewel, his life can't be so short! Isn't there any way to extend it?"

"I don't know," he replied. "But let's make sure we have him stay around for another year." As I walked out, I wondered what he could have meant.

༄༅

After this, I made the journey from Chamdo to Tsikey monastery to see Uncle Tersey. I told him about the Karmapa having ordered me to go to Tsurphu and about his premonition that the local people at my monastery back home would certainly object and cause trouble. I asked for his advice.

"If I hear that you went into retreat," Uncle Tersey replied, "or that you are riding around collecting offerings given in good faith—but have gone against the Karmapa's wishes—I will be deeply disappointed. Here's a good excuse for you to use: from Chokgyur Lingpa's time until today, our lineage has never gone against the Karmapas, nor should you. If you find it in yourself to be the first to go against the Karmapa's word, I will lose every good feeling I have for you."

How could anyone be clearer?

"On the other hand," he continued, "if I hear that while obeying the Karmapa's wish you got killed on the desolate northern plains by a gang of bandits preying on travelers on the way to Lhasa, I won't feel the slightest remorse. Just do what the Karmapa says and I will never worry about you—that is my heartfelt advice!"

So that sealed my decision to go to Tsurphu, come what may.

31

Brilliant Moon

It was at this meeting that Uncle Tersey told me about his time with a tulku named Rabsel Dawa, Brilliant Moon. "Old Khyentse was amazing and there's no doubt that, as people said, he was the return of Longchenpa in the flesh. But as far as I'm concerned, the Khyentse of our time is this tall young tulku, Rabsel Dawa. I feel that he will become a replica of the great Khyentse, just like Dzongsar Khyentse. I trust that Dzongsar Khyentse has outstanding qualities, both in learning and in realization, and his activity to influence beings is beyond compare—but what good is that to me? Every time I go to Derge I find out he is somewhere else. Four times it's happened! I longed to meet him, but now instead I have unexpectedly met this tulku from the Dilgo family, who is definitely a sublime being. Honestly, he can even read the yellow parchment with the secret script of the dakinis."

I myself fully rejoice at having met this Khyentse incarnation, whose greatness really doesn't require my adding anything. Today, we know him as Dilgo Khyentse. Loter Wangpo[223] was the first to recognize him as a reincarnation of the great Khyentse. He predicted that an emanation of Old Khyentse had been born as a son of the Dilgo family in the district of Denkhog. Dzongsar Khyentse also confirmed that this son of the Dilgo family was an authentic tulku of the great Khyentse and placed him on a throne. Then, after he was recognized and enthroned by Dzongsar Khyentse, whom he regarded as his root guru, the Karmapa also verified him as an authentic incarnation.

51.
A tulku named
Rabsel Dawa,
Brilliant Moon

Later the tulku was brought to Shechen monastery where he entered the great Dharma college.[224] Seen from the viewpoint of ordinary people, he had reached preeminence in education due to his outstanding intelligence and diligence. But in actuality, he was an emanation of both Vimalamitra and the great Khyentse—so what do I need to add? Such a precious master!

He came to be the guru not of just one or two people but the entire world. Like the sun rising in the sky, his deeds and activity reached everywhere. His eyes were so clear, his tongue so eloquent! His virtues were truly extraordinary! If you ever met him, you would know what I mean.

Wherever he went there would be a commotion. On first seeing him I heard some Nepali people exclaim, "Padmasambhava must have looked like that! He's so big!"

When Dzongsar Khyentse departed to the invisible realms, Dilgo Khyentse appeared and continued to shine like the sun for the Buddha's teachings and all beings. This is the special quality of the Khyentse incarnations: when one of them passes away another tulku appears to work for the Dharma in an even greater way. In our present time no one equals Dilgo Khyentse in spreading the teachings of Khyentse, Kongtrul and Chokling.

52. Early photo of Dilgo Khyentse Rinpoche

༄

After Könchok Paldrön had passed away, her special possessions were given to family members. I received a yellow parchment that was written in the coded language of the dakinis. Afraid I might lose it, I entrusted it to Uncle Tersey's safe hands. Only realized beings who are treasure revealers can decipher this secret language. Rabsel Dawa was such an individual.

Uncle Tersey had met Rabsel Dawa on several occasions, including once at the hermitage above Tsikey. On that visit, Uncle Tersey showed him that small piece of yellow parchment with dakini script. Unfortunately the great master Chokgyur Lingpa had never decoded it himself, but he had told Könchok Paldrön that it contained a lot of teachings. Uncle Tersey told me what then happened.

"People say that you can read sign script," he told Rabsel Dawa. "I don't have this ability myself. Is this true—can you really decode the script of the dakinis?"

The Khyentse tulku replied, "It depends. Sometimes I can, sometimes I can't. There's no guarantee."

Uncle Tersey showed him the piece of parchment from Chokgyur Lingpa, telling him it supposedly contained a terma that the great tertön never succeeded in writing down, and asked if he would be willing to give it a try.

Dilgo Khyentse replied, "Since you are a descendant of Chokgyur Lingpa, we could try working together to perform the sadhana of Padmasattva—Chokgyur Lingpa's pure form—and then see what happens.[225] We should do it together in the shrine room where the body of the great treasure revealer is enshrined.[226] Let's wait a couple days and go there on the tenth day of the lunar month."

Uncle Tersey had been staying at the retreat center above Tsikey known as Mindrolling, the Sanctuary of Ripening and Liberation. The path down to the monastery was very steep and quite hazardous; Tersey, quite old by now, was escorted down on the early morning of the tenth day. Just the two of them, sitting together, performed the sadhana with a lavish feast offering. This is a unique sadhana that had been revealed by the great Khyentse as a mind treasure after Chokgyur Lingpa passed away. To allow them to concentrate on the dakini script undisturbed, at some point Tersey went and locked the main door so that no one could enter.

"The yellow parchment needs to be soaked in amrita made of the five nectars," Dilgo Khyentse then said. "Dissolve some sacred *mendrub* medicine in barley wine, then place the parchment on top of it."

Interestingly, terma paper does not react to liquids in the same way normal paper does. It never gets damaged.

They then began the sadhana in front of the golden stupa and continued all the way to the recitations, which took about an hour. At that point, Dilgo Khyentse asked for the amrita vessel containing the parchment to be brought over to him.

"Do you see anything?" Tersey asked.

"Not a thing."

So they continued the practice. In particular, they repeatedly sang the blessed supplication, a prayer to the pure form of the great tertön.

After a while, Dilgo Khyentse said, "Let's take another look." As they removed the lid, he exclaimed, "Now I can see! Bring over some paper to write on."

Tersey thought to himself, "There is a correlation between the decoding and auspicious coincidence. One should make sure to avoid any extreme—in this case, neither too much paper nor too little. I wonder how much paper I should get."

He went to the cupboard and found some blank sheets of handmade paper with dimensions the same as a parchment Chokgyur Lingpa had once found as a terma. He took forty sheets and went back to his seat.

Dilgo Khyentse took the sheets, noting, "This is going to take a while," then began to write rapidly. They kept the door locked the whole time; the attendant wasn't even able to deliver their lunch. By five o'clock, all forty sheets were filled.

Uncle Tersey told me that from ten until five, the sign script of the dakinis had transformed itself before Dilgo Khyentse's eyes and he had simply copied down what he saw, completing the last words of the last sentence on the last piece of paper.

When Dilgo Khyentse was done writing, he told Uncle Tersey, "It appears you must be the primary recipient of this teaching, since you are the reincarnation of the tertön's son. I have merely acted as his assistant. Chokgyur Lingpa's terma parchment is authentic and in my vision I received his complete blessings for this task. This terma has three levels of detail: extensive, medium and condensed. If I had written down the extensive version, it would have filled a large volume, which is more than needed these days. I wrote down the medium version, complete as it is. Now the time is up and the script is no longer visible. So let's complete the sadhana."

With that, they continued with the feast offering and concluded with the dedication of merit. Then Tersey requested Dilgo Khyentse to give him the empowerment. "Now that you have decoded the script, it should be put to use for the benefit of the Dharma and all sentient beings. So, please give me the empowerment for it right now."

Dilgo Khyentse replied, "I will surely do so, don't worry. But first we need to have it verified by my guru, Dzongsar Khyentse, who is the lord of the Dharma in our age. Even though I have no doubt about the authenticity of the parchment, I am not fully confident in my ability to decode it. So first let me show it to him. If he confirms that it is a true Dharma teaching and gives his consent for propagating it, then I will certainly come back and offer you the empowerment and reading transmission. Otherwise, it is not enough just to have decoded a terma, as I cannot justify authenticating it on my own."

Uncle Tersey went back up to his retreat center and that evening he slowly read through the text. It contained a sadhana for the eight consorts of the eight *herukas* in the *Eight Sadhana Teachings*. There exist many versions of the sadhana with the male herukas, but this terma was unusual in being based upon their consorts.

The scripture Dilgo Khyentse wrote down began with a root tantra, resembling a short version of the *Guhyagarbha Tantra,* of astounding beauty and clarity yet containing in full the ten main aspects of tantra. This tantra was followed by a sadhana, then the empowerment ritual, both the general and superior levels. Each of these levels had an explanation whose profundity amazed my uncle.

This is how Chokgyur Lingpa's terma on the eight consorts was established in written form. Uncle Tersey later told me, "There is no question that Dilgo Khyentse knows the symbolic script! I haven't the slightest doubt about it."

Dilgo Khyentse took the text with him to show Dzongsar Khyentse, but he never got the opportunity to give this empowerment to Uncle Tersey.

However, this story gives us a glimpse of Dilgo Khyentse's capacity. Wasn't he just amazing! He was unique, truly incredible, a master in the truest sense of the word.

❧

Dilgo Khyentse once told me that he had asked Uncle Tersey to give him the empowerment for a mind treasure containing dakini teachings.[227] This empowerment had great meaning to him, since it had been revealed by the great Khyentse and Tersey had received it straight from him.

Since Tersey had a direct lineage from the mind treasure's very revealer, Jamyang Khyentse Wangpo, he replied, "There is no one between me and the great Khyentse; I got this from him directly. And isn't it true that you are his reincarnation? I'm nothing special, but I can offer you this teaching, since I see we have the karma of being linked as master and disciple." He then proceeded to give the empowerment.

Uncle Tersey had gotten this empowerment when he was quite young and went with his mother and his grandmother, Lady Degah, to see Old Khyentse. He remembered how "the great Khyentse personally came all the way out into the courtyard holding incense and a scarf in the traditional gesture of welcome, looking very impressive and tall. He had deep appreciation, not only for the tertön but for his entire family and treated us all with great respect and affection."

When Tersey was finished, he said, "I do not have any extraordinary qualities concerning the view, meditation and conduct. But from the beginning of the empowerment ritual until this moment, I have maintained the vivid presence of being Jamyang Khyentse Wangpo myself, without a single moment of distraction. So, there might be a tiny bit of blessing from this empowerment."

Even this low-key claim was very much out of character for Uncle Tersey, who never spoke of his abilities in any way.

❧

Before my return to Nangchen I spent three days together with Uncle Tersey at the retreat center above Tsikey. We slept in the same room, ate meals together and talked a lot. He gave me some presents including a remarkable little statue of the Lotus-Born master made of a precious mixture of bronze. He had used this small *kutsab* statue during an empowerment that he most graciously bestowed upon me.

I didn't receive that many transmissions from him, but the ones I did get were amazing. I was also hesitant to ask him for any empowerment, because I knew how meticulous he was and how long it would take, especially if you asked for a whole series of transmissions. So I never dared to request more than a few empowerments. On meditation practice, however, I received a good deal of instruction during my last meeting with him.

Upon giving me the statue he said, "It seems to me the time has come when the future transmission of Chokgyur Lingpa's teachings will rest primarily on your shoulders. So when the opportunity arises for you to pass them on, please do so. I have heard that you are still pretty open-minded and make no real distinctions between all the various termas revealed by past tertöns, such as the practice of the peaceful and wrathful deities revealed by Karma Lingpa, the dakini practices and so forth. But don't you see that we already have them all in the *New Treasures*? Since you're the great-grandson of Chokgyur Lingpa, it would be better if you practiced our own terma teachings."

Basically he was somewhat annoyed that I practiced all these different sadhanas, but his displeasure was more an expression of wanting me to appreciate our own heritage. I had been particularly fond of a terma by Yongey Mingyur Dorje for a longevity practice, as well as a practice of the peaceful and wrathful deities by Karma Lingpa. Both were quite popular where I was from.[228]

I had often done these practices in the homes of benefactors, and this fact must have weighed on his mind, because he insisted, "You sit in the east with the tormas in the west. You sit as you should, but you don't chant what you should. Of course, past termas still have great blessings—I'm not denying that. But by using them instead of the *New Treasures*, you are casting away our own tradition. Mark my words when I say that this is a great mistake."

His advice struck my heart like a knife, because what he said was true. He put a fright in me that lasted a long time. The rest of my stay, though, he was very affectionate toward me.

On the third day we walked down to the main monastery at Tsikey. Two days later, when I asked to take leave, he firmly declared, "You and I will never see each other again. You will go to Lhasa and spend many years in Central Tibet; I feel certain the Karmapa won't let you leave there so easily. Even if he did, it seems you aren't burning to come back here. I myself am old now and, thanks to the gung-treng"—the communists—"bad times are headed our way. You will find there is no point in wanting to return to Nangchen.

"Don't plan to see me again. I don't plan on seeing you either. In these bodies we have now, I don't expect we'll ever meet again. But I pray we will do so in Chokgyur Lingpa's pure land, the Lotus-Covered Realm.

"Don't you agree?" he added, jokingly. "This is the Vajrayana tradition—wherever the guru goes, the disciples go too, to assemble in a single mandala. So, since Chokgyur Lingpa manifested a pure realm, we should all form the wish to go there."

With canes in his hands to support his large, magnificent frame, he walked with me all the way through the main gate—something quite unusual for him. We walked together slowly to a little pass almost a mile away. There he remained standing with palms joined, watching me walk away, and uttering good wishes and prayers for my protection.

That was the last time I ever saw him.

&

From Tsikey I rode back to Lachab but didn't stay for long. If Uncle Tersey hadn't told me I had to follow the Karmapa's command and go to Tsurphu, I would have been obligated to remain in my monastery a few months longer. The season for visiting benefactors' homes was upon us and I would surely have collected generous offerings for Lachab. However, as soon as winter set in I would have been stuck, because my physical ailment prevented me from tolerating the outdoors in the winter.

Instead I followed a very tight schedule, arranging to visit four or five benefactors daily over just nineteen days. I drastically shortened every ritual, whether for the longevity of the living or for the benefit of a recently deceased relative. All the money and yaks that I received I left behind for the care of Samten Gyatso's reincarnation at Lachab. For myself, I took along little more than the animals that the Karmapa had given me.

Understandably, the immediate reaction to my plans at Lachab was that there was no way in the world I could leave. Everyone connected to the monastery shared the sentiment that their tulku shouldn't go anywhere but stay right there.

However, taking Uncle Tersey's advice to heart, my response was, "You must be very important, since you want to go against the explicit wish of the Karmapa, whose title is Lord of Conquerors! So please, whoever opposes him, each of you raise a hand to show that you individually want to break the Karmapa's command

and stop my departure. I would like to see who you are, so I can write a letter to the Karmapa mentioning you by name as the ones who are preventing me and who pay no heed to his wishes. As soon as I have written this letter, I will send it by messenger to him on a fast horse and stay put right here!"

All of a sudden everyone seemed to have changed their minds, pleading, "Don't talk like that! If you must go, you must go."

It seems that my karmic nemesis, the governor who had tried to prevent my three-year retreat at Fortress Peak, had to show up one final time to create obstacles. For some reason, he thought he could rebuke me whenever he felt like it—not that I was at all afraid of him.

"I hear you are about to leave once again," he said. "That is definitely inappropriate. Samten Gyatso's tulku is, of course, the main lama, but he is still a child, while you are an adult. It is *your* responsibility to make sure that offerings keep coming in. You do agree that people need to eat, don't you? You may want to play and frolic your way through life, but it is neither responsible nor appropriate at this time."

"Very well. Do you mean to say that I should go against the Gyalwang Karmapa's command?" I retorted, using the Karmapa's special title, King of All the Buddhas. "Are you in a position to override him? If you are, perhaps I should listen to you instead."

"Don't use the Karmapa as an excuse," he retorted. "Of course I'm not personally going against his word. But you are not leaving!"

He was the kind of person who would speak impulsively as if he were in charge. So using similar tactics, I snapped, "I would rather be dead than disobey the Karmapa—so I *am* leaving!"

After this battle of wills, he just kept quiet, went home and didn't interfere any longer. No one else opposed my leaving and I began preparing for my departure.

You probably have no idea how stubborn Khampas can be, but let me tell you, unless you can yield on a small point, you could be heading for a major dispute. However, the Karmapa is the one person whom Khampas universally respect; otherwise I might never have gotten out of Kham.

So in the end, it was the Karmapa who helped deliver me from that particular form of samsara known as monastery management.

༄

Thanks to the Karmapa's letter, I was able to escape to Central Tibet in midsummer, the sixth Tibetan month. I left there feeling like someone who has been released from a dark dungeon. At that time of year, the rivers swell with summer rain, so you don't find a single soul traveling the road to Central Tibet. But I had no choice if I was to reach Tsurphu by the eighth month.

Shortly before leaving, I went to spend some time with my brother Penjik.

"Do you have a firearm you could lend me?"

"Well, well, a gun!" he said, "I have one I can *give* you."

"Don't give it to me; I just want to borrow it. I'll bring it back," I promised.

He brought out a Tibetan-made rifle that was practically useless and he also forced a precious dagger on me, a family heirloom. I rode off soon after.

Normally, Khampas travel in large caravans, but since no one makes such a journey that late in the summer, there were only the fourteen of us in our party. I was probably around thirty-five and my two sons were still toddlers. They sat in boxes hanging from the sides of one of the horses.

The area we were traveling through was notorious for holdups. Several times we had to stop and wait when we heard that other travelers had been attacked.

One day we had stopped for tea along the way, when suddenly four bandits on horseback rode up to us. Two were mere teenagers, but the adults looked pretty tough. They were dressed in sheepskin coats and had rifles slung over their shoulders. My attendant had packed my things in a rush, putting the rifle and knife inside the luggage. Now, when we needed them, they were nowhere to be found.

"Keep your hands up and don't try anything," the leader shouted. "And you over there, keep brewing that tea! Bring us some! Looks like you're heading to Tibet. You must have a bundle of that stuff." With all their long and short firearms, daggers and knives pointing here and there, they almost looked like thorn bushes.

A nun in our company soon walked over with a cup of tea for each of them. During all this I had been sitting on a large box in the middle of the camp. My hands were tucked inside the shawl I had wrapped around my shoulders and I hadn't moved. Slowly I had lifted my index finger and they couldn't tell if I had a gun or not. The teenagers were getting antsy and kept fidgeting.

"Hey, you!" the leader shouted at me. "You're just sitting there—what are you thinking about?"

I didn't say a word.

"Which bags have the tea?" the leader demanded.

"We haven't brought any tea to sell in Lhasa," I said. "There's nothing for you here." I still had my finger raised under the shawl.

"I don't like this," one of the kids said. "Why don't we leave them alone?"

One of my attendants was a true Khampa; he had already grabbed his knife inside his jacket. "Keep your hands to yourself," I whispered to him.

The tense standoff went on. "This is it!" I thought at one point. "They're going to kill the lot of us. Sometimes this kind of thing happens: one intends to practice the Dharma but winds up getting killed. If my servant pulls out his knife now, what good will that do against four men with rifles? I'm not a fighter and I don't intend to become one now."

All I could think to do was sit there and act as if I had a gun trained on them.

The youngsters couldn't sit still on their horses; you could see by their faces there was no question in their minds I had a gun.

But not their leader. He simply said, "Look at this guy! He's trying to act tough and play games with us. Is that what you're doing? Are you playing with us?"

I still didn't say a word or make a move. That was good, because even if I'd had a gun, I wouldn't have known how to shoot it. Of course, I could have tried using a knife, but I wouldn't have stood a chance against those guys.

The teenagers seemed to have already made up their minds to leave as quickly as possible. Something must have made their leader change his mind as well—for all of a sudden he grinned and said, "Let's go."

The other bandit, who was somewhat older, glanced at me. "He looks like a lama. If we kill him, we'll get bad luck."

"Hey, you two!" the leader yelled to the young bandits. "Let's not hang around in this wretched valley!" One of the teenagers gave a whoop and off they went.

Two of the nuns were petrified and couldn't walk any further. It was a while before any of us dared to laugh.

Had we brought along some tea or other items to trade in Lhasa, we probably could have avoided trouble by handing it over. But who knows? Down the road, we ran into other travelers who told us that they had been robbed by the same four guys—and one man had even been killed.

But by the blessings of the Three Jewels, the rest of our journey was safe.

32

My Last Visit to Central Tibet

Our first stop was Drong monastery, where they wanted to enthrone Chökyi Nyima as the tulku of Gar Drubchen. We stayed there for ten days, then all proceeded to Drigung and on to Lhasa and Tsurphu.

On arriving in Central Tibet, I went first to Pawo Rinpoche's monastery at Nenang.[229] Uncle Tersey had spent a lot of time there, and he and Pawo Rinpoche were very close friends. His monastery was near Lhasa on the way to Tsurphu and I had some presents for him from Uncle Tersey. He asked me about Tersey and how my trip was going. I told him about a new highway from Chamdo to Lhasa on which you could travel with motorized vehicles. He was happy to see me and I had a delightful stay at his hermitage with its astounding beauty.

During my stay Pawo Rinpoche once told me, "You should go back to Chamdo and invite Tersey Tulku to Central Tibet; I'll put him up here at my hermitage. We've always gotten along very well. I have only been able to receive a few of the *New Treasures* from the fifteenth Karmapa, not enough to fully use them to benefit others. Invite him here so I can get the rest; I'll pay for everything."

I was very pleased to hear this and readily agreed, "Thank you very much; this is very kind of you. Because it is *you* making the invitation, I think he will come. Since he is old, he will only be able to come by traveling on the new road."

Pawo Rinpoche enthusiastically repeated his invitation adding, "In the present day he is the main holder of the *New Treasures*."

Right then and there I promised to do what Pawo Rinpoche had asked. Uncle Tersey was not only one of my teachers but also like a second father to me, so of course I would see to inviting him.

But it wasn't so easy. In those days a decision of such importance would first have to be presented to the Karmapa for his approval. Besides, Tsikey monastery would never let Uncle Tersey travel—as he was their main lama at the time—unless it was at the Karmapa's explicit wish.

So Pawo Rinpoche decided to get the Karmapa's consent. And I would soon have the chance to make the request.

൞

Just before I arrived at Tsurphu, the Karmapa told a prominent man from Nangchen to go down to the road to watch for me.

"Wouldn't it be better to wait?" the man retorted. "We haven't even received word that he has reached Lhasa yet. Besides, it's already getting dark."

"Don't worry," the Karmapa reassured him. "Just go and wait. I have a pretty strong feeling he's almost here."

This turned out to be a good idea, because by the time I arrived dusk was falling and it was quite late when we entered Tsurphu; having the guide was helpful.

Karmapa's attendant was waiting for me and said we were to come right in, so I didn't even have time to get the traditional white scarf for greeting or the special offerings I had brought for him. Before we had a chance to enter, another servant came out who told us that the Karmapa was asking for "the tulku" to come in immediately.

The servant lent me a scarf as I went in to greet the Karmapa. At the end of our conversation, the Karmapa asked me, " Why are you so late—did you stop along the way? The road from Lhasa isn't that long!"

I told him that along the way I had stopped at Nenang to visit Pawo Rinpoche.

"What were you two talking about that was so important?" the Karmapa asked.

This was another time my stubbornness surfaced. I told him about Pawo Rinpoche's wish to invite Uncle Tersey up to Central Tibet, "How about I catch a ride from Lhasa to Chamdo, go to Tsikey and bring him back with me? The decision, of course, is yours—it can only happen with your consent."

"What?!? Forget about it. There's no point," the Karmapa responded.

What a disappointment!

"Wish-Fulfilling Jewel, how can you say it's pointless? It's now possible to drive in a motor car. That way the trip from Chamdo to Lhasa takes no more than three days. The Pawo tulku will cover all expenses and it will be no inconvenience whatsoever to the monastic household in Tsurphu."

This wasn't the right thing to say, but it was all I could think of at the time. The Karmapa responded, "Are you insinuating that I can't feed Tersey Tulku? I can feed not just him but twenty of his kind, no

53. Pawo Rinpoche of Nenang monastery

problem! Food isn't the issue. What I mean is that bringing him to Central Tibet would be of no use, so you should forget about it!"

His words saddened me and I wondered what he meant.

A few days later I had the chance to see the Karmapa again, and this time I brought along some presents from Uncle Tersey and tried again. But the Karmapa would hear nothing of my hopes to bring Tersey Tulku to Central Tibet. I didn't dare mention it again and gave up on the plan for eight or nine days, when I found the opportunity to get the Karmapa's attention.

"Hey, tulku! What are you up to now?" he asked.

"I just have a small request, but it's really on my mind. Tersey Tulku has been like a father to me, as well as one of my teachers. So I feel I must bring him to Central Tibet. Of course, I would remain here as your assistant while he stays at Nenang monastery with Pawo Rinpoche. From time to time, he can easily come here to offer you any necessary empowerment from the *New Treasures,* as well as perform a ritual for your health.

"Isn't it true that you have set your mind on receiving the entire *New Treasures*, and at present Tersey Tulku is not only the main lineage holder but also the most learned and accomplished master of the lineage? Chokgyur Lingpa is gone and his two tulkus are gone as well; so in this lineage there is only Tersey Tulku left. You must invite him."

What I didn't say was that Uncle Tersey was in Kham, and the way things were going there with the communists, I wanted to get him out.

"Huh! I know he's a good lama. I met him when I visited Tsikey. But isn't it enough to tell you twice? By the Three Jewels, don't invite him! It's useless."

But I could be very persistent. Two or three days later, as we were engaged in some pleasant conversation, I found a moment to bring the matter up one more time.

"By the Three Jewels!" he exclaimed. "It's pointless, it won't amount to anything. Don't bring it up again!"

I had merely displayed how pushy I could be; nonetheless I guess I finally got the point. Just to be sure, the Karmapa's attendant came over and whispered to me, "When he speaks like that, it's no use to go on and on asking him. Your Khampa tenacity won't help." That was the last straw, I finally gave up the idea.

Two months later I got the news that Uncle Tersey had passed away. I recalled the Karmapa's earlier remark, "Let's try to make him stick around another year." But he hadn't even stayed a full year.

It would seem that all the while the Karmapa knew Uncle Tersey would soon die.

One day at Tsurphu, the Karmapa went down to see the protectors' shrine, a separate temple containing a statue of Mahakala, the guardian of the Buddha's teachings. This temple is quite dark as it has no windows. By tradition a person's name can be placed in a small container for a divination on whether a connection with them will be helpful, harmful or neutral.

When the Karmapa goes somewhere, he is rarely alone, so immediately his attendants prepared for the walk. There were five or six of us, including the Karmapa's general secretary and his chamberlain.

The Karmapa placed a piece of paper with the question in front of a sacred mask that had been crafted many centuries before by a great master—a huge Mahakala mask hanging on the wall flanked by Dusölma and another protector. Then he returned to his quarters.

When we went back the next morning, we all saw that something looking like blood had begun to flow from the eyes of the mask, especially the left eye. This reddish liquid had already filled three bowls up to the brim.

Something like this had happened once before, many centuries ago, during a battle between the Tibetan government and China. That time the "blood" had dripped from the curved knife instead of the mask.

After verifying that the shrine had been locked up for the night, we were sure no one had entered. We felt that the dripping liquid was quite ominous.

The Karmapa just said, "What a pity!" and fell silent.

For a day or so, he said nothing about the divination. It wasn't until the next evening that he spoke. "I think we better go back and take another look. I want to know how much blood has flowed from the left eye."

This time we saw that the red liquid was flowing from both eyes equally.

"What a pity!" the Karmapa repeated. "Previously when blood flowed from this mask, our government was fighting the foreign power to the east. That time, Tibet won the battle and, as a sign of victory, blood dripped from the curved knife.

"Now it seems that Mahakala is crying tears of blood. The Buddha's teachings in Tibet will probably disappear. What a tragedy!"

At this point, the red liquid had spilled onto the floor—we all saw it. I'm not talking about just a few drops.[230]

Around this time, Dudjom Rinpoche told me he had seen something similar to this in the Kongpo district south of Lhasa, when "blood" flowed for seven days straight from a statue of a heruka made by the master Tsele Natsok Rangdröl. He said it flowed so much it almost reached the entranceway.

There was a rule that whenever omens like this occurred, whether auspicious or not, a letter describing them should be sent to the government in Lhasa. And

54. (left) The Moon Cave at Drak Yerpa

55. (right) View from the Moon Cave

soon a minister replied in writing, "There is no need to worry. At the three large monasteries of Sera, Drepung and Ganden the recitation of a particular form of wrathful Manjushri will be repeated six million times. This will ensure that the threat will be eliminated."

This was the only response that was offered, even though the omen foretold the destruction of Buddhism in Tibet.

It is amazing how a country like Tibet could have the merit to host so many great masters and at the same time lose everything.

❧

The Karmapa was about to leave on a pilgrimage to India and we parted ways. That gave me the chance to visit the famous sacred place Drak Yerpa near Lhasa, where I stayed in a cozy little cave that opens into the Moon Cave. I must admit, however, this was not a time of true solitude, for I had brought along my two children, their mother, an old nun related to my mother and two attendants.

One night I had a dream. It seemed that I had awoken inside a cave and somewhere close-by there was a dakini of incredible beauty, captivating to behold and wearing exquisite jewelry. During the dream I somehow knew that it was a dream and that I was actually still in the Moon Cave. The thought that this beauty must be a wisdom dakini gave rise to strong feeling of devotion. At first she stood still; then she began a graceful dance with swift movements.

At one point I asked her, "Our Wish-Fulfilling Jewel, the Karmapa, has gone on a pilgrimage to India. I hear that the king of Bhutan may invite him there as well. Is this true?"

"He has been invited, but it is not an insistent request and the Karmapa will not go to Bhutan," she replied. "The king will instead send offerings."

"What will happen to Tibet?" I asked. "Will the Chinese invade or not? We hear over the new telephone line from the east that people are getting killed there."

"The Chinese will come."

"When?"

"Thirty-six months from now the Buddha's teachings in Tibet will be stamped to the ground and the land left in darkness."[231]

"Will the Dalai Lama go into exile? Some people say he will stay."

"He will leave. There is no doubt. He will go to India."

I ended the conversation by asking a simple question about the Dalai Lama's whereabouts in the near future, so that I could verify the accuracy of her other statements.

She was so pretty I didn't want to wake up, thinking that opening my eyes would cause her to vanish. But awash with hope and fear, I eventually opened them anyway, expecting to wake up in my normal surroundings, and was surprised to see the dakini still visible at a slight distance. I was actually quite fascinated by her, she was so beautiful, but as I gazed at her, she slowly disappeared.

Since my big mouth won't stay closed, upon returning to Lhasa I had to tell someone about the dream. So I told Dudjom Rinpoche that I had had an unusual dream. Then I asked whether the Karmapa had gone to Bhutan.

"The king sent an invitation with offerings," he replied, "but our Wish-Fulfilling Jewel didn't go."

I then continued to relate my dream and what the dakini had said. By this time, my question about the Dalai Lama's whereabouts had also been confirmed.

"Oh my!" exclaimed Dudjom Rinpoche, "I believe you have received a prophecy about the future of Tibet." Then he muttered, "Oh my" a few more times before adding, "We must prepare for the worst."

Not long after, being the blabbermouth that I am, I shared my dream with both the Karmapa and Dzongsar Khyentse, who replied, "That is definitely bad news."

I'm not the type who usually has lucid dreams, but this one has stayed in my memory as clear as when it happened. It was too vivid to forget—its message haunted me day and night.

56. The young Dudjom Rinpoche

When I returned to Kham the last time, I realized how the political situation had taken a turn for the worse. Even then I saw what was soon to befall Tibet. From whatever angle I looked at things, it was obvious that Tibet would lose its independence. I felt certain—a sentiment that no one around me seemed to share.

If I raised the topic in Kham, people would make a contemptuous sound and refuse to even consider it. If I mentioned it in Central Tibet, it seemed no one lost any sleep worrying that the end of the Dharma was fast approaching.

But I had no peace. "What's going to happen to Tibet?" I would worry. "When the flood of communists sweeps in from the east, how can a bundle of grass and a few twigs restrain it? The whole of Tibet will be inundated. The Khampas look to the Central Tibetan government for support, but who will be the final support? The Tibetan government has no one to turn to. I am sure this will not end well."

Those were the thoughts I agonized over.

Isn't it a fact that everything comes to an end? The Chinese army numbered in the hundreds of thousands, while I doubt there were more than ten thousand Tibetan soldiers in the entire country. How could such a small force turn back an invasion?

The Central Tibetans were shrewder than the Khampas, but what good would that do them? This shrewdness had caused them to postpone making any solid alliances because of a belief in their independent strength. Now it seemed obvious there wasn't a single other country that would come to the aid of Tibet in a time of trouble. Meanwhile, the nobility and government officials busied themselves living off whatever they could extort from the common people, never using the funds for anything useful, let alone what they were intended for. How could that possibly end well?

Most people in Kham were not what you would call politically astute. They would simply repeat empty platitudes like "The snowy ranges of Tibet are like a beautiful painted scroll with Lhasa in the center. How could the communists ever damage that?"

Though such foolish beliefs were quite popular, how can I fault them? They didn't know any better. Still, this is the same as saying, "I won't die because I haven't experienced it."

I'm not sure where the Khampas got the idea that the government in Lhasa could protect them against the Red Army and that powerful India was standing behind Tibet ready to help. To top it off, they believed that the rest of the world, including the United States, was just waiting to come to Tibet's assistance—all they had to do was send the word.

I am not making this up. Many Khampas actually believed it. Why don't we just call it wishful thinking?

33

Amazing Masters in Lhasa

Dzongsar Khyentse

While in Lhasa I was able to spend time with a wonderful master, the beloved Dzongsar Khyentse. In Kham this tulku became as famous as the great Khyentse himself; he was not just a tulku of the first Khyentse but a near replica. He was learned, noble and accomplished, and had an amazing presence.

In the latter part of his life, he fell seriously ill and remained so for three years, with no cure in sight. Finally he was requested to accept a consort to improve his health. He replied, "If there is no way around it, I will give back my monastic vows."

He then went on to describe a particular young woman and her whereabouts. She and her family were sent a letter of invitation, and she came to live with him.[232] No longer a monk, Dzongsar Khyentse now became a ngakpa—and a perfect one at that.

When the political situation in Kham became untenable, he used the pretext of a short trip to leave for Central Tibet without letting anybody know. That way no one was able to stop him. He passed through Nangchen on the way.

As I mentioned, Dzongsar Khyentse had earlier visited Fortress Peak, Samten Gyatso's mountain hermitage. There Dzongsar Khyentse requested my guru to give him the transmissions for the sections of the *New Treasures* composed by the fifteenth Karmapa that he had not received. But I did not meet him then.

One day, while I happened to be in front of the statue of Buddha Shakyamuni at the Jokhang in

57. Dzongsar Khyentse Rinpoche

Lhasa, word went around that Dzongsar Khyentse was arriving. He came striding in with immense presence, wearing the Lotus-Born master's famous lotus crown and Dharma robes.[233]

All around people were whispering, "Look there! Who is that? Looks like a great master. He's dressed like Padmasambhava." Almost instantly he became renowned all over Lhasa. While he was staying at the house of an important dignitary, I went to visit him; he was transmitting the *Four Branches of Heart Essence,* a most important set of Dzogchen teachings.

"Who are you?" he asked.

"I am a Khampa," I replied.

"From where in Kham?"

"I am from Chokgyur Lingpa's family. I am his great-grandson."

"Neten Chokling has no children." Dzongsar Khyentse was very close to the Chokling of Neten. He continued, "So whose son are you?"

"Neten Chokling is the reincarnation, but I am the descendant of Chokgyur Lingpa himself, since my father was born from his daughter."

"Ohhhh ... so maybe you're the one who's the descendant of Chokgyur Lingpa that everyone is talking about—the one who is giving the *Three Sections* empowerments to Karmapa Rigpey Dorje! Is that you?"

What could I say other than "Yes, that's me"? I guessed this meant that we had now been formally introduced.

"Well, well, if that's the case, then you must arrange for me to meet the Karmapa," he said. "He holds the lineage for an empowerment that enables the disciple to master the display of awareness.[234] I must receive it from Rigpey Dorje in person. Please assist me by asking him on my behalf."

To help facilitate such an auspicious meeting, I first took the Karmapa's general secretary and several members of the Karmapa's family to see Dzongsar Khyentse. This meeting went well, and soon Dzongsar Khyentse was invited to Tsurphu to give teachings and empowerments. I remember clearly that Dzongsar Khyentse arrived on the twenty-third and remained at Tsurphu until the eighth day of the following month.

Our Wish-Fulfilling Jewel treated Dzongsar Khyentse with great respect, putting him up in some of the best quarters. I was fortunate enough to receive the empowerments from them both and could see with my own eyes how fond they had become of each other. Dzongsar Khyentse stayed at Tsurphu during the New Year's celebrations, where he was treated with great honor and placed on the lofty Dharma throne.

In private the Karmapa told me, "I am deeply thrilled that we could host such a great master. Even though these times are troubled, he puts me totally at ease."

The Karmapa requested a mind treasure of the first Khyentse concerning *Chandali, the Mother of Longevity* in a form that had a seal of secrecy.[235] In turn Dzongsar Khyentse requested the empowerment of the red form of Avalokiteshvara known as *Ocean of Conquerors*, the single most important yidam of all the Karmapas since the time of Karma Pakshi, the second Karmapa. Connected to this empowerment there is a particular aspect known as "the empowerment for the play of awareness" that the Karmapa also gave him.[236] Only Ponlop Rinpoche, who was the Karmapa's brother, and I were allowed inside the inner chamber during these empowerments.

After the transmissions, the conversation turned to the future of Tibet. Dzongsar Khyentse said, "It seems obvious to me that the communists are up to no good. My main reason for coming here was actually to ask you personally what you see about me going to Pemakö," a very remote mountain region on the Indian border.

After a short while the Karmapa said, "Pemakö, Pemakö . . . It doesn't look good. The mountains are very steep, and the river on the way is difficult to cross—but in the end the communists will invade there as well. That's what I see. Rinpoche, you must go to Sikkim."

"Very well, Wish-Fulfilling Jewel, I have faith in you as someone who can clearly see past, present, and future. I will follow your advice. Eventually I had planned on leaving Tibet through the district of Kongpo, but I had my doubts. That is why I came to ask you."

During his time at Tsurphu, Dzongsar Khyentse became one of my teachers. I got to clarify many important points with him since, for many days in a row, some conceited Tsurphu secretaries barred him from meeting the Karmapa. This was nothing new; the same thing had happened to many other great lamas as well. Also, when he first arrived at Tsurphu, no one seemed to appreciate what an extraordinary, great master Dzongsar Khyentse truly was. Other than me, not a single person came to request teachings from him. One reason was that he was living in the Karmapa's quarters, which were difficult to get access to. Another reason was that people close to the Karmapa seemed to lose all appreciation for other lamas; they found it hard to have faith in anyone else. So for that period it was my good fortune to have no competition to see Dzongsar Khyentse.

But, as the days went by, the Tsurphu Khandro, who had been the consort of the previous Karmapa, the Tsurphu vajra master, and I were seen going in and out getting teachings. Eventually the word got around and soon people were standing in line to see him.

～

Before leaving Tsurphu, Dzongsar Khyentse asked for eight sets of the medium-length sadhana for *Tukdrub Barchey Kunsel*, saying, "This is a special terma meant specifically for this time. Please ask our Wish-Fulfilling Jewel if I may get copies of it."

Then he asked to borrow a small image that the first Karmapa had consecrated by biting into the bronze. These statues had never been seen before in Kham, but Dzongsar Khyentse knew that the Karmapa had several. The Karmapa seemed quite pleased with this request and, when he had his store of relics searched, he found two.

"I want to give one to you," he suddenly told Dzongsar Khyentse.

Dzongsar Khyentse tried to refuse, but the Karmapa forced him to take it. You should have seen the ripple it created throughout Tsurphu. Every time two monks crossed paths, it was the main topic of conversation, "This Sakya lama from Dzongsar has gotten one of our most valued treasures—the statue that our first Karmapa, Dusum Khyenpa, bit into. If our Wish-Fulfilling Jewel gives away treasures like that, I don't know what will happen to the Dharma! He is giving away our very heart!"

A critical attitude was in the air. I tried to stop the monks by telling them, "Don't talk like that! The Karmapa is the lord of the Dharma and there must be a good reason if he gives away a statue like that. Besides, it is only one of two; the other is still here at Tsurphu."

"Yes, yes, but two is better than one!" came the reply.

Clearly, the Karmapa did not see it the same way. When Dzongsar Khyentse was about to end his stay, the Karmapa commented, "When this old lama leaves Tsurphu, the place is going to seem empty."

～

When Dzongsar Khyentse returned again to Lhasa, I had the opportunity to receive some more teachings from him. In particular, he gave an instruction from the great Mipham to town yogis.[237] It begins this way:

Without the need for lengthy study, thought and meditation,
But by maintaining mind-essence through pith instruction's way,
A common town yogi can reach a knowledge-holder's stage with minor hardship—
This is the power of the most profound of paths.

He taught very slowly in the early mornings over several days, and I enjoyed our sessions together immensely. We also had the chance to exchange other teachings. For instance, I had some clarifications by Karmey Khenpo on the practice of the Lotus Dakini from the *Sevenfold Cycle of Profundity* I had brought along. Dzongsar Khyentse had a copy made and I was happy to offer him the reading transmission.

While in Lhasa I also met Dilgo Khyentse—the other incarnation of the great Khyentse. Though I had heard about him and his revelation of the dakini scroll I had given to Uncle Tersey, I had never met him. As it happened, Uncle Tersey had passed away that very winter; some of his special possessions were to be given to Dilgo Khyentse and I was given the task of bringing them to him at Samye.

Dilgo Khyentse was tall and impressive. He told me about his Dharma connection to my family through Uncle Tersey and that he would be delighted to give me some transmissions. Just then he was on his way to Tsurphu to meet the Karmapa and he said that when he came back we would discuss it further.

I took the occasion to remind him of the story that Uncle Tersey had told me about the dakini terma of the *Eight Consorts*, adding that he had ordered me to request the transmission from this Khyentse tulku.

Dilgo Khyentse replied, "Back in Kham I showed the forty pages to Dzongsar Khyentse and he told me, 'You must give me that empowerment and the reading transmission. I had been aware of one of Chokgyur Lingpa's dakini cycles that hadn't been put into writing till now and this seems to be that very one. You have done an impressive job!' I offered the empowerment and reading of the entire cycle to him.

"But as for your request, we are out of luck right now, as I left the text with him, so I can't give it to you now. You'll have to ask Dzongsar Khyentse when you see him; he said he wanted to take charge

58.
Dilgo Khyentse Rinpoche in Lhasa

of that teaching." Still, Dilgo Khyentse seemed quite pleased that I had asked and he was very kind to me.

"It's a magnificent terma," he went on, "but what can I do—I gave it to Dzongsar Khyentse and I don't have the text. Because of the deteriorating situation in eastern Tibet, I had to escape to Lhasa and had no idea that Dzongsar Khyentse would already be here. I expected him to come later. Dzongsar Khyentse told me that he sent someone to Kham in order to pick up those texts, but he doesn't know what has happened to them."

So, some time later, in one of the many wonderful conversations that I had with Dzongsar Khyentse, I told him Uncle Tersey's story about the terma Dilgo Khyentse had transcribed. "Rinpoche," I asked, "he told me you have the text. Did you bring it?"

Dzongsar Khyentse replied, "This was no ordinary terma that tulku wrote down! He landed something quite marvelous. It even included a tantra—and, let me tell you, not all tertöns can manage to do that! The great Khyentse and Kongtrul could, and Chokgyur Lingpa received a couple as well.[238]

"I made Rabsel Dawa give me the transmission and immediately afterward I had woodblocks carved for the entire text, with the intent to propagate it. But now look what has happened! The enemies of the Buddha's teachings suddenly arose from the east and began their invasion. Since I had to leave in such a hurry, there was no way I could bring it along. Let me tell you how little I managed to carry with me: only the three tiny *kutsab* statues that Padmasambhava concealed as his representatives for the benefit of Tibet.[239] That was it! All the other sacred images, scriptures and relics—there just wasn't any chance. Our sublime scriptures are lost to the enemies of the Dharma!"

In short, even though Dzongsar Khyentse had secured the transmission, he was now unable to pass it on. He lost everything else as well—all the sacred objects that represent enlightened body, speech and mind.[240]

So when it comes to receiving this terma as Uncle Tersey advised, I feel I have tried my best, requesting it first from Uncle Tersey himself, then from Dilgo Khyentse and finally from Dzongsar Khyentse.

One day Dzongsar Khyentse said, "I'm going on a pilgrimage around Central Tibet, and if you come along there are some empowerments and reading transmissions I can share with you. There are also a few rare pieces from the *New Treasures* that I haven't received and I think you have. Don't you think it would be nice if we traveled together for a bit? Why don't you ask the Karmapa for permission to come with me?"

It didn't turn out as we had planned though, as the Karmapa wanted very specific rituals done those days and we were in the middle of performing a ritual of exorcism connected to the Lion-Faced Dakini that took nine days. So when I told Dzongsar Khyentse that the Karmapa had refused to let me go, he had no choice but to leave without me.

Dudjom Rinpoche

I have already mentioned Dudjom Rinpoche but I never explained how we met.

One day while Dzongsar Khyentse was still in Lhasa, I went over to meet him. But I was told at the door he would be gone for the rest of the day; he had gone to a tent camp on the outskirts of Lhasa to ask Dudjom Rinpoche to give him an empowerment. When I next saw him, he expressed his deep admiration for Dudjom, "In our present time, I don't believe there is any vidyadhara more accomplished than Dudjom. That's why I had to request an empowerment from him!"

59. Dudjom Rinpoche

Soon after, I met Dudjom Rinpoche myself. He was staying at the home of an aristocrat of good character whom I knew. Now this dignitary wanted to perform one hundred thousand feast offerings in his household temple and had invited Dudjom Rinpoche to preside. Since he knew I was in town, he invited me to come. It was during these one hundred thousand feasts that Dudjom and I met, and spent time together.

"Who are you?" he asked me.

"I am from Kham," I replied.

"Where in Kham are you from?"

"From Nangchen."

"Which lineage do you belong to?"

"I belong to the Barom Kagyu lineage."

"What do you practice?"

"I practice the termas of Chokgyur Lingpa."

"You might be related to him then."

"Yes, in fact, I am one of his great-grandchildren."

"Explain your family line."

I told him that I was the son of Chimey Dorje and the nephew of Samten Gyatso.

"Oh really!" Dudjom replied. "I received parts of the *Three Sections of the Great Perfection* from Samten Gyatso and regard him as one of my root gurus. I recently heard about a Khampa lama who gave the Karmapa the *Three Sections* empowerment at Tsurphu—is that you?"

Obviously, word had gotten around, so I admitted, "Yes, that's me."

"Do you have the books with you?"

"Yes, I do; they are back in my quarters at Tsurphu."

"Do you have the icons?"

"Yes, I have them as well."

"Excellent, because you will have to give that teaching to me. I got the first three empowerments at Tsurphu, but I definitely want it in full."

Dudjom Rinpoche was very insistent, so I had to dispatch my attendant to Tsurphu immediately to get the books and icons while the Karmapa was away on a journey to Sky Lake, northwest of Lhasa. Soon after, I had to offer Dudjom this transmission, to the best of my meager abilities.

༂

60. Chatral Rinpoche

A few days into offering these empowerments, I met Chatral Rinpoche. His appearance was striking: he wore coarse felt garments and had a prominent nose and a Khampa bearing. Our conversation began like this:

"You, lama! Where are you from?" he demanded brusquely.

"I am from Nangchen."

"From where in Nangchen?"

"I am a descendant of Chokgyur Lingpa."

"I've been to Tsikey and I didn't see you there."

"I didn't always stay at Tsikey."

"Then where are you from? Out with it!"

"Chokgyur Lingpa's daughter, Könchok Paldrön, had four sons one of whom was my father."

"Hmmm . . . hmmm . . . I had heard that you were supposed to be the nephew of Neten Chokling. I know him from Dzongsar, where he came to visit Dzongsar Khyentse, but I've never heard that he had a lama nephew. Now I hear that *our* Dudjom Rinpoche is receiving the *Three Sections* from such a nephew, and we all know that plenty of these so-called Khampa lamas come here to Central Tibet to try out their various tricks. So, I was wondering if you were just another one of them. Hmmm . . ."

He was staring at me with his big eyes glaring the whole time. "A lot of Khampa lamas come here and cheat people by giving empowerments to which they have no lineage."

Dudjom Rinpoche, who was sitting right there, broke in and said, "It was I who asked him to give this transmission."

And soon they began to crack one joke after another, during which Chatral Rinpoche turned to me with a smirk and said, "Okay, I guess you are not a fake after all—you can go ahead and give him the empowerment then."

❧

While I was offering the empowerments to Dudjom Rinpoche, the Chinese communists were already in Lhasa. Yet only a few people were aware of their plans to take over Tibet. Ta Lama, one of the important ministers at that time, kept a fine, dignified face in public, but as soon as we saw him in private, he would ask, "Do you have any terma predictions from the Lotus-Born master concerning our time?"

It seemed that the Tibetan government didn't exactly have the fearless and unshakable confidence of mastery, and they were hoping to find a solution to the crisis through Padmasambhava's prophecies. In fact, there were several clear terma prophecies by the Lotus-Born about the imminent destruction of Tibet, some even mentioning invasion from the east.

But people paid no heed, or else they misinterpreted the omens. For instance, one text of predictions said that in the future, "Like a flower amid a lake, the Jowo will be worshipped from afar," which was interpreted to mean that the Jowo statue was so precious that it was indestructible. The real meaning was that people would be prevented from seeing it or forced to live in exile from Tibet.

I asked Ta Lama if they had tried to establish diplomatic relations with foreign powers like the United States, India and Great Britain. He replied that they had but had not received any firm commitments. Meanwhile, the Chinese communists had only one aim in mind: to devour Tibet.

This threat weighed on my mind, so much so that I often could not sleep. I had a feeling that sooner or later Tibet would be lost and I needed to flee somewhere free of communist invaders. It was not in my heart to remain in Tibet—not in the least. I am sorry to say so, but a great many Tibetan government officials were enticed by the silver coins that the Chinese gave out lavishly, and so many officials claimed that that there was nothing to worry about—everything was just fine.

One day, Dudjom Rinpoche confided that he felt we still had about one year left. "We should take advantage of the Chinese while we can. I plan to stay here for about one year, and to use their silver coins to ensure the Dharma's future."[241]

"There is no way I will remain that long," I replied. "I've already asked for the Karmapa's permission to leave. I'm going to get out before anybody else."

⁂

Around this time, a Committee of Religious Affairs was established in Lhasa, composed of the heads of the various schools. Meetings of the group were orchestrated by the Chinese occupation forces in order to control the Buddhists from above.

Not wishing to attend in person, the Karmapa sent me in his place. I couldn't excuse myself because of the Karmapa's wish that I represent him in Lhasa, so I had to go. Dudjom Rinpoche represented the Nyingma school. There were also representatives of the Sakya, Gelug, and Bönpo—five Dharma traditions in all.

Our main activity at these meetings was to while away the hours as one person after another gave lengthy lectures extolling the virtues of Dharma practice—while in reality our time for practicing the Dharma was quickly running out. Under the pretext of encouraging Dharma lectures to a large audience, the communist leaders were pulling the wool over everyone's eyes. Each speech had to start out with a salute to the "authentic reign of the great helmsman, Mao Tse-tung," thanking him for his "immense kindness, which has finally allowed the five spiritual traditions to assemble under one roof."[242]

In a typical display of Chinese cunning, at each event the communist officials would hand out bags of money, twenty-five large silver coins a day. Even my attendant, who was a secretary from Tsurphu and a very good man, got fifteen. So simply sitting there would earn me twenty-five large silver coins, which was a significant amount in those days. If you could grin and bear it for a month, you could collect a considerable sum.

However, I didn't keep any of those silver coins, feeling in the core of my heart no desire to form a concrete link with the communists. Rather than using that money even for transportation, I opted to represent all the Kagyu lineages by walking everywhere on foot. After twenty-five days, I got a chance to visit Tsurphu, and along the way I threw away all the silver coins.

"Why are you here and not at the assembly?" the Karmapa asked.

"I don't want to attend any longer, even if you threaten to chop off my head!" I said.

"Very well, we'll find someone else," he replied.

I then told him another tulku had volunteered to take my place and asked if that would be acceptable. The Karmapa consented and I was off the hook.

Later, when things got really bad in Lhasa, my replacement failed to escape. Even though they had regularly given him silver coins for two or three years, the Red Army executed him.

Shechen Kongtrul

As I was preparing to leave Tibet, a wonderful master named Shechen Kongtrul gave me a letter to deliver to Dzongsar Khyentse, who was already in Sikkim. Handing me the letter, he said, "These days it is definitely justifiable to say that Dzongsar Khyentse is Old Khyentse in person. Nowadays it seems very easy for people to meet him down in Gangtok, which is actually quite incredible. Please take this letter to him."

It was extremely unusual for this master to offer such praise about anyone. But when I later gave Dzongsar Khyentse the letter, he put it on his head and said, "This is from someone who is like Old Kongtrul in person. It may seem as though it was very easy for you to meet him, but it is amazing good fortune." They had this remarkable mutual admiration for, and pure perception of, each other.

Shechen Kongtrul had reached the collapse of delusion. Noble beings at this level very often act in a totally spontaneous way, like children, without any second thoughts regarding social conventions—and that's how Shechen Kongtrul seemed during the last years of his life.

Once, while he was in Lhasa, one of the ministers of Central Tibet came to visit him. The officials of the Lhasa governing body of that time all kept their hair tied up on their head, decorated with a golden relic box. Yogis often tie their hair up too, with a small relic box containing sacred scriptures or relics. Even though this man was clearly dressed as a Tibetan dignitary, Shechen Kongtrul said to him, "Hey, yogi, where are you coming from?"

61. The Kongtrul of Shechen

"Rinpoche, psstt," someone leaned over to him and whispered, "He's not a yogi, he's a minister."

"Oh, so you're a minister," Shechen Kongtrul blurted. "I thought you were a yogi. Where are you from?" The minister was very embarrassed.

On another occasion, Ngabö, a high government official, had invited Chung Rinpoche of Mindrolling, Shechen Kongtrul, Dilgo Khyentse and many other monks to perform a ceremony at the Jokhang. They all sat together.

Ngabö did not come in person but sent his wife, a woman of high standing who was addressed as Lhacham Kusho, Her Ladyship. Because she was a VIP, when she gave a white scarf with an envelope of money to Chung Rinpoche, she also lowered her head—not as low as an ordinary person would to receive a blessing from the lama's hand, but only to the level of touching foreheads.

At that, Shechen Kongtrul nudged Dilgo Khyentse with an elbow and burst out loudly, "Hey Khyentse, quick! What am I supposed to do with that woman? I've never touched heads with one before." Meanwhile the woman had stepped over and was standing right in front of him.

"Just keep quiet and touch heads!" Dilgo Khyentse whispered. So, Shechen Kongtrul bent down and touched heads with her in the manner of greeting between equals.

She then presented him with a scarf accompanied by a traditional envelope of money as an offering. While Dilgo Khyentse was seated next to him receiving his scarf and offering, Shechen Kongtrul had already torn open his envelope and looked inside—breaking every rule of decorum.

He took out the money and spoke up for all to hear, "Hey Khyentse, look what I got! How much did you get?"

I wasn't there, but Dilgo Khyentse himself told me the story and warned, "It's impossible to sit next to him in public."

※

When Shechen Kongtrul spoke about mundane affairs, he could often be quite childish, but when he spoke about the Dharma, his wisdom was like the rising sun dispelling the darkness. In Lhasa I once had the chance to ask him who he felt were the most realized masters in Tibet.

"Take a look at Dudjom," he replied. "His eyes are so bright and present, almost like a hawk. In the eyes you can see the quality of complete open awareness. If anyone has realization, he does. Compared to him everyone else seems quite dull and absentminded."

"What about that master Drukpa Yongdzin, who is so greatly renowned?" I then asked.

"He's definitely got it too. His mind is wide open, without a shred of ignorance," replied Shechen Kongtrul. "I hear that he doesn't even sleep."

Then I asked him what he meant by *high realization.*

"It is when your awareness is unimpeded and free of fixation, and yet you are acutely present and attentive to detail."

He then precisely demonstrated just this. I felt sure that he was a highly realized master himself and I had deep trust in him.

※

There had been an uprising against the Chinese occupation forces in Kham, although Central Tibet was still calm. While I was still at Tsurphu with the Karmapa, Shechen Kongtrul stopped there.

He told me of a premonition, "Whenever I see a Chinese communist these days, I immediately get a pain in my chest. I feel extremely uncomfortable. Probably I will be taken off by the communists someday."

He made this comment several times. Once I asked, "Why would you be taken off by the communists? Karmapa is sending you to Sikkim to become the main guru of the Sikkimese king. Our Wish-Fulfilling Jewel has already made the arrangements, telling the Sikkimese, 'I'm sending this lama to you to be the guru of the court.'

"Since you are leaving Tibet so soon," I asked him, "why do you think the Chinese will take you?"

Shechen Kongtrul replied, "I don't know why, but I just feel it will likely happen."

Before leaving for Sikkim he wanted to visit different places in Central Tibet. But Karmapa told him, "Don't. You should remain right here. Soon, you must leave straight for Sikkim. The main sponsor of Mindrolling is already there. You must join him; you will have perfect circumstances there."

But Shechen Kongtrul objected, "I must go to Mindrolling first. Mindrolling is like the cornerstone of the Nyingma tradition. I must pay just one visit there."

They argued back and forth, until finally the Karmapa said, "All right, if you must go, I will make all the arrangements for you and provide the servants. But you can stay there no more than two weeks. Then you have to come straight back here and go on to Sikkim."

Shechen Kongtrul promised to remain not a day longer than two weeks at Mindrolling. In accord with the Karmapa's command, he stayed only two weeks, then headed back to Tsurphu.

On the way back, he encountered a group of people at the crossing of a large river. It just so happened that they were members of the Lingsang family who had revolted in Kham and fled to Central Tibet, chased by the Chinese communists.

Since these people were Shechen Kongtrul's sponsors back in Kham, he was obligated to perform rituals for their support, for which he lingered on the banks of the river for five days. This turned out to be disastrous—the Chinese communists arrived, and he was arrested and whisked off to China.

I don't know how he died. He must have been transported from Central Tibet back to Derge in the east, because people saw him there, and then he was taken to China.

It was very sad. He was only about fifty years old.

⁂

Unfortunately, now I must give you another example of my own headstrong tenacity. As I was preparing to go to Sikkim, the Karmapa told me, "At first, stay at my disciple Banyak Ating's estate in Sikkim for a while, then go on to Nepal to the Great Stupa at Boudha in the Kathmandu valley. You should build a monastery next to it.

"Someone at the stupa has promised to give me land and I have a letter from one of the rulers in the valley pledging building materials. It has been six months since I was supposed to send a lama to oversee this project and I think you would be ideal for the job."

The next day, as I sat in front of our Wish-Fulfilling Jewel, someone walked in with a stack of eight letters. As he handed them to me one by one, he told me whom the letters were for. Each was addressed to a specific official in the Nepali government, as well as one to the land sponsor and one to the secretary of King Mahendra of Nepal. There was even a letter to Khunu Lama, an Indian master, asking him to come, though I doubted he would.

"Bad times will befall the country of Tibet," the Karmapa said. "I want you to build a monastery in Nepal. I am already making preparations to send half of our statues, books and ritual implements to Nepal, little by little. But there has to be a place to receive them—a monastery. You must go on ahead and build one."

He continued, "I have chosen you for good reason; you are capable of being my representative. I will send all the necessary attendants and secretaries, and give you a high position as lama. So pack all your things and go south to Kyirong, on the border of Nepal. From there proceed to the Kathmandu valley and immediately begin construction on a major monastery. The construction must be of fine quality and must be completed within three years. We should agree on this right now—there's no point lingering here in Tibet in the blind belief that everything will turn out okay."

"Pardon me, Wish-Fulfilling Jewel!" I said in disbelief. "How on earth can someone like me fulfill such a command? I am not that educated. I am not an eloquent teacher nor am I tall and handsome. It appears to me that you've chosen the poorest candidate. Sending me not only would be an unwarranted punishment, but I am sure would also end in failure."

Looking back on it, I can't help laughing at my audacity.

"In Kham there are so many great Kagyu monasteries including Surmang," I continued, "each with capable and distinguished lamas. You have the power to command the best to be your representative and they will obey you—wouldn't that be better? All you have to do is express your wishes and I am sure any of them will do as you say. That's what you should do—because I can't possibly take such a position. Even if I did go, no one would listen to me. I couldn't possibly promise to complete the monastery in three years. I am more like a hungry ghost in human form who has been given the name 'lama.' Choosing me to represent you will result in nothing but disgrace to the Dharma."

Then I stood up and did three prostrations in order to demonstrate the firmness of my resolve.

"When someone like me takes the position of a high Buddhist master," I added, "it will turn people against the Dharma and cause them to break their samayas."

"Don't you bother worrying about such things—leave them to me," the Karmapa replied, undeterred. "And, by the way, I think people will have faith in you."

"I'm not trying to say that you are wrong," I protested, "but it seems to me you are trying to make a dog behave like a lion—and I just don't see how it's possible."

"You really are an obstinate man!" the Karmapa exclaimed. "Senselessly stubborn. What a shame! You obviously don't realize what great benefit this would be to both the Buddha's teachings and sentient beings. I have great hopes for you.

"I am not in short supply of important lamas clamoring for a higher rank and position; many of them are eager to go and do exactly what I am asking of you. It's a shame, but forget about it—at least for the time being."

That's what he said, but it was of no help. I still wouldn't obey him.

This exemplifies my obstinate pride. I now regret not using that opportunity to fulfill his wish, because of course he was right: that was exactly when a monastery in Nepal would have brought great benefit.

But what did I know? I'm just an ordinary fool—and yet I was totally convinced of my own judgment.

Around this time the Karmapa inquired, "You are going to Nepal anyway, aren't you?"

"Why?" I asked.

"There is a place there called Maratika. That is where you should go to do your three-year retreat."

"Where is it located, Rinpoche?"

"Not too far from the Kathmandu valley. If you can do some longevity practice there during the three years, you will have good results."

"Please, don't force me to do that!" I pleaded. "Of course, I have heard of Maratika, where the Lotus-Born master attained accomplishment. But how will I be able to obtain provisions? I don't know anyone there. Please, don't ask me to do this."

So I didn't obey his wish that time either.

The Karmapa was very unusual in how he spoke. When he formulated his wishes, they often didn't sound so much like suggestions, but rather like possibilities that would actually happen. Still, in those days, I obviously didn't trust in him enough to listen.

And so those were two times when I failed to fulfill his explicit wishes.

❦

When I think of all the precious treasures that were lost from those days, I can hardly believe my foolishness. In particular, the books in the library at Tsurphu were impressive; knowing what later happened to that priceless library, I regret not having asked to borrow a few books for my trip to Sikkim.

One in particular comes to mind: Karmey Khenpo's annotated version of the *Treasury of Knowledge*. Not only was it in his own large calligraphy, but between the lines he had inserted clarifications that he had personally requested from the author, Kongtrul. The whole text with Kongtrul's own commentary filled three volumes. At Tsurphu I asked to borrow these and the Karmapa agreed. But when I tracked down the books, they had already been borrowed by Dilyak Drubpön, the retreat master.

"I have already asked our Wish-Fulfilling Jewel to lend these books to me. Could you please have them sent over?" I requested.

"By the Three Jewels I will not!" Dilyak Drubpön responded. "I am not parting with these books—not for anything! And I'll tell you why: Karmapa is always sending people over to ask me questions. Without these books, how can I give proper answers? You know I didn't do extensive studies while young, except for the rudimentary texts, the *Way of a Bodhisattva* and the *Triple*

Precepts. I am not that well educated and these three volumes are all I've got to back me up.

"It doesn't help that you say our Wish-Fulfilling Jewel has sent you; he's the one I'm working for too. Now you come here proclaiming you want to tear out my two eyes and leave me blind! By the Three Jewels, I swear I'm not parting with these books."

We were very close friends, so what could I do? I couldn't argue with him, so I tried another angle, "You don't need to hold on to them like that. The Karmapa really said I could borrow them for just a short time; let me take them for a little while."

"No, by the Three Jewels, you will not!" he exclaimed emphatically.

Dilyak Drubpön was a real meditator and a first-class person. But once he swore "By the Three Jewels!" there was nothing you could do. Had it been anybody else, there is no doubt I would have requested the Karmapa to lean on him. But not wanting to make it into a bigger issue, I let it pass and I never got the chance to read the books.

※

One day at Tsurphu, I was sitting with Dilyak when a close friend and relative of his, who had just finished studying dialectics and logic at Sera College, came into the room. Drubpön himself was more the simple meditator type.

"What do you understand by emptiness?" his friend asked, teasingly.

"Emptiness is very simple. It is what we call Mahamudra and Dzogchen," Drubpön replied.

"You silly man! You can't define emptiness by using just another word; it's supposed to be the basis of all the teachings, and yet you can't describe it. You sit here, pretending to be the Karmapa's assistant teacher, you fraud!"

"Okay, you define it, if you're so eager," demanded Drubpön.

"How can any meaning be communicated without using defining characteristics? Do you think the ultimate truth will just dawn on you by surprise? You need to use words and concepts. You idiot!" replied his friend.

Drubpön replied, "If you think you can demonstrate emptiness using words and concepts, then you're the foolish man, beyond compare!"

They went on bickering and laughing like this.

Drubpön then turned to me and said, "You see, without Karmey Khenpo's annotated version, how can I fend off guys like this?"

※

Later, when Dilyak Drubpön managed to get out of Tibet and reached Sikkim, he told me, "I didn't get to bring the books with me. I wanted to bring them and I really tried, but it didn't work out."

"How could you have lost them?" I lamented.

"By the Three Jewels! You weren't there to see the chaos and confusion. No one knew whether the next morning they would be alive or a corpse. Like clouds moving across the autumn sky, nothing was predictable. It was a time of intense turmoil and danger.

"That's the state we were in, while you were here in Sikkim relaxing and having a good time."

Still, it often comes to my mind that those notes—Kongtrul's own replies to Karmey Khenpo—would have been such a wonderful embellishment to the *Treasury of Knowledge*!

❦

At Tsurphu I had been lucky enough to see *The Great Scroll Depicting the Hundred Wondrous Deeds*. I consider it to be one of the most impressive examples of meaningful art in this world. In one painting after the other, this enormous scroll depicts all one hundred of the miracles performed by the fifth Karmapa at the Chinese emperor's court. Its text is in four languages: Chinese, Mongolian, Tibetan and another I couldn't recognize.

This remarkable scroll is more than forty arm spans long and several feet in height. It shows the sixteen arhats as saints appearing in cloudbanks, plus all the amazing events that took place inside the emperor's private chambers during empowerments, such as how the emperor saw the mandala of the deities and the day three suns arose.

I didn't know the scroll existed until Dzongsar Khyentse came to Tsurphu and asked to see it. When we unrolled it, Dzongsar Khyentse remarked, "I have never seen anything like this in this world! Other masters have displayed miracles while in China, but nothing like this." One morning, Dzongsar Khyentse and I looked the scroll over, reading through all the narrations from beginning to end.

I heard that three copies of the scroll had been made: one in China, this one at Tsurphu and one other that was destroyed in a fire many centuries ago. On the paintings were nineteen seals of verification by the emperor's own stamp. It would be a wonderful thing to preserve in book form.

I also tried to tease Dilyak Drubpön about not having carried out this precious scroll. But again he retorted, "Who are you to say I'm not a tough guy? You think you're tough, lolling around in Sikkim while we were on the verge of death?"

What could I say to that?

But then I remembered something and teased him a bit more, saying, "So who packed the Karmapa's bags? I hear there were one hundred porters merely to carry the tsampa flour, dried cheese and meat. Couldn't you have just replaced just one bag of food with the scroll? Didn't you know that the king of Bhutan had offered to be the Karmapa's benefactor? Who would starve to death with the king as sponsor? And while I'm at it, how about all the other representations of body, speech and mind that were left behind?"

All joking aside, I really was worried that this precious treasure had been lost. But I later discovered it was safe in Sikkim.[243]

Part Four
In Exile

34

Leaving Tibet

Shortly before I left Tsurphu, I told the Karmapa, "I don't feel it's appropriate for me to stay here any longer."

"Why not?" he asked.

"I have two children and their mother to worry about. While you can fly off like a bird in the sky wherever you desire; I, on the other hand, cannot move about so freely and I'm afraid I'll get stuck here in Tibet. My only wish is to go somewhere without a single Chinese communist. I have a short list of several places for your consideration. First, there is the Khenpa valley, a small hidden place in Bhutan. My next choice is lower Bhutan itself and my third choice is Sikkim. There is also a hidden valley in the district of Solu Khumbhu in Nepal and in the western part of Nepal there is a place called Nubri."

I mentioned the connection my uncle had to some people in Nubri, explaining, "A lama living there descends from King Trisong Deutsen and, since he's a disciple of my uncle, if we go there at least we won't starve. Please give me your advice as to the best place to go. The thought of staying in Tibet keeps me awake at night."

One of the Karmapa's lamas leaned over and said, "You don't have to worry about a thing; you are under our Wish-Fulfilling Jewel's protection. Just stay with our Wish-Fulfilling Jewel and he will take care of everything."

I replied, "That wouldn't be appropriate. I have a family I must worry about. And if I came along, I would not only diminish his stature but also be an embarrassment, since I'd be the only non-monk in his retinue. I would rather go on ahead."

62. Chökyi Nyima, Chokling and their mother Kunsang Dechen

While I was at Tsurphu, a group of practitioners from Nubri happened to come; they insisted on being given the entire transmission for the *Tukdrub Barchey Kunsel*. The Karmapa gave me the task, which took nineteen days. After that the Karmapa said, "Write down your choices on a piece of paper for me; I'll tell you the result of my divination tomorrow morning."

Early the next day the Karmapa said, "Forget about your other choices. Go to Sikkim. I will give you a letter of introduction to my disciple Banyak Ating, and he will take care of you. In any of the other valleys, it will be more difficult for you and, anyway, you are not familiar with their dialects."

With those words I had his permission to leave Tibet.

❧

I had left my two sons and their mother at Drong monastery, north of the city, and sent a messenger to fetch them. When they arrived I told them of my decision to go to Sikkim.

Hearing of this my brother-in-law Wangdu, who was a Central Tibetan aristocrat, exclaimed, "The Potala palace in the heart of the Lhasa valley is like a splendid tangka painting upon which the Dalai Lama shines like a radiant sun. How can the Chinese communists be any match for such a lofty presence? The communist army may run over you Khampas without any problems, but there is no way in the world that they can conquer the Central Tibetan government."

"The Chinese army has an incredible number of battalions, each with thousands of soldiers," I replied. "Please tell me the exact number of conscripts in the Central Tibetan army, which you consider so formidable. I wonder if they can muster any more than a mere ten or twenty thousand troops. When a mountain comes crumbling down in an avalanche, simple trees and bushes are unable to hold it back."

My brother-in-law would hear nothing of it. His attitude was typical of most the Central Tibetan aristocracy: unwilling to entertain even the

63.
Tulku Urgyen
Rinpoche early
photo

thought that his country was about to be crushed. So, my wife and her family simply refused to go.

As one of them put it, "There is no way we can just abandon our property and wealth!"

So I left on my own.

⁂

Just before my departure for Sikkim, a Tibetan woman told me she had good news, "The Panchen Lama, who is the Buddha of Boundless Light in person; the Dalai Lama, who is Avalokiteshvara; and Mao Tse-tung, who I am sure is the bodhisattva Vajrapani, are meeting together. This is a good omen for world peace."

Undaunted, and long before any fighting broke out in Lhasa, I left, with only my trusted servant at my side. Probably no one else ran away as early as I did—and so I managed never to hear a single shot fired from a communist's rifle. As they say, when the fox comes, the biggest chicken is the first to run into the henhouse.

It didn't take that long to get from Lhasa to Sikkim. Our small party traveled on horseback at a pleasant pace, with yaks carrying our luggage. If you don't stop along the way, you can get to Gangtok, the capital of Sikkim, in twenty days.

In Sikkim, I was received by the Karmapa's disciple, Banyak Ating, a generous and dignified statesman and a chief minister in the Sikkimese government. He had become an important benefactor and given many rice fields to the Karmapa, enough to produce five hundred bushels of rice annually. He said I could stay with him as long as I lived, offering me enough cornfields to feed ten people. Later, he rebuilt the house I was in, transforming it into a small temple. Over the next few years, I tried to persuade my brother, Tenga Tulku, to leave Kham and join me in Sikkim—but one day I received news that he had already gotten sick and died.

After receiving several insistent letters from me, my brother-in-law Wangdu eventually brought my wife and sons to join me. But after he arrived in Sikkim, he wanted us all to turn around and head back to Tibet.

"You've come to this unknown, godforsaken valley," he said. "I'm sure the Red Army won't follow you here—and if they did, they would starve to death! I've heard there is no proper food hereabouts, and it's so hot you can barely survive. I certainly won't stay. And I will not allow my old mother to stay here. I am sure she will die from hunger or the heat."

We had quite a lively discussion and it ended only when I swore that there was no way I was going to return to Tibet.

"Even if someone were to bind and drag me, I won't go, nor will I let my two children go back," I told him. "You are free to do what you want. When someone escapes from death row, they don't care whether the landscape goes up or down—they just run. For me, leaving Tibet was like getting out of prison. There's no way I'm going back!"

Wangdu retorted, "I don't sleep well here; I toss and turn, longing to be back in Tibet." So finally Wangdu packed up his things and took his mother back to Tibet.

I didn't see him again for many years—when the Chinese government released him after twenty years in prison.

～

Looking back I see it's only thanks to the Karmapa that I survived outside of Tibet—it certainly wasn't on my own merits. I had a wife and children, and I hadn't brought a single possession from Kham—just a few minor articles from Lhasa.

I sent a trusted servant to Kham to tell my close relatives, friends and those under my care in the monasteries all to join me in Sikkim. But many of them were too distracted by their yaks and sheep, and taking care of what they considered important matters, to even consider leaving.

I had requested from Lachab—which was still very prosperous thanks to Samten Gyatso's tulku—some important articles and funds, but my wishes went unheeded. Of my Dharma possessions, I hadn't brought a thing from Kham. By the time I was living in exile, Nangchen already had survived so many invasions and political upheavals over the centuries that people found it unimaginable that things might be unsafe in a monastery this time.

Chökyi Nyima's monastery was also very wealthy. If we had had the chance to bring some valuables from there, we would have been well off. But before a messenger could be sent there, all links to Tibet—both transportation and communication—were cut. Besides a few personal possessions and the daily necessities that we could carry, I arrived in Sikkim utterly destitute.

I was quite sad about some things that were lost. For instance, my teacher Kyungtrul's *Treasury of Nyingma Songs* in two volumes was a dear treasure; back in Kham, I had used it frequently to chant at funerals, healing ceremonies or feast offerings. Of course, I brought it with me to Central Tibet, but I couldn't bring it to Sikkim without risking strong suspicions or outright objections. The same went for other valuable articles, such as shrine objects. So I brought only a set of average-quality ritual objects, leaving behind all the heirlooms.

Because Samten Gyatso had been extremely exacting when commissioning statues, the images in the new shrine room at Fortress Peak were of the highest possible quality for his time. But I couldn't bring a single statue nor even one book from his extensive library. They were all supposed to belong to his reincarnation, the young tulku.

Anyway, this lost book by Kyungtrul had been one of my prized possessions.[244] The first Kongtrul had written a practice in which one honors all the masters in the lineage of the Great Perfection. In his text, he mentions that right after the feast offering, "at this point you can include a suitable number of songs from the lineage gurus." He also mentions great benefits from singing these spiritual songs, quoting from the tantras that "the wakefulness of knowing the natural state will expand boundlessly within one's personal experience."

Kyungtrul took upon himself the task of collecting these songs. One might think he got slightly carried away, since he began his search with Longchenpa's vast *Treasury of Dharmadhatu*.[245] His justification was this: "If you want to have songs that express the ultimate view of the three sections of the Great Perfection, I personally don't see any way to exclude Longchenpa's masterwork."

Following that, he collected songs from all the early Dzogchen masters, as well as from every important lineage master of Tibet. In the end, the collection itself filled two volumes. At one point, he even wanted to include a lengthy scripture containing profound songs by Longchenpa, the *Treasury of the Way of Abiding*.[246]

Samten Gyatso convinced him not to keep endlessly expanding his collection, saying, "Of course these too would be appropriate, but then there would be no end if someone wanted to chant all the songs during the feast offering—unless you want to make it last two days."

⁌

A few other precious texts did, however, manage to make their way out of Tibet in those days; for example, Samten Gyatso had an exquisite calligraphic version of the *Three Sections of the Great Perfection* that I was able to get out.

When he saw my personal copy of the *Three Sections*, Dudjom Rinpoche was extremely impressed by its high quality. "What a wonderful level of craftsmanship in both writing and spelling you have in eastern Tibet!" he exclaimed. "How amazing! I haven't seen anything this perfect before. Who did it?"

I answered that Samten Gyatso had an old attendant who was extremely meticulous and renowned for rarely making a spelling mistake. Samten Gyatso personally sponsored the handcopying of thirty volumes of scriptures connected to Chokgyur Lingpa's *New Treasures* and this attendant was the one who did most of the work.

My aunt, Tashi Chimey, and her husband were the caretakers of my gompa, and her husband was extremely fond of this text. He wrapped it in several layers of special brocade, always taking extreme care. Later on, when I was ordered by our Wish-Fulfilling Jewel to come up to Central Tibet, I sent for the text. My uncle then had a copy made for himself by a monk from my father's monastery, who was passing through on a pilgrimage.

Later, by the grace of the Three Jewels, the person who was carrying the text back to Kham got lost in the turmoil of the Chinese invasion and, having no idea what a treasure he was carrying, handed it over to a tulku from my gompa with the words, "This book belongs to Fortress Peak." That's why we have this very accurate version of the text today.

35

Sikkim

My Sikkimese host and benefactor, Banyak Ating, was a very special person. While young, he had been a secretary to the fifteenth Karmapa, Khakyab Dorje; Banyak loved him dearly. He spent three years with the Karmapa in Kham and had immense faith and devotion.

Once he returned home to Sikkim, Banyak married and raised a family. Most of his household shared his deep devotion to the Karmapa; you rarely see such a level of faith. One day, after our Wish-Fulfilling Jewel had returned from visiting the major sacred places in India, Banyak invited the Karmapa to the estate. Banyak himself was holding a white scarf and a bundle of incense, as he stood at the head of a long line of monks wearing special yellow shawls.

Banyak later told me that his wife—who, incidentally, was Tibetan—wasn't so pleased that her important husband was bowing to a Tibetan priest. In a critical tone, she asked, "Oh my! If you treat this Karmapa Lama in such a fashion, what will you do if the Dalai Lama comes?"

Banyak, however, was not so easily influenced and replied, "The Karmapa has been the guru of all my ancestors, as well as of the Sikkimese kings. He is our refuge and protector; it is from him that we get our teachings. There is no one more important than one's own root guru—not even the king of another country, even if he happens to be the Dalai Lama."

Banyak's family were descendants of the old Sikkimese kings, though not in the main royal lineage; instead they held positions as minister or governor, which were passed on from father to eldest son. He once heard that the queen herself had said, "Maybe Banyak should be called King Ating, he's so powerful. What's the use of having another king?"

Banyak just laughed and said, "I wouldn't do anything against His Majesty. But if that is the talk of the court, it's not a good omen for Sikkim's future and perhaps I should retire." And he did so soon after.

One evening, we were sitting around talking with two of Banyak's daughters. One said, "It would have been much better if the Karmapa had never come here. It was no good—he really shouldn't have come."

"Why?" I asked.

"Well, he wasn't a buddha after all," was the reply. "We cooked his food and we saw with our own eyes that he ate it. Later, we looked in the toilet after he had been there and we saw what was lying inside the bowl! So, realizing that he is just a human being, we have now lost half of our faith. It would have been much better if he hadn't come to our house at all."

"Oh, hush!" their father said. "Don't go on with this childish talk. Of course he's a human being! What did you expect?"

They had expected him to be a deity without a real physical body. The whole household did not use the Karmapa's name when referring to our Wish-Fulfilling Jewel; they called him "our buddha"—not *the* buddha, but *our* buddha.

Of course he was a human being. When the Buddha was in Sarnath and Bodhgaya, he too had a human body.

Banyak himself was not that childish; he was a person of great sophistication. He was also a man of means, with generosity to match. Every year, on a particular date, he had five hundred porters each carry a full load of rice up to Rumtek, the Karmapa's monastery in Sikkim. Whatever the monastery couldn't use, they were free to sell.

Wouldn't you call someone like that a benefactor?

༞

At Banyak's estate I went into a three-year retreat. While I was in retreat, my sons Chökyi Nyima and Chokling were learning to read. There was a village school nearby and Banyak insisted that they enroll there. But after just three days, Chökyi Nyima came home, appalled.

64.
The family in Sikkim

"That school is useless!" he complained. "The older kids show the younger ones how to trap birds and kill them. In the afternoon, behind the school, they pull out the feathers, roast the body over a small fire and eat the dead birds. How can I stay in such a place? I'm never going back!"

"So what?" The young Chokling seemed unperturbed. However he only lasted a couple more days.

For his part Chokling was impossible to discipline. Once he was so naughty I was forced to dangle him out the window by his ankles, threatening to drop him if he didn't behave. Yet even hanging there upside down, he was still defiant.

Sure enough, shortly afterward, he crawled out the same window trying to grab a branch and he fell. His playmate came running in, yelling that Lungtok—Chokling's name in those days—had fallen out the window. Miraculously, he escaped with only a twisted ankle. And though his eyes were moist with tears, he bravely proclaimed that nothing was wrong.

~

The two boys were very different.

Threatening Chökyi Nyima *did* have an effect: It made him worse, ensuring he would never listen. So I soon figured out it was best to use the voice of reason with him.

"What's the use of having the name of a big lama," I would tell him, "when your monastery is lost in Tibet? Here we are, penniless in a foreign country and some children aren't interested in being educated. Even though they might have been a big lama in their last life, without proper education their only chance for a job will be as a porter, carrying heavy loads down the road in the scorching sun, with sweat pouring down their faces. How sad!

"If only they could have studied while they were young tulkus! There is a Khampa saying: 'Today's meat and cream is tomorrow's shit.'

"Back in Kham we were like cream, and now we are like shit. Unless you study and learn to read and write now, you are going to be in trouble one day, I'm sure. You must have noticed how the porters sweat on the road; you're going to be like them if you don't do your daily lessons."

Once he got the point, Chökyi Nyima had no trouble studying. These gentle reminders were more effective than a hundred slaps with a cane. He would then even reprimand his younger brother, lecturing him on the virtues of a good education.

However, no matter what you tried with Chokling, it had no effect at all; he would merely laugh at your attempt to reason with him, saying, "What's there to worry about? I can carry a porter's load—I don't care!"

~

After I finished my retreat I was able to go on several pilgrimages. First, I visited Bodhgaya, one of the most sacred places in this world. As sutras tell us, the vajra throne in Bodhgaya is the site where the one thousand buddhas of this eon awaken to complete enlightenment.[247]

65. The Vajra Throne in Bodhgaya

Samten Gyatso once told me that all who visit Bodhgaya just once in their lifetime have not wasted their life and can die without regret. With that in mind, and not wanting to die without having seen it, I headed off for Bodhgaya soon after arriving in Sikkim. I was looking forward to making prayers and pure wishes at that sacred place, though I didn't get to stay long on that first visit.

I was also able to visit Bhutan several times. The first time, a Bhutanese dignitary named Puntsok Wangdu of the *drashö* rank sent someone to invite me there. He had met Uncle Tersey and was quite devoted to the *New Treasures;* in fact he had repeatedly asked if any lamas from this lineage had left Tibet. When we met it was clear that he had a strong connection to our lineage and had especially great faith in Tsewang Norbu. In the Bumtang valley Puntsok Wangdu had built a new temple at a place called Moon Meadow.[248] The Bhutanese way of making statues is to mix unspun cotton with clay, beat them together and then mold the statue from the mixture. In the shrine hall were exquisite life-size statues of the twelve manifestations of the Lotus-Born master, in fine detail according to the tradition of *Tukdrub Barchey Kunsel.*

While we were visiting Moon Meadow, Puntsok Wangdu told me, "I'm delighted that you have escaped the Chinese. Why don't you leave Sikkim and stay here? Although I am near the end of my life, I will sponsor you—I'll give you the Padmasambhava temple and build you a monastery."

"I can't stay right now," I replied. "The Karmapa sent me to Sikkim and he has placed me with his benefactor Banyak. I can't just abandon that situation. It is very kind of you, but now is not the time." He died not long after that meeting.

It was during this trip that I met the Queen Mother of Bhutan, who had been Uncle Tersey's patron. I was on a visit to a temple in Kalimpong, built in the style of the Lotus-Born master's Glorious Copper-Colored Mountain, and it happened that she was also this temple at the time.

"It's good you have left Tibet," she told me. "Near the Tibetan border is Lion Fortress Meadow, one of the five sacred places of Padmasambhava, where Yeshe Tsogyal meditated.[249] I have some land just below it, and if you would like to stay there, I will support you. Its fields are big enough to support about ten people."

Having no plan to settle in Bhutan, I thanked her but said that for the time being I was fine in Sikkim, being supported by our Wish-Fulfilling Jewel and Banyak.

༄

While Dzongsar Khyentse was staying in Gangtok, I had the opportunity to visit him every morning for twenty-five days and to ask many questions. Since he was in semi-retreat, ordinarily he received no visitors; but because I was a descendant of Chokgyur Lingpa, he showed me special kindness and allowed me to visit. Often he was alone, without any attendant whatsoever.

Banyak Ating had deep faith in the Karmapa but not in many others—not even in Dzongsar Khyentse. But one day after seeing me walk into Gangtok every morning to meet Dzongsar Khyentse, Banyak asked me why I was going there.

"In the entire land of Tibet and Kham, there is no equal to this master known as Dzongsar Khyentse. So I go to clear up a few points, even though I don't request any large body of teachings." Dzongsar Khyentse was familiar with the writings of every single master I mentioned to him and he also knew all the termas of the different tertöns; people said he was the most learned master of his time. Don't forget, this was no small achievement: There were many learned and accomplished masters during his day, but he was regarded as the "crest of the victory banner."

Hearing this Banyak wondered, "Hmmm . . . is he really all that special?"

"Don't speak about him with even a hint of doubt," I replied. "There is no one else like him."

66. Dzongsar Khyentse under the Bodhi Tree

It seems I raised some questions in Banyak's mind, for soon after, he began to visit Dzongsar Khyentse as well. And, being a steady-minded person, he never lost faith in him again.

~

One day I asked Dzongsar Khyentse what teaching I should practice. "The Great Perfection will blaze like a wildfire during this coming age," he replied, paraphrasing the famous prophesy, "When the flames of the Dark Age rage rampantly, the teachings of the vajra vehicle of Vajrayana will blaze like wildfire."

Dzongsar Khyentse explained that during the early days of Buddhism in Tibet, when the Dharma was just beginning to spread, three masters—Padmasambhava, Vimalamitra, and Vairotsana—brought many tantric and Dzogchen teachings to Tibet. Several centuries later, when Atisha came to Samye and looked through all the original Indian manuscripts kept in the libraries there, he saw many that were no longer available in India. He was so impressed he exclaimed, "Such an abundance of teachings! Those three masters must have brought tantras directly from the secret treasury of the dakinis."[250]

For a while, the teachings on the three inner tantras—Maha Yoga, Anu Yoga and Ati Yoga—flourished widely in an oral lineage from master to disciple. Later on, the Dzogchen teachings were mainly sustained by means of terma revelations.

As Dzongsar Khyentse told me, "Terma teachings were concealed to be revealed at particular periods later in history, and they appear in the forms most appropriate to the particular time periods in which they are revealed. Each major tertön must reveal a minimum of three major themes: Guru Sadhana, Great Perfection, and Avalokiteshvara. In our time Old Khyentse and Chokling were specifically endowed with seven transmissions."

Dzongsar Khyentse continued explaining that over the centuries, various cycles of Dzogchen teachings came to light and spread among people. The older tradition flourished all the way until the time of Chetsun Senge Wangchuk. Later on, Longchenpa codified the teachings into the *Four Branches of Heart Essence*. Later still, there were many other revelations until Jigmey Lingpa, who was the reincarnation of Longchenpa, revealed the famous Nyingtig cycle, the *Innermost Essence*.[251]

So each age has had its particular teaching of the Great Perfection meant especially for that time. Recently Khyentse, Kongtrul and Chokgyur Lingpa brought to light several cycles of the Great Perfection. And, as is well known, Chokgyur Lingpa personally revealed seven different cycles of Dzogchen instructions.

In our time, two particular teachings will be very influential: one revealed by the great Khyentse (the *Chetsun Nyingtig*) and one by Chokgyur Lingpa (the *Heart Essence of Samantabhadra*). These cycles of teachings were practiced by the two siddha kings who lived in recent times: the great masters Shakya Shri and Adzom Drukpa, both disciples of Old Khyentse.

"Which Dzogchen practice should I focus on?" I then asked.

Dzongsar Khyentse recommended that I focus on the *Heart Essence of Samantabhadra,* praising its suitability for this age. He quoted the last statement made by the Lotus-Born master in the sadhana section of the text:

> These ultimate instructions
> Of extreme secrecy
> Will, at the ultimate end of this age,
> Spread the heart teachings of Samantabhadra.

Another day, I asked Dzongsar Khyentse, "People like myself, who don't know much of anything, have a hard time discerning which are the most important among all the revelations contained in the *Treasury of Precious Termas*. We are like children picking flowers in a huge meadow, trying to choose the most beautiful. Which do you consider the most important?"

"For the guru aspect, there is none greater than Guru Chöwang's *Tenth Day Practice in Eight Chapters*; it is sovereign among all guru sadhanas," Dzongsar Khyentse answered. "For the yidam aspect, the Lotus-Born master taught the *Eight Sadhana Teachings,* and Nyang-Ral's version is eminent. The most important dakini practice is the *Black Vajra Yogini*, also revealed by Nyang-Ral Nyima Özer. These three are the most important among all terma revelations."[252]

I also asked about the *Three Sections of the Great Perfection*.

"It is the combined heart essence of Padmasambhava, Vairotsana and Vimalamitra that they received from their guru Shri Singha, their primary guru for the teachings of the Great Perfection.[253] So far it hasn't been widely propagated and practiced in Tibet; it's a concealed teaching, meant to be practiced in hidden places. I believe the time is yet to come when it will benefit a great many beings. I wouldn't suppose those three masters combined their efforts for no purpose—enlightened beings who can see the future wouldn't do something pointless, would they?" That's all he would say.

"There are some precious guidance manuals in the *Three Sections*, but it all seems very short to me," I said.

"Only the Lotus-Born guru can condense so many teachings into a single volume, no one else. And, by the way, do guidance manuals have to be extensive? Tell me, what exactly do you think is missing in those teachings?"

Of course he wasn't expecting an answer—it was obvious the *Three Sections* lacked nothing.

"When I look at the *Three Sections*," he continued, "I see something complete, without a single aspect missing. I have heard others say that they felt it wasn't all written down, but I don't see it that way."

Then I requested, "Tell me about the Dzogchen teachings."

"They are incredibly precious. Instructions on the Great Perfection are found in both the oral lineage of the Nyingma school, transmitted from master to student, and in the terma revelations. Among the termas, the foremost collection is the *Four Branches of Heart Essence*, containing teachings from both Padmasambhava and Vimalamitra. In their particular time, these instructions benefited multitudes and many practitioners ascended to the vidyadhara level by applying them.[254]

"The Lotus-Born master, with great compassion and wisdom, ensured that each generation would have a specific teaching meant for that time. Moreover, they would be guaranteed a short lineage, unpolluted by damaged samayas and with the blessed breath of the dakinis still warm. That is why we now have so many sadhanas from over various centuries based on the Three Roots.

"Some people wonder what is the point of having such variety—but there are many good reasons. One is the immediate effect at the time of revelation: it's like having a fresh crop, rather than food from last year. In each age, there are worthy disciples ready to be brought to maturity and they must be given the proper empowerments. Other beings must be benefited indirectly, by planting the seeds for their future liberation. And the Buddha's teachings must be supported to ensure the happiness of beings. This was Padmasambhava's concern and he made certain of this for many generations into the future. His was indeed an immense kindness."

"What do you suggest I personally practice?" I then asked.

"Take *Tukdrub Barchey Kunsel* as your main teaching," he replied. "Since you are a descendant of its revealer, Chokgyur Lingpa, regard him as your main guru and supplicate him one-pointedly. In this way, you have a practice complete with guru, yidam and dakini. Don't forget this! Among all of Chokgyur Lingpa's termas, *Tukdrub* was revealed without any hindrance and is extremely profound. Practice it and you will find nothing lacking. When obstacles are removed, realization occurs spontaneously, so focus on that practice!

"As you are a descendant of Chokgyur Lingpa, the sublime deity you practice should be connected with your family line. The *Tukdrub* cycle is unexcelled in that the Lotus-Born master has a circle of twelve distinct deities, each of which is indivisible from him. *Tukdrub* represents a unique kind of sadhana, in which the guru and the yidams are practiced indivisibly."

"Whom should I regard as the guru?" I asked.

"Supplicate Chokgyur Lingpa!" Dzongsar Khyentse replied. "That will be sufficient!"

In this way I found the answers to a wide range of questions.

67. Dzongsar Khyentse Rinpoche

During this same time, Trulshik Rinpoche was in Gangtok and also received teachings from Dzongsar Khyentse, who was one of his main root gurus. Trulshik later told me that he too had asked whom he should follow in the future. Dzongsar Khyentse told him there would be no one better for him than Dilgo Khyentse.

Dzongsar Khyentse later passed away in Gangtok.

⚜

One day, three of the people from Nubri whom I had met at Tsurphu showed up in Sikkim and insisted I return with them to Nubri to give the *New Treasures*. They refused to leave without me. During this time the Karmapa was giving some very important teachings on two of the great Kongtrul's five famous treasuries: the *Treasury of Kagyu Tantric Teachings* and the *Treasury of Oral Instructions*. This event took place at Rumtek and I encouraged them to remain in order to receive these. But after those teachings ended, they again refused to leave without me.

Even though Banyak happily provided my family with loads of rice, I didn't feel we should continue being a financial burden on him. And instead of assisting the Karmapa, I became worried that I was diverting funds from him, since Banyak Ating was the Karmapa's main sponsor. So I began to think about how we could move.

Since I was still occasionally the Karmapa's assistant, I had to ask his permission to leave. One day, I went over to pay my respects to our Wish-Fulfilling Jewel, with a plan in mind.

68. Trinley Norbu Rinpoche with his wife and the tulku of Dzongsar Khyentse

69. The sixteenth Karmapa

"I would like to ask your permission to leave Sikkim," I told him.

"Where are you planning to go?" asked the Karmapa.

"I am heading for Nubri in the mountains of Nepal," I replied. "I know some people there that I once met in Tibet. Those asking me to come are the descendants of King Trisong Deutsen I told you about. They are gentle people and their devotion is steadfast. I know the people of Nubri are of humble means, but they are persistent in their requests for me to come."

In fact, the three of them were waiting outside at that very moment.

I added, "But I'm afraid of hurting Banyak Ating's feelings by leaving abruptly."

The Karmapa replied, "No need to worry. Banyak is a good man, all he wants to do is benefit the Dharma. I'm sure he won't mind your leaving."

"If that's the case, I'll prepare to leave as soon as possible," I said. But the Karmapa asked me to stay on for a few more days. Banyak Ating, on the other hand, had other news for me.

Around this time, Banyak discovered something more about my background. "I know you are a descendant of Chokgyur Lingpa," he announced. "Dzongsar Khyentse asked me what lamas I have living at my estate and I told him the Karmapa had sent me some lama descending from Chokgyur Lingpa's family line. To that Dzongsar Khyentse replied, 'Excellent! He's first class! The profound terma teachings he holds are very precious, believe me. You should help him to build a small monastery on the mountainside, accept him as your lama and embrace his Dharma lineage.' He continued to extol Chokgyur Lingpa until I agreed.

"We don't need to build a new monastery," Banyak continued, "since there is already a small gompa on my property. I would like to give it to you, so you can establish the *New Treasures* here, and I would like to help you restore it."

I replied, "I have no such ambition, so I don't need to take you up on your kind offer."

In short, though Banyak's intentions were good, his offer came a bit late. Since the folks from Nubri had no intention of leaving without me, my mind was already made up.

"You are a very strange man," he said. "We've just received word that a border skirmish has broken out between the Chinese and Nepali armies. Don't you know that if China decides to, they can take over Nepal in less than one hour? Nepal does not have the resources to withstand an invasion. And now you think you can take refuge in such a small, helpless country? Sikkim, on the other hand, is defended by India and if China decides to take on India, it will take at least ten days." He repeated how foolhardy my plan was and chuckled.

"I am sure I'll be fine, as the Karmapa has given me his assurance," I replied. "But I would be quite grateful if you could provide me with a letter of passage."

"I understand your reasons for leaving," Banyak answered, "since it looks like these people from Nubri won't leave unless you go with them. Although I had hoped to be able to do more for you, as I recently mentioned to our Wish-Fulfilling Jewel, I will do what I can to help."

❦

Before leaving, I visited Dudjom Rinpoche once again to request the Kilaya empowerment from his own mind treasure. While there, I heard him tell several lamas from Ladakh and Khunu who were with him, "Don't waste your time with me. Go up to Gangtok, because a real Jamyang Khyentse lives there! Don't you know that he is an emanation of Vimalamitra? Not only are you mistaken in coming to see me instead, but it makes me uneasy that you are ignoring such a great master!"

After the others left, he turned to me and said, "These days I'm sending many people over to Gangtok to see Dzongsar Khyentse."

When I told him that I was going to Nepal, he asked, "What does the Karmapa say?" The Karmapa and Dudjom Rinpoche had great respect for each other.

I assured him that I had received the Karmapa's blessing and Dudjom gave me his as well. Dudjom remarked that he had pure perception of my kids as being from the vidyadhara lineage of Chokgyur Lingpa and was pleased that they would be going with me. "Nothing bad will happen to them," he assured me.

As I was leaving, Banyak wished me well and said that if things didn't work out, I was always welcome to come back and take him up on his offer. He also supplied me with a letter of passage for local authorities, which was very kind, though it only got me as far as the Nepali border. I had spent a very enjoyable three years at Banyak's; it was very beautiful.

70. Trulshik, Dudjom and Tulku Urgyen, Rinpoches

Some of our host's household were weeping at our departure, worried that we would never meet again. As long as they could see us, they kept waving their white scarves.

We soon arrived in Nepal—and, indeed, I never have had the chance to go back to visit my friends in Sikkim.

71.
Dudjom and
Nyingma lamas
in exile

36

Nepal

When I arrived in Nepal in 1961, some of the Karmapa's disciples took me to the Great Stupa in Boudha and I was put up by Chini Lama. The Karmapa had sent money to Chini Lama in order to build a monastery in Boudha.

This was not an auspicious time to arrive in Nepal; the country was under a king, but the Congress Party had been mobilized for the first time, and the dream of democracy had made villagers swarm to the capital and fill the streets. They surrounded the royal palace waving sticks, crawling over the fence and yelling for the king to come out. With all the turmoil, it was hard to get any government official's attention, let alone deliver any of the letters the Karmapa had given me.

Nevertheless, along with several of the Karmapa's benefactors, I went looking for land near the Swayambhu hill. I told Chini Lama, "The Karmapa will pay for the purchase, but there has to be room for five hundred monks."

"Well, well," Chini Lama replied, "and who do you suppose is going to feed five hundred monks? These days people think twice before giving food to even a couple of monks. We have tried to maintain a temple for only four monks and it has been hard to find food just for them.

"This is not a good time; the Congress Party is revolting against the monarchy. You should have come earlier. The official who made the promise to the Karmapa to provide cement and rebar at government expense may have done so in writing, but what good is that now? He's not in charge any longer; his written promise isn't worth a glass of water! And by the way, the lama the Karmapa sent with money for the project brought only two thousand rupees, not twenty thousand. I understood that the money was for maintaining the stupa, so it's all spent—not a coin is left."

He was correct about many things, for one—I never got a single rupee from him.

72. The Great Stupa in Boudhanath, 1956

That evening, I sat down and drafted a report of all this news to the Karmapa and had it delivered to our Wish-Fulfilling Jewel. I thought how stupid I had been not to do the Karmapa's bidding at the right time; circumstances had been very different three years earlier, when he told me to go to Kathmandu. Clearly, the time he wanted to send me there was just right.

Now one benefactor was dead, another was attending to his dying son, the former secretary to the king was in prison and I had no one to deliver the rest of the letters to.

After a short stay in the Kathmandu valley, I proceeded to Nubri, together with my family, our welcoming party and some porters. I didn't stay there that long on my first trip; I arrived in the first month and came back to Kathmandu five months later.

My two young sons were at an unruly age, so I tied a rope around their waists and kept them on a leash just like dogs. People were laughing, but there was no other way. Some complained, "What an evil man, treating his poor children like animals!"

Chokling was particularly brazen and always looking for trouble. Sure enough, if it hadn't been for that rope, we would have lost him into the abyss on one of those steep roads. We had to pull him back up by the rope several times.

At one point, in order to consecrate a large prayer wheel, we came within a day's walk of the Tibetan border, which was now patrolled by Chinese soldiers. Some

73. Swayambhu Stupa, 1965

Tibetans we met along the way told us we shouldn't go up there, since it was too close to the border—they asked us why we would want to go back after having just escaped. But we went anyway. Looking across the valley, we could see our lost homeland.

Because we already had enough to carry and we had been told we could buy rice along the way, we hadn't brought any rice with us. To our dismay however, we discovered that, in that desolate region between Nepal and Nubri, there wasn't much food.

When they were small, Chökyi Nyima would only eat if the food was well prepared and tasty, but Chokling was far less picky—if there was food on the table, he would eat it. Once, we arrived in a village late at night after the shops had closed; that evening for dinner someone prepared big lumps of parched millet flour that had a distinctive brown color. Chökyi Nyima took one look and exclaimed, "It's poop! I'm not going to eat poop! No way! How can people live here eating poop every day? Don't try to feed me poop ever again!"

He would only eat some dried meat. I must admit it didn't take much imagination to think that it was excrement, so who could blame a small child for not wanting to eat it?

On the other hand, Chokling said, "I don't care if it looks like shit—it's delicious!" and he wolfed down both their servings.

⁂

Before I left Rumtek, the Karmapa had told me, "In a letter to me, the Dalai Lama says that we should accumulate a great number of the VAJRA GURU mantra as a support for the Buddha's teachings. So, arrange for a VAJRA GURU accumulation in Nubri."

I kept this command in mind, and it was the first thing we did at Lama Tashi Dorje's gompa in Nubri. He is a very stable, solid person, without a speck of deceit. His father had been a disciple of both Samten Gyatso and Karmey Khenpo. We met for the first time at Tsurphu, because Tashi Dorje's family was connected to Karmey Khenpo; the family had come to Central Tibet to find his reincarnation, who turned out to be a cousin of mine.

At Nubri, for forty days the whole village participated in this VAJRA GURU accumulation, from morning until night, eating meals together. The villagers were tantric householders and they all joined in, husbands and wives together. All told, about three hundred people participated in the ceremonies and each evening they would all hand in the number of recitations they had done that day.

I continued the same practice in other villages in Nubri, as well as in the Manang district. By the end of this trip, we had reached a total of nine hundred million recitations of the Lotus-Born master's mantra. The villagers also gave me offerings, so I returned to Kathmandu with a comfortable sum.

74.
Lama Tashi Dorje of Nubri

37

The Chokling of Neten

One of the most inspiring experiences on this trip was meeting the third Neten Chokling incarnation, who accompanied me to Nubri with his family.[255] Like all Chokling incarnations, he was very unusual.

His previous incarnation had been a siddha, whose personality was such that once he began giving someone the pointing-out instruction, he would not allow that person to leave the room until he or she had recognized the nature of mind. The second Neten Chokling incarnation was predicted by Chokgyur Lingpa himself in a letter he gave to Karmey Khenpo, whereas Tsikey Chokling was recognized by the great Khyentse.[256]

It is due to the third Neten Chokling that we have any of the *New Treasures* books at all. The Tsikey Chokling was both affluent and influential, and he managed to have almost every single terma carved in woodblocks. Tsikey Gompa was known for its first-rate woodblock printing facility. The books printed from those blocks were disseminated far and wide, but the woodblocks were all destroyed—burned during the Cultural Revolution.

Fortunately Neten Chokling managed to carry out a twenty-four volume set made from the Tsikey woodblocks, which he presented as an offering to Dzongsar Khyentse in the Sikkimese capital of Gangtok. This set forms the basis of what we use today as our present edition of Chokgyur Lingpa's *New Treasures*. After Dzongsar Khyentse passed away, Neten Chokling asked to borrow the books from his estate and used them to give the complete transmission at Tashi Dorje's gompa in Nubri.

75. The third Chokling of Neten—Pema Gyurmey

The third Neten Chokling was outstanding in many ways. His benefactor told me that one morning while the master was staying in his house, Neten Chokling repeated everything the benefactor had been thinking and dreaming during the night—he just saw it all very clearly.²⁵⁷

76.
The Chokling of Neten with his oldest son Orgyen Tobgyal Rinpoche

After our trip to Nubri, I saw Neten Chokling one last time, in Kathmandu. He tried to get me to travel with him to India, where he was headed. Since I was unable to come, he gave me his watch as a farewell present, saying he wanted me to have it since we would not meet again. He must have known that he would not live long. He was of tremendous service to the Chokling teachings; it was a great shame he died when he did—he was just forty-seven.

Later on, after Neten Chokling had passed away, the *New Treasures* were reprinted, and I have a set of those books bound in a large format. Oddly enough, the Bönpos arranged the first printing of our *New Treasures* outside Tibet. Later on, due to the kindness of Dilgo Khyentse and Lama Putse, and with the cooperation of American libraries in New Delhi—all of whom provided funds—a new edition was published.²⁵⁸

Surely Lama Putse ranks highly among those who have upheld these teachings. First of all, once outside Tibet, he collected every single text available to him in print. Then he searched and added whatever others he could find. Many of these were from those brought back from Orgyen Tobgyal's first visit to Kham, a great kindness on his part.

Lama Putse was the one who really knew all the scriptures of the *New Treasures* tradition and put the collection back together. So we can say that it is largely thanks to him that we have these written teachings of Chokgyur Lingpa in their present form.²⁵⁹

Though Tsikey Chokling had block prints made for the whole collection, nowadays you probably can't find a single full set in all of eastern Tibet—thanks to the Chinese communists, who were so meticulous in their destruction.

77.
The fourth Chokling of Neten

⁂

I hadn't left my obsession with caves behind in Tibet. I knew about a cave in Yölmo, one of Nepal's hidden lands, called the Sun and Moon Cave, where the Lotus-Born master once stayed.²⁶⁰ The cave was also under the care of Chini Lama and he generously gave me his consent to stay there until I died, which was very kind of him. So, one day I packed my bags and gathered the necessary provisions for a long retreat. I had five loads that included such things as dried meat, butter and even blocks of salt that had been brought down from Nubri. I sent one of my trusted servants ahead to prepare the cave.

The main effect from staying in solitude is that pointless activities naturally diminish. There is a famous statement, "By abandoning activities, you approach the nature of nonaction." That's the entire reason for staying in mountain retreats. Otherwise, without meditation practice how could there possibly be any point in staying in a cave. The beauty of a cave is that you don't have to build one, some people however miss this point and spend time interior decorating and making improvements. Forgetting the real purpose, they wind up thinking what a great cave they "own" and live an ordinary life.

At any rate, the Karmapa was due to arrive in Nepal for a visit. By the time he arrived, I was firmly resolved to stay in retreat at the Sun and Moon Cave until the end of my days. Everything was ready for my departure; four loads of provisions had already been packed and sent ahead. I had sent my sons to be educated at the monastery of our Wish-Fulfilling Jewel in Rumtek as I was planning to entrust their education to him.

So when we met at the Boudha Stupa, I asked the Karmapa about going to the cave in Yölmo. Unfortunately, however, an ownership dispute had broken out over the Swayambhu temple and the Karmapa refused to let me go, saying, "You must stay in Kathmandu until this case is resolved." My plan to go to the cave was thwarted—the court case took nine years.²⁶¹

But it wouldn't be my last attempt to try to stay in a cave.

78. Chökyi Nyima and Chokling, Rinpoches

As in India, the society of Nepal was divided into a large number of different clans and castes. Each caste had its own position in relation to the others, comprising a rigid hierarchy.

I found the Nepali people to be very gentle and generous. The family I stayed with belonged to the lowest caste of all. The head of the family was a very solid and kind man named Ram Lal. He had been the benefactor of Kharsha Rinpoche, the lama who had founded Nagi Gompa.

Ram Lal had a humble little house in the center of Kathmandu and important people would never cross the doorstep. Until the old king eliminated some sections of the caste system, you couldn't even drink water poured from the hand of a person below your own caste—so no one would drink water from Ram Lal's house. Nonetheless that's where I lived when I first arrived.

Some castes regarded themselves as very important. One of the dignitaries for whom I had a letter asked our Wish-Fulfilling Jewel, "What is wrong with this Tulku Urgyen? I don't know why, but he's staying in the house of someone in the lowest caste in Kathmandu. He must be able to find better accommodations. It's hard enough for us to meet with him, but if we use the old rules, I wouldn't even be able to get a cup of water."

Our Wish-Fulfilling Jewel later came to Kathmandu and asked me about this dignitary's complaint.

"Whether these Newari people are high or low caste," I explained, "Ram Lal is a benefactor of the Dharma and of noble character. I merely need mention some intention in passing and he does not rest until he has satisfied it. Such selfless dedication is hard to come by."

So it came to pass that Ram Lal's house would have to suffice as my "cave." And through the many years of legal wrangling about the temple at Swayambhu, Ram Lal was the most helpful person of all.

Thanks to Kharsha Rinpoche, I immediately had a group of supportive benefactors.

When Kharsha Rinpoche passed on, his family, disciples and benefactors offered his small hermitage Nagi Gompa to the Karmapa.

One day, the Karmapa told me, "You must stay at Nagi. You are an appropriate choice, since you are both Kagyu and Nyingma," as was Kharsha Rinpoche.

As soon as the Karmapa had installed me as Kharsha Rinpoche's successor, his benefactors all accepted me and carried out my wishes.

Back then, Nagi Gompa was very poor, as was the surrounding area; the local villagers didn't even fire the bricks they used to build their homes. Rain would leak through the roof of the room I stayed in, and the walls had large cracks. Such were the conditions while I lived at Nagi for the first few months.

I had the thought—not based on any profound sense of clairvoyance—that this was not going to be a stable dwelling for the future. "What," I wondered, "is the use of fixing this house?" So instead, I encouraged a few of Kharsha Rinpoche's benefactors to sponsor workers to begin digging into the hillside above, to create a flat area.

Later, I put an end to farming on the land around Nagi, thinking, "What's the use of killing insects just for a little food to eat?" However, I did allow Kharsha Rinpoche's daughters and his extremely haughty bursar to keep some fields for farming.

So now I had two tasks: I divided my time between developing Nagi Gompa and supervising the legal proceedings. It was two years before I could start construction on the new temple at Nagi. In those days, there was no road to Nagi; everything had to be carried by porters. We all had to walk up and down the hill countless times.

Intending to benefit the future of Buddhism in the valley, we began building. I thought to myself that constructing a large Buddha statue would not only counteract the negativity accumulated through the legal dispute but also benefit sentient beings. In those days, a big Buddha statue of the size I intended could only be built of clay; without a building for protection, it would surely deteriorate in this climate.

So, with the help of our local benefactors, I arranged to buy some more land to expand the acreage of the monastery. In those days, no one had the foresight or courage to spend considerable amounts for land. They habitually thought about the price of land in square feet. I bought all the adjacent land I could, while Kharsha Rinpoche's tract only surrounded the old temple below.

79. View of Nagi Gompa

By adding together many smaller purchases, we managed to acquire a decent sized property on which Nagi Gompa now stands.

During the construction, I was called down to the city below at least once a month to attend to another step in the endless legal proceedings. Then once again, I would walk up to Nagi and continue the work. I participated, building the three main statues in the shrine hall myself. Every so often, the statues had to be left to dry for a bit and then I would go back down to the valley.

※

During the legal proceedings in Kathmandu, I made a short visit to Rumtek. Border skirmishes had again broken out between India and China, and I asked our Wish-Fulfilling Jewel if it might not be better for me to go stay at Paro in Bhutan.

"Not at all," he abruptly replied. "You are definitely not allowed to go to Bhutan. Just stay in Nepal. Nothing is going to happen there with Chinese communists; I'll personally vouch for it."

Shortly after I left, the Red Army's presence at the borders became even more aggressive, and people began to evacuate Kalimpong and head for other places in India. The Karmapa, however, refused to leave Rumtek.

The king of Sikkim paid him a visit and said, "Wish-Fulfilling Jewel, I would like to suggest that you come and spend a little time across the valley in Gangtok. If the Chinese army invades, I'm not sure we can protect you at Rumtek. So should the need arise, it would be much more convenient to go to India from there. Please consider moving your residence, if only temporarily."

"Nothing will happen to Sikkim and I am definitely not going anywhere," the Karmapa replied. "If you believe in me, drop all these worries. Don't go to India. Nothing is going to happen here."

Then all the officials at Rumtek held a meeting and went before our Wish-Fulfilling Jewel. The general secretary, with tear-filled eyes, presented a white scarf, pleading, "We have just fled our homeland, barely escaping the Chinese invaders with our lives. Once again, that dreaded army is too close; it would take them no more than a few minutes to fly here from the border to bomb us. We know that China and India are at war up in Assam, and it is not just a skirmish. Please consider leaving Rumtek."

"You can leave if you want to, but I'm definitely not going," came the reply.

The Karmapa did not leave and nothing untoward happened.

As for me, whenever I even broached the subject of my going to Bhutan, the Karmapa refused to consider it for even a moment. He simply said, "From now on, you just stay put in Kathmandu and quit moving around!"

I've lived in Nepal ever since, where I have been able to survive without any threat to life or limb.

⁂

I must admit however that I did try to get to a cave one last time.

Once, on a visit to Bhutan, I was staying at Paro and, looking up, saw that below the famous Taktsang cave was an enticing little hermitage. It wasn't rightfully a cave, but it did have a lot of exposure to the sun and appeared to have wonderful properties for retreat.

The Karmapa was also in Bhutan at the time and I pointed out the hermitage to him, saying, "I would like to stay up there."

To strengthen the point, I reminded him, "The court case in Nepal has been settled."

"No way," he replied, "Definitely not! I want you in Nepal." So, once again, my plans were thwarted.

The Karmapa is my refuge and protector in this life as well as in the life to come. So how could I live with myself if I kept going against his word?

38

The Hearing Lineage from Bomta Khenpo

My next trip to Bhutan was primarily to meet and receive teachings from an incredible master named Bomta Khenpo. I had been yearning deeply to connect with him for quite some time and was worried that it might never happen. I had met him once at the hermitage Tashi Gang two days journey from the capital and, though we spent only an hour together, I was thrilled to the bone by his words. I had a strong feeling that if I could just spend a little more time with him, I could gain just a tiny bit of understanding. It was mainly due to that one hour together that I persisted, finally visiting him in Bhutan.

He was living at a hermitage in the mountains above the capital, a little wooden house provided by his royal benefactor. The queen mother kindly provided for my stay, and I moved into a comfortable small hut next to his that had been vacated by his bursar, who had gone to India on a pilgrimage. How I cherish the three months we were able to spend together!

If Bomta Khenpo felt close to you, it was very easy to get teachings. "Just come early every morning," was all he said, and so every morning I came at the break of dawn. There was ample opportunity for him to clarify every single point on Dzogchen about which I was not clear.

During this precious time I received Khenpo Ngakchung's profound *Hearing Lineage* from Bomta Khenpo. A hearing lineage is one that is given from the master's voice to the disciple's ears, and only to one person at a time, rather than being a printed text. I received the major part of these teachings from Bomta Khenpo.[262]

Many years later I also received parts of the same hearing lineage from Nyoshul Khen. However by then

80.
Bomta Khenpo

81. Nyoshul Khen Rinpoche

his voice was so feeble and my hearing so weak that we couldn't communicate unless we used a hearing aid and a microphone! Also, I was afraid of disturbing his fragile health and didn't want to pursue any of the points too deeply. This doesn't mean that Nyoshul Khen couldn't transmit that lineage—far from it. But he would only give it as a one-to-one transmission, with no one in the room but him and me.²⁶³

On the other hand, during the months with Bomta Khenpo, my ears had not yet gone half deaf, and his voice was bold and strong. Even though we didn't spend that much time together, I was able to receive some very solid teachings and ask key questions, concerning both personal guidance and the traditional instructions on the Great Perfection, from beginning to end.

&

Bomta Khenpo was a remarkable master and also very eccentric. "You and I have become very close," he remarked one day, "and you seem able to understand what I say. We are now connected as master and disciple."

He continued after a pause, "I'm an old man now and I tell you this without bragging, but this old man here is a bearer of the authentic Dzogchen teachings. Still, what good does that do? No one comes here to request them and even when they do, they rarely understand. A lecturer without an audience is no more than a barking dog. What's the use of me teaching into the air?

"No one from Kham, Central Tibet or these southern mountain ranges has come to request the view with a sincerity coming from the core of their heart. My health is now failing, yet I am still the old bearer of the true Dzogchen teachings—and it seems that I am going to take them with me when I die."

It stung me to hear these moving words, so I requested as many teachings as I could.

&

One day Bomta Khenpo told me, "In my life I have received plenty of teachings on the view and the scriptures of the Great Perfection, as have many others. But I'm one of the rare people who have met both Vimalamitra's emanation and Vimalamitra in actuality."

"Please, Rinpoche," I requested, "tell me the story."

"Vimalamitra's emanation is my teacher Khenpo Ngakchung. Once every hundred years, Vimalamitra sends an emanation to Tibet to clarify the innermost essence of the Dzogchen teachings. Paltrul once told his disciple Lungtok of Nyoshul that he didn't get to meet this emanation of Vimalamitra, but 'you will probably meet him in your time.' Lungtok identified his own disciple Khenpo Ngakchung as an unmistaken emanation of Vimalamitra and Khenpo Ngakchung became my root guru.

82. Khenpo Ngakchung

"When I met Khenpo Ngakchung, I already had a fairly good comprehension of emptiness, but that degree of theoretical learning didn't satisfy me. I still felt an acute need to clarify every point and gain a thorough understanding, to the fullest degree.

"So I asked for the job of Khenpo's tea server—not that I was that young at the time, but I thought it would be a good way to get close to the master. Each time I poured him a cup of tea, I whispered a short question and each time I received an answer. That was the only practical way to approach him; otherwise you had to advance to the position of assistant teacher to be allowed to ask questions. For eight years, I held on to my menial chore, serving his tea—and at the end of that time, I couldn't find a single question that I still needed to ask."

Later on, I got a chance to ask the Karmapa about Bomta Khenpo's teacher, "What do you think of Khenpo Ngakchung?"

"Oh, he's definitely an emanation of Vimalamitra," he replied in his deep voice.

That settled it.

☙

"The time I met Vimalamitra in person," Bomta Khenpo continued, "I had gone to stay in a cave up on a mountain above Shechen monastery. On the way up the mountain, I ran into a beggar-yogi, who volunteered to accompany me as an attendant.

"At one point we stopped to rest and I asked, 'How about the two of us cooking up a meal?' There was ample firewood and we prepared to make some

83. Vimalamitra— the Dzogchen master

tsampa soup. The fire was burning quite nicely and all of a sudden the soup began to boil over.

"'Quick! Quick!' I anxiously cried out. 'The soup is boiling over!'

"The beggar turned around, pointed his staff at me, and said, 'Hey, you! Forget the soup! You should worry about knowing the wakefulness that is your own nature.'

"At that very moment, I looked toward my mind and, all of a sudden, it was more vividly clear than ever before—untainted by even a shred of conceptual thinking. For a while I remained suspended in that experience.

"'Hey, you!' the beggar exclaimed. 'The awakened state! That's it!'

"In the meantime he had rescued the soup, though, and we sat down to lunch.

"In the afternoon, we walked down the mountain and, as we neared Shechen, the beggar told me to walk on ahead. After reaching the monastery, I sat down and had a cup of tea. Then I went outside and looked all over the hillside but couldn't see anyone in any direction. Then I went all around the entire monastery—but not a single person had seen this yogi. Finally, the head lama of Shechen told me, 'You won't find that fellow; he's no regular human being.'

"I objected, saying, 'What do you mean he's not a human being? I was with him.'

"'No, no,' the lama declared. 'He was an emanation of Vimalamitra.'

"So I've met such an emanation and he's the one who introduced me to the natural state so that I recognized it in actuality—what we call the ineffable natural face of awareness. From that point on, my practice became merely a matter of training in not being distracted from it—the natural state itself never changed. I did, however, have to pursue this nondistraction with great perseverance!"[264]

※

One day, Bomta Khenpo pointed into the air and asked me, "Do you see these Dharma protectors?"

"No, I don't see anything," I replied.

"There she is again! This Dusölma always comes around when you are here. Don't you see her? Right there!"

"No," I had to admit.

"What about all the others?" he asked, pointing around.

"I don't see any of them either," I said.

As Bomta Khenpo's moments of ordinary deluded perception became less and less frequent, his pure experience increasingly unfolded. Eventually he could see all the Dharma protectors as clear as daylight.

He would often give blessings by putting sacred objects on people's heads. Every once in a while, he would bang someone really hard and everyone else would run away; then, for a few days no one would come. This banging became known as a "wrathful blessing" among the local people. Once I met someone who claimed to have been cured from a serious illness after receiving one of these generous blessings.

He told me, "Bomta Khenpo hit me so hard I totally forgot my illness and after a few days I was all better."

❧

While I was there Bomta Khenpo was teaching an important Dzogchen text, the *Guidance Manual of Unexcelled Wisdom,* to a group of eighty or ninety lamas, monks and Bhutanese nobles. He gave an amazing exposition of these teachings.

Then suddenly he exclaimed in a loud voice. "Hey, you, old fellow! You talk and talk, but who is there to hear? Why don't you just shut up!" And he slapped himself on the cheek.

For quite a while he just sat there quietly. Then he began teaching, until another slap on the cheek interrupted him. And again he would say, "Shut up, old geezer! Who is here to understand these teachings?"

Apparently my own lack of merit meant I couldn't stay to receive the teaching in full; I received a message from the Karmapa asking me to come immediately to participate in some important ceremonies. So at the end of Bomta Khenpo's lecture that day, I told him that our Wish-Fulfilling Jewel had called for me.

Bomta Khenpo gave his permission for me to go and then as an aside, mentioned, "The expanse of the all-ground has begun to overflow. So many 'untaught treatises' now spontaneously manifest from within.[265] If I don't watch out, they seem to take on a life of their own, pouring out through my mouth. If I'm not careful, I become just a helpless witness. But what's the use of voicing these teachings when there is no one here to comprehend? The only thing that seems to help is when I slap myself on the cheek as a reminder."

"How does this happen?" I asked him.

"I once had a conversation with some old geshe teachers of the highest rank from Sera, Ganden and Drepung monasteries," Bomta Khenpo replied. "One of them told me, 'I have studied so much and learned so many teachings, but most have been forgotten.'

"'What?' I said. 'Can you forget what you have understood? You mean you forget the words, right? Not that you've forgotten the meaning. The tantras mention that untaught treatises are supposed to inexhaustibly pour forth spontaneously from the adept practitioner. So how can you complain about forgetting?'

"But the old geshe repeated, 'I am forgetting all I have learnt.'"

Bomta Khenpo continued his explanation, "Once you truly understand the teachings, it is impossible to forget the meaning, no matter how old you might be. My problem is the opposite: there seem to be more teachings than I can possibly contain. Sometimes they slip out, so I have to tell this old geezer to shut up and slap him until he stays quiet.

"But it doesn't help. He just continues talking about how all phenomena are interconnected, how the world and all beings are interconnected on both an outer and inner level, and how the manifest quality of spontaneous presence is related to essence, nature, and capacity. Then the old geezer goes on to how the empty essence has a cognizant quality of natural experience that can be either pure or impure, unfolding as either the inconceivable wisdom displays or as the proliferations of dualistic mind. Sometimes incredibly detailed explanations come out, describing the scenery and the adornments of the world as the illusory city of the aggregates, elements and sense-bases.[266] Isn't it true that the forests and greenery resemble the hairs on our bodies?"

He went on and on like that.

He would also cover in incredible detail the properties of the major and minor elements that compose the phenomenal world and our human bodies, and how they are linked—and then go on to how the sense faculties have a place within all this, both in the context of pure wisdom experience and that of the deluded way of perceiving samsara. He had an amazing ability to describe the basic condition of every human being, in ways I have never encountered on the written page.

Nor have I ever seen any master tell himself to shut up while slapping himself in the face—and then stay silent until gradually starting to teach again.

꩜

While our Wish-Fulfilling Jewel was performing the Black Crown ceremony in Bhutan, one day Bomta Khenpo came to attend. He had great difficulty walking at this point, but he forced himself to walk all the way.

"I need to meet the one who is Avalokiteshvara in person at least once," he said. "I have not yet had the chance to meet him. My background is Sakya, but he is the one in whom I have the deepest faith."

The Karmapa had traveled there with a large following. At the ceremonies, many great tulkus and lamas were seated in the front row, including Shamar, Situ, Jamgön and Pawo Rinpoches. I sat in the opposite row with Thrangu Rinpoche.

At one point, during a break in the ceremony, I saw that the Karmapa had tears in his eyes. I went over to inquire what the matter might be.

He leaned toward me so that no one else could hear. "In my dreams last night, I saw that the king of Bhutan is near the end of his life. There is nothing to be done. He has been a great benefactor and quite close to me, so I feel saddened."

The Karmapa treated Bomta Khenpo with great affection and after the ceremony he said to me, "Tell him to stay. I would like to have lunch with him."

84. The Black Crown ceremony of the Karmapa

After lunch, when Bomta Khenpo had departed, I saw that the Karmapa again had tears in his eyes.

"What's the matter, Rinpoche?" I asked.

"The merit and life are running out," was all he said.

The king passed away not long after and it was barely two months before the great khenpo left his body as well. For two or three days after the khenpo passed away, there wasn't a cloud to be seen in any direction, not even a wisp.[267]

Dudjom Rinpoche later told me that at Bomta Khenpo's funeral, suddenly a huge white light was seen coming from his cremation stupa. There were also a large number of relic pills found in the ashes.

Having trekked over to another gompa, I was only aware that someone was being cremated, but somehow I knew it was this great master. People in the area said that they had never seen such a clear sky in their entire lives. Bomta Khenpo was an astounding master.

It was in Bhutan that I asked our Wish-Fulfilling Jewel to give a name to a son I had with a girl from Nubri. The next morning he said, "A ngakpa lama named Drubwang Tsoknyi appeared to me wearing a white shawl and skirt. Your new son is his reincarnation."

39

Conclusion

At the Karmapa's suggestion, I went to Malaysia with three attendants. Our little gang of four robed people were the first Tibetan lamas to visit. The trip lasted three months and I was able to accumulate a fair amount of funds from faithful Chinese Buddhists there.

I had decided to use the money to improve the temple at Nagi Gompa. However, once I got back to Nepal and started conferring with Ram Lal about how best to use the funds, a letter arrived from my two older sons, Chökyi Nyima and Chokling. They were finishing up their studies at Rumtek with the Karmapa and other great masters.

The letter said:

> Dear Father and Mother,
> The Karmapa has told us both that we must build a monastery. We are too young to do anything about it now, but we have heard that the Chini Lama offered you some land at the Great Stupa. Please build a small monastery there. It doesn't have to be two stories; one is fine.

85. The Boudha Stupa and Ka-Nying Shedrub Ling Monastery—old air photo by Toni Hagen

The Karmapa hadn't singled out Chökyi Nyima and Chokling to build a monastery—he had told the same thing to every single tulku and lama at Rumtek that year. Anyway, this is how I embarked on building Ka-Nying Shedrub Ling, the monastery at the Boudha Stupa.

86. (left) The sixteenth Karmapa with the tulkus at Ka-Nying Shedrub Ling Monastery

When the building was completed, I thought, "The Karmapa is my ultimate object of refuge; it would be wonderful if he could come and perform the consecration." So on my next visit to Rumtek, I told the Karmapa, "I have finished building a small monastery in Boudha, and I have great hopes that you will pay it a visit. I am here to request you to go there and give the *Treasury of Kagyu Tantric Teachings*."

The Karmapa replied, "That is very sweet of you; I will definitely come. You have my word. I need to go to India first, but after that I will come to Nepal."

He came soon after. He also consecrated the temple and statues at Nagi Gompa. He gave the empowerments and then returned to Rumtek.

So, many years after he directed me to build a monastery in Nepal, I was finally able to fulfill my Wish-Fulfilling Jewel's command.

❧

We have reached the end of most everything of major importance that has taken place in my life. I'm sorry my story's a bit dull, but I have don't anything impressive.

I have told you about my family history, where I was born, my childhood in eastern Tibet and where I have lived. Even though I have been asked many times, I can't come up with anything spectacular to relate about myself.

My only important accomplishment is that I have been able to pass on a few of the transmissions I have received.

87. The sixteenth Karmapa & King Birendra of Nepal at the inauguration

The responsibility for the future transmission of the *Three Sections* did land squarely on my shoulders; these days it seems I'm the only one who holds both lines of transmission. I have very carefully given the *Three Sections* empowerments to several important incarnate lamas. In this way, the transmission for this teaching and the rest of the *New Treasures* remains unbroken.

I gave the *Three Sections* nine times. The first time was to our Wish-Fulfilling Jewel at Tsurphu. The second time was to Dudjom Rinpoche in Lhasa. Next was to Kangsar Khenpo of the Ngor monastery. Later, in Bhutan, I gave the *Three Sections*

88. Chatral, Dudjom and Dilgo Khyentse, Rinpoches

to the Bhutanese incarnation of Palpung Khyentse. The next time I gave it was to Depuk Rinpoche at Nagi Gompa and later to Khampa Gomchen, a lama who lived at our monastery at the Boudha Stupa. The seventh time was to the Karmapa's regents and many other incarnate lamas here at Nagi. Following that I offered this transmission to Adeu Rinpoche and Tarthang Tulku. The last time I gave it was to Tenga Rinpoche. That sums it up.

I have told some of the details of how the *Three Sections* has been transmitted and also hinted at how many great masters have shown deep appreciation for this teaching, including Dudjom Rinpoche. I also related the interest with which they pursued receiving it, such as the fifteenth and sixteenth Karmapas. In fact, these great masters had such appreciation for this extraordinary teaching that four of them undertook to write the empowerment manual for it.[268]

⁓

Dilgo Khyentse gave the *New Treasures* in our monastery at the Boudha Stupa, Ka-Nying Shedrub Ling monastery, because I told him, "My second son has been recognized as an incarnation of Chokgyur Lingpa.[269] He is also his descendant, and I don't feel I can give the empowerments and all the reading transmissions. An important master is required, and I feel there is no one superior to you, Rinpoche. So, Rinpoche, please bestow the *New Treasures* upon my sons."

When I made my request for him to give the empowerments, Dilgo Khyentse simply replied, "Yes, yes. I will definitely do as you ask." As was typical for Dilgo Khyentse he responded with great kindness and care, and not long after was able to complete the transmission—when Dilgo Khyentse said he would do something, he always did. There were many tulkus and lamas present. Near the end of the

89. (left) Enacting the drama of Padmasambhava, Shantarakshita and King Trisong Deutsen—Dilgo Khyentse, Trulshik & Chökyi Nyima, Rinpoches

90. (right) Lamas at the Boudha Stupa, at the end of the transmission for the New Treasures

91. (left) Five lamas in Boudha—Tulku Urgyen, Trulshik, Dilgo Khyentse, Dabzang and Depuk, Rinpoches

92. (right) Dilgo Khyentse Rinpoche with lamas at the Yak & Yeti

empowerments, because he was very learned, he wrote a fine text explaining the lineages from the treasure revealer through the great Khyentse, Kongtrul and the other chief disciples, how they were gathered into Tsewang Norbu and from him to Neten Chokling and Dzongsar Khyentse from whom Dilgo Khyentse had received the lineage.[270]

So we have two main lines of transmission for the *New Treasures,* one through Tsewang Norbu to Samten Gyatso, the other through Tsewang Norbu to Neten Chokling, Katok Situ and Dzongsar Khyentse, then to Dilgo Khyentse. Most important, though, the lineages have now been transmitted and continue to be upheld to this very day.

This has been my feeble attempt to briefly explain the stories of the lineage masters. I am seventy-six now, but I haven't performed any remarkable feats. So all you have are these stories linking together what I have seen and heard.

Personally, I have eaten a lot of meals and slept in between. That's my life story in short.

93.
Dilgo Khyentse Rinpoche with Tulku Urgyen Rinpoche's family

Afterword

Let's go back to Tulku Urgyen Rinpoche's grandmother loading up the yaks. Why would an old lady go to so much trouble? The journey that she was about to undertake was a highly daunting one. Traveling in 1919 from Nangchen in eastern Tibet to Lhasa in Central Tibet was arduous. The terrain to be traversed was dangerous, with huge rock formations of mammoth heights and steep gorges bordered by raging rivers. The weather was unpredictable and harsh. Anything could happen, from sudden hailstorms or torrential rains to blinding blizzards.

This is, of course, not to mention the vast distance that lay ahead of the traveling party. It took a minimum of one month on horses, yaks, and on foot. And finally, don't leave out the bandits and murderers who might rob and possibly kill them or leave them helpless, without animals or supplies to survive the elements.

So why undertake such a risky journey? Her mission to bring back her famous lama son was not to save him from the distractions of a well-fed clergyman amid the wealthy. Her aim was to put him to work codifying and collecting the precious teachings of her father. This would ensure the continuation of the body of masterpieces and the propagation of his rich legacy.

But it was not merely family pride that made the *New Treasures* so special and important to protect. By now you know that the *New Treasures* are teachings and practices revealed by Chokgyur Lingpa, who was the last of one hundred and eight great tertöns that Padmasambhava mentioned by name in his *Golden Garland Chronicles*. Chokgyur Lingpa met the Lotus-Born master face to face many times and discussed important points directly with him.

These teachings are Padmasambhava's heart essence, made available to the fortunate who want to put an end to samsaric existence and reach liberation and enlightenment. This amazing legacy continues to benefit countless beings to this very day.

Jamgön Kongtrul had complete faith and confidence in Chokgyur Lingpa's termas, and received from him as many empowerments for them as he possibly could. In his autobiography, he relates his various meetings with the tertön and the blessings he received from practicing his sadhanas. The great Kongtrul even acted, in his own words, as "the scribe" for Chokgyur Lingpa on several occasions. Not only that, but he collected the tertön's most important treasures and placed them in the *Treasury of Precious Termas*, (*Rinchen Terdzö*), his mammoth work that contains the choicest jewels from the revelations of the one hundred and eight major and one thousand minor tertöns over a millennium.

In his unpublished work on *Hidden Teachings*, Orgyen Tobgyal Rinpoche explains the Dharma in general and termas in particular:

> Hidden treasures were first buried in earth or rock and later taken out, revealed again. Moreover, hidden treasures can also mean treasure mines, the powers of the five elements, self-existing in nature. Termas can be divided into seven different types. Among all the tertöns, only Jamyang Khyentse Wangpo and Chokgyur Lingpa seem to have had all seven types of Dharma treasures. The texts of the terma teachings, such as the earth termas—whether the original handwritten manuscript was hidden in the form of Tibetan writing or written down in the symbolic script of the dakinis—remain completely unharmed by the four elements and cannot be destroyed, even if the world were to turn upside down, though they may stay concealed for one or two thousand years or more before being revealed by the tertön at the appropriate time.
>
> An authentic treasure teaching is comprised exclusively of the words of Guru Rinpoche and is not interpolated by other people's thoughts or opinions. It is as if the buddhas had examined what would be of the most benefit for the present times. Terma teachings are closely linked to their recipients, just as a master gives guidance closely linked to the mind of a disciple. In the same way, the Dharma treasures of Guru Rinpoche are closely related to the present age, like a direct link from the past to the present.
>
> Dharma treasures are transmitted directly from Guru Rinpoche to his authorized tertön, thus the lineage is very short. Therefore, since the tertön's mind is indivisible from Guru Rinpoche's, the transmission of blessings is like meeting Guru Rinpoche in person—there is no difference. It is therefore definite that a tertön has recognized nondual awareness and possesses an eminent level of realization. Moreover, the blessings of the lineage transmitted from mind to mind cannot possibly be impaired in any way.
>
> Because of the tremendous and unimpaired blessings of the lineage received from a true tertön, even if the practitioner manages to receive just a short empowerment, there will be immense blessings, unlike when receiving other empowerments. We can find this to be true when we truly examine our own experience.

Tulku Urgyen Rinpoche was born into the family line of Chokgyur Lingpa. His grandmother and the early masters who helped mold his character were committed to gathering, practicing, preserving and propagating the termas of Chokgyur Lingpa. They exhibited a profound appreciation for them and dedicated their lives to maintaining the lineage. Tulku Urgyen Rinpoche devoted his life to practicing and upholding these teachings as well. Many realized masters sought him out to receive the empowerments for the *New Treasures*. With utmost enthusiasm and commitment, Tulku Urgyen Rinpoche filled this need for dissemination. *Blazing Splendor* is a testament to this tradition that was one of the focal points of Tulku Urgyen Rinpoche's life.

Even though Tulku Urgyen Rinpoche downplayed his own achievements, we feel it is appropriate to mention some of them briefly here. We will not reveal his inner life story and level of realization; that is for great masters to do. Being as he was a hidden Dzogchen yogi like the rest of his family, it was not his style to laud himself. We will simply give a sketch of some of his accomplishments.

By the time Tulku Urgyen Rinpoche passed away in 1996 at the age of seventy-six, he had built five major monasteries in Nepal and a number of smaller ones, as well as establishing centers in Malaysia and Denmark, and had planted the seeds for an eventual center in the USA. His most important monasteries are in the Kathmandu

94. Tulku Urgyen with Tsoknyi and Mingyur, Rinpoches, and their mother Sönam Chödrön at Nagi Gompa

95. Tsoknyi Rinpoche with Adeu Rinpoche of Nangchen

96. (left) Yongey Mingyur Rinpoche—the youngest son

97. (left) Tenga Rinpoche with Tenpa Yarpel

98. (left) Ka-Nying Shedrub Ling monastery in Boudha

99. (right) The temple at Asura Cave in Pharping

100. Ngedön Osel Ling monastery

valley at Boudhanath, the site of the Great Stupa, at the Asura Cave, where the Lotus-Born master manifested the Mahamudra Vidyadhara level, and at the hill behind the Swayambhu Stupa. He primarily lived at the Nagi Gompa hermitage above the Kathmandu valley. Under his care and the ensuing care of his sons are over a thousand practitioners, including monks, nuns and laypeople. Of his six sons, four are major incarnations: Chökyi Nyima, Tsikey Chokling, Tsoknyi and Mingyur Rinpoches.[271] His grandsons include the reincarnation of Dilgo Khyentse and Phakchok Rinpoche, a master from Riwoche monastery. Tulku Urgyen's two other sons are Tenpa Yarpel, a close attendant to Tenga Rinpoche, and Urgyen Jigmey, one of Uncle Tersey's tulkus.

Tulku Urgyen Rinpoche gave the transmission of the *New Treasures* to his sons and eldest grandson as well as many other incarnate lamas. He insured that these precious teachings were passed on and upheld. He was however most well known for his Dzogchen instructions. In 1980, when Tulku Urgyen Rinpoche went to the West, he was among the first Tibetan masters to teach the most essential instructions of Dzogchen outside of Tibet. He did so at the express direction of the sixteenth Karmapa, who instructed him "Make the wisdom-sun rise on the Western skies." And that is exactly what he did.

101. Chatral and Tulku Urgyen, Rinpoches, with Kunsang Dechen and Phakchok Tulku

He conveyed the Dzogchen teachings with a brilliance that was unequalled in our times. He was famed for his pro-

Afterword

102. (left) Chokling Rinpoche with his first son—Phakchok Tulku

103. (right) Chokling Rinpoche with his second son—the incarnation of Dilgo Khyentse Rinpoche

found meditative realization and for his concise, lucid, and humorous style with which he imparted these essential teachings. His method was "instruction through one's own experience." Using few words, this way of teaching pointed out the nature of mind, revealing a natural simplicity of wakefulness that enabled the student to actually touch the heart of awakened mind. He changed the lives of many practitioners who received these teachings, recognized their mind nature and persevered in the practice. Until his death, many Buddhist students from the world over found their way to Nagi Gompa to receive these vital oral instructions in Dzogchen directly from the mouth of this master. His memoirs provide a glimpse into the influences and experiences that shaped the man whose simplicity and humility could attract such a cross-section of humanity.

104. (left) The fourth Chokling of Tsikey in Nepal

105. (center) The fourth Chokling of Tsikey in Kham

106. (right) Tulku Urgyen Rinpoche with Tsikey Chokling, Dechen Paldron and the incarnation of Dilgo Khyentse Rinpoche

107. Neten Chokling and Tsikey Chokling

108. Three sons and Phakchok Tulku at Nagi Gompa

Acknowledgements

It is with great honor, inspiration and encouragement that we could offer this wonderful book, *Blazing Splendor*. Tulku Urgyen was an amazing storyteller. I first heard many of these stories while he was on a world tour with his eldest son, Chökyi Nyima Rinpoche, in 1980-81. More often than not, Tulku Urgyen Rinpoche would spice up a lecture on profound topics with a story from his life. But, unfortunately, I had no tape recorder.

In 1981-2 we had the fascinating fortune to hear the story of Chokgyur Lingpa and his lineage from Orgyen Tobgyal Rinpoche, an avid patron of the *New Treasures*. These stories were written down and published as *The Life of Chokgyur Lingpa*. He suggested that we ask for more details from Tulku Urgyen Rinpoche about his uncles and grandmother.

After an eye operation in 1983, Tulku Urgyen Rinpoche had to convalesce in bed for several weeks, lying on his back. His German student, Andreas Kretschmar, had the foresight to install a small microphone right above Rinpoche's bed. Then we requested him to talk about the main masters in his lineage. When Rinpoche began to tell a story, Andreas would immediately press the RECORD button. Most of those stories are included in this book.

Years later, we decided to continue gathering these stories. They had been so moving that we wanted to preserve them so that other people might benefit. We embarked on this pursuit in 1992 when Rinpoche was supervising the building of one of his several monasteries in the Kathmandu valley. Marcia, Graham Sunstein and I would drive from Boudha to Swayambhu every morning and trek up to Ngedön Ösel Ling to record many wonderful tales. The quest continued when Rinpoche lived at the Asura Cave temple, the following year. Primarily, though, we gathered the most material while he stayed at his hermitage Nagi Gompa. It seemed that with each story we became increasingly enthused, requesting more and more augmentation. In the end, we had close to fifty tapes. We supplemented these with all the story fragments Marcia had managed to glean from Rinpoche's innumerable teachings tapes of seminars, answers to questions and private meetings.

The task of translating those tapes and editing them came much later, after Tulku Urgyen Rinpoche's passing in 1996. I translated most of the tapes while

Michael Tweed took dictation. Then began the immense task of weaving the stories into the single narrative presented here—a task undertaken with incredible diligence by Michael Tweed (who additionally monitored all aspects of this work), as well as Marcia and myself. Years later my good friend Daniel Goleman helped wash and iron this well-tailored narrative, while his wife, the gracious and beautiful Tara Bennett Goleman, lent a keen eye for the final polish.

We could not have endeavored in this project without many helpful Dharma friends and the consistent financial assistance they offered. Our list of benefactors include: Jes Bertelsen and the Center for Growth, Daniel and Tara Goleman, George MacDonald, Jean-Marie Adamini, Graham Sunstein, and Richard Gere.

We would also like to thank Quentin English for Michael Tweed's airfare, Josh Baran for marketing advice, James Shaheen at Tricycle for believing in and supporting this book, and Tsewang Dechen, the tulku of Samten Gyatso, who arranged for us to visit many of the places in Nangchen mentioned.

We take this opportunity to express gratitude to the all-accomplishing noble incarnation, Sogyal Rinpoche who with amazing generosity has given us his beautiful foreword. Once again we wish to show appreciation to the exuberance of Daniel Goleman in providing his introduction as one more way to offer life to the book. Special mention goes to the different photographers, the photo and line drawing donors who are listed on the page for art credits. Final thanks goes to Kerry Moran, to our expert copy editor, Tracy Davis and to the talented type-setter, Rafael Ortet and our ever keen eyed proof reader, Daniel Kaufer.

This publication of *Blazing Splendor* has come to life thanks to this continual support and enthusiasm, without which it would have remained a mere aspiration. There has been so much joy and heartfelt devotion in working with this material. Words cannot express the sense of purpose and love we have experienced while walking in Tulku Urgyen's landscape, literally and figuratively. It has been a shower of his blessings for sure. We rejoice in our collective achievement and harmony.

109. (left) Marcia Binder Schmidt in Nangchen 2003

110. (right) Tulku Urgyen Rinpoche and Erik Pema Kunsang at Nagi Gompa

Please forgive the inevitable faults we might have made. Accept the result as a praise and an offering combined with the heartfelt wish that the pure lineages and masters will continue and flourish without any obstacles, that the incarnation of Tulku Urgyen Rinpoche be blessed with similar abilities, that all beings may benefit from the Buddha's teachings and that we disciples may assemble with all the characters we have met here in the Lotus-Covered Realm of Padmasattva!

Art Credits

Ani Jinpa 48, 61
Ani Lodro Palmo 76, 77
Erik Pema Kunsang 11, 19, 21, 25, 26, 27, 28, 29, 30, 33, 34, 35, 36, 38, 41, 42, 49, 106, 109
Ganesh Man Chitrakar 73
Gelong Rinchen 18
Gloria Jones 37, 39, 45
Graham Sunstein 15, 54, 55, 63, 65, 69, 80, 93, 95
Greg Rabold 107
Gyangtse Lhadripa 8
Jean-Marie Adamini 1
Jeff Sable 108
Jocelyn Sylvester 60, 70
Kathy Morris 62, 86, 87
Kungo Kalsang 64
Larry Mermelstein 46
Lobpon Norbu La 50
Mani Lama 72, 85
Marcia Binder Schmidt 4, 22, 43, 68, 79, 94, 102
Mathieu Ricard / Shechen Archives 31, 32, 40, 44, 51, 52, 53, 56, 57, 58, 59, 66, 71, 75, 84, 89, 90, 105
Mayum Sönam Chödrön 74
Michael Tweed 9
Mingyur Rinpoche 96
Namdol Gyatso 91, 96, 99
Ngawang Zangpo 2, 6, 12, 13, 14, 47, 82
Raphaele Demandre 103
Rose Marie Sudan 24
Sangye Yeshe 78, 92
Sogyal Rinpoche 5
Soktse Rinpoche 23
Steven Goodman 83, 86
Tashi Lama 100
Tenpa Yarpel 16, 97
Ugyen Shenpen 10

Appendix:
The Lineage of the New Treasures

Chokgyur Lingpa had four close disciples who were like his own sons, who upheld his teachings in eastern Tibet. You could call them the "owners of his termas." One of the four was Deypa Tulku. As an old lama he requested the *Three Sections* empowerment from the Chokling of Tsikey, who then said, "I promised to give this to only one person, but we need an empowerment assistant, otherwise we can't do it. You are old, and I can't run back and forth to the shrine myself. Who would be best as shrine attendant?" He decided on my uncle Sang-Ngak, but they didn't manage to get hold of him, as he was staying with Könchok Paldrön, at the time. When Tsikey Chokling managed to contact him, he said to my uncle, "You must be the empowerment assistant," which he then became. While Sang-Ngak was helping during the ceremony, he also received it.

In this way, my uncle received via Tsikey Chokling the lineage from Karmey Khenpo's vision of the wisdom-body of Chokgyur Lingpa. Later on, at Fortress Peak, Samten Gyatso first received it from Uncle Sang-Ngak with the remark, "You're the one who has Karmey Khenpo's lineage, so you must give it to me!" After that, Samten Gyatso gave the entire transmission again to Uncle Sang-Ngak, to my father and to me. That's how I came to have both lineages. Samten Gyatso died soon after.

So we can see that not all the lineages pass through Tsewang Norbu, but Tsewang Norbu possessed all the lineages that he received from Khyentse, Kongtrul, Karmey Khenpo, and the learned Rinchen Namgyal. He had everything, in its entirety. Later on, Samten Gyatso was the one who was in possession of the entire transmission, some of which he even received from his mother, Könchok Paldrön. Samten Gyatso passed all these transmissions on to me.

Recently, Orgyen Tobgyal told me, "You say you have the entire transmission, but there is no record describing it. We need to find some account that gives the details of how the teachings were passed down. You say that whatever Tsewang Norbu had was passed on to Samten Gyatso. Samten Gyatso told you that you now have everything that he had received. That's not precise enough. The details of the transmission are important; we need to have a written account. There was one list of transmission details at Neten, but it was kind of vague. It simply mentions that Neten Chokling received this from Tsewang Norbu. Later on, the next

Neten Chokling, my father, received the lineage from Dzongsar Khyentse. But he also doesn't know who Dzongsar Khyentse got it from.[272] Therefore, you must make clear the way in which your family passed these teachings on. Otherwise, people won't feel sure later on."

What he said is true, but it is also true that I can't write such an account because I don't know all the details. I don't have the slightest doubt that I received everything that Samten Gyatso had of the *New Treasures*. He emphatically told me that he had given me all that he had and he had everything in its entirety. I don't know any more than that.

Luckily and by the grace of the Three Jewels, we later got hold of the sixteenth Karmapa's record of teachings received belonging to the *New Treasures*, which his regents brought me when they came to receive the *New Treasures* at Nagi Gompa. The Karmapa had instructed his regents to come, saying, "You must receive the *New Treasures* from Tulku Urgyen."

The main one who made the request was the third Kongtrul incarnation, who came here twice to ask me personally. On his second visit, I said okay. Anyway, the text they brought is a real eye-opener. It tells exactly which of the empowerments passed from the treasure revealer to Tsewang Norbu, which went through Khyentse or Kongtrul or Karmey Khenpo, and which went through the master-scholar Rinchen Namgyal and then to Tsewang Norbu and through him to Samten Gyatso. Some of the lineages pass through Könchok Paldrön before reaching Samten Gyatso, and all the details are found in that text.[273] That is the text Orgyen Tobgyal was insisting should exist and that I never knew existed before. It proved quite helpful that he brought this up, since it encouraged us to get hold of the text.

The same text mentions separately everything I offered the Karmapa. When Orgyen Tobgyal came here last time, I showed him this text, and he said, "Good, good! Everything is there: the lineage of every single empowerment, all the way back to the dharmakaya buddha Samantabhadra." From him the lineage passes through Garab Dorje and Vajrasattva; other lineages come from the Lotus-Born master to King Trisong Deutsen's son, and so forth. Fortunately, now we do have the Karmapa's lineage list.

In the beginning, there was no empowerment manual arranged for the *Three Sections*. The first empowerment manual was begun by the great master Kyungtrul, who met Samten Gyatso and was given the command to write an arrangement for the *Three Sections* empowerments. Kyungtrul wrote while Samten Gyatso gave the empowerments and they discussed many details. However, because of Kyungtrul's broad erudition, when he finished with the first of the three sections, the Mind Section, it already filled a whole volume.

A learned master could still transmit the *Three Sections* without an empowerment manual. Dzongsar Khyentse received the transmission from the second Chokling of Neten, who was deeply realized and able to give it without having a detailed arrangement as support. Neten Chokling was very unusual, a true siddha. Of course, he was also learned, but he didn't put on airs about his scholarship. He told Dzongsar Khyentse, "I can give you the empowerments, but the written arrangement for doing so is beyond my abilities. You will have to compose the arrangement for how to pass these empowerments on in the future." This is how this draft of that empowerment manual came about: while Neten Chokling was giving one empowerment after the other during the day, Dzongsar Khyentse meticulously wrote the empowerment manual at night.

Dzongsar Khyentse was in such a rush to get the manual done by the following morning that he had to abbreviate all the inserted sections, so later it was quite difficult to follow when giving the empowerment. An uneducated lama like me would find sweat pouring down his neck trying to use it. Luckily, Dilgo Khyentse had the time to make a first-class script for people like me, so we don't have to flip back and forth between texts. Dzongsar Khyentse's text was used when Samten Gyatso passed the *Three Sections* on to me.

The manual Dilgo Khyentse wrote was done to fulfill his guru's last words. Dzongsar Khyentse wasn't satisfied with the one he had earlier written when Neten Chokling transmitted the *Three Sections* to him, Shechen Rabjam and Katok Situ. And anyway that text was eventually lost and so he asked his disciple Dilgo Khyentse the last time they spoke, over the radiophone from Sikkim, to write a second one. Dilgo Khyentse's version is the one that is now included in the *Treasury of Precious Termas* and it is extraordinary.

Dudjom Rinpoche also wrote an empowerment manual for the *Three Sections*, partly at my request. As I mentioned, when he asked me to give the empowerment back in Lhasa, it was very difficult with the arrangement text I had. So I said, "You are so learned and eloquent—it would be wonderful if you could write one." I also asked the Karmapa for permission to ask Dudjom to write it, and he said, "By all means, you must ask him to do so!" Later, in Kalimpong, I asked him again and he agreed to slowly write a nice one that is now included in his collected works.

"An empowerment manual for transmitting the essence of Ati Yoga," Dudjom Rinpoche once told me, "doesn't serve its purpose by giving intricate details from the Maha and Anu Yoga perspectives. It should be lucid unto itself, just like pure gold studded with emeralds and diamonds. That terma in one volume the size of my forearm has brought to the light of day not only the three sections of Dzogchen but also the three inner tantras, Maha, Anu and Ati, unified into a single intent within Padmasambhava's extraordinary framework. All of this is in one single book! Each of the three sections has between twelve and fifteen sets of instructions. Other than the Lotus-Born master, who would be able to condense all of that into one book the size of my forearm? The quotations inserted from the original terma in the manual should be like studding pure gold with emeralds and diamonds." As you may see, Dudjom Rinpoche's own empowerment manual clearly reflects his opinion, in its conciseness and brilliance using nothing but the Dzogchen perspective itself.

In this way there were four empowerment manuals for the *Three Sections*, two of which survive today.

Endnotes

1. Although Buddhism of Tibet possesses a vast array of written literature, it relies heavily on oral transmission—the direct imparting of knowledge from master to student in an unbroken line of succession spanning centuries. These teachings not only impart words and intellectual knowledge, equally important is the direct personal experience conveyed, which keeps the transmission alive. According to traditional protocol, the student visits the teacher to request instruction on a specific meditation practice, usually bearing gifts and a sincere wish to practice the advice. In the case of a lineage holder like Tulku Urgyen Rinpoche, he not only practices the teachings he receives but also becomes qualified to pass on the same transmission to worthy disciples at a future date. [epk]
2. Seen from the Khampas' perspective, Tibet is a different country a long journey away to the west. To show this distinction we use the name 'Central Tibet'. [epk]
3. As Dzongsar Khyentse, one of my teachers, told me, "Terma teachings were concealed to be revealed at particular periods later in history, and they appear in forms most appropriate to the particular time periods in which they are revealed. Each major tertön must reveal a minimum of three major themes: Guru Sadhana, Great Perfection, and Avalokiteshvara. In our time, Old Khyentse and Chokling were specifically endowed with seven transmissions." [tur]
4. The 'four enlightened activities' refer to how a buddha or deity benefits sentient beings: pacifying, enriching, magnetizing and subjugating. [epk]
5. Shakya Shri's biography mentions "the descendant of Chokgyur Lingpa, Tersey Tulku" among the disciples who practiced Dzogchen. [tur]
6. My uncle, Samten Gyatso, encouraged the second Tsikey Chokling to compile a life story of Chokgyur Lingpa. This Chokling Tulku was extremely learned and well-spoken and embellished many statements with quotations from the old scriptures. But the end product didn't completely please Samten Gyatso; instead, Tsikey Chokling got rebuked for neglecting to consult Könchok Paldrön and merely condensing a previous life story elaborately written by Karmey Khenpo. Samten Gyatso said, "The real story you can hear from my mother." We have another version by Neten Chokling in addition to the shorter version by Old Khyentse and Kongtrul, which is based on the *Supplication to the Life Story* of the great tertön. [tur]
7. A detailed story about this stupa is presented in *The Legend of the Great Stupa*, translated by Tulku Pema Wangyal and Keith Dowman (Berkeley: Dharma Publishing, 2003).
8. Vimalamitra's life can be found in Tulku Thondup, *Masters of Meditation and Miracles*, and Vairotsana's detailed biography is available in English as *The Great Image*, translated by Ani Jinpa Palmo, both from Shambhala Publications.
9. All together, eight transmission lineages flourished in Tibet and were later known as the Eight Chariots of the Practice Lineage. One was Nyingma, literally the Old School, and the others Sarma, or New Schools, which include the Marpa Kagyü, the Shangpa

Kagyü, and the *Lamdrey* (Path and Fruit), which belonged to the Sakya tradition. There was also the Kadampa, later reformed into the Gelug school, as well as the Shijey and Chö, which respectively mean Pacifying and Cutting. The *Jordruk*, or Six Unions, and the *Nyendrub*, or Three Vajra Practices of Approach and Accomplishment, likewise appeared among the many practice lineages in Tibet. [tur]

10 Tibetan historians sometimes write that India is like the father of the Buddha's teachings, Nepal is like the mother, and the teachings that arrived in Tibet were like their offspring. [tur]

11 The earliest mention of the Tsangsar family is by Ga Lotsawa, a great translator who visited India, as well as being a great siddha. Another reference is found in the tale of King Gesar of Ling, whose guru was also a member of the Tsangsar family. [tur]

12 The beginning of the Kagyü lineages is described as the Four Greater and the Eight Lesser schools. Each of these appears to have its own individual way of continuing the lineage: one from uncle to nephew, one through "bone line," which means father to son, and one where guru and disciple are both monks. The Barom Kagyü was continued through both hereditary and monk lineage, and my ancestors trace their origin back to the masters of this lineage. [tur]

For more details about the various Kagyü lineages, see *The Rain of Wisdom, translated by Nalanda Translation Committee* (Boston: Shambhala Publications, 1989), and Tsang Nyön Heruka, *The Life of Marpa the Translator* (Boston: Shambhala Publications, 1995). [epk]

13 According to the profound system of the Buddhist tantras, each experience—whether profane or sublime—has an inner correlation in the structure of the subtle channels, energies and essences. [epk]

14 Gampopa became known as World-Renowned master from Dakpo (Dakpo Dzamling Drakpa), hence the lineage known as the Dakpo Kagyü. Phadru Dorje Gyalpo, one of Gampopa's chief disciples, was an incredibly realized master. His mind was as open as the sky. Each of his disciples gave rise to an individual lineage known as the eight lesser Kagyü schools. Phadru died when leprosy swept through the region; in order to save the others, he took everyone's disease upon himself and hence passed away. While carrying his body toward the funeral pyre, they set it down for a moment on a large rock. The body sank into the rock, and when they lifted it out a very clear imprint was left behind. The great master Sakya Pandita heard this story and wrote in a teasing manner, which is actually a concealed form of praise, "The footprints made from Phadru's corpse were definitely needed, but they were too late." He meant that it would be more appropriate to leave footprints when one is still alive. [tur]

15 This Barom Gompa, known as the Upper Seat, was at Sangzhung, situated in the Nakchu province northeast of Lhasa. [tur]

16 To this day, Nangchen is still known as Gomde. Local balladeers have even composed a beautiful song explaining how this land of meditators is a true homeland. [mbs]

17 People could even find relic pills—a sign of extremely high spiritual attainment—in his urine and excrement. The first Karmapa, Dusum Khyenpa—who was one of Phadru's Dharma brothers—practiced for many years under a simple rock overhang where he built a simple stone wall. At some point, people found that tiny relic pills known as *ringsel*, relic pills, were appearing in his feces. Sakya Pandita wrote, "The ringsel in Dusum's

shit were definitely needed, but they came too soon"—meaning they should have been found in his remains after he died. It is said that even many centuries later, people were still finding them at the same spot. [tur]

18 Tishi Repa is known to have said, "Darma Wangchuk introduced me to the unmistaken state of natural mind. Lama Shang Tsalpa introduced me to boundless interconnectedness. Kyobpa Jigten Sumgön taught me unceasing devotion. Taklung ensured that I could forsake all worldly concerns, regarding them as nothing more than ashes, so that I could never forget it." In this way, the four outer peaks symbolized his own teachers. [tur]

19 This story of Chögyal Pakpa's visit to China exemplifies the traditional relationship between Tibet and China as accepted by most Tibetans, called "master and benefactor." [mbs]

Chögyal Pakpa was invited to China, where he became the guru of the Mongol emperor. Together they became renowned everywhere by the saying "In the sky are the sun and the moon; on the earth are the guru and patron." Chögyal Pakpa was Sakya Pandita's nephew, and it is interesting to note that Sakya Pandita once had a vision of the female deity Kurukulle, the Lotus Dakini, in which she told him, "The time for my serving you will not appear during your life, but I will accomplish your nephew's every wish."

The second Karmapa, Karma Pakshi, accompanied Chögyal Pakpa to China. During their journey, war broke out in the kingdom of Ling, and it became very difficult to proceed. To avoid the turmoil, the caravan turned south and went through lower Kham, where they stopped at the first Nyingma monastery in the area, the Vajra Throne of Katok. The visiting lamas were requested to perform a consecration of the new Buddha statue. While Chögyal Pakpa chanted his benediction, Karma Pakshi literally turned the temple inside-out in a single moment. A third accomplished master who was there said, "We can't leave it like this!" and proceeded to put the temple back to normal.

Chögyal Pakpa and Karma Pakshi then proceeded to China, where the story goes that Karma Pakshi performed one incredible miracle after another. One day, the queen said to Chögyal Pakpa, "It is fine that you let your disciple perform miracles, but the emperor is beginning to prefer him to you. Until now, you haven't displayed any special signs, so if you have some sign of accomplishment to show, you better do so soon." When the emperor arrived the next morning Chögyal Pakpa cut off his own head and left it hovering in midair above his still-seated body. In despair, the emperor cried out, "My lama has died! My lama has died!" and prostrated in front of Chögyal Pakpa. Finally Chögyal Pakpa let his head descend back to its original position and declared, "The ultimate truth is beyond birth and death." After he witnessed this, the emperor's trust in Chögyal Pakpa became unshakable. Chögyal Pakpa and Karma Pakshi then received the highest honors as religious dignitaries—Chögyal Pakpa as the supreme and Karma Pakshi one rank below.

During empowerment ceremonies, the previous emperors had received the blessings from the empowerment vase and other implements on their thumb rather than on the crown of their head. Chögyal Pakpa had begun to do likewise so that the emperor, who was not in the habit of bowing to anyone, simply remained seated with his head held high while Chögyal Pakpa raised the empowerment vase. Karma Pakshi, however, had a siddha-type personality and tolerated no nonsense, and so one time he said, "Empowerments and rivers do not flow uphill; you need to bow your head!" and physically "helped" the emperor bow his head, which was a cause for severe punishment to be meted out. If you read the supplication to Karma Pakshi, you will see the list of these punishments and the miracle he performed in response to each. No matter what his torturers tried, they were unable to execute him, and the imperial court finally gave up on trying to execute him. There is also a story about how Karma Pakshi transported a gift of a copper roof to Tsurphu by throwing it in the river in China and picking it up in Central Tibet. [tur]

20 Marpa's disciple Ngog Chöku Dorje (1036-1106) became the student foremost in mastering the explanations of the Tantras. Thrangu Rinpoche is regarded to be a reincarnation of this master. [epk]

21 This lama was Geshe Chayulwa (1075-1138), a master in the old Kadam tradition which emphasizes mind training (*lojong*), the Mahayana way of developing the awakened attitude of a bodhisattva by treasuring others higher than oneself. [epk]

22 With 'half-wisdom and half-mundane' he means a guardian of the Dharma who appears in a form that is not completely enlightened. Dharma protectors are often nonhuman spirits who vow to protect and guard the teachings of the Buddha and its followers. They can be either 'mundane' i.e. virtuous samsaric beings or 'wisdom protectors' who are emanations of buddhas or bodhisattvas. [epk]

23 Lumey Dorje moved into the Nangso Chenmo palace that Repa Karpo modeled after the Jokhang in Lhasa. [tur]

24 Over the centuries, the heads of the monasteries in Nangchen became followers of the Drigung Kagyü lineage, and in recent times the king's gurus were from the Drukpa Kagyü school. The king's main temple, Tsechu Gompa, is Drukpa Kagyü; the head lama of this monastery is Adeu Rinpoche. Several of the other major monasteries are Drigung Kagyü. [tur]

25 These included Kyodrak, Surmang, etc. [tur]

26 Three brothers were born in the Tsangsar lineage: Ngaktrin, Sönam Yeshe, and Namgyal Tulku. Sönam Yeshe was nicknamed "the bird voice of Tsangsar," for not only did he sound like a bird, but he twisted his head in an unusual way. All three grew up to become lamas, and each built a monastery. Ngaktrin founded Lachab Gompa, Sönam Yeshe founded what is now known as Tsangsar Gompa, and Namgyal Tulku founded Demo Gompa. [tur]

27 Every one of Tulku Urgyen Rinpoche's ancestors left ringsel (relic pills) after the cremation pyre was opened, including Tulku Urgyen Rinpoche. [epk]

28 I would also like to mention Lhasung, one of the most important masters among my ancestors. He was one of five brothers who all became siddhas and he manifested a rainbow body at the end of his life. This happened during the lives of the great child tertön Namchö Mingyur Dorje and his disciple Karma Chagmey. Mingyur Dorje received a mind treasure, thirty-seven folios long, concerning Lhasung, which included a sadhana as well as other practices involving the various activities of enlightenment. In his vision, the young Mingyur Dorje saw that Lhasung had emanated from the navel center of Mahakala, the guardian of the Buddha's teachings. The tertön gave the scripture to Lhasung's disciples and told them, "If you can perform these practices, it will ensure the protection of your lineage for many generations." I have some of the hairs Lhasung left behind after his body vanished into rainbow light, which I put into one of my amulet boxes. [tur]

29. From eldest to youngest, their four sons were Samten Gyatso, Chimey Dorje, Sang-Ngak Rinpoche, and Tersey Tulku. Their two daughters were Tashi Chimey and Rigdzin Paldrön. [tur]

30. Mahakala is the main Dharma protector of the male class, while Dusölma is the main female, and there is one other important deity called Shinje Trochu. These Dharma protector chants I have chanted many times. That is the extent of my Barom Kagyü practice. [tur]

31. In the *Bhadrakalpa Sutra* the Buddha describes how he is the fourth among one thousand truly and completely awakened ones to appear within our world system. [epk]

32. Dakini script—A type of coded or magic script used to record Padmasambhava's teachings on scrolls which were then hidden in rocks, lakes, and caskets. [epk]

33. The seven transmissions are: 1) oral tradition (Kahma), the early translated Tripitaka and tantras passed on in an unbroken line from master to disciple; 2) earth treasure, revealed by the tertön; 3) rediscovered treasure, revealed for the second time from a past treasure; 4) mind treasure, revealed from the mind of the guru; 5) hearing lineage, received directly from an enlightened being; 6) pure vision, received in a pure experience; and 7) recollection, remembrance from a former life. [epk]

34. The first two tertön masters, Nyang-Ral and Guru Chöwang, were known as the Two Tertön Kings, and the other hundred tertöns are described as their attendants. There are also the Three Eminent Tertöns, the Eight Lingpas, the twenty-five major tertöns, and so forth, all of equal importance. But among the 108 tertöns, the main ones are the outstanding Two Tertön Kings: Nyang-Ral Nyima Özer and Guru Chöwang. The first among all tertöns was known as Sangye Lama, who, by the way, is not the same as Sangye Lingpa. [tur]

35. You can find the details of his remarkable change in his extensive biography (Vol. 38 of *New Treasures*). [Tur]

36. During a vision of Padmasambhava, Chokgyur Lingpa received this advice, which is included in the famous *Ngakso* text, which is based on the terma treasure *Tukdrub Barchey Kunsel*: "During this part of the dark age there is almost no Tibetan who hasn't received an empowerment for Vajrayana. The sacred samaya bond is what sustains the life-force of empowerment. Without observing the samayas, the life-force of the empowerment vanishes, like a feather blown away in the wind, and will not bring you any benefit." For this reason Chokgyur Lingpa requested a method for regularly restoring the samayas, the tantric commitments, which he then received, based on the *Tukdrub Barchey Kunsel* teachings. This practice is now widely known as the *Ngakso*. [tur]

37. Sangye Lingpa was the great tertön who revealed the *Lama Gongdü* cycle of teachings. [epk]

38. The *Three Sections of the Great Perfection* is known among Tibetan lamas as *Dzogchen Desum*. We will hear much more about them later. [epk]

39. For further details about revealing termas in front of crowds, see *The Autobiography of Jamgön Kongtrul: Gem of Many Colors*, translated and edited by Richard Barron (Ithaca, N.Y.: Snow Lion Publications, 2003), p.112.

40. Terma revelations, in the form of representations of enlightened body and speech, include statues and yellow parchment with the secret sign script of the dakinis. [epk]

41 Such a guardian is often also called a *kasung*, a guardian of the teachings. The highest type of guardian is known as *yingkyi kasung*, "guardian of the dharmadhatu teaching," which includes such protectors of the male and female classes as Ekajati and Damchen Dorje Lekpa. There are also guardians who are half wisdom beings and half mundane, such as Tsering Che-nga, the Five Sisters of Long Life, or the Twelve Tenma Goddesses, who protect Tibet. Mundane protectors include the eight classes of gods and spirits. [tur]

42 In each terma there is also the prophecy of the tertön, how Chokgyur Lingpa himself was an incarnation of Prince Damdzin, and to which of the guardians it was entrusted. [tur]

43 The word *gyalpo* refers to a particular type of spirit. [tur]

44 In his *Life of Chokgyur Lingpa*, Orgyen Tobgyal Rinpoche adds many details to this journey to Lhasa. [epk]

45 Lady Degah (Mayum Degah) was the affectionate name for my great-grandmother Dechen Chödrön, who was Chokgyur Lingpa's consort. [tur]

46 Several generations later, I traveled through that area on the trail to Lhasa and saw the remains of the throne where the tertön once sat in the middle of the plain. [tur]

47 Life force is our vital energy that keeps us alive. Realized beings can see this force. If it is damaged or degenerated, it can sometimes be summoned back by ritual or blessings. It also can vanish in which case the person is sure to die. [mbs]

48 According to Orgyen Tobgyal Rinpoche, "The first Tsoknyi Rinpoche often served as Chokgyur Lingpa's cook. He carried water and tended the animals. He was a hard worker." [epk]

49 This story is told in detail in *The Great Image*. [mt]

50 *Lamrim Yeshe Nyingpo* is the original Tibetan title for this Dharma treasure. [tur]

51 The Gönchen at Derge, a monastery belonging to the Sakya tradition. [tur]

52 An extraordinary level of realization may result in the practitioner dissolving his or her body into rainbow light and departing from the human realm in this form. This is not always possible for a master with many disciples. [epk]

53 In the scriptures, Kongtrul is often respectfully referred to as Jamgön Kongtrul Lodrö Thaye. For more details of this amazing master's life, see *The Autobiography of Jamgön Kongtrul: Gem of Many Colors*. Snow Lion Publications.

54 In this book we use the English translation for *Rinchen Terdzö* as *Treasury of Precious Termas*. [epk]

55 Jamyang Khyentse Wangpo "revived" some of these precious teachings in the manner of 'rediscovered treasures', by writing them down again, conferring the empowerments and explaining the teachings. Due to his outstanding realization and being a tertön, he had access to all the termas of former treasure revealers and could write them down at will. Kongtrul included most of these rediscovered treasures (*yangter*) in the *Treasury of Precious Termas*. [epk]

56 I have already mentioned *Gem of Many Colors* while a medium length biography of Jamyang Khyentse Wangpo is included in Dudjom Rinpoche, *The Nyingma School, Its Fundamentals and History*, (Gyurme Dorje, transl.). Wisdom Publications. [epk]

57 The need for tertön to have a consort in order to "unlock the treasure chest" of the termas has to do with a profound connection between consort practice and realization. A terma is essentially concealed within an "indestructible sphere" in the tertön's heart center—indelibly sealed in his stream of being when in a past incarnation he received the transmission from Padmasambhava in person—and an extraordinary yogic practice is now necessary to bring it forth. The failure to do so can often incur the wrath of the dakinis in that he neglects a past pledge to benefit sentient beings. [epk]

58 Zilnön Namkhai Dorje was one of the main teachers of Dudjom Rinpoche. This tertön appeared shortly before the fifteenth Karmapa and is regarded as authentic. His termas include some prophecies about the future. [tur]

59 When referred to respectfully, her full name was Urgyen Tsomo, the Great Dakini of Tsurphu (Tsurphu Khandro Chenmo Urgyen Tsomo), as she was born in a valley behind Tsurphu. [tur]

60 This was the hermitage of the first Kongtrul. It was called Tsari-like Jewel Rock (Tsadra Rinchen Drak). [epk]

61 This way of speaking shows Samten Gyatso's deep respect for the Karmapa. The same wording would be used for making offerings to the buddhas and bodhisattvas. Tulku Urgyen Rinpoche also mentions that his guru had commented on this: "In the past, I couldn't refuse the second Kongtrul, so how can I refuse the Karmapa? Moreover, if Khakyab Dorje doesn't receive the *New Treasures*, its continuation will be in danger in the future, so I must consent." [epk]

62 Karmey Khenpo's collected works contain innumerable answers from Chokgyur Lingpa on various topics and practices. [epk]

63 The reincarnation of Chokgyur Lingpa at the great tertön's seat at Tsikey monastery. [epk]

64 In this way, Tsikey Chokling received two lineages: one from Tsewang Norbu and the other from Karmey Khenpo. Jamgön Kongtrul never received the *Three Sections of the Great Perfection* from Chokgyur Lingpa either, but had to wait until Khyentse gave it to him. [tur]

65 Tulku Urgyen Rinpoche told Erik and I the following story he heard from his grandmother, which unfortunately, we did not tape. Könchok Paldrön was at an encampment with both Karmey Khenpo and the first Tsoknyi. One day they were debating and of course Tsoknyi could not defeat the Khenpo. At one point Tsoknyi shouted, "I don't care what you *say* about emptiness; when you *realize* it, it's like this!" Then he flew over Chokgyur Lingpa's tent. Könchok Paldrön told her mother who was inside another tent that Tsoknyi had just flown in the sky. Lady Degah responded by saying, "Oh, that is merely Tsoknyi showing off again." Moreover, the yogi-master did not impress Karmey Khenpo either, but got scolded for being disrespectful by flying over the great tertön's tent. [mbs]

66 It is often the case that the "bone-line" from a great revealer of terma treasures is regarded as having special blessings, perhaps encoded with the DNA. Cutting the hair implies becoming a monk and having no offspring and consequently no direct lineage-holders in the family line. [epk]

67 This remark meant that Wangchok Dorje had the ability to establish in writing the ter-

mas that Chokgyur Lingpa had missed. [tur] There were quite a few still waiting to be revealed. [epk]

68 There were also copies at Tsikey and Neten, the monasteries of the other incarnations of Chokgyur Lingpa. Dzongsar Khyentse, in western Kham, had a huge library that contained copies as well. Tsoknyi's monastery Gebchak also had a large library, but it, as were the other libraries, was burned down by the communists. [tur]

69 Since this time, Chokgyur Lingpa's writings have been found and comprise the final two volumes of Lama Putse's edition of the *New Treasures* (*Chokling Tersar*). [epk].

70 The one Chokgyur Lingpa had taken as his consort, as was necessary for revealing the terma for the *Three Sections of the Great Perfection.* [tur]

71 When the great translator Vairotsana had been exiled to an eastern region in Kham, he met a vassal king's son named Yudra Nyingpo. Amazingly, it is said that his realization was perfected simply upon seeing Vairotsana. [tur]

72 The *Three Sections of the Great Perfection* are also sometimes known as *Vairotsana Dzogchen* or *Heart Essence of Vairotsana* (*Vairo Nyingtig*). The *Vairo Nyingtig* should therefore first be conferred to an incarnation of Yudra Nyingpo, and such an incarnation appeared as Chokgyur Lingpa's own son. Chokgyur Lingpa revealed this terma in the presence of both Jamyang Khyentse Wangpo and Jamgön Kongtrul and immediately conferred the empowerment of *Three Sections* upon Jamyang Khyentse and Yudra Nyingpo; the latter was only about six months old at the time. This is why Tsewang Norbu is regarded as an emanation of Yudra Nyingpo. [tur]

73 According to the biography of Jamgön Kongtrul, this was on the third day of the twelfth month of the fire dragon year (1857), which puts Tsewang Norbu's birth in 1856, six months prior. [mbs]

74 Being a disciple of Paltrul Rinpoche, Tsewang Norbu originally followed *Longchen Nyingtig*. This was true of both brothers; due to a connection from former lives, they had immense devotion for Paltrul. Later, he only practiced the termas of Chokgyur Lingpa, to such an extent that near the end of his life he embodied the very life force of the *New Treasures* in terms of continuing the empowerments, reading transmissions, and instructions. One reason was the early demise of his brother, who had never been able to pass the lineage on in any significant way. When you look at the lineage records, you find Tsewang Norbu's name in almost all of them. Above him are only Chokgyur Lingpa, Jamyang Khyentse, or Jamgön Kongtrul. Since the great tertön died in his forties, Tsewang Norbu didn't receive much of the lineage directly from his father, but he did get the *Three Sections,* as we know. [tur]

75 Mastery in yoga, including full control over subtle channels and energies, includes the ability to extract essence from air and space, enough to keep the body alive for a long time. [epk]

76 Throughout all of Tibet the Karmapas was regarded not as an ordinary man but as a living buddha, hence Tsewang Norbu's reluctance to give an empowerment to someone of such stature. [epk]

77 A prediction had been contained in a terma from the Lotus-Born master indicating that the family line of Mindrolling would be maintained by a descendant of Chokgyur Lingpa. As Tsewang Norbu explained, "Old Khyentse knew that the family line at Mindrolling

was in danger of being interrupted. But he had revealed a prophecy that the daughter of the Mindrolling family was destined to marry a son of Chokgyur Lingpa. Even so, he simply sent me off without telling me any of that." Since the bone line has been broken, today the family lineage of Mindrolling is considered a blood line, carried on through the chief lama's daughter. [tur]

78 This could be the time when the thirteenth Dalai Lama had fled to India in 1909, after a Chinese invasion. There was a Tibetan uprising, and by April, 1912, the Chinese troops surrendered and were permitted to leave Tibet via India. The Dalai Lama returned to Lhasa in January 1913. See Melvyn Goldstein, *A History of Modern Tibet 1913-1951: The Demise of the Lamaist State* (Berkeley: University of California Press, 1991), pp. 54-59. [mbs]

79 This would have been the drubchen entitled *Gongpa Kundu*. [epk]

80 The Kechu is quite wide near its confluence with the Tsichu River, which, by the way, is where Tsikey gets its name. [tur]

81 Tsewang Norbu was not only Chokgyur Lingpa's son but also Khyentse's nephew. [epk]

82 She was adept in the Mindrolling style of tangka painting from Central Tibet, which is distinct from the Karma Gardri style of the east. [tur]

83 Khyentse's main residence in Derge was at Dzongshö. The drubchen performed was *Gongpa Kundu*. [epk]

84 Sometimes a tulku may be regarded as an emanation of a past master, sometimes of a deity. The Dalai Lamas, for instance, are said to be emanations of Avalokiteshvara. Four-Armed Mahakala is a wrathful form of Avalokiteshvara. [epk]

85 The first Ngawang Trinley was one of the three Tsangsar brothers who became known as the "three wish-fulfilling sons." In his succeeding lives, Ngawang Trinley's incarnation was known as Ngaktrin, the abbreviated form of the name, together with where he was born, thus Argong Ngaktrin, Chiltsa Ngaktrin and Tsangsar Ngaktrin. [tur]

86 These included Rinchen Namgyal, Khewang Chögyal and Söntar Chönchok, who was one of his close Dharma friends and an extraordinary Dzogchen master. [tur]

87 Kyasu being Chokgyur Lingpa's family name. [tur]

88 The practice of *phowa*, the ejection of consciousness, is a skillful way of making sure that one takes rebirth in a buddhafield, or at least in one of the higher realms, and is performed right at the moment of death. This is necessary because we human beings are usually lazy and busy ourselves with futile pursuits so that our precious life is over far too soon. [epk]

89 Chökyi Nyima Rinpoche recently received one of those handwritten manuscripts and has it in his possession in Boudhanath, Nepal. [epk]

90 When you look back through the history of who succeeded in transmitting Chokgyur Lingpa's *New Treasures* for future generations, it is obvious that Tsewang Norbu spoke from his clairvoyant point of view when he singled out Samten Gyatso at Riwoche. During his life, Samten Gyatso had taken upon himself the task of meticulously tracking down every single text, empowerment, and reading transmission and collected them all within himself. This was no small feat if you consider the geography of Kham and

how far-flung the people possessing the texts and lineages were. It is largely thanks to Samten Gyatso that we now have such an extensive version of not only Chokgyur Lingpa's terma treasures but also all the additional teachings related to them. Moreover, on his visit to Central Tibet, he personally requested Khakyab Dorje to compose any additional arrangements that were still required, while he himself was offering empowerments to the Karmapa. You can find out how many when you look through the index to the *New Treasures*. It is a Tibetan tradition that the author always mentions in the colophon the name of the person who requested the writing, and in the index you find Samten Gyatso's name more than a few times. It is such a kindness that someone took so much trouble for future generations. [tur]

91 After this, Tsewang Norbu went to Central Tibet, while Samten Gyatso remained in Kham. When Samten Gyatso went to Central Tibet with his mother two years later, Tsewang Norbu had already passed away. [tur]

92 Outwardly, he was a virtuous monk strictly adhering to the monastic precepts; inwardly, he adhered to the bodhisattva trainings; and on the innermost level, he adhered to the commitments of Vajrayana. [tur]

93 Karmey Khenpo had been reborn as the son of Samten Gyatso's sister. [tur]

94 Nang Tsangsar Gompa had been founded by my father's previous incarnation, Tsangsar Sönam Yeshe, who was believed to be an emanation of the Crow-Headed Protector (Jarok Dongchen). [tur]

95 Dzigar Kongtrul had one of Lady Degah's bones that had an image of the female buddha Tara on it. He kept this relic in a small sandalwood box. I saw it with my own eyes, and it was definitely not a fake. He kept many bones from great lamas as his secret shrine objects. [tur]

96 Tsikey Chokling is her father's current incarnation at Tsikey monastery. [epk]

97 These four periods here are explained as the age of bringing practice to fruition, simply practicing, teaching the words, and wearing only the dress. [epk]

98 As a boy, I attended him just as a servant would. For two years, I managed his household; before that, I was his cook and sometimes made him the special *momo* dumplings. I never even heard him scold a servant. He never once spanked me—but then I never went against his wishes. [tur]

With 'transference of realization' is meant that Chimey Dorje realized the basic state of wakefulness that is unchanging and identical with that of his teacher. [epk]

99 For these four, see 'four levels of Dzogchen and Mahamudra' in the Glossary. [epk]

100 Even a hidden yogi cannot prevent special signs from manifesting at the time of death. Tulku Urgyen Rinpoche once said that "A practitioner shouldn't show off except at the time of death, when best is to laugh, next best to be unafraid and third best is to have no regrets." The body shrinking is considered a lesser version of the "rainbow body" and Tulku Urgyen Rinpoche sometimes said that disciple's were known to hasten the cremation of their master to "at least retain some tangible relics." The *ringsel*—tiny, shiny pearl-like pills—can often be found in the ashes. The ancient Dzogchen tantras describe the various types, colors and reasons why they appear as signs of inner realization. [epk]

101 One of the eight main traditions in Tibetan Buddhism, Chö is the tradition of letting go. Chö practice is done to relinquish selfishness and is an eminent method for abandoning

attachment, to be free. Cutting, the meaning of *Chö*, refers to cutting through subject-object fixation, cutting through dualistic experience. This Chö teaching was the only one that was translated from Tibetan into the Indian languages—showing how special it is. Chö is practiced out of the unity of emptiness and compassion. In this courageous compassion there is no hesitation, no doubt in acting for the welfare of beings. As Machik Labdrön said, "Compared to begging one hundred times, 'Save me, protect me!' it is much more effective to say once, 'Devour me!'" [tur]

Chö is the instruction in giving away the 'body of illusion' as a feast offering, the reason being that we human beings have strong attachment to the material body. For detailed teachings on Chö practice, see *Machik's Complete Explanation, Clarifying the Meaning of Chod*. (Sarah Harding, trans.) Snowlion Publications, Ithaca, NY, 2003. [epk]

[102] Sarah Harding calls these the four devils of the material, the immaterial, of exaltation & inflation, where inflation is defined as ego-fixation, pgs. 117-120 in *Machik's Complete Explanation*. Tulku Urgyen Rinpoche explains indecision as the subtle wavering of consciousness due to ignorance which then necessitates latching on to a solid sense of self and world, which is ego-fixation. [epk]

[103] A rebirth of a lama from the old Sertsa monastery in the Gegyal Riwo district. [tur]

[104] Uncle had received Karmey Khenpo's lineage for these empowerments from the Tsikey of Chokling while Samten Gyatso received his from Tsewang Norbu. These were regarded as two different streams of blessings in that Tsewang Norbu received it from his father, the great tertön, in person, while Karmey Khenpo received his from the Chokgyur Lingpa's wisdom body, after the tertön had passed away. [epk]

[105] I believe Uncle Tersey was about sixty-six years old when he died, as he died during my second visit to Central Tibet. [tur]

[106] The height of a lama's throne is often a measure of his rank or stature, either political or spiritual. [epk]

[107] The retreat center above Tsikey was called Mindrolling, the "Sanctuary of Ripening and Liberation." The lamas at Riwoche monastery had great trust in my Uncle Tersey and so invited him there to give teachings. And after Samten Gyatso passed away, Tersey was invited to Fortress Peak to give teachings. [tur]

Uncle Tersey later did have offspring. His granddaughter, a nun, was recently attending the Chokling tulku at Tsikey monastery. [epk]

[108] The integrity consists in not wanting to distract people away from what is more important than miracles—renunciation, compassion and the true view. [epk]

[109] A great meditator who realizes the awakened state to such an extent Samten Gyatso mentions has no basis whatsoever of falling back into samsara. The reason is, as Tulku Urgyen Rinpoche taught, "stability in nondual wakefulness is free of the ignorance required to take rebirth." [epk]

[110] Uncle Tersey had no interest in the respect and social status arising from giving empowerments to exalted masters like the Karmapa. [epk]

[111] An empowerment can be given as a ceremony of conferring blessings on a practitioner who is then authorized to begin a particular sadhana. It can also be given in the real sense of authorizing the disciple through introducing the nature of reality, which essen-

tially is the deity's body, speech and mind. For more details, see Tsele Natsok Rangdröl, *Empowerment*, Rangjung Yeshe Publications. The six types of liberation are specific to this vision and involve liberation through seeing, seeing, hearing, remembering, touching, wearing and tasting. [epk]

[112] In particular, I remember an explanation of the deities for the *Tukdrub Trinley Nyingpo* that amazed all who read it. I still haven't seen a surviving copy of that text, but who knows—it may still surface in Kham. He wrote the *Side Ornament* for the *Heart Essence of Samantabhadra* and many similar texts that are included in the *New Treasures*. [tur]

A terma treasure is often very concise and contains many implied references, which are obvious to a master or lineage holder. For ordinary practitioners to use in their daily sadhana practice it is necessary to have the obvious spelled out, the implications explained and the references inserted. [epk]

[113] This is how the particular type of statue known as *jema atrong* was made. Chokgyur Lingpa once gave one such statue to the king of Nangchen. Several people, including Dilgo Khyentse, have one of these. [tur]

Infused with his wisdom-being means blessed and empowered to be an extension of himself so that everyone who comes into contact with this image has the seed of liberation planted in their stream-of-being. [epk]

[114] Among his other teachers were Khamtrul Tenpey Nyima and the first Tsoknyi. [tur]

[115] Drubwang Tsoknyi's mind treasure is named *Ladrub Kunzang Tuktig*. [tur]

[116] There was also a very good lama from Ladakh named Pema Chögyal, who belonged to the Mahamudra group. [tur]

[117] My father was also a disciple of Shakya Shri, although not as close as Uncle Tersey. Samten Gyatso went to stay with Khakyab Dorje and never met Shakya Shri. Uncle Tersey told me that at Shakya Shri's hermitage, Uncle Tersey himself and Drukpa Yongdzin, below the Drukchen Jamgön, were among the chief disciples. Shakya Shri practiced the *Heart Essence of Samantabhadra*, though he had never met Chokgyur Lingpa, but was, as mentioned in the text, a disciple of the first Khyentse. [tur]

[118] This biography is presently being translated by Elio Guarisco. [epk]

[119] These precious and profound teachings are now primarily contained in two collections of canonical scriptures: *Collected Nyingma Tantras* and the *Nyingma Kahma*. [epk]

[120] Khyentse of Palpung, who was the young Karmapa's tutor, was then sent to China in his place. [tur]

[121] Another Neten Chokling was identified by Dzongsar Khyentse and was the father of Orgyen Tobgyal Rinpoche and Dzigar Kongtrul. [tur]

[122] Tsagah lived in Nepal and toward the end of her life she became a nun and was an inspiration to all who met her. We met the youngest sister in 2003; she was a very sweet elderly woman who had suffered quite a bit under the communists. Her husband, a lama from Tana Monastery, a day's horse ride to Lachab, was executed and she stayed with nomads for many years after that with her young daughter. Penjik's daughter still lives in Kham in Jekundo. His son's family—which includes several tulkus—has rebuilt the Tsangsar family monastery at Lhalam Gön. Kungo Kalsang is still alive and lives in retreat at Ngedön Osel Ling monastery in Nepal. [mbs, epk]

123 Life-Lake of Yeshe Tsogyal, known as Tsogyal Lhatso, is situated at Drakda some 20 km from Samye. [epk]

124 This *ngadrama*, or likeness, was a very small statue known as Guru Tsokye Dorje revealed by Nyang-Ral Nyima Özer as a terma treasure. [tur]

125 This was the tenth incarnation in the Drukchen lineage, Mipham Chökyi Wangpo (1884-1930) whose monastery was Druk Sang-Ngak Chöling. [epk]

126 This included the complete transmission for *Tukdrub Barchey Kunsel*, at the request of Tubwang Rinpoche, who was Lama Tendzin Dorje's brother. Bong Gompa had three main lamas. Gampo Tulku, an incarnation of Gampopa whose residence was at Gampopa's original seat, also attended this transmission. He had deep appreciation for the *New Treasures* of Chokgyur Lingpa, and even though he didn't receive them all, he wanted at least the *Tukdrub* empowerments that Samten Gyatso gave. [tur]

127 The seventh Karmapa, Chödrak Gyamtso (1454-1506). [epk]

128 'Undeserved earnings' (*kor*) refers to material things offered out of faith to a monastic community or an individual lama for the benefit of a living or deceased person, which—when used for another purpose than the intended—have dire karmic consequences. [epk]

129 Abum Rinchen Pungpa, or Mount Abum, is situated eight hours' drive on dirt roads from Sharda in Nangchen. [epk]

130 The magical phenomenon of self-appearing syllables is found on rock faces all over Tibet and the Himalayan regions. A letter or the image of a deity appears to become increasing clear over the course of months or years. [epk]

131 As a *nyerpa*, Tulku Urgyen Rinpoche was managing the affairs of his father's household in both secular and ritual matters. [epk]

132 On a visit in 2003 to this nunnery, which is once again home to many fine female practitioners, we saw that the juniper trees have grown back. There is now a rule that not one single branch is allowed to be cut from any of these beautiful trees, although the needles may be collected for the preparation of a sacred incense. [mbs]

133 And rebuilt finely indeed by the many nuns living there! Dechen Ling faces south towards a beautiful valley. There is plenty of sunshine, water and trees. When we visited there were 32 nuns in long term retreat, 12 of whom were in life retreat. [mbs]

134 The vajra guru mantra is OM AH HUNG VAJRA GURU PADMA SIDDHI HUNG. [epk]

135 Tsang-Yang Gyamtso's "emanation basis" is supposed to be Gyalwa Cho-Yang, one of Padmasambhava's twenty-five disciples. [tur]

136 Tsoknyi had access to several mind treasures, one of which was very similar to one of Chokgyur Lingpa's termas for realizing the dharmakaya aspect of the guru. When Chokgyur Lingpa saw it, he told Tsoknyi teasingly, "You stole my terma!" then laughed. The first Tsoknyi was a master with that kind of capacity. [tur]

137 This is different from a *drubdra* or sadhana retreat. Prior to entering a *gomdra* meditation retreat the practitioner would usually have gone through one or several sadhana retreats, covering the preliminaries, yidam practice and the inner yogas. The practice now would focus on the unelaborate training in the four yogas of Mahamudra or on Trekchö and Tögal. [epk]

[138] In 2003, Marcia and I were told that one third of the three hundred nuns living at Gebchak are capable of this feat. [epk]

[139] The implements used to bless people in an empowerment can be a vase, torma, icon, *kapala* or the like. [epk]

[140] While Kyungtrul Rinpoche gave the *Treasury of Oral Instructions* (*Dam-ngak Dzö*), it was Lama Pemba of Tana Monastery who gave the collected works of the first Kongtrul (*Gyacher Kadzö*) and the *Treasury of Knowledge* (*Sheja Dzö*). [tur]

[141] The yearly rituals of exorcism based on Vajra Kilaya are usually performed right before the Tibetan New Year, with the main torma being hurled on the 29th day of the 12th month. The purpose is to drive negative forces out that may otherwise harm the Dharma and sentient beings. The primary demons are of course ignorance and selfish emotions. [epk]

[142] *Chanting the Names of Manjushri—Manjushri Nama Sangirti* consists of six hundred verse lines. [epk]

[143] Free-flowing, perfect eloquence is often considered to be a special power bestowed upon a person by either a deity or a demonic force. [epk]

[144] The great Situ of Palpung, Pema Rigdzin of Riwoche, Shingkyong of Katok and Kuching of Palyul monastery. [tur]

[145] Sey Phakchok is known for carrying on his father's lineage and for two important scriptures of meditation instruction—one on Mahamudra and one on Dzogchen. [epk]

[146] Drubwang Tsoknyi (the first) was one of his gurus. [tur]

[147] A genuine Buddhist doesn't think of himself or herself as shopping for the scriptures and then as their owner, but rather as a benefactor and then as their temporary custodian. [epk]

[148] The Sakya master was Sachen Kunga Nyingpo and his disciple was Galo. [epk]

[149] In the case of the attainment of the "lesser" rainbow body, the physical elements do not vanish within seven days but may take longer time, the size of the body decreasing every day. The hair and the nails, having neither physical nerves nor subtle channels of energy, usually don't shrink but are left behind. [epk]

[150] In those days, only fifteen or sixteen people lived there at a time. [tur]

[151] Sure enough, the monastery was destroyed during the Cultural Revolution and subsequently rebuilt in the late 1980s by the current Samten Gyatso incarnation, Tulku Tsewang Dechen, who spent twenty-three years in a Chinese prison camp. [mbs]

[152] This is Tsoknyi's maternal grandfather, Lama Tashi Dorje's father. [epk]

[153] One of the major trade routes between Ziling on the Mongolian border and Lhasa to the west used to pass through Nangchen. This location corresponds to Jekundo in the present Qinghai province. [epk]

[154] The Japanese had taken over Manchuria in 1931. The Chinese communists appeared in east Tibet with the Long March around 1935-6. The Japanese surrendered in 1945. The Chinese civil war began around that time and ended in 1949 with the communist victory. [mbs]

155 "Remaining absentminded and unaware in the state of the all-ground" means that the meditator has decided to simply rest in a peaceful and serene state of mind while ignoring not only the mindful presence of shamatha and vipashyana, but also the knowing of the unformed natural state that defies every concept. [epk]

156 The instructions in being liberated during the *bardo* states are necessary since we human beings too often create causes that develop the phenomena of the lower realms—out of hatred, greed and uncaring apathy. [epk]

157 Although, in essence, the natural state is identical with the mind of a fully awakened buddha, for most people the experience of the natural state passes by like a flash of lightning in the sky. A buddha, on the other hand, has attained complete stability in the natural state. The training to attain stability requires instructions from a qualified master. [epk]

158 Tana is the seat of the Yerpa Kagyü, one of the original schools of the Kagyü lineage. The name means "horse's ears" because the mountain peaks above have the clearly recognizable shape of two pointed ears. They can be seen looking south from Lachab. [epk]

159 We are assuming that Tulku Urgyen Rinpoche refers to the 1936 intrusion by the communist forces, who were chased by the nationalists into eastern Tibet as noted earlier. [mbs]

160 In addition to Situ and Khyentse of Palpung, two other masters—Karsey Kongtrul and Ongtrul—had their own sections of the monastery which they personally supervised. [tur]

161 The reason Karsey Kongtrul was close to Tsikey goes back to the trouble on the border between Tibet and China that had forced the Karmapa to detour to Nangchen instead of going to Derge. Because of this dispute, Karsey Kongtrul was forced to flee Palpung. After a while, the political situation quieted down. In my monastery, we only heard news about fighting between the various factions over in China. At one point, we heard that the communists had been defeated and had withdrawn their soldiers from Kham. It was to be several years before another upheaval would begin. During this lull, Karsey Kongtrul, who had been staying at Tsikey, was able to return to Palpung. Prior to his arrival at Tsikey, Karsey Kongtrul had gone to Riwoche monastery and from there the Chokling of Tsikey now invited him to his monastery at Könchok Paldrön's urging. Karsey Kongtrul stayed there for three weeks. Tsikey Chokling was ill as well and stayed next to the monastery at his house, which was called Norbu Ling, Jewel Sanctuary. [tur]

162 The reminder for samadhi is usually given by one's teacher or a close Dharma friend. To be truly effective it must be given before the "inner circulation of energies" has ceased. For more details, see Chökyi Nyima Rinpoche, *Bardo Guidebook*.

163 I feel uncomfortable including this private conversation in a book because not only would it be out of character for Samten Gyatso, but some people might think that we were only bragging about our own family. [tur]

164 In an unrecorded conversation, Tulku Urgyen Rinpoche told me that approaching the representative of the Chinese emperor was no simple matter—if he felt you were wasting his time, you could get slapped on the cheek with his infamous spiked glove, which was sure to rip the skin off your face. [epk]

[165] In one of Tsikey Chokling's visions, he saw my father, Chimey Dorje, holding a transparent curved knife, his long streaming hair curling upward. "Your father," he told me, "is without a doubt an emanation of the Crow-Headed Protector," a particular guardian of the Buddha's teachings. [tur]

[166] It is interesting to note that most tertöns have similar visions when they visit this pure land; in fact, they often see the exact same details. [tur]

[167] To a person brought up in the materialistic-nihilistic world view it is hard enough to be open-minded to the idea of rebirth, and now we hear of someone being an incarnation of several bodhisattvas or former masters, simultaneously! Tulku Urgyen Rinpoche explained that an incarnation of a tulku is like the reflection of the moon in the surface of water and several reflections can easily appear in the same pool. [epk]

[168] He was famous for this habit of scrutinizing Dharma scriptures, which allowed him to spot and collect many important—but rare or missing—meditation manuals and other scriptures. [tur]

[169] For details of the hell realms, see *Words of My Perfect teacher,* pages 63-72. [mbs]

[170] The *inner space of primordial purity* is the buddha-nature itself in its unmanifest aspect—empty in essence, cognizant by nature and unconfined in its capacity. [epk]

[171] About "fourfold confidence," let me quote Tsele Natsok Rangdröl, *Circle of the Sun* (Rangjung Yeshe Publications, 1990): "Practitioners who have perfected the four visions [in Dzogchen] also attain the fourfold confidence of liberation. There are two types of downward-directed confidence. The first is confidence free from dread, hence one is beyond intimidation by anything whatsoever, such as danger or the hellish sufferings of heat and cold. The second is confidence free from fear of wandering into the birthplaces of the six classes of beings and through the three realms of samsara. There are two types of upward-directed confidence. There is confidence free from fascination with the qualities of buddhahood and the happiness of the buddhafields and so forth, and the confidence free from expectation, which means not having the hope or desire to achieve the reward of nirvana. These four types of confidence result from having resolved that all of samsara and nirvana is self-cognizance beyond concepts." Self-cognizance beyond concepts refers to our basic state of being, the buddha-nature. [epk]

[172] From the Mahayana and Vajrayana perspective—and this makes the story more amusing—the hell realms are not real, physical locations but resemble horror movies played out in the minds of the beings there. [epk]

[173] This is where all the early kings of Tibet used to live. [epk]

[174] Tramdruk Temple is renowned as one of the three Dharma Wheels of Central Tibet, the others being Samye and the Jokhang in Lhasa. [tur]

[175] The lama was from the same family as the Sakya master Tarik Rinpoche and the Kagyü master Sabchu Rinpoche. [tur]

[176] The "restricted empowerments" may include certain secret practices or entrustment to particular guardians of the teachings and are often given only to lineage holders. [epk]

[177] The "warm breath of the dakinis" is a metaphor for effective teachings through an unimpaired, short lineage. Between Padmasambhava and Samten Gyatso were only two other masters: Chokgyur Lingpa and one of the lineage holders from whom Samten Gyatso received a particular empowerment, for instance Tsewang Norbu or Karmey Khenpo. [epk]

178 The Indian master Khunu Rinpoche related to Chökyi Nyima Rinpoche that he had also received the *Lamrim Yeshe Nyingpo* from Jamdrak this way. [epk]

179 Jokyab Rinpoche was born in the Gegyal district. He was the son of a government official in an important family. From an early age, he had sincere interest in following a spiritual path and was allowed to go to Gebchak Gompa, where he became a disciple of Lama Wangdor, who gave him teachings on the *Guhyagarbha Tantra*. After gaining some sound understanding, he became a monk at Dilyak Gompa, where he studied with a disciple of the great Karmey Khenpo. At some point, he met Samten Gyatso, from whom he received the complete *New Treasures*. He also told me that he received some key instructions from Kyungtrul Rinpoche. [tur]

180 Thanks to Jokyab's tenacity and commitment, we have Jamdrak's learned commentary recorded as a complete volume. Today it's a vital aid to understanding the full depth of the *Light of Wisdom*; it can be found in the English version in the form of extensive endnotes to the main text. It's hard to say why Jamdrak delayed so long in giving the teachings. Maybe he was testing the sincerity of these students. [epk]

181 This was likely in 1931-32 when the Mongolian warlord Ma Pu-Fang attacked Nangchen see pp. 221-2 in Goldstein. [mt]

182 This ritual involving the "summoning of life force" can be based on Buddha Amitayus, his consort Chandali or one of the many other deities for longevity. [epk]

183 It was the same in the palace of the Derge king, in whose presence only lamas such as the great Situ or the Karmapa were welcome, and probably not that many others. [tur]

184 It is thought that one's personality relates to the elemental properties: the earth type is stable, water is flexible, fire volatile, wind swift, and space accommodating.

185 The title "lord of the teachings" refers to the head of a lineage or monastery. [epk]

186 Prior to this time, there was not one single complete collection of Chokgyur Lingpa's terma revelations. The great tertön on many occasions had immediately handed the treasure—consisting of a statue, sacred substances or decoded scripts from the celestial dakinis—to one of the prophesied recipients, who would become the main lineage holder of that particular terma. In Samten Gyatso's youth, around the turn of the century, thirty years had already gone by since the great master's passing, and during this time some of the lineages had spread far and wide, while others were almost nonexistent. In those days, Nangchen had neither transportation nor any modern means of communication, and Samten Gyatso began a treasure hunt in the most meaningful sense of the word. These days the collection consists of more than forty huge volumes. [epk]

187 An entrustment to the guardians of a terma teaching involves confirming the master's position as 'lord of the mandala' and then placing the particular guardian in his service. The protector of these teachings is then supposed to carry out the master's noble wishes and activities. [epk]

188 After having practiced a sadhana for a specific amount of time or a particular number of recitations, the practitioner can make use of certain applications, such as the preparation of sacred substances to carry out various activities to protect and serve the living and the dead. [epk]

189 Based on a mind treasure of the great master Khyentse known as *Chandali, the Mother of Longevity*. [tur]

[190] This medical treatment is much more radical than moxibustion. The heat from the instrument's iron or gold tip reaches quickly into the affected part of the body. At times a blister is instantly formed. [epk]

[191] The glorious conch refers to the throat chakra of a supreme incarnation such as Buddha Shakyamuni. This power of speech results from immeasurable merits—surpassing all the other major and minor marks added together—and is said to produce sounds that can be understood by people in their own language. [epk]

[192] Taking the first syllable of someone's name and then adding *gah*, meaning "dear," is a common Khampa way of abbreviating names, Tulku Urgyen Rinpoche's name being Karma Urgyen. [epk]

[193] Great practitioners are in complete control over their mental state when they pass away. There is never any anxiety as with ordinary people because changing bodies is like changing clothes for them. Some can even determine how and in what circumstances they will expire. Samten Gyatso chose the moment of his passing to coincide with those last poignant lines. Remaining in samadhi—an extraordinary state of meditative stability—after exhaling their last breath is a phenomenon often seen in high lamas and advanced Buddhist practitioners. This state, known as *tukdam*, is characterized by some warmth around the heart, the skin not fading or discoloring, no onset of rigor mortis and the body remaining in an upright sitting posture. It can last from several hours to a week or more. [epk]

[194] When the funeral stupa was opened after Tulku Urgyen Rinpoche's own cremation, his skull was found completely intact too. It is presently kept in Chökyi Nyima Rinpoche's private shrine room in Ka-Nying Shedrub Ling monastery in Boudha, Nepal. A self-appearing AH is visible on its surface. [epk]

[195] I repeated some recitations from *Tukdrub Barchey Kunsel*, *Kunzang Tuktig* and a couple other small practices. After I received the *Treasury of Precious Termas* I stayed at the Lotus Garuda Fortress (Pema Kyung Dzong) for about three years. [tur]

Marcia and I saw Tulku Urgyen Rinpoche's room, and the people at Lachab said that it was a sealed retreat, the door walled up with stones and sealed with mud for the entire time, leaving only an opening to pass food. [epk]

[196] Barwey Dorje's former life was Lady Degah's brother. He became a disciple of Chokgyur Lingpa and sometimes acted as his bursar and at other times as his household manager. After the tertön's passing, he moved to his own monastery and spent his remaining years practicing. I am told he attained a very high level of realization. [tur]

[197] Do tertöns require the Karmapa's approval? Not necessarily, but Tulku Urgyen Rinpoche once mentioned that their benefit for beings greatly increases when validated by a Karmapa because the Karmapa incarnations represent the activity of enlightenment. [epk]

[198] A manual is a concatenation of the tantric root text, explanations, notes to the vajra master about implements and what should be said aloud for the disciple during the ceremony. These can be quite complex. The *Three Sections of the Great Perfection* is quite an elaborate collection of teachings, as well as being incredibly profound in depth and scope. Each section has many parts, both sadhanas and instructions. Today the *Three Sections* fill more than two large volumes. See *Appendix 1* for more details. [epk]

[199] While Dudjom was there, he received some reading transmissions and instructions from Kyungtrul on three major tantric scriptures of the New Schools; from Jampal Tsultrim he requested some of the more important parts of Khakyab Dorje's collected works, and from Samten Gyatso he requested the complete version of the *Three Sections of the Great Perfection*, but it seems he only received the first three empowerments. [tur]

[200] One day, Dudjom asked to be excused and left. So while Samten Gyatso bestowed the remaining empowerments, Kyungtrul continued laboriously composing the arrangements. At some point, it became clear they would not be able to complete the whole thing in this way. So as Samten Gyatso had to return to Kham, he stopped the empowerments and Kyungtrul stopped working on the text. [tur]

[201] He was referring to a saying common among the people living at Tsurphu that if you stay only a day, you'll want to leave, but if you stay a year, you'll never want to. The Khampas who come there find it difficult when they first arrive; it's hard to find anyone who will even give you the time of day. [tur]

[202] This is no small event: the *Treasury of Precious Termas* consists of sixty-three large volumes full of empowerments and profound instructions. The transmission of these teachings can take anywhere between three and six months, depending on the master, the number of recipients and the level of detail. It may also be interspersed with group practices and therefore may take even longer. [epk]

[203] The *Collected Nyingma Tantras* in a special annotated edition may be one Tulku Urgyen Rinpoche often mentioned as including notes from the Dzogchen master Melong Dorje. [epk]

[204] What makes the remark even more amusing is that the name of Samten Gyatso's hermitage—the Mansion of Lotus Light—is also the name of Padmasambhava's celestial palace. [epk]

[205] Obviously, Kyungtrul was not referring to physical space but rather the basic space that is the very nature of awareness already and transcends dimensions. [tur]

[206] Tulku Urgyen Rinpoche once explained that Kyungtrul's teaching style was to include profound meditation instructions in stories about the lives of past masters. [epk]

[207] These three young prodigies were receiving teachings in philosophy from the great master Tutob Namgyal. During this time, there were six major monastic centers for the Nyingma tradition in Tibet: Shechen and Dzogchen in lower Kham, Katok and Palyul in the middle, and Dorje Drag and Mindrolling in upper Tibet. While Tutob Namgyal was in charge of higher studies at Shechen monastery in Kham, Khyentse, Kongtrul and Paltrul were classmates. Khyentse was nobility from the influential Dilgo clan, which included a line of ministers in charge of one quarter of the Derge kingdom. Kongtrul was born into the Kyungpo clan, the same as Milarepa and Kyungpo Naljor, the founder of the Shangpa Kagyü school. The Kyungpo clan included both Buddhists and Bönpos, as shown by one of Jamgön Kongtrul's aliases: Chimey Tennyi Yungdrung Lingpa, which has a Bönpo connotation. Later Paltrul departed for the district of Dzachukha, while Kongtrul went to reside at the great Kagyü monastery Palpung. [tur]
Yungdrung is often used by Bönpos as the equivalent for vajra. [epk]

[208] The great master Shabkar Tsokdrug Rangdröl. See *Life of Shabkar: The Autobiography of a Tibetan Yogin*. (Snow Lion Publications).

209 Gods take birth in an instantaneous or miraculous manner, not requiring nine months of gestation like humans do. [epk]

210 The "teachings of the ultimate transmission" refer to Mahamudra and Dzogchen, especially a type known as Essence Mahamudra—the transmission of the wisdom lineage, so vital in ensuring the purity of Buddhist practice. When receiving the pointing-out instruction the disciple is brought face to face with the innate nature of his mind—as have all the masters in the lineage before him. You can compare such an experience of nondual awareness with daybreak on a cloudless sky: the clouds of ignorance, emotions and conceptual thinking are absent—at least for a short while. Once this is experienced, ahead of the practitioner now lies the path of growing ever more familiar with this cloudless sky—a steady and repeated training in dissolving the tendencies to recreate further clouds—until one reaches true realization, a state that is compared to the unchanging sky itself. [epk]

211 Karma Pakshi, the second Karmapa, stayed there, and many of the Shamarpas practiced there as well. Sometimes it is called Lofty Fortress of Conquerors. [tur]

212 Near the end of his life, Tendzin Dorje gave a young woman a necklace of precious stones, a considerable gift, with the remark, "One day I may come to visit you in your house." The young woman blushed with embarrassment and didn't know what to think. Not long after she was informed by messengers from the sixteenth Karmapa that the child she was carrying was the tulku of Tendzin Dorje. The woman was Kunsang Dechen and the child, her first-born, is Chökyi Nyima Rinpoche. [epk]

213 Today, in 2005, we know that both Dilgo Khyentse Rinpoche and Tulku Urgyen Rinpoche began to give the empowerments for the *Three Sections* to smaller groups of tulkus and close disciples; in this way, they both mark the third generation of lineage holders. [epk]

214 Dzongsar Khyentse was originally known as Katok Khyentse, but after he was invited to reside at Dzongsar monastery, eventually he assumed the position of Lord of the Dharma. He was known to be like the great Khyentse in person, and his fame spread far and wide. [tur]

215 The fifteenth Karmapa was the immediate reincarnation of Tekchok Dorje. There had been a mutual link of teachings between Tekchok Dorje and Chokgyur Lingpa. Several generations later, Tekchok Dorje's reincarnation as the fifteenth Karmapa, Khakyab Dorje, was again closely connected to my guru and uncle, Samten Gyatso. So it seems this connection was about to continue. [tur]

216 Tendzin Dorje's main practice was *Chetsun Nyingtig* and *Heart Essence of Noble Tara* (*Pagma Nyingtig*), which were both mind treasures revealed by the great Khyentse. [tur]

217 The yearly ceremonies included the extremely detailed version of the *Eight Sadhana Teachings* as revealed by Nyang-Ral Nyima Özer, *Lama Ngödrub Gyamtso* revealed by Pema Lingpa, as well as other termas, although the monastery itself belonged to the Drigung tradition. [tur]

218 This disciple was Tralek Jamgön, who resided at Thrangu Gompa. The two large monasteries Thrangu and Benchen are the seats of the current Khenchen Thrangu Rinpoche and Venerable Tenga Rinpoche. [epk]

219 The messenger was referring to the custom of monasteries providing horses free of cost to people in the service of great masters. [epk]

220 The new incarnation of Samten Gyatso at Lachab was a nephew of the two masters Sabchu and Tarik. [tur]

221 When I visited Lachab in 2003, Tulku Urgyen Rinpoche's room had been rebuilt in the same place as when he lived there. The manager told me that during Tulku Urgyen's retreat, he had it sealed off with stones and mud and only a small opening allowed food to be passed through. [epk]

222 A detailed account of this visit and its implications is given in Tsering Shakaya's *Dragon in the Land of Snow: A History of Modern Tibet since 1947* (Middlesex, England: Penguin Compass, 1999), p. 122. [mbs]

223 Loter Wangpo was a lama from the great Ngor monastery in the Tsang province of Central Tibet. He was one of the principal disciples of both Khyentse and Kongtrul and reached the level of indivisible realization through them. He requested many important teachings and was a great master of outstanding importance. He was educated in the Sakya lineage when young, but he was really nonsectarian. Despite being chiefly Sakya, he was the compiler of two collections—*Drubtab Kuntu* and *Gyudey Kuntu*—containing tantric teachings from all the Sarma schools, which he supervised in accordance with the advice of Khyentse and Kongtrul. [tur]

224 This is why he was sometimes called Shechen Khyentse [tur]

225 Padmasattva—Chokgyur Lingpa's pure form—is also known as the bodhisattva Lotus-Sprout. After the great tertön's passing, Old Khyentse saw him in a vision as residing in his own buddhafield and received empowerments, blessings and teachings. Today these teachings are known as *Kusum Rigdu Zabtik*, the Profound Essence Embodying the Families of the Three Kayas, and the sadhana practice is the *Sphere of Great Bliss*. These words appear at the end of the sadhana text where Old Kongtrul writes: "Pema Ösel Do-Ngak Lingpa (Old Khyentse)—the great monarch of all the vidyadhara tertöns and siddhas—had on the fifteenth day of the eleventh month of the year of the Iron Horse, a vision in which he personally received—in the Lotus-Covered Buddhafield—from Bodhisattva Lotus-Sprout, indivisible from the great treasure revealer Chokgyur Lingpa—the nectar-like transmission of the sadhana, empowerment and instructions. For one month he kept the samaya seal of secrecy. Then, on the tenth day of the twelfth month, they were established in writing in combination with a feast offering, the task which I—Chimey Tennyi Yungdrung Lingpa Tsal (Old Kongtrul), a fortunate disciple of both great vidyadharas—undertook with deep respect. At this time the entire ground outside was suddenly warmed up, so that the ice and snow melted into a river, an auspicious sign which was visible to everyone. Since also the few connecting passages of this sadhana are written according to the Lord Guru's command, may this cause whoever connects with it to attain the state of being indivisible from these two vidyadhara masters' three secrets and may it cause the teachings to flourish and remain for a long time! May virtuous goodness increase!" [epk]

226 This was a very large assembly hall where the large golden stupa containing Chokgyur Lingpa's remains were kept. This stupa was made using the gold that Chokgyur Lingpa had found from a terma; it had an unusual brilliance to it. [tur]

227 This mind treasure focused on the dakini aspect was revealed by Jamyang Khyentse Wangpo and is named *Khandro Sangwa Kundu*. [epk]

228 The *Union of Means and Knowledge* (*Tabshe Khajor*) and *Karling Zhitro*. [tur]

The teachings on the intermediate states between death and rebirth connected to *Karling Zhitro* are commonly known in English as *The Tibetan Book of the Dead*. [mt]

229 Tulku Urgyen Rinpoche treated Pawo Rinpoche with immense respect and told me that he was the living embodiment of the great master Rinchen Lingpa. Having spent many years in Dordogne, France, Pawo Rinpoche passed away in Boudhanath a decade ago. [epk]

230 Around the same time, word went around that water had been pouring continuously from the mouths of the sea monsters' heads on the corners of the roof of the Jokhang temple in Lhasa. [tur]

231 We assume this happened in 1956. The Lhasa uprising and the subsequent suppression took place three years later, in 1959. [mbs]

232 Khandro Tsering Chödrön is currently living in Sikkim. She is the aunt of Sogyal Rinpoche. [mbs]

233 Padmasambhava's lotus crown is regarded as an object that "liberates though seeing". [epk]

234 The empowerment to master the display of awareness is a most profound transmission; it brings the disciple face to face with the nature of nondual knowing after which the training is to realize that thoughts and emotions are the display of this awareness. [epk]

235 A "seal of secrecy" often restricts a terma's propagation to masters who will be holders of that particular lineage, or to people who pledge to practice it wholeheartedly. [epk]

236 To explain this empowerment, let me quote Padmasambhava: "The empowerment for the awareness-display is taught by the buddhas who are by nature spontaneously perfected and, sending out compassionate emanations from the dharmadhatu of Akanishtha, they teach it for the sake of awakening instantaneously the people who are of the highest fortune. It is therefore not possible to attain buddhahood without having received the empowerment for the awareness-display. All the buddhas of the past awakened after receiving the empowerment for awareness-display. Everyone who presently attains enlightenment also awaken after receiving the empowerment for awareness-display. And, every buddha who attains enlightenment in future times will awaken as well after having received the empowerment for awareness-display. It is impossible to attain enlightenment unless you have obtained this." [epk]

237 Full title: *A Lamp to Dispel Darkness: An instruction that points directly to the nature of mind in the tradition of the Old Realized Ones*. (*Crystal Cave*, Rangjung Yeshe Publications, 1990).

238 Chokgyur Lingpa revealed and decoded several tantras. Some are among the treasures known as the *Sevenfold Cycle of Profundity*. He also brought forth a tantra as profound as the *Guhyagarbha*. Sadhanas, of course, are plentiful, but extremely rare is the tertön who lands a tantra of this type. But our tulku did so, together with the cycle on the *Eight Consorts*! [tur]

239 Those revealed by Nyang-Ral, Guru Chöwang and Chokgyur Lingpa. [tur]

240 Another version of the *Eightfold Sadhana Teaching* does exist in the *Three Sections of the Great Perfection* and the Instruction Section of the *Three Sections* also includes a cycle of teachings on the nine dakinis that are the protectors of basic space. In essence, these dakinis are identical with the eight consorts who manifested as guardians of the Dzogchen teachings. In this way, you could say that the essence of these teachings is still intact. The male aspect is present in the form of many sadhanas, but because that one text was lost, the female aspect is now only found in the form of Dharma protectors of Ati Yoga. [tur]

Recently Orgyen Tobgyal brought this text back from Tibet so it is now part of the *New Treasures*. The carved edition was twenty folios. I am not sure if he has managed to receive its transmission. [epk]

241 Dudjom Rinpoche was able to build a house close to the border of southern Tibet near Sikkim, ship many books there, and later carry them out to India. [mbs]

242 According to Tsering Shakaya's *Dragon in the Land of Snow*, "Among the newly involved figures promoted by the Chinese were prominent leaders from other religious sects (than Gelugpa). For the first time since the seventeenth century, lamas belonging to the Sakya, Kagyü and Nyingma schools were invited to participate in Tibetan polity. In this way the Chinese were able to broaden their support but it aroused deep suspicion among the traditional Gelugpa hierarchy." p. 132. [mbs]

243 I believe it is still at the Karmapa's monastery Rumtek in Sikkim. [epk]

244 This *Treasury of Nyingma Songs* by Kyungtrul Rinpoche surfaced in the spring of 2003 and is now being translated under that title. [epk]

245 Longchen Rabjam, *The Precious Treasury of the Basic Space of Phenomena*, (Chöying Dzö), transl. by Richard Barron (Padma Publishing).

246 Longchen Rabjam, the *Treasury of the Way of Abiding*, transl. by Richard Barron (Padma Publishing).

247 There is a relative and an ultimate meaning of the term *vajra throne*. The ultimate is the awakened state of primordial purity, which is the real location for attaining enlightenment. The vajra throne in Bodhgaya is an external version of the inner throne of basic space. In Kham, everyone had heard that when the deceased's spirit flounders through the bardo, there are only two places it cannot choose to go: the mother's womb and the vajra throne. But Samten Gyatso once told me, "It's not the throne in Bodhgaya, it's the vajra throne of inner basic space, the awakened state of primordial purity. After conception, you can't come and go from the mother's womb. You can only go in once, then you stick like a fly in glue and the spirit begins to be enveloped in a body composed of the aggregates, elements, and sense bases, from which there is no escape until the death of that rebirth." [tur]

248 Puntsok Wangdu was the father of the Bhutanese tulku of Palpung Khyentse. Later, he offered this temple to his son, who was in charge of it until he died. [tur]

249 Lion Fortress Meadow, *Neuring Senge Dzong*, is one of the five principal retreat places of Padmasambhava. It is situated on the Bhutanese side of the border.

250 Only a few of the tantras taught in this universe are available to humans; the rest are

kept in the storehouse of the dakinis in their celestial realms. Sometimes the dakinis are described as the custodians of the terma teachings. [epk]

[251] Some of these very important Dzogchen treasures included Tawa Long-Yang, the *Vast Expanse of the View,* revealed by Dorje Lingpa, and Rigdzin Gödem's *Samantabhadra's Realization Directly Revealed.* Dzogchen teachings were also revealed by Jatsön Nyingpo. Dzongsar Khyentse also mentioned, "The chief termas throughout all these centuries were revealed by the three eminent tertöns: Nyang-Ral Nyima Özer, Guru Chöwang, and Rigdzin Gödem, 'the vidyadhara with vulture feathers.'" [tur]

[252] Dzongsar Khyentse added, "Guru Chöwang's *Tenth Day Practice in Eight Chapters* is based on the form of Padmasambhava known as *Lama Sangdü,* the 'master who embodies all secrets.' There were three major versions of the *Eight Sadhana Teachings.* Among all the various dakini practices, Nyang-Ral's black wrathful form of Vajra Yogini is extremely profound.

"Of the major collections of termas, Padmasambhava codified three main sets, each under the name Gongdü: *Lama Gongdü, Yidam Gongdü,* and *Khandro Gongdü*; he then supplemented these with the *Chökyong Gongdü.* Sangye Lingpa received the mandate for receiving *Lama Gongdü,* Taksham Lingpa revealed the *Yidam Gongdü,* and Chokgyur Lingpa had the mandate to reveal the *Khandro Gongdü.* But the right coincidence wasn't formed and he became unable to reveal them; otherwise they would have filled quite a few volumes. It is the same for the *Chökyong Gongdü,* as all he wrote down was a short sadhana. Padmasambhava indicated that the *Khandro Gongdü* was concealed at the White Cliff in present-day Bhutan, but Chokgyur Lingpa was prevented from going there." [tur]

[253] Interestingly, these four masters were all from different countries: Padmasambhava from Uddiyana, Vairotsana from Tibet, and Vimalamitra from Kashmir, while their guru, Shri Singha, was born in China, probably in one of the Central Asian countries beyond the Pamir and Karakoram mountain ranges. They all met Shri Singha in Bodhgaya, though not at the same time. [epk]

[254] The oral lineage of the Nyingma school, the *Kahma,* contains all the nine gradual vehicles of the buddhas, but it emphasizes the three inner tantras. The ninth of these is the Ati, which refers to the Dzogchen teachings. [tur]

The *Four Branches of Heart Essence* are highly respected and famous under the Tibetan name *Nyingtig Yabzhi.* These two sets of *Heart Essence*—the *Khandro Nyingtig* of Padmasambhava and the *Vima Nyingtig* of Vimalamitra—has each a *Quintessence* written by Longchenpa, the *Khandro Yangtig* and *Lama Yangtig.* In addition, there is the *Profound Quintessence* (*Zabmo Yangtig*). Together these are called the *Mother and Child Heart Essence.* [tur]

Tulku Urgyen Rinpoche mentions these under the famous abbreviation *Do, Gyü,* and *Sem,* short for *Düpedo, Gyutrül,* and *Semde. Düpedo* is the main scripture of Anu Yoga. *Gyutrül* is the main Mahayoga tantra. *Semde* here refers to the Mind Section of Dzogchen Ati Yoga and in this context includes the other two of the *Three Sections*: the Space Section and Instruction Section. [epk]

[255] This Neten Chokling incarnation was Pema Gyurmey. He was recognized by Dzongsar Khyentse, who also became his guru. He was the father of Orgyen Tobgyal Rinpoche, Khyentse Yeshe and Dzigar Kongtrul. [epk]

256 These were the two official reincarnations of Chokgyur Lingpa and were commonly known after their places of residence—the Tsikey and Neten monasteries. See glossary for more details. [epk]

257 For the adept yogi, clairvoyance is an indelible part of the luminosity of deep sleep. [epk]

258 Since the books were sold to the U.S. Library of Congress preservation project priced by volume, each book was made shorter. The result was that the *New Treasures* came to comprise forty or so volumes, rather than the original twenty-four. For example, Chokgyur Lingpa's life story was originally included in the volume with the *Lamrim Yeshe Nyingpo*. [tur]

259 Lama Putse was a disciple of the third Chokling of Neten, the chant leader of the monastery and editor of the *New Treasures* published in the early nineteen-eighties. He knew the contents of the forty seven-hundred-page volumes better than anyone. [epk]

260 The Sun and Moon Cave is located near Melemchi in the Helambhu region (Yölmo in Tibetan), three days walk north of Kathmandu. On the ceiling inside the main cave is a very clear design of the sun and moon. [epk]

261 The important point about the court case is not the details of why, but the unwavering steadfastness with which Tulku Urgyen Rinpoche undertook a task out of devotion to the Karmapa. For nine years he pursued the case, getting nothing from it but a lot of trouble. [mbs]

262 However, it is now written down thanks to Gyurmey Dorje, the son of the great siddha king Adzom Drukpa, who felt compelled to have it done. The origin of this lineage is Jigmey Lingpa, who at Samye Chimphu had three visions of the wisdom body of Longchenpa, the omniscient lord of speech, from which he received the complete transmission of Dzogchen. Since then the lineage has been passed on to only one disciple at a time. This lineage was unique in its profound and extensive nature. Jigmey Lingpa's chief disciples were Tradrub and Dodrub. The former of these was Paltrul's lineage master. Paltrul then passed it on to Khenpo Lungtok, whose disciple was Khenpo Ngakchung. Another lineage went through the great scholar Zhenga and this particular lineage comes through Khenpo Lungtok, who spent around fifteen years at Paltrul's feet. Both Mipham and Zhenga were students of Paltrul. [tur]

263 Quite a few tulkus and khenpos opened their eyes to this Hearing Lineage from Nyoshul Khen after Tulku Urgyen Rinpoche had requested it, especially because it was difficult to get as only one person at a time was allowed to receive it. [epk]

264 This is quite an understatement. According to Soktse Rinpoche, who was his close disciple, Bomta Khenpo practiced for nine years at one hermitage in Central Tibet, having given up every type of extraneous activity. [epk]

265 As a master's meditative experience deepens and the 'expanse of the all-ground begin to overflow', profound and intuitive understanding unfolds and untaught treatises—topics never before studied—are easily comprehended. [epk]

266 The illusory city of the aggregates, elements and sense-bases is every sentient being's domain of experience—in other words, the state of samsara. [epk]

267 The utterly cloudless sky is, according to the ancient Dzogchen tantras, the external sign that often accompanies a master's inner realization of dharmakaya. It is considered the best sign of all. [epk]

[268] The details are in the appendix: "*The Lineage of the New Treasures.*" [mt]

[269] After the young Tsikey Chokling's unfortunate demise many years earlier, Tulku Urgyen Rinpoche had been given the task by Tsikey monastery—as was tradition—to ask the Karmapa about the Tsikey Chokling's whereabouts. When Rigpey Dorje replied that the tulku had been reborn as his second son, Tulku Urgyen Rinpoche refused to bring the news back to Nangchen, being concerned with accusations of nepotism. It was only when the Karmapa was visiting Dabzang Rinpoche's monastery in Boudha that he declared the fact in front of many lamas—Dabzang, Sabchu, Andzin and Tulku Urgyen Rinpoches. [epk]

[270] On one occasion, Dzongsar Khyentse visited Fortress Peak to receive some of the remaining *New Treasures* from Samten Gyatso. He stayed there for about a week, and this was when he conferred upon Samten Gyatso the extensive empowerment of Padmasattva (Pema Nyugu), which Samten Gyatso didn't have. In return, Samten Gyatso gave him the short Padmasattva empowerment. [tur]

[271] When I requested a name for my youngest son, Mingyur Rinpoche from the sixteenth Karmapa, he simply said, "He is a noble incarnation." Situ Rinpoche was His Holiness' attendant at the time and he told Rinpoche this son was the reincarnation Yongey Mingyur Dorje (whose incarnations had been closely related to the Situ Rinpoches). Later, Dilgo Khyentse Rinpoche indicated that Mingyur Rinpoche "would be the best choice for the tulku of Kangyur Rinpoche," who was the father of Tulku Pema Wangyal. This was fine by me as we often see cases of tulkus being simultaneous reincarnations of several masters, as well as one master reincarnating in three or five forms. The tulku is something much more flexible than a samsaric sentient being who takes one rebirth after another, and not by their own choice. For instance, Chokgyur Lingpa saw that Dabzang Rinpoche was the simultaneous incarnation of Gampopa, Yutok Gönpo and Drimey Dashar, one of Padmasambhava's twenty-five disciples. [tur]

[272] Dzongsar Khyentse Rinpoche received this transmission from Neten Chokling, who gave it to Katok Situ as well. [epk]

[273] This text, entitled *Garland of Gemstones*, was composed for the young sixteenth Karmapa by Uncle Tersey and Samten Gyatso, together, while using the record written by the second Chokling of Tsikey, Könchok Gyurmey Tenpey Gyaltsen. It was later annotated with notes about which transmissions the Karmapa received from Karma Orgyen (Tulku Urgyen Rinpoche). In other words, it contains the exact details of Tulku Urgyen's lineage of the *New Treasures*. A similar record also entitled *Garland of Gemstones*, listing the lineage received by Dilgo Khyentse Rinpoche, is found in his *Collected Works*, Vol. 25, page 219-276. [epk]

Endnote authors:

Tulku Urgyen Rinpoche [tur]

Erik Pema Kunsang [epk]

Marcia Binder Schmidt [mbs]

Michael Tweed [mt]

Glossary

abra—local type of mouse-hare or prairie dog.

Abum Rinchen Pungpa—Mount Abum; situated eight hours' drive on dirt roads from Sharda in Nangchen.

accomplishment—realization; signs of accomplishment include clairvoyant abilities, miraculous powers, and the inner heat of *tummo*.

Achen—prince of Nangchen during the time of Samten Gyatso.

Adeu Rinpoche (b.1930)—guru of the Nangchen kings whose monastery, Tsechu, is located next to the former royal palace.

Adzom Drukpa (1842-1924)—Drodul Pawo Dorje; one of the great Dzogchen masters of the early part of the twentieth Century, a tertön and a disciple both of Jamyang Khyentse Wangpo and Paltrul Rinpoche.

all-ground—*alaya*, a sentient being's basic state of mind; 'expanse of the all-ground' refers to the vastness of basic being.

amban—Chinese ambassador in Lhasa.

Amdo—one of the provinces of Kham.

Amnye—region of East Tibet.

amrita—nectar of immortality; drink of the gods; tantric rituals often use blessed liquor or fruit juice.

Angi Tendar—yogi from Nangchen; disciple of the first Tsoknyi.

Anu or Anu Yoga—second of the three inner tantras corresponding to the eighth of the nine vehicles; emphasizes knowledge (*prajna*) rather than means (*upaya*) and the completion stage rather than the development stage. The view of Anu Yoga is that liberation is attained through growing accustomed to the insight into the nondual nature of space and wisdom.

Argong—*see* Ngaktrin of Argong.

arhats, sixteen—disciples of the Buddha who vowed to preserve the Dharma until the coming of Maitreya, the future awakened one.

Armor Against Darkness—*Munpey Gocha*; commentary on Anu Yoga in more than 1,400 pages by Sangye Yeshe of Nub, according to an original tantra known as the *Scripture of the Great Assemblage*. The *Armor* has since been published in Delhi, India, as part of Dudjom Rinpoche's monumental publishing effort to preserve the early teachings of the Nyingma school. It is in volume 50–51 of his *Nyingma Kahma* edition.

Asura or Asura Cave—sacred place where the Lotus-Born master subdued the evil forces of afflicting negative conditions on Nepal through the practice of Vajra Kilaya and manifested the Mahamudra Vidyadhara level. Situated near Pharping in the Kathmandu valley.

Ati or Ati Yoga—third of the three inner tantras; emphasizes, according to Jamgön Kongtrul the First, the view that liberation is attained through growing accustomed to insight into the nature of primordial enlightenment, free from accepting and rejecting, hope and fear. The more common word for Ati Yoga nowadays is 'Dzogchen,' the Great Perfection.

Atisha (982-1054)—great Indian master who visited Tibet; from him springs the Kadampa and then the Gelugpa lineages.

Avalokiteshvara—bodhisattva of compassion, often depicted with four arms.

Banyak Ating (20th cent.)—governor of Sikkim and benefactor of tulku Urgyen.

bardo—intermediate state between death and the next rebirth.

Barom Kagyu lineage—begins with Dharma Wangchuk of Barom, a disciple of Gampopa.

Barwey Dorje (1836-1920)—master based in Raktrul Monastery in Sharda, Nangchen. Present incarnation (third) is Bardor Tulku Rinpoche, living in the USA.

basic nature of reality—*dharmata*; unformed and unconditioned nature of things which can be realized in personal experience.

basic space—fundamental nature of experience.

Benchen monastery—one of the main Kagyu monasteries in Nangchen; seat of the Sangye Nyenpa incarnations, Chimey and Tenga Rinpoches.

Black Crown ceremony—ritual of 'liberation through seeing' during which the Karmapa wears the crown exclusively worn by the Gyalwang Karmapas.

Black Vajra Yogini—important female deity.

Bodhgaya—site where Lord Buddha attained complete enlightenment situated in Bihar, India.

bodhisattva vow—pledge to bring every sentient being to liberation and enlightenment.

Bomta Khenpo (19th-20th cent.)—Polo Khenpo Dorje; disciple of Khenpo Ngakchung.

Bönpo—religion prevalent in Tibet before the establishment of Buddhism in the 9th Century.

Boudha; Boudhanath—location of the Great Stupa in the Kathmandu valley.

Brahma realm—celestial world of the god Brahma within the Realms of Form.

Buddha—enlightened or awakened one who has completely abandoned all obscurations and perfected every good quality. A perfected bodhisattva after attaining true and complete enlightenment is known as a buddha. The Buddha generally referred to is Shakyamuni Buddha, the buddha of this era, who lived in India around the 6th century B.C. There have been innumerable buddhas in past eons who manifested the way to enlightenment. In the current Good Eon—from the beginning to the end of human beings—there will be one thousand buddhas of which Buddha Shakyamuni is the fourth.

buddha activity—activity of an enlightened one to influence other beings and guide them to liberation and enlightenment.

Buddha Shakyamuni—the historical Buddha, regarded as the chief teacher of our present age.

buddhafield—*see* pure lands

Buddhaguhya (8th-9th cent.)—renowned Indian master who visited Mount Kailash at the time of King Trisong Deutsen and transmitted the *Guhyagarbha* tantra to the Tibetan translator Jnana Kumara of Nyag.

buddhahood—state of true and complete enlightenment, endowed with the ability to benefit countless other beings.

Bumtang valley—sacred valley in mid-Eastern Bhutan, traditional home to the master Pema Lingpa.

Calling the Guru from Afar—famous devotional chant written by Jamgön Kongtrul.

Chakrasamvara—main yidam deity and tantra of the New Schools.

Chamdo—province south of Nangchen, presently included within the Tibet Autonomous Region.

Chandali, the Mother of Longevity—consort of Buddha Amitayus; in *Blazing Splendor* a mind treasure of the first Khyentse, Jamyang Khyentse Wangpo.

chang—Tibetan beer brewed primarily from barley.

Chanting the Names of Manjushri—Manjushri Nama Sangirti Expressed in Songs of Praise. A tantra in six hundred verses belonging to Kriya Yoga known to all Tibetan Buddhists as *Jampal Tsenjö*. It is text number 424 in the Tsamdrak edition of *Collected Nyingma Tantras (Nyingma Gyuma)*. Translated as *Chanting the Names of Manjushri*, A. Wayman, Shambhala Publications.

Chatral Rinpoche—Sangye Dorje; prominent Nyingma master living at Pharping in the southern part of the Kathmandu valley.

Chetsun Nyingtig—see Heart Essence of Chetsun.

Chetsun Senge Wangchuk (11th-12th cent.)—great master of the Nyingma lineage. As a result of his high level of realization, his physical body disappeared in rainbow light at the time of death. See also *Heart Essence of Chetsun*.

Chimey Dorje (1884-1948?)—Tulku Urgyen Rinpoche's father and an adept Chö practitioner.

chinghu—religious dignity which is one rank below *goshir* but still higher than a *wang*. See also *tishi*.

Chini Lama—lama of Chinese descent who was the custodian of the Great Stupa of Boudhanath.

Chö—The practice of cutting through attachment to body and ego. See also *Machik's Complete Explanation: Clarifying the Meaning of Chod* by Sarah Harding, Snow Lion Publications.

Chögyal Dorje (1789-1859)—the first Tsoknyi's guru.

Chögyal Pakpa (1235-1280)—Sakya master and nephew of Sakya Pandita; ruled Tibet and was preceptor to the Mongolian Kublai Khan.

Chokgyur Lingpa (1829-1870)—important revealer of hidden treasure from Padmasambhava; Tulku Urgyen Rinpoche's great-grandfather.

Chokling—short for Chokgyur Lingpa; *see also* Chokling of Tsikey, Chokling of Neten.

Chokling of Tsikey—Tsikey Chokling; the incarnations of Chokgyur Lingpa residing at Tsikey monastery. Presently there are two, one in Boudhanath, Nepal and one in Tsikey monastery, Tibet.

Chökyi Nyima Rinpoche (b.1951)—oldest son of Tulku Urgyen Rinpoche, and abbot of Ka-Nying Shedrub Ling Monastery in Boudha, Nepal.

Chökyong Gongdu—terma revealed by Chokgyur Lingpa related to the protectors of the Dharma.

Chöwang Tulku (19th-20th cent.)—Tulku Urgyen Rinpoche's immediate former life.

chuba—traditional Tibetan dress used by lay people for both men and women, but with different style and folds.

cognitive obscuration—most subtle veil that covers our buddha nature; consists of holding notions of subject, object and interaction. *See also* emotional obscuration.

collapse of delusion—disappearance of erroneous ideas and concepts; rather than saying that someone "attained realization" the phrase shows realization's the real nature—that something extraneous has vanished, just like when the sun is cleared from clouds.

Collected Nyingma Tantras—Nyingma Gyubum; Literally the "One Hundred Thousand Nyingma Tantras." The website for The Collected Tantras of the Ancients at Virginia University lists around 388 different titles.

composure—state of meditation or equanimity; often opposed to post-meditation, the state of involvement in daily activities.

Dabzang Rinpoche (?-1992)—Dilyak Dabzang; master at Dilyak monastery in Nangchen and an emanation of Gampopa. The late Dabzang Rinpoche counted Kyungtrul Kargyam as one of his main teachers.

Dagger of the Sevenfold Profundity—Zabdun Purpa, belongs to the cycle of Kilaya, which is one of the seven sets of revelations among the *Sevenfold Profundity*, a terma treasure revealed by Chokgyur Lingpa. "Dagger" stands for Kilaya. This practice was also performed at Tsurphu.

dakini—goddess or female tantric deities who protect and serve the tantric doctrine.

dakini script—code script, symbolic script or writing used by the dakinis.

Dakpo Kagyu—synonym for the Kagyu lineages, since Gampopa became known as the master from Dakpo.

Darma Wangchuk (1127-1199/1200)—Gampopa's disciple who founded the Barom monastery in northern Latö and who is regarded as the father of the lineage.

Dartsedo—*Chinese name*: Kangding; the old border town between Kham and China.

Dechen Ling—the hermitage on Mount Abum Rinchen Pungpa where Chimey Dorje spent the second half of his life; presently a nunnery and retreat center.

Denkhog—district located in the Derge province.

Depuk Rinpoche (19th-20th cent.)—master from south-western Tibet; built a monastery in Solu Khumbhu, Nepal.

Derge—large independent kingdom in Kham that used to occupy the present-day counties of Jomda, Derge, Palyul, and Sershul.

development and completion—two main aspects of Vajrayana practice; development stage means positive mental fabrication while completion stage means resting in the unfabricated nature of mind.

Deypa Tulku—one of Chokgyur Lingpa's four close disciples who spread his teachings in eastern Tibet.

Dezhin Shekpa (1384-1415)—the fifth Karmapa, who performed numerous miracles in China and was given the famous black crown by Emperor Yunglo (Yongle) after converting him to Buddhism.

Dharma—teaching of the Buddha.

Dharma protector—nonhumans who vow to protect and guard the teachings of the Buddha and its followers; can be either 'mundane' i.e. virtuous samsaric beings or 'wisdom protectors' who are emanations of buddhas or bodhisattvas.

Dharmadhatu—realm of phenomena; the suchness in which emptiness and dependent origination are inseparable; nature of mind and phenomena that lies beyond arising, dwelling and ceasing.

dharmakaya—*see* kayas.

Dharmaraja—religious rulers, Dharma kings.

Dilgo Khyentse (1910-1991)—one the five immediate re-embodiments of Jamyang Khyentse Wangpo. Regarded by followers of all four schools as one of the foremost recent masters of Tibetan Buddhism. In the early days of his life, Tulku Urgyen first knew him as Tulku Salgah or Rabsel Dawa.

Dilyak Drubpön (1908-1963)—accomplished meditator who completed numerous three year retreats at Dilyak monastery; retreat master at Tsurphu.

Dilyak monastery—Dabzang Rinpoche's monastery in Nangchen, founded by the first Dabzang Rinpoche.

Dorje Ziji—one of the names of Jamyang Khyentse Wangpo (Old Khyentse); means Indestructible Resplendence.

Drak Yerpa—One of five sacred places blessed by Padmasambhava. Situated 30 km northeast of Lhasa, it is famous for caves used for meditation by the Lotus-Born master and his consort Yeshe Tsogyal, as well as by the 10th century scholar Atisha.

Drakda—birthplace of Tulku Urgyen Rinpoche near the Life-Lake of Yeshe Tsogyal (Tsogyal Lhatso), situated at Drakda some 20 km from Samye.

drashö—rank of government official in Bhutan.

Drepung—one of the three major Gelukpa monasteries around Lhasa.

Drigung—major branch of the Kagyu lineage, founded by Kyobpa Jigten Sumgön (1143-1217), a disciple of Phamo Drupa.

Drimey Dashar, one of Padmasambhava's twenty-five disciples. Same as Jnanakumara of Nyag.

Droma—a sweet root used as a delicacy; sweet potato of Tibet.

Drong Gompa—(Bong Gompa) the monastery of Lama Tendzin Dorje, Chökyi Nyima's previous life, which is situated several days' journey north of Lhasa on the route to Kham through Nakchukha. Drong means wild yak.

Drönyer—an attendant in charge of receiving guests.

Drowo—Valley of Birches, residence of Marpa the Translator, presently in Lhodrak county in southern Tibet.

drubchen—"great accomplishment practice"; an elaborate tantric practice undertaken by a group of people which goes on uninterruptedly for seven days.

drubdra—the "practice center" where the traditional three-year retreat takes place.

Druk Sang-Ngak Chöling—The seat of the Drukchen Jamgön. Literally, the "Dharma Garden of Secret Mantrayana" at Jar in southern Tibet was built by the fourth Drukchen, Pema Karpo (1527-1592) who transferred the seat of the Drukpa Order to this place.

Drukchen—respectfully referred to as the Drukchen Jamgön. His monastery's name is Druk Sang-Ngak Chöling. The Drukchen incarnation in residence during Tulku Urgyen Rinpoche's early childhood was Mipham Chokyi Wangpo (1884–1930) whose principal guru was the great siddha, Drubwang Shakya Shri.

Drukpa Kagyu—The Kagyu teachings transmitted from Gampopa through Phamo Drubpa to Lingje Repa.

Drukpa Yongdzin Rinpoche (d.1958)—the eighth Druk Kharag Yongdzin/ Dechen Chokhor Yongdzin Ngagi Wangpo; a prominent Drukpa Kagyu master of Central Tibet.

Dudjom Rinpoche (1904-1987)—incarnation of the great treasure revealer Dudjom Lingpa. He was the supreme head of the Nyingma lineage after exile from Tibet and is regarded as one of the most prominent scholars of our time.

Dudul—Samten Gyatso's attendant and Tulku Urgyen's childhood friend.

dur—ritual performed after someone's death to disengage certain spirits from the vital energy of the deceased which otherwise can slow down or create obstacles to liberation in the bardo.

duruka—negative influences mentioned in old prophecies as three kinds: invading armies, infectious diseases, and material substances.

Dusölma—protector; a female guardian protector of the Buddhist teachings.

Dusum Khyenpa (1110-1193)—first Karmapa and disciple of Gampopa.

Dzigar Kongtrul—one of the main incarnations of Jamgön Kongtrul the first. His present tulku is the youngest son of Neten Chokling.

Dzogchen—Also known as Great Perfection and Ati Yoga. The highest teachings of the Nyingma School of the Early Translations. The early lineage masters include Garab Dorje, Manjushrimitra, Shri Singha, Jnanasutra, Vimalamitra, Padmasambhava and Vairotsana. Numerous Dzogchen teachings were concealed as *termas* treasures by these masters and revealed through the following centuries. These teachings are embodied in the oral instructions one receives personally from a qualified master.

Dzongsar Khyentse (1893-1959)—Jamyang Khyentse Chökyi Lodrö of Dzongsar monastery; one of the five reincarnations of Jamyang Khyentse Wangpo. He upheld the Rimey (nonsectarian) tradition, and was one of the two main root gurus of Dilgo Khyentse.

Dzongsar monastery—the seat of Jamyang Khyentse Wangpo in Derge county, home of the famous Buddhist college and subsequently the seat of the successor, Dzongsar Khyentse Chökyi Lodrö.

Dzongshö—also Sugata Assemblage of Dzongshö, the sacred place of hidden qualities where Chokgyur Lingpa revealed implements belonging to the master Padmasambhava, the abbot Shantarakshita and the king Trisong Deutsen. The great tertön also revealed a guidebook explaining the lay-out and benefits of practicing there.

earth terma—A revelation based on physical substance, often in the form of dakini script, a vajra, a statue, etc. See also 'mind terma'.

egolessness—the fact that the seemingly real identity in a person or phenomenon cannot be found to be of a permanent, partless and independent nature.

eight classes of spirits—the sutras mention: devas, nagas, yakshas, gandharvas, asuras, garudas, kinnaras, and mahoragas. All of them were able to receive and practice the teachings of the Buddha. These eight classes can also refer to various types of mundane spirits who can cause either help or harm, but remain invisible to normal human beings: *ging, mara, tsen, yaksha, raksha, mamo, rahula,* and *naga*. On a subtle level, they are regarded as the impure manifestation of the eight types of consciousness.

eight *herukas*—eight wrathful manifestations of the eight main bodhisattvas. They symbolize the transformation of the eight consciousnesses.

Eight Sadhana Teachings—Eight Commands; eight chief yidam deities of Mahayoga and their corresponding tantras and sadhanas: Manjushri Body, Lotus Speech, Vishuddha Mind, Nectar Quality, Kilaya Activity, Liberating Sorcery of Mother Deities, Maledictory Fierce Mantra, and Mundane Worship.

Eighteen Mahayoga Tantras—eighteen important scriptures translated into Tibetan during the time of King Trisong Deutsen.

emanation—a magical creation or divinely manifested rebirth of a buddha or past enlightened master.

emanation basis—the enlightened being in a buddhafield who emanates or 'incarnates' into the world.

Embodiment of Realization—(Tukdrub Gongpa Kundu) A terma treasure revealed by Chokgyur Lingpa that combines all levels of guru sadhana.

empowerment—The conferring of power or authorization to practice the Vajrayana teachings, the indispensable entrance door to tantric practice. Empowerment gives control over one's innate vajra body, vajra speech and vajra mind and the authority to regard forms as deity, sounds as mantra and thoughts as wisdom.

empowerment for the play of awareness—The empowerment for practicing Dzogchen or Mahamudra. Sometimes it also refers to a stage of realization achieved through Dzogchen practice.

emptiness—The fact that phenomena and the ego are empty of, or lack, independent true existence.

entrustment—for instance to the life force of Tseringma; a short empowerment ritual, usually for receiving the blessings of the body, speech and mind of the deity.

eruption test—a local spirit may challenge the yogi's stability in meditation by creating magical apparitions of varying degrees of intensity.

Essence Manual of Oral Instruction—(Sheldam Nyingjang Yishin Norbu) the first volume of Chokgyur Lingpa's *New Treasures* and the major scripture in the *Tukdrub Barchey*

Kunsel cycle. Tulku Urgyen Rinpoche regarded this important text as being a tantra in itself.

essence, nature, and capacity—The three aspects buddha nature according to the Dzogchen system. Essence is the primordially pure wisdom of emptiness. The nature is the spontaneously present wisdom of cognizance. The capacity is the all-pervasive wisdom of indivisibility. This is, ultimately, the identity of the Three Roots, the Three Jewels and the three kayas.

evil influence—the influence of mischievous spirits that can cause misfortune and/or disease.

exhaustion of concepts and phenomena—the fourth of four levels of realization in Dzogchen practice. To quote Tsele Natsok Rangdröl, "the body, experiences, sense faculties and all thought forms become exhausted, so there is no way one can avoid attaining enlightenment and dissolving into the space of dharmata beyond thought and description."

five sciences—language; dialectics; science of medicine; science of arts and crafts; religious philosophy.

Fortress Peak—Dzong-Go Ling, the lofty hermitage of Samten Gyatso and Tulku Urgyen Rinpoche administrated by Lachab monastery, which lies one day's horse ride away. In recent years it has been rebuilt by the incarnation of Samten Gyatso.

Four Branches of Heart Essence, the—(*Nyingtig Yabzhi*) One of the most famous collections of Dzogchen scriptures, in which Longchenpa combined the streams of teachings from Padmasambhava and Vimalamitra together with his own mind treasures.

four levels of Dzogchen and Mahamudra—The four visions in Dzogchen practice: *dharmata* in actuality, increase in experience, culmination of awareness and exhaustion of phenomena. Four stages in Mahamudra practice: one-pointedness, simplicity, one taste, and nonmeditation.

four mind-changings—The reflections of the four mind-changings cover the topics of precious human body, impermanence, karma and samsaric suffering. These contemplations are like loosening up the hard soil and preparing a field to be fertile and ready to grow the seeds of enlightenment.

four modes and six limits—The indispensable keys for unlocking the meaning of the tantras. The four modes are the literal, general, hidden, and the ultimate. The six limits are the views of the expedient and definitive meaning, the implied and the not implied, the literal and the not literal.

Four-Armed Mahakala—guardian protector of the teachings.

Ga Lotsawa—great siddha and translator who visited India; also known as Palchen Galo ['Galo' is an abbreviation of Ga Lotsawa, or "the translator of the Ga clan"]. He stayed at Nalanda monastery and meditated in the Cool Grove Charnel Ground, where he had a vision of a wisdom-protector and received predictions. [tur]

Galo—*see* Ga Lotsawa.

Gampo or Dakla Gampo—the mountain where Gampopa lived, in the southeastern part of Central Tibet.

Gampopa (1079-1153)—forefather of all the Kagyu lineages; foremost disciple of Milarepa who possessed both supreme realization and great scholarship. He was the author of

The Jewel Ornament of Liberation. More details can be found in *The Life of Milarepa* and *The Rain of Wisdom*, Shambhala Publications.

Ganapati—a monkey-faced guardian of the Buddha's teachings.

Ganden—major Gelukpa monastery near Lhasa, founded in 1409 by Tsongkhapa.[map]

Gangtok—capital of the former (up to 1975) independent kingdom Sikkim, situated between Tibet, Bhutan, Nepal, and India.

Gar Drubchen—A Tibetan accomplished master of the Drigung Kagyu school who was an emanation of Nagarjuna and also Phamo Drupa (1110-70), one of the three foremost disciples of Gampopa.

Garab Dorje—Prahevajra; incarnation of a god who earlier had been empowered by the buddhas. Immaculately conceived, his mother was a nun, the daughter of King Dhahena Talo of Uddiyana. Garab Dorje received all the tantras, scriptures and oral instructions of Dzogchen from Vajrasattva and Vajrapani in person and became the first human master in the Dzogchen lineage. Having reached the state of complete enlightenment through the effortless Great Perfection, Garab Dorje transmitted the teachings to his retinue of exceptional beings. Manjushrimitra is regarded as his chief disciple. Padmasambhava is also known to have received the transmission of the Dzogchen tantras directly from Garab Dorje's wisdom form. Garab Dorje means 'Indestructible joy.'

garuda—The mythological bird, able to travel from one end of the universe to the other with a single movement of its wings. It is also known to hatch from the egg fully developed and ready to soar through the sky.

Gathering Palace of Sugatas—(Deshek Dupey Podrang). The hermitage of Jamyang Khyentse Wangpo (Old Khyentse) above Dzongsar monastery. Sugata is a synonym for a buddha.

Gebchak—gompa, monastery. Retreat center and nunnery founded by Tsang-Yang Gyatso, half a day's horse ride from Fortress Peak or Lachab.

Gelug—The Tibetan school of Buddhism founded by Tsongkhapa as a reformation of the tradition of Atisha Dipamkara.

genyen—the twenty-one *genyen*, guardian spirits of the Dharma who, when Padmasambhava was in Tibet, were bound under oath to protect the Buddha's teachings.

geshe—a learned Buddhist scholar or teacher.

Geshe Chayulwa (1075-1138)—a master in the old Kadam tradition who was also one of the teachers of Gampopa, the great Kagyu master.

Glorious Copper-Colored Mountain—the terrestrial pure land of Padmasambhava.

Golden Garland Chronicles, the—the extensive biography of the Lotus-Born master, Padmasambhava; a terma revealed by Sangye Lingpa (1340-1396).

Golok—large province in northeastern Kham.

Gomde, the Land of Meditators—a name for Nangchen.

gomdra—meditation retreat, often for groups staying three years in seclusion, where the practice is focused on Dzogchen or Mahamudra. Compare with *drubdra*.

Gompa—a monastery or temple hall connected to a hermitage.

gönchung—a shrine room, often small for the Dharma protectors.

Gongdu—Assemblage of Realization, or 'gathering all the intentions into one'; a name used for certain revealed treasures, for instance *Yidam Gongdu*.

gönla—the lama in charge of the chants for the protectors.

goshir—religious rank, *see* tishi.

Great Mother of Transcendent Knowledge, the—the twelve thick volumes of the *Prajnaparamita* scriptures, one of the most famous sutras in Mahayana.

Great Perfection—Dzogchen; the third of the three inner tantras of the Nyingma School. The Great Perfection is the ultimate of all the 84,000 profound and extensive sections of the Dharma, the realization of Buddha Samantabhadra, exactly as it is. Synonym for 'Dzogchen' or 'Ati Yoga.'

Great Scroll Depicting the Hundred Wondrous Deeds—the famous Tsurphu Scroll an early Ming dynasty silk-backed painting with Chinese, Tibetan, Mongolian, Uighur and Arabic inscriptions. It depicts the miracles performed by the Fifth Karmapa Dezhin Shekpa during his 22-day visit to the Yunglo (Yongle) emperor in Nanjing in 1407. The emperor also offered the Karmapa the famous Black Hat, which he had seen in a vision during a religious ceremony.

Great Stupa of Boudha—The Jarung Khashor Stupa at Boudhanath, Nepal, situated in the Kathmandu valley. For details, see Keith Dowman, *The Legend of the Great Stupa*.

Guhyagarbha—the *Tantra on the Essence of Secrets*, which is the most vital of all the tantras in the Old School (Nyingma) of Tibetan Buddhism.

gungtreng—the Chinese name for communists.

Guru Chöwang (1212-1270)—one of the five tertön kings and former life of Tulku Urgyen Rinpoche. For details, see Dudjom Rinpoche's *The Nyingma Lineage, its History and Fundamentals*, pages 760-70.

Guru Mahasukha—Great Bliss Master, a peaceful form of Padmasambhava, usually depicted as wearing the pandita hat and with hands in equanimity.

guru yoga—the final and most important part of the preliminary practices. The practice of supplicating for blessings and mingling the mind of an enlightened master with one's own mind.

gyaling—a reed instrument close to the Persian *shanai* and one of the principal ritual instruments in Tibetan Buddhism.

Gyalpo Pehar—a powerful spirit and guardian of the Dharma; the Dharma protector of Samye.

Gyalwa Cho-Yang—one of Padmasambhava's twenty-five disciples.

Gyalwang—King of All the Buddhas, a special title for certain lamas such as the Karmapa or the Drukchen.

Hayagriva—Tantric deity shown with a horse's head within his flaming hair; wrathful aspect of Buddha Amitabha. Identical with Padma Heruka, Lotus Speech, among the *Eight Sadhana Teachings*.

hearing lineage—given from the master's voice to the disciple's ears, and only to one person at a time, rather than being a printed text.

Heart Essence of Chetsun—(*Chetsun Nyingtig*), one of the most important Dzogchen instructions of recent times, revealed by Jamyang Khyentse Wangpo.

Heart Essence of Samantabhadra—(*Kunzang Tuktig*), one of the most important Dzogchen instructions of recent times, revealed by Chokgyur Lingpa.

heart essence of the Great Perfection—(*Dzogchen Nyingtig*), teachings of Dzogchen brought to Tibet by Vimalamitra and Padmasambhava as for instance arranged by Longchenpa in the *Four Branches of Heart Essence*, the *Nyingtig Yabzhi*.

Heru Gompa—a monastery in Nangchen near Tana south of Lachab; the seat of Kyungtrul Kargyam.

heruka—a wrathful deity, for instance Hayagriva or Vajra Kilaya.

Hinayana—The vehicles focused on contemplation of the four noble truths and the twelve links of dependent origination, the practice of which brings liberation from cyclic existence, samsara.

Hinayana; Mahayana; Vajrayana—the three levels of the Buddha's teachings.

hundred peaceful and wrathful deities—The 42 peaceful and 58 wrathful deities. The are often related to the after-death experience of the *bardo* state. The details are found in the *Liberation Through Hearing in the Bardo*.

hungry ghost—One of the six classes of sentient beings, tormented by their own impure karmic perception, which causes them to suffer tremendously from craving, hunger and thirst.

Inexhaustible Garland of Lightning—a petition chant to the guardians of the Dharma, especially those who protect the Dzogchen teachings.

inner heat, blissful—*see* tummo yoga

Jambhala, Black—a particular manifestation of Jambhala, the god of wealth.

Jamdrak (1883?-1945?)—Dru Jamyang Drakpa. A close disciple of Jamyang Khyentse Wangpo and a very learned master. one of the destined disciples predicted in the root text *Lamrim Yeshe Nyingpo*.

Jamgön Kongtrul—Lodrö Thaye (1813-1899); prophesized by the Buddha Shakyamuni in the *King of Samadhi Sutra* and by Padmasambhava in many of his termas. He studied and mastered all the Buddha's teachings. His primary teachers were the Fourteenth Karmapa, Situ Pema Nyinje Wangpo and the Great Khyentse. He became the teacher of the fifteenth Karmapa, Khakyab Dorje. He is renowned as an accomplished master, scholar, writer, poet, and artist, and authored and compiled more than 100 volumes of scriptures. Among these, the best known is the *Five Treasuries*. In *Splendor* he is referred to as Old Kongtrul or simply Kongtrul.

Jamgön: loving protector—a title used for the greatest masters, for instance the first Kongtrul or the Drukchen.

Jampal Tsultrim—one of the fifteenth Karmapa's chief disciples.

Jamyang Khyentse Wangpo (1820-92)—the first Khyentse; great master of the 19th century. He was the last of the Five Great Tertöns and was regarded as the combined reincarnation of Vimalamitra and King Trisong Deutsen. He became the master and teacher of all the Buddhist schools of Tibet and the founder of the Rimey movement. There are ten volumes of his works in addition to his termas. Jamyang means 'Manjushri, gentle melodiousness', Khyentse Wangpo means 'Lord of loving wisdom.' In this book he is referred to as Old Khyentse or simply Khyentse.

Jangchub Shönnu—Lumey Dorje's nephew and successor; early master in the Barom Kagyu lineage.

Jatsön Nyingpo (1585-1656)—revealer of terma, especially known for the *Könchok Chidu* teachings.

Jewel Garland, the—a long collection of Chö songs composed by the third Karmapa and codified by Karma Chagmey.

Jigmey Lingpa (1729-1798)—reincarnation of Longchenpa, revealed the famous *Nyingtig* cycle, the *Innermost Essence.* Among his immediate reincarnations are counted Jamyang Khyentse Wangpo, Paltrul Rinpoche and Do Khyentse Yeshe Dorje.

Jokhang—the famous temple and most important pilgrimage site in Lhasa, houses the Jowo statue of Buddha Shakyamuni.

Jokyab—the gifted khenpo sent to receive teachings on *Lamrim Yeshe Nyingpo* from Jamdrak Rinpoche.; one of Tulku Urgyen Rinpoche's teachers.

Jordruk—One of the Eight Practice Lineages. Literally it means "Six Unions" and is according to the system of Kalachakra.

Jowo—the Jowo Rinpoche or Jowo Shakyamuni in the Jokhang, the main temple of Lhasa originally called Rasa Trulnang Temple. This statue is said to have been made while Buddha Shakyamuni was still alive and personally blessed by him.

Kadam—tradition; one of the eight chariots of the practice lineages, brought to Tibet by Atisha Dipamkara in the eleventh century.

Kadampa—a follower of the Kadam lineage.

Kagyu—The lineage of teachings brought to Tibet by Lord Marpa, received from the dharmakaya buddha Vajradhara by the Indian siddha Tilopa, Saraha, and others. Transmitted by Naropa and Maitripa to the Tibetan translator Marpa, the lineage was passed on to Milarepa, Gampopa, Karmapa and others. The main emphasis is on the path of means which is the Six doctrines of Naropa, and the path of liberation which is the Mahamudra instructions of Maitripa.

Kahma—the "long lineage" of the Nyingma school, the canonical scriptures, which has been transmitted in an uninterrupted way from master to disciple since Padmasambhava and before.

Kailash—the sacred mountain in west Tibet.

Kalachakra—'Wheel of Time'. A tantra and a Vajrayana system taught by Buddha Shakyamuni himself, showing the interrelationship between the phenomenal world, the physical body and the mind.

Kalimpong—city near Darjeeling in northern India, the old trading post between Calcutta and Lhasa.

Kalpa—Chöwang Tulku's attendant.

Kangsar—see Mount Kangsar; Samten Kangsar.

Kangsar Khenpo—a Sakya teacher from the Ngor monastery.

Kangyur—the translated words of the Buddha; the 103 or 104 volumes of the Tibetan canonical scriptures that contain the direct words of Buddha Shakyamuni.

Ka-Nying Shedrub Ling monastery—founded by Tulku Urgyen Rinpoche at the great stupa of Boudhanath in Nepal; abbot and vajra master are Chökyi Nyima Rinpoche and Chokling Rinpoche.

Kargah—Tulku Urgyen Rinpoche's nickname.

Karma Chagmey (1613–1678)—great saint and tertön, belonging to both the Nyingma and Kagyu traditions. His monastery was Neydo (Nemdho) Tashi Chöling in Chamdo. Known for his *Union of Mahamudra and Dzogchen*.

Karma Gön—The monastic seat of the Karmapa incarnations in Kham, situated in Lhatö, on the road between Surmang and Chamdo, south of Nangchen. Seat of the first incarnations of Situ Rinpoche.

Karma Gyaltsen—Kyungtrul Kargyam's main name.

Karma Lingpa—14th cent. Tertön mostly known for revealing the text now famous as *The Tibetan Book of the Dead* or more correctly *The Great Liberation Through Hearing in the Bardo*.

Karma Pakshi (1204-1283)—second Karmapa and therefore the first Karmapa tulku.

Karmapa—the Karmapa incarnation line. Chokgyur Lingpa predicted the names of the first twenty-five. The present is the seventeenth.

Karmey Khenpo (b.19th cent.)—Karmey Khenpo's full name was Karmey Khenpo Rinchen Dargye. My teacher, Samten Gyatso, described Karmey Khenpo as "the great tertön's disciple, who was a reincarnation of Khenpo Bodhisattva and repeatedly certified by the great masters Khyentse, Kongtrul, and Chokling, and an outstanding master in his own right." [tur]

Karmey Khentrul—the reincarnation of Karmey Khenpo, the cousin of Tulku Urgyen Rinpoche.

Karpo Sabchu—yogi and attendant of Chokgyur Lingpa.

Karsa Yuri—Tulku Urgyen Rinpoche's mother.

Karsey Kongtrul (1904-1953)—alias Jamgön Palden Khyentse Özer, the immediate reincarnation of Old Kongtrul, reborn as the son of the 15th Karmapa. One of Tulku Urgyen Rinpoche's root gurus.

Kathmandu—the capital of Nepal.

Katok monastery—one of the four main monasteries of the Nyingma tradition in Kham. Situated south of Derge, near Palyul.

Katok Situ (1880-1925)—Chökyi Gyatso; a great scholar from Katok monastery. One of the teachers of Uncle Tersey.

kayas—the three kayas: dharmakaya, sambhogakaya and nirmanakaya. Dharmakaya is the 'body' of enlightened qualities, which is devoid of constructs, like space. Can be either an aspect of the yogi's experience or of final enlightenment. Sambhogakaya is the sublime form of a buddha in the buddhafields endowed with the 'major and minor marks'. Nirmanakaya is the incarnations to influence and benefit sentient beings.

Kechu River—one of the rivers between Nangchen and Derge; it joins the Tsichu River in front of the Tsikey monastery.

Khakyab Dorje (1871-1922)—fifteenth Karmapa; disciple of the old Kongtrul and teacher of Karsey Kongtrul.

Khala Rong-go—the place where Chokgyur Lingpa revealed the terma treasure *Tukdrub Barchey Kunsel*. Situated in Nangchen on the road between Jekundu and Sharda.

Kham—independent kingdoms east of Chamdo, including Nangchen, Derge Amdo and Golok; presently occupies parts of the TAR (Tibetan Autonomous Region), Yunnan, Qinghai and Sichuan provinces. It is known as eastern Tibet among non-Tibetans.

Khampa—a person from one of the regions in Kham.

Khampa Gomchen—an eccentric meditator and doctor who passed away in Nepal in the '80s.

Khamtrul Tenpey Nyima (1849-1907)—one of the main masters of the Drukpa Kagyu lineages. His present incarnation resides in Tashi Jong, Himachal Pradesh, India.

Khandro Chenmo—the Great Dakini of Tsurphu; consort of the fifteenth Karmapa. Her reincarnation, Khandro Rinpoche, lives in Himachal Pradesh, India, but teaches around the world.

Kharsha Rinpoche—a master from Kharsha (Lahoul) in northern India.

khenchen—great scholar/khenpo; a title only given to teachers of the highest degree of learning.

Khenpa valley—a small hidden place in Bhutan.

khenpo—a learned teacher in a monastery or the one who gives precepts of monastic ordination.

Khenpo—see Bomta Khenpo; Kangsar Khenpo; Karmey Khenpo; Khenpo Bodhisattva.

Khenpo Bodhisattva—Usually known under the name Shantarakshita. The Indian pandita and abbot of Vikramashila in India and of Samye who ordained the first Tibetan monks.

Khenpo Lekshey—teacher at Tsurphu between the fifteenth and sixteenth Karmapas.

Khenpo Ngakchung (1879-1941)—scholar-teacher at Katok monastic college and a very important reviver of the scholastic lineage of expounding the Dzogchen scriptures. Considered to be incarnation of both Vimalamitra and Longchenpa. Chatral Sangye Dorje is one of his last living disciples. Khenpo Ngakchung got his name because there was an older khenpo with the name Ngawang, so he became the "Younger Khenpo Ngawang." One of his works is available in English with a short biography in the introduction: Khenpo Ngawang Pelzang, *A Guide to the Words of My Perfect Teacher* (Shambhala Publications, 2004).

Khentrul—"Khenpo's reincarnation" here in this book refers to Karmey Khentrul, the tulku of Karmey Khenpo.

Khunu—a province in the northern part of Himachal Pradesh, India.

Khunu Rinpoche (1885-1977)—Khunu Lama Tendzin Gyaltsen; lama from India who traveled all over Tibet and Kham and became a teacher of the Dalai Lama. For more details, see his book on bodhichitta in English: *Vast as the Heavens, Deep as the Sea*.

Khyentse—*see* Dilgo Khyentse; Dzongsar Khyentse; Jamyang Khyentse Wangpo; Khyentse of Palpung.

Khyentse of Palpung (1896-1945)—reincarnation of Old Khyentse residing at Palpung monastery.

kilaya—dagger used in tantric rituals, often the blade has three sides.

Kilaya—deity usually known as Vajra Kilaya or Vajra Kumara; wrathful form of Vajrasattva.

kilaya dagger—same as *kilaya*.

King Jah—Indian king who received the eighteen Mahayoga tantras on the roof of his palace approximately one hundred years after Buddha Shakyamuni's passing. The lineage of these teachings continues to the present day.

King Nyatri—first ruler of all of Tibet, took the throne in 247 BC.

King Trisong Deutsen (790–844)—second great Dharma king of Tibet who invited Padmasambhava, Shantarakshita, Vimalamitra, and many other Buddhist teachers to Tibet; built Samye, the great monastery and teaching center modeled after Odantapuri, established Buddhism as the state religion of Tibet, and during his reign the first monks were ordained. He arranged for panditas and lotsawas to translate sacred texts, and he established centers for teaching and practice. Among his later incarnations are Nyang Ral Nyima Özer (1124-1192), Guru Chöwang (1212-1270), Jigmey Lingpa (1729-1798), and Jamyang Khyentse Wangpo (1820-1892).

Könchok Gyurmey Tenpey Gyaltsen (1871-1939)—second Chokling of Tsikey.

Könchok Paldrön (1858?-1939?)—Tulku Urgyen Rinpoche's grandmother; daughter of Chokgyur Lingpa. Her name means Precious Lamp of Splendor.

Kongpo—province near the Indian border, straight east of Lhasa, and southwest of Nangchen.

Kongtrul—Jamgön Kongtrul; *see* also Karsey Kongtrul; Dzigar Kongtrul.

kudung—sacred remains of a master's body, either before or after cremation. Sometimes the entire body was embalmed an enshrined in a stupa, as was the case with Chokgyur Lingpa.

Kungo Kalsang—son of Chimey Dorje; Tulku Urgyen Rinpoche's half brother.

Kunsang Dechen—Tulku Urgyen Rinpoche's consort; mother of Chökyi Nyima and Chokling Rinpoches.

Kunzang Dorje—Tulku Urgyen Rinpoche's youngest brother; supposedly an incarnation of Neten Chokling.

Kunzang Tuktig—*Heart Essence of Samantabhadra*; collection of terma teachings revealed by Chokgyur Lingpa focused on the peaceful and wrathful deities as the development stage and on Trekchö and Tögal as the completion stage.

kutsab—representative, usually refers to a statue of the Lotus-Born master, Padmasambhava.

Kutsab Lhakhang—shrine room dedicated to a special statue representing Padmasambhava.

Kyasu Tertön—treasure revealer of the Kyasu clan; Kyasu being Chokgyur Lingpa's family name. One wall of Kyasu mansion is still visible an hour's walk from Tsechu monastery in Nangchen.

Glossary

Kyipuk—retreat encampment of the great master Shakya Shri, near Druk Sang-Ngak Chöling, at Jar in southern Tibet.

Kyirong—southwest of Lhasa, on the old border of Nepal directly north of Kathmandu.

Kyungpo clan—same family line as Milarepa; rulers of west Tibet in the days of the early king Songtsen Gampo.

Kyungpo Naljor (1002-1064)—Tibetan master who brought teachings back from India later known as the Shangpa Kagyu and is thus regarded as its founder; disciple of the female siddha Niguma.

Kyungpo region—presently situated in Tenchen county, south of Nangchen one the road between Chamdo and Lhasa. Kyungpo is the name of a district in Kham and means garuda.

Kyungtrul Kargyam—Karma Gyaltsen; one of Tulku Urgyen Rinpoche's teachers and regarded as one of the emanations of Jamgön Kongtrul the first. Kargyam is an abbreviation of Karma Gyaltsen. The king of Nangchen had four gurus; one of them, Kyungtrul's father, resided at Heru Gompa.

Lachab monastery/Gompa—Lachab Jangchub Nordzin Chöling; main monastery of Samten Gyatso and Tulku Urgyen Rinpoche in Nangchen.

lachen—title of grand master, imperial priest.

Ladakh—area to the far west of Tibet, presently in India, north of Kashmir.

Lady Degah—Dechen Chödrön; Chokgyur Lingpa's consort and Tulku Urgyen Rinpoche's great-grandmother. Her name means Dharma Lamp of Great Bliss.

Lake Manasarovar—famous lake and pilgrimage site near Mount Kailash in west Tibet.

Lama Latsey—one of Karmey Khenpo's disciples; important holder of the monastic precepts in Kham.

Lama Putse—Pema Tashi; learned disciple of the third Chokling of Neten and of Dilgo Khyentse Rinpoche.

Lama Sangdu—terma treasure revealed by Guru Chöwang.

Lamdrey—(*Path and Fruit*) vital teachings of the Sakya tradition that come from the India master Virupa.

Lamrim Yeshe Nyingpo—spontaneous song by the ninth-century Indian master Padmasambhava, covering the entire Buddhist path to enlightenment, especially that of Vajrayana. Its commentary is the *Light of Wisdom*.

Langdarma (841-906)—evil oppressor who almost succeeded in eradicating Buddhism in Tibet; brother of King Ralpachen; assassinated by Palgyi Dorje.

Lhabsang—one of the two potential successors to the fifth Dalai Lama, the other being Sangye Gyamtso.

Lhacham Kuchok—Her Ladyship; polite way to address the wife of a dignitary.

Lhagsam—Chokgyur Lingpa's cook.

Lhakhang—shrine room.

Lhasa—capital of Tibet.

Lhodrak—district south of Lhasa, north of Bhutan.

Lhundrub Teng—Palace of Spontaneous Perfection in Derge; founded by Tangtong Gyalpo (1361-1485); since then the main temple for the Derge Kings.

Light of Wisdom—famous set of teachings covering the entire Buddhist path to enlightenment, especially that of Vajrayana. Based on *Lamrim Yeshe Nyingpo*, a spontaneous song by the ninth-century Indian master Padmasambhava, this scripture is highly revered and played a pivotal role in Tulku Urgyen Rinpoche's education and personal practice. He knew the entire root text by heart and referred to it continually in his own teaching throughout his life.

lineage holder—disciple who receives a teaching and/or empowerment, realizes its intent and is capable of passing it on to others. A lama may hold many lineages of teaching.

lineage masters—teachers through whom a certain teaching and/or empowerment has been transmitted.

Lingpa—title usually referring to a revealer of hidden treasures, for instance Sangye Lingpa, Ratna Lingpa, Chokgyur Lingpa.

Lion-faced Dakini—one of the chief deities for averting obstacles and negative forces.

Longchen Nyingtig—*Heart-Essence of the Vast Expanse*; mind treasure of mystical teachings discovered by the great scholar and adept Jigmey Lingpa, transmitted to him by Longchenpa; lineage of the Nyingma school of Tibetan Buddhism. See *Masters of Meditation and Miracles: Lives of the Great Buddhist Masters of India and Tibet*, Tulku Thondup, Shambhala Publications 1999.

Longchenpa (1308-1363)—major lineage master and writer of the Nyingma lineage; an incarnation of Princess Pema Sal, the daughter of King Trisong Deutsen, to whom Guru Rinpoche had entrusted his own lineage of Dzogchen known as *Khandro Nyingtig*. He is single-handedly regarded as the most important writer on Dzogchen teachings. His works include the *Seven Great Treasuries*, the *Three Trilogies* and his commentaries in the *Nyingtig Yabzhi*. A more detailed account of his life and teachings is found in *Buddha Mind* by Tulku Thondup Rinpoche, Snow Lion, 1989.

longevity practice—practices for restoring vital energy that has been degenerated and dissipated which causes illness, aging and death to occur.

Loter Wangpo (1847-1914)—lama from the Ngor monastery in the Tsang province of Central Tibet; one of the principal disciples of both Khyentse and Kongtrul.

lotsawa—translator of the canonical texts; usually worked with Indian panditas.

Lotus Essence Tantra—(Pema Nyingpo Gyu), short tantra that gives liberation through hearing or reading.

Lotus Garuda Fortress—Pema Kyung Dzong, retreat place high up on the mountain above Tsurphu.

Lotus-Born master—English translation of Padmasambhava.

Lumey Dorje—of the Tsangsar clan; one of the masters in the Barom Kagyu lineage; Tulku Urgyen Rinpoche's ancestor.

Lungtok—childhood name of Tulku Urgyen Rinpoche's second son. The sixteenth Karmapa later recognized him as the fourth Chokling of Tsikey.

Lungtok of Nyoshul (1829-1901/2)—one of Paltrul Rinpoche's disciples; main teacher of Khenpo Ngakchung.

Machen Pomra—the mighty Amnye Machen Range, also called Magyal Pomra; sacred mountain said to be the abode of Machen Pomra, powerful protector of the Dharma in Tibet.

Machik Labdrön (1055-1153)—great female master and incarnation of Yeshe Tsogyal who set down the Chö practice of cutting through ego-clinging. Machik Labdrön means 'Only Mother Lamp of Dharma.'

Maha—short for Mahayoga; the first of the three inner tantras: Maha, Anu, and Ati Yoga.

Maha, Anu, and Ati Yoga—short for Mahayoga, Anu Yoga and Ati Yoga; the three inner tantras of the Nyingma school.

Mahakala—one of the main Dharma protectors; a wrathful form of Avalokiteshvara.

Mahamudra—literally, 'great seal,' one of the most direct practices for realizing one's buddha nature; system of teachings which is the basic view of Vajrayana practice according to the Sarma or New schools of Kagyu, Gelug, and Sakya—just as Dzogchen is for the Nyingma school.

Mahayana—'greater vehicle;' connotation of 'greater' or 'lesser' refers to scope of aspiration, methods applied and depth of insight. Central to Mahayana practice is the bodhisattva vow to liberate all sentient beings through compassion and insight into emptiness.

Mahayoga—first of the three inner tantras of the Nyingma school; emphasizes sadhana practice and the view that liberation is attained through growing accustomed to the insight into the indivisibility of the superior two truths—purity and equality. The pure natures of the aggregates, elements and sense factors are the male and female buddhas and bodhisattvas. At the same time, everything that appears and exists is of the equal nature of emptiness.

Mahayoga tantras—primarily the eighteen main tantras now contained in the *Nyingma Gyubum*, chief of which is *Guhyagarbha Tantra*.

Mahayoga, Anu Yoga and Ati Yoga—the three inner tantras of the Nyingma school; profound methods for awakening to buddhahood in one lifetime.

Manang—district in northwestern Nepal.

Mandala—'center and surrounding;' usually a deity along with its surrounding environment. A mandala is often a symbolic, graphic representation of a tantric deity's realm of existence.

mandala offering—an offering visualized as the entire universe, as well as the arrangement of offerings in tantric ritual, often placed as a circular, ornate plate. To present a teaching "as a mandala offering" shows the utmost respect for the recipient.

mani stones—stones carved or engraved with the *mani* mantra of Avalokiteshvara: OM MANI PADME HUNG. They are often made under commission by a devotee to increase the merit of the living or the dead and placed where other people can benefit from seeing or circumambulating them.

Manjushri—one of eight main bodhisattvas; personification of the perfection of transcendent knowledge.

Mao Tse-tung—helmsman of Communism in China; seen by many Tibetans as possessed by a demonic force bent on destroying the Dharma and happiness of sentient beings.

Mara—demon of obstacles; anything that distracts a practitioner from the Dharma and the pursuit of lasting happiness and liberation.

Maratika—sacred cave where Padmasambhava and Mandarava attained immortality; these days believed to be in southeastern Nepal.

Margyenma—one of King Trisong Deutsen's queens who made obstacles for Vairotsana, resulting in his exile.

Marpa (1002/12-1097)—great forefather of the Kagyu lineage. See *Life of Marpa the Translator*.

means and liberation—refer, in the Kagyu context, to Naropa's Six Doctrines and Mahamudra.

meditative composure—*see* composure.

Melemchi—village in the Helambu region (Yölmo), three days walk north of Kathmandu.

mendrub—sacred medicine made from herbs and relics and consecrated in a particular ritual known as *mendrub drubchen*.

metsa—old-fashion fire kit using flint, steel and dry moss or bark.

Milarepa (1040-1123)—one of the most famous yogis and poets in Tibetan religious history; much of the teachings of the Karma Kagyu schools passed through him. See *The Life of Milarepa* and *The Hundred Thousand Songs of Milarepa*. His name means 'Cotton-clad Mila.'

mind essence—nature of mind. Pointing out the mind essence: the main aim of the 'pointing-out instruction' is to make obvious to the meditator what it is that knows and thinks—not as a theory but a direct experience. See *pointing-out instruction*.

Mind Section; Space Section; Instruction Section—the *Three Sections of the Great Perfection*; after Garab Dorje established the six million four hundred thousand tantras of Dzogchen in the human world, his chief disciple, Manjushrimitra, arranged these tantras into three categories: the Mind Section emphasizing luminosity, the Space Section emphasizing emptiness, and the Instruction Section emphasizing their inseparability. They represent the most profound or subtle spiritual literature present in this world.

mind treasure or terma—revelation directly within the mind of a great master, without the need for a terma of material substance. The teachings revealed in this way were implanted within the 'indestructible sphere' at the time when the master in a former life was one of Padmasambhava's disciples.

Mindrolling—one of the two primary Nyingma monasteries in Central Tibet (founded in 1670, by Terdag Lingpa), the other being Dorje Drag.

mind-stream—individual continuity of consciousness; like the stream of a river, it is neither permanent nor interrupted.

Mingyur Chödrön—Tulku Urgyen Rinpoche's sister.

Mingyur Dorje—the tulku of Yongey Mingyur Dorje; he was a disciple of Chokgyur Lingpa and though being a tulku himself was the tertön's servant.

Mipham (1846-1912)—student of Jamgön Kongtrul, Jamyang Khyentse Wangpo and Paltrul Rinpoche. Blessed by Manjushri, he became one of the greatest scholars of his time; his collected works fill more than 30 volumes. His chief disciple was Shechen Gyaltsab Pema Namgyal, the root guru of Dilgo Khyentse Rinpoche.

momo—Chinese style dumplings, filled with meat or cottage cheese.

Monkey-Faced Ganapati—a protector of the Dharma.

Mount Dakpo—Dakla Gampo; eight-peaked mountain in the region in Southern Central Tibet.

Mount Gegyal—presumably in the Gegyal Riwo district southwest of Nangchen, west of Tengchen on the main road from Chamdo to Lhasa.

Mount Kailash—sacred mountain in west Tibet.

Mount Kangsar—mountain on the old route between Nangchen and Lhasa.

Mount Karma—sacred mountain south of Nangchen on the way to Chamdo.

Mount Sumeru—mythological mountain of giant proportions at the center of our world-system surrounded by the four continents; abode of gods of the Desire Realms. It is encircled by chains of lesser mountains, lakes, continents, and oceans and is said to rise 84,000 leagues above sea-level. Our present world is situated on the southern continent called Jambudvipa.

mudra—sacred gesture; symbolic hand gesture.

naga—powerful long-lived serpent-like beings who inhabit bodies of water and often guard great treasure. Nagas belong half to the animal realm and half to the god realm. They generally live in the form of snakes, but many can change into human form.

Nagi Gompa—Tulku Urgyen Rinpoche's hermitage on the northern slope of the Kathmandu valley.

name-burning—ritual that guides the dead to a better rebirth; can only be performed by a realized master.

Namkhai Nyingpo (8th cent.)—one of the twenty-five close disciples of the Lotus-Born master.

Nangchen—independent kingdom in eastern Tibet; presently situated in the southern part of the Qinghai province.

Nangso Chenmo—monastery built by Lumey Dorje of Tsangsar, one of the early Barom Kagyu masters; the ruins are situated on a small hill a half a day's walk south from Tsechu Gompa.

Naropa—siddha of India, chief disciple of Tilopa and guru of Marpa in the Kagyu Lineage. See *Rain of Wisdom* and *The Life of Marpa*.

nature of mind—synonym for mind-essence or buddha nature; should be distinguished from the thinking mind (*sem*), which refers to ordinary discursive thinking based on ignorance. This nature is the basic space from and within which these thoughts take place.

Nenang—Pawo Rinpoche's monastery in Central Tibet, 60 km from Lhasa on the way to Tsurphu.

Nendo—(Neydo) one of the branches within the Karma Kagyu lineage; originates from Karma Chagmey. The main monastery (Nemdho Tashi Chöling) is in Chamdo south of Nangchen.

Neten Chokling—*see* Chokling of Neten.

Neten monastery—one of the three main 'seats' of Chokgyur Lingpa. When the tertön went there, he had a vision of the Sixteen Arhats or the Sixteen Elders. "Neten" means "elders" in Tibetan. It is situated on the border between Nangchen (Qinghai) and Chamdo (Tibet Autonomous Region) near Tsechu Gompa.

Neuring Senge Dzong—Lion Fortress Meadow, one of the five principal retreat places of Padmasambhava, situated just inside the border of Bhutan north of Lhuntse Dzong.

New Schools of the Later Translations—*see* Sarma schools.

New Treasures—*Chokling Tersar*; collection of termas in the forty thick volumes revealed by Chokgyur Lingpa together with connected teachings, arrangement texts and commentaries written primarily by Jamyang Khyentse Wangpo, Jamgön Kongtrul, Khakyab Dorje, Tsewang Norbu, Tersey Tulku and Dilgo Khyentse Rinpoche.

neydag—lord of the locality, local spirit.

Ngabö—high government official in the nineteen fifties' Lhasa.

Ngadrama—likeness; statue or painting that is supposed to look exactly like the person depicted.

Ngakchung, Khenpo (1879-1941)—*see* Khenpo Ngakchung.

ngakpa—practitioner of Vajrayana who keeps long hair, wears a different robe than monks, and can be married.

Ngaktrin—Ngawang Trinley; incarnation line of Samten Gyatso who was the fourth Ngaktrin tulku.

Ngaktrin of Argong—second Ngaktrin Tulku; disciple of the twelfth Karmapa, Jangchub Dorje (1703-1733) and the eighth Situ, Chökyi Jungney.

Ngari—provinces in the western part of Tibet.

Ngawang Trinley—contemporary of the eleventh Karmapa, Yeshe Dorje (1675-1702); former life of Samten Gyatso; first of the Ngaktrin incarnations who built Lachab monastery.

Ngedön Ösel Ling—one of the monasteries built by Tulku Urgyen Rinpoche situated on the hilltop behind Swayambhu in the Kathmandu valley; now the seat of Tsoknyi Rinpoche in Nepal.

Ngor monastery—Sakya monastery in the Tsang province of Central Tibet.

nine vehicles—nine gradual vehicles of the Nyingma school: Shravaka, Pratyekabuddha, Bodhisattva, Kriya, Upa, Yoga, Maha, Anu, and Ati. They are meant to be alternative approaches to liberation and enlightenment for people of various types of capacity and inclinations.

nondual awareness—(especially in the context of the pointing-out instruction to the awakened state) state of consciousness that is totally free from ignorance and clinging to the duality of perceiver and perceived. It is consequently free from selfish emotions and the creation of unvirtuous karma. The recognition of and training in this nondual awareness is the central issue in Dzogchen and Mahamudra.

nonmeditation—fourth of four levels of Mahamudra. For more details, see Dakpo Tashi Namgyal, *Clarifying the Natural State*. (Rangjung Yeshe Publications).

Norbu Lingka Park—summer palace of the Dalai Lamas in the vicinity of Lhasa.

Nubri—situated in Ganesh Himal, northwestern part of Nepal.

Nyagla Pema Dudul (1816–1872)—master who attained rainbow body.

Nyang-Ral Nyima Özer (1124-1192)—first of five king-like tertöns and a reincarnation of King Trisong Deutsen. Several of his revealed treasures are included in the *Rinchen Terdzö*, among which the most well known is the *Kabgye Deshek Dupa*, a cycle of teachings focusing on the *Eight Commands*, and the biography of Guru Rinpoche called *Sanglingma*, now published as *The Lotus-Born*. Nyang Ral means 'Braided one from Nyang,' and Nyima Özer means 'Ray of sun light.'

Nyemo—area southwest of, but close to, Lhasa.

Nyenchen Tanglha—important protector of the Nyingma teachings, regarded as a bodhisattva on the eighth level; name of mountain range north of Lhasa.

Nyendrub—*Three Vajra Practices of Approach and Accomplishment*; one of the eight chariots of the Practice Lineage brought to Tibet by the master Orgyenpa (1230-1309) who had traveled to the terrestrial pure land Uddiyana where he met the female buddha Vajra Varahi.

nyerpa—steward managing the affairs of a monastic household in both secular and ritual matters.

Nyingma Kahma—Oral Transmissions of the Old School; 56 volumes in the expanded edition published by Dudjom Rinpoche. The predominant number of scriptures concern the three inner tantras.

Nyingma school—teachings brought to Tibet and translated mainly during the reign of King Trisong Deutsen and in the subsequent period up to Rinchen Zangpo in the ninth century, chiefly by the great masters Padmasambhava, Vimalamitra, Shantarakshita, and Vairotsana. The two main types of transmission are Kahma and Terma. Practices are based on both the outer and inner tantras with emphasis on the practice of the inner tantras of Mahayoga, Anu Yoga and Ati Yoga.

Nyingtig—heart essence; usually refers to the innermost aspect of the Dzogchen teachings, such as the instructions of Vimalamitra or Padmasambhava.

Nyingtig Yabzhi—see Four Branches of Heart Essence.

Nyoshul Khen (1932-1999)—Jamyang Dorje; one of the greatest recent khenpos of the Nyingma tradition; renowned for his spontaneous poetry and songs of realization; disciple of Shedrub Tenpey Nyima and one of the holders of the *Hearing Lineage of Nyingtig* which came through Jigmey Lingpa and Paltrul Rinpoche.

Old Khyentse—in this book, short for Jamyang Khyentse Wangpo.

Old Kongtrul—in this book, short for Jamgön Kongtrul the First.

om mani peme hung—famous mantra of Avalokiteshvara, the bodhisattva of compassion.

One Hundred Chö empowerments—*Chöwang Gyatsa*; collection of one hundred empowerments for the practice of Chö.

Orgyen Chöpel—Tulku Urgyen Rinpoche's paternal grandfather.

Orgyen Tobgyal (b.1952)—oldest son of the third Neten Chokling. Lives in Bir, Himachal Pradesh in Northern India, where he has rebuilt Neten monastery.

Padmasambhava—the Lotus-Born master who brought Vajrayana to Tibet in the eight century; also referred to as Guru Rinpoche, the precious teacher. For more details on this master's life, see *The Lotus-Born*.

Padmasattva—chief deity in a mind treasure revealed by Old Khyentse after Chokgyur Lingpa's passing. In a vision, he saw the great tertön in his sambhogakaya form and, receiving an empowerment and teachings, wrote them down.

pakshi—see under *tishi*.

Palbar—Tibetan word translated here as *Blazing Splendor*.

Palpung—large Kagyu monastery near Derge in Kham; seat of the Situ incarnations; founded in 1717 by Situ Chökyi Jungney.

Paltrul Rinpoche (1808-1887)—one of the foremost masters of his time known not only for his scholarship and learning but also for his example of renunciation and compassion. His most famous works include *Words of my Perfect Teacher* (*Kunsang Lamey Shellung*) and his commentary on *Three Words Striking the Vital Point* (*Tsiksum Nedek*), the quintessence of the Dzogchen teachings.

Palyul—Namgyal Jangchub Ling, one of the four main Nyingma monasteries in Kham; founded in 1665 by Rigdzin Kunsang Sherab.

Panchen Lama—incarnation line of the abbots of Tashi Lhunpo monastery, established in the time of the Fifth Dalai Lama; first Panchen Lama was Lobzang Chögyen (1570-1662).

pandita—learned master, scholar, professor in Buddhist philosophy.

Paro—famous pilgrimage site in Bhutan, ninety minutes drive from the capital Thimphu.

Pawo Rinpoche (b.1912)—Tsuklag Nangwa Wangchuk; one of the main masters of the Kagyu lineage in recent times.

peaceful and wrathful deities—42 peaceful and 58 wrathful deities representing the basic qualities of buddha nature, the transformation of samsaric traits on the path, and the perfect virtues of complete enlightenment. The practice connected to their mandala is very popular in the Nyingma and Kagyu traditions.

Pema Kyung Dzong—*see* Lotus Garuda Fortress.

Pema Ösel Do-Ngak Lingpa—Jamyang Khyentse Wangpo's (Old Khyentse) tertön title, given by Padmasambhava.

Pema Trinley—the great tertön's servant; told many stories to Tulku Urgyen Rinpoche.

Pemakö—region in southern Tibet famous for its hidden land of sacred places; one third is inside Tibet and two-thirds in Arunachal Pradesh of India.

Penjik—Tulku Urgyen Rinpoche older half-brother.

Phakchok—Tulku Urgyen Rinpoche's grandson; Tsikey Chokling's oldest son. *See also* Sey Phakchok.

PHAT—sacred, tantric syllable used in the practices of *phowa*, *Chö* or *Trekchö*

phey—an exclamation used in Chö practice; same as PHAT but with different pronunciation.

phowa—tantric practice of ejection of consciousness through the crown of the head at the time of death to effectuate a rebirth in a buddhafield. This is often accompanied by visible sign of success.

pith instructions—practical and concise advice on how to carry out a spiritual practice in the most simple and effective way.

pointing-out instruction—direct introduction to the nature of mind, of paramount importance in Dzogchen and Mahamudra; given by a root guru so that the disciple recognizes the nature of mind.

Ponlop Rinpoche—incarnation line of masters connected to Dzogchen monastery in Kham. The sixth Dzogchen Ponlop Rinpoche, Tubten Jigdral Tsewang Dorje (1925-62), was the brother of the sixteenth Karmapa.

pönpo—local chieftain, similar to district governor.

Potala—famous palace of the Dalai Lamas and the landmark of Lhasa.

Prajnaparamita—transcendent knowledge; Mahayana teachings on insight into emptiness, transcending the fixation of subject, object and action; associated with the Buddha's second turning of the wheel of Dharma. Since Prajnaparamita eliminates the most subtle obscuration, this insight is often called Mother of All Buddhas.

Prajnaparamita sutras—teachings that describe insight, transcendent knowledge, and other practices of a bodhisattva, as well as a buddha's omniscient state of enlightenment. These sutras exists in varying degree of details, the shortest being the famous *Heart Sutra* memorized by most monks and nuns and the longest being the *Hundred Thousand* in twelve large volumes.

preliminary practices of the four times hundred thousand—(four foundations), traditional basis for a Vajrayana practitioner's development: refuge and bodhisattva vow, Vajrasattva recitation, mandala offering and guru yoga, each of which are repeated one hundred thousand times.

Prince Murub—second son of King Trisong Deutsen; close disciple of Padmasambhava, attained enlightenment and took the vow to come back repeatedly to reveal the hidden treasures of the Lotus-Born master; later incarnated as Chokgyur Lingpa.

protectors—guardians of the Dharma teachings.

Puntsok Wangdu—Bhutanese dignitary of the *drashö* rank; father of one of the incarnations of Jamyang Khyentse Wangpo.

pure realm or lands—buddhafields; manifested through the aspirations of a bodhisattva in conjunction with the merit of sentient beings. According to the tantras, a buddhafield is an expression of the awakened state. A practitioner can take rebirth in Sukhavati, the pure land of Buddha Amitabha, at the moment of death or during the bardo through a combination of pure faith, sufficient merit, and one-pointed determination.

Rabjam—*see* Shechen Rabjam; Longchen Rabjam/ Longchenpa.

Rabsel Dawa—one of the names of Dilgo Khyentse Rinpoche.

rainbow body—at the time of death of a practitioner who has reached the exhaustion of all dualistic clinging through the Dzogchen practice of Tögal, the five gross elements which form the physical body, dissolve back into their essences, five-colored light. Sometimes the only remainder is the hair and the nails are left behind. In the chapter on Accomplishment, *Rainbow Painting*, Tulku Urgyen Rinpoche gives a fascinating account of an old nun attaining rainbow body in the shed of a benefactors house. [epk]

rakta vessel—sacred implement in tantric rituals.

Ralpachen—great religious ruler and grandson of Trisong Deutsen; also known as the third of the great Dharma kings who established Buddhism in Tibet.

Ramoche—temple in Lhasa; contains one of the two most famous Buddha statues in all of Tibet.

Ratna Lingpa (1403-1478)—one of the major revealers of treasures whose termas are still practiced today in Nangchen.

reading transmission—authorization to study a scripture by listening to it being read aloud.

Realization Directly Revealed—teachings on the Great Perfection entitled *Samantabhadra's Realization Directly Revealed* (*Kuntu Zangpö Gongpa Sangtal du Tenpa*) from the great revealer of hidden treasures Rigdzin Gödem's tradition of Northern Treasures.

Reding—(Reting), regent between the thirteenth and fourteenth (present) Dalai Lamas.

rediscovered treasure—terma that is brought forth after having been revealed in the past, even centuries before.

refuge—source of protection, place of trust, object of support.

reliquary box—(*gau*), amulet box to carry around ones next or place on the shrine; may contain relics from a past master.

Repa Karpo (b.1198)—early master in the Barom Kagyu lineage; Tishi Repa's chief disciple.

representations of enlightened body, speech and mind—shrine objects; statues, scriptures and stupas.

Rigdzin Gödem (1337-1408)—one of the five king-like tertöns; great treasure revealer of the tradition of *Northern Treasures*. Among his termas are the Dzogchen teachings *Gongpa Sangtal*.

Rigpey Dorje (1924-1981)—sixteenth Karmapa; disciple of the eleventh Situ and Karsey Kongtrul; established numerous monasteries and Dharma centers outside of Tibet and was profoundly instrumental in preserving the Buddha's teachings.

Rinchen Lingpa (1295-1375)—one of the eleven great revealers of hidden treasures with the name Lingpa.

Rinchen Namgyal (b.19th cent.)—master-scholar and disciple of Jamgön Kongtrul and Jamyang Khyentse Wangpo.

Rinchen Terdzö—see Treasury of Precious Termas.

Rinchen Zangpo (957-1055)—important translator at the time of Atisha; known as the first *lotsawa* of the New Schools.

ringsel—pills, tiny white pearls; often found among the ashes of sublime people and great meditators.

Rinpoche—venerable; respectful way of addressing one's guru, abbot or Buddhist teacher.

ritual of burnt food—(*sur*), smoke produced by burning flour mixed with pure food and sacred substances; can nourish bardo spirits and hungry ghosts.

Riwoche monastery—important monastic center for the Taklung branch of the Kagyu lineage, situated to the south of Nangchen a little more than one hundred kilometers from Chamdo.

rolang—Tibetan-style zombie; walking dead or a re-animated corpse. This unbelievable type of resurrection is believed to be a goblin that occupies a dead body, rather than the deceased spirit coming back to life in his own body.

root guru—vajra master who confers empowerment, who bestows reading transmission, or who explains the meaning of the tantras. A practitioner of Vajrayana can have several types of root guru. The ultimate root guru is the master who gives the pointing-out instruction so that one recognizes the nature of mind.

ropani—measurement for land in Nepal; eight ropanis are approximately one acre, sixteen one hectare.

Rumtek—chief seat of the Karma Kagyu lineage established in Sikkim, India, by the sixteenth Karmapa.

Sabchu Rinpoche—lama from Dilyak monastery in Nangchen.

Sachen Kunga Nyingpo (1092-1158)—one of the five forefathers of the Sakya lineage.

sadhana—means of accomplishment; tantric liturgy and procedure for practice. The typical sadhana structure involves a preliminary part including the taking of refuge and arousing bodhichitta, a main part involving visualization of a buddha and recitation of the mantra, and a concluding part with dedication of merit to all sentient beings.

Sahor—kingdom in ancient India; believed to be identical with Mandi, Himachal Pradesh.

Sakya lineage—one of the four major schools of Buddhism in Tibet; began in the eleventh century when Drogmi Lotsawa 993-1050), disciple of the Indian master Virupa, brought his teachings back to Tibet.

Sakya monastery—one of the main seats of the lineage in Central Tibet.

Sakya Pandita (1182-1251)—Kunga Gyaltsen; renowned scholar and Tibetan statesman; staved off a Mongolian invasion (1244) by converting Emperor Godan Khan to Buddhism.

samadhi—state of undistracted concentration or meditative state; in the context of Vajrayana can refer to either the development stage or the completion stage. Tulku Urgyen Rinpoche often uses it to means stability in the awakened state.

Samantabhadra—primordial buddha who awakened to enlightenment many eons before this world was formed; forefather of the Dzogchen teachings.

samaya—sacred pledges, precepts or commitments of Vajrayana practice; essentially consist of maintaining harmonious relationship with the vajra master and Dharma siblings and not straying from the continuity of the practice. A samaya violator is someone with severely damaged or broken samaya, comparable to a traitor or demon.

Samgya—abbreviation of Samten Gyatso.

Samsara—'cyclic existence', 'vicious circle' or 'round' of birth and death and rebirth within the six realms; characterized by suffering, impermanence, and ignorance; the state of ordinary sentient beings fettered by ignorance and dualistic perception, karma and disturbing emotions. It also means ordinary reality, an endless cycle of frustration and suffering generated as the result of karma.

Samten Gyatso (1881-1945/6)—master of the Barom and *New Treasures* lineages; based at Lachab monastery in Nangchen; Tulku Urgyen Rinpoche's uncle & root guru.

Samten Kangsar—powerful spirit and guardian of the Dharma.

Samye—temple complex and monastery in Central Tibet founded by Padmasambhava, King Trisong Deutsen, and Shantarakshita; center of the early transmission.

Sangha—community of practitioners usually the fully ordained monks and nuns or the *ngakpas*, tantric practitioners distinguished by their long braided hair, white skirts, and striped shawls.

Sang-Ngak—(Uncle Sang-Ngak); the uncle of Tulku Urgyen Rinpoche.

Sangwa Yeshe—(Secret Wisdom), enlightened dakini.

Sangye Gyamtso (1653-1703/5)—regent-king after the fifth Dalai Lama, and one of Chokgyur Lingpa's former lives.

Sangye Lama (990?-1070)—earliest tertön in Tibet.

Sangye Lingpa (1340-1396)— reincarnation of the second son of King Trisong Deutsen; major tertön and revealer of the *Lama Gongdu* cycle in 13 volumes.

Sangye Yeshe of Nub (b.9th cent.)—Nubchen Sangye Yeshe; one of the twenty-five disciples of Padmasambhava; chief recipient of the Anu Yoga teachings and visited India and Nepal seven times. When the evil king Langdarma attempted to destroy Buddhism in Tibet, Sangye Yeshe instilled fear in the king by causing an enormous scorpion, the size of nine yaks, to magically appear by a single gesture of his right hand. Tulku Urgyen Rinpoche is considered one of his reincarnations.

Sarma schools—New schools: Kagyu, Sakya, and Gelug as well as Shijey and Chö, Jordruk, Shangpa Kagyu, and Nyendrub (Kalachakra).

Sarnath—sacred site near Varanasi where Buddha Shakyamuni gave the first teaching on the four noble truths.

Scripture of the Great Assemblage—(*Do Gongdu*), fundamental tantra in the Anu Yoga category.

Secret Essence Kilaya—(*Sangtik Purpa*), terma revelation of Chokgyur Lingpa.

Secret Mantra—synonym for Vajrayana.

self-appeared—images, syllables, etc. The Himalayan region abounds with divine images that supposedly are not made by the human hand.

semtri—guidance in understanding and experiencing the nature of mind; vital part of Mahamudra and Dzogchen.

Seven Treasuries—seven profound writings by Longchenpa.

Sevenfold Cycle of Profundity—(*Zabpa Kordun*), a most extensive set of revelations by Chokgyur Lingpa; contains the sadhana of the Lotus-Dakini, Kilaya, etc.

Sey Phakchok—son of Shakya Shri who continued his teaching and encampment.

shabdrung—vajra master in charge of tantric ceremonies, a religious rank two steps below the highest hierarch of the Sakya school.

Shabdrung Rinpoche—early name for Jamyang Khyentse Wangpo (Old Khyentse).

Shabkar Tsokdrug Rangdröl (1781-1851)—great master-bodhisattva; see *Life of Shabkar*.

Shakya Shri—Tibetan mahasiddha of the nineteenth century; belonged chiefly to the Drukpa Kagyu lineage.

Shakyamuni—the historical Buddha, regarded as the chief teacher of our present age.

shamatha and vipashyana—stillness and insight; two basic meditation practices common to most schools of Buddhism.

Shangpa Kagyu—one of the eight practice lineages; brought to Tibet by Kyungpo Naljor (1002-1064).

Shantarakshita—abbot of Vikramashila who ordained the first Tibetan monks at the invitation of King Trisong Deutsen.

Shantideva (685-763)—one of the eighty-four mahasiddhas of India; composed the famous *Bodhisattva Charya Avatara* (*The Way of the Bodhisattva*).

Shechen Kongtrul (1901-1960)—Pema Drimey; one of the incarnations of Jamgön Kongtrul (Old Kongtrul); guru of Chögyam Trungpa.

Shechen monastery—one of the four main Nyingma monasteries in Kham: Shechen, Dzogchen, Katok, and Palyul.

Shechen Rabjam (1910-195?)—one of the main masters at Shechen monastery.

Shigatse—(Zhigatse), Tibet's second largest town, location of Tashi Lhunpo, seat of the Panchen Lamas.

Shijey—one of the eight practice lineages; brought to Tibet by Padampa Sangye.

Shri Singha—chief disciple and successor of Manjushrimitra in the lineage of the Dzogchen teachings; born in Khotan; his disciples were four outstanding masters: Jnanasutra, Vimalamitra, Padmasambhava and the Tibetan translator Vairochana; the latter three were responsible for bringing the canonical scriptures of Dzogchen to Tibet.

Shri Singha College—school of higher Buddhist studies at Dzogchen monastery.

siddha—perfected one, realized one, adept who has attained realization.

Side Ornament to the Light of Wisdom—Jokyab's collected notes on *Light of Wisdom* that he received from Jamyang Drakpa of Dru.

Sikkim—(until 1975) independent kingdom in the Himalayas, between Nepal and Bhutan.

sindhura—red or deep orange substance often used in tantric rituals.

Single Child of the Buddhas (*Sangye Seychig*)—primordial tantra that give liberation through hearing, touching, or tasting.

Single Seat Session—short liturgy text for Chö practice by Jamgön Kongtrul.

Situ Chökyi Jungney (1700-1774)—eighth in the line of Situ incarnations; great scholar and visionary, doctor and painter; founded Palpung in 1727.

Situ Pema Nyinje Wangpo (1774-1853)—ninth Tai Situ; root-teacher of Jamgön Kongtrul the Great.

Situ Pema Wangchok Gyalpo (1886-1953)—enthroned by the fifteenth Karmapa and studied with Jamgön Kongtrul and the great scholar Zhenga. He later enthroned and offered the transmission of the Kagyu lineage to the sixteenth Gyalwang Karmapa, Rangjung Rigpey Dorje.

Six Doctrines of Naropa—*tummo*, illusory body, dream, luminosity, bardo, and *phowa*; subtle yogic practices usually undertaken after yidam practice.

sixteen arhats—disciples of the Buddha who vowed to preserve the Dharma until the coming of Maitreya.

Smritijnana—Indian master-scholar who entered Tibet early in the eleventh century.

Sogyal Rinpoche—incarnation of the treasure revealer Lerab Lingpa, based in France; author of *The Tibetan Book of Living and Dying*.

Solu Khumbu—district in the northeastern mountains of Nepal.

Sönam Yeshe of Tsangsar—former life of Chimey Dorje, Tulku Urgyen Rinpoche's father; founder of Lhalam monastery in Nangchen.

Songtsen Gampo, King (617–698)—first great Dharma King, who prepared the way for transmission of the teachings; regarded as an incarnation of Avalokiteshvara. He married Princess Bhrikuti of Nepal and Princess Wen Cheng of China who each brought a sacred statue of Buddha Shakyamuni to Lhasa. Songtsen Gampo built the first Buddhist temples in Tibet, established a code of laws based on Dharma principles, and had his minister Tönmi Sambhota develop the Tibetan script. During his reign the translation of Buddhist texts into Tibetan began.

Söntar Chönchok—teacher of Chimey Dorje and close friend of Samten Gyatso.

Spontaneous Fulfillment of Wishes—terma treasure of Chokgyur Lingpa that contains a supplication to Padmasambhava famous under the same name.

Stupa—dome-shaped monument housing relics of the Buddha or an accomplished master.

Subjugator of All Appearance and Existence—one of the names of Padmasambhava.

Summary of Logic—scholastic text composed by Mipham.

Surmang monastery—(Zurmang), refers in *Blazing Splendor* to the Namgyal Tse in east Nangchen near Tsikey monastery.

Surmang Tentrul—learned and accomplished master at Surmang Namgyal Tse; later gave most of the *New Treasures* to the sixteenth Karmapa.

Sutra and Tantra—Sutra refers to the teachings of both Hinayana and Mahayana; Tantra refers to Vajrayana.

Sutra system—exoteric teachings belonging to Hinayana and Mahayana that regard the path as the cause of enlightenment, as opposed to the esoteric, tantric teachings.

Swayambhu—one of the three main stupas of the Kathmandu valley.

swift walking or swift feet—yogic ability to walk extremely fast, covering huge distances in a short time, through control over the inner currents of energy.

Taklung—Kagyu monastery 150 km northwest of Lhasa founded in the twelfth century.

Taklung Tsetrul—lama of Taklung monastery.

Taksham Lingpa (1682-?)—also known as Nuden Dorje or Samten Lingpa; tertön and emanation of Atsara Sale, Yeshe Tsogyal's Nepalese consort.

Taktsang—Tiger's Nest, sacred place of Padmasambhava above the Paro valley of Bhutan.

Tana—monastery in Nangchen originally Yelpa Kagyu, named Horse-Eared after distinctively shaped mountain peaks above it; site of Ling Gesar's tomb.

tangka—sacred painting on cloth; can be rolled up as a scroll.

Tantra on the Essence of Secrets—see Guhyagarbha Tantra.

Tantra system—canonical scripture in which the Buddha taught Vajrayana in his sambhogakaya form. The real sense of tantra is 'continuity,' the innate buddha nature, which is known as the 'tantra of the expressed meaning.' The general sense of tantra is the extraordinary tantric scriptures also known as the 'tantra of the expressing words.' Can also refer to all the resultant teachings of Vajrayana as a whole.

tantric—of or pertaining to Vajrayana.

tantric ornaments—jewelry and garments of silk for a peaceful deity and bone-ornaments for a wrathful.

tantrika—person who has received empowerment, continues the sadhana practice and keeps the commitments; could be a monk or nun but refers mainly to lay practitioners.

Tarthang Tulku—Nyingma master based in the United States; prolific publisher of sacred scriptures.

Tashi Chimey—Tulku Urgyen Rinpoche's aunt.

Tashi Gang—two days east from Thimphu, the capital of Bhutan.

Tashi Lhunpo—monastery, seat of the Panchen Lama in Shigatse; founded in 1447 by Gedun Drub (1391-1475), Tsongkhapa's nephew and disciple; used to house up to four thousand monks.

Tashi Özer (1836-1910)—abbot of Paljor and Palpung monasteries and a student of Jamgön Kongtrul.

Tendzin Dorje—previous life of Chökyi Nyima Rinpoche; lama at Drong monastery near Nakchukha.

Tendzin Rabgye—healer and accomplished master from one of the old temples of the Barom Kagyu.

Tenga Rinpoche—master from Benchen monastery in Nangchen; close friend of Tulku Urgyen Rinpoche.

Tenga Tulku—brother of Tulku Urgyen Rinpoche.

Tengyur—collection of translated commentaries by Indian masters on the Buddha's teachings; second part of the Tibetan Canon in 213 volumes.

Tenpa Tsering (1678-1738)—King of Derge at the time of Situ Chökyi Jungney.

Tentrul of Surmang—see Surmang Tentrul.

terdag—guardian deity of a specific terma treasure.

Terdag Lingpa (1646-1714)—Gyurmey Dorje, built Mindrolling in Central Tibet, one of the most important Nyingma monasteries.

terma—transmission through concealed treasures hidden, mainly by Padmasambhava and Yeshe Tsogyal, to be discovered at the proper time by a *tertön* for the benefit of future disciples; one of the two chief traditions of the Nyingma school, the other being Kahma; said to continue even long after the Vinaya of the Buddha has disappeared.

terma objects—concealed treasures of many kinds, including texts, ritual objects, relics, and natural objects.

Tersey Tulku (1887/9–1955/7)—*see* Uncle Tersey.

tertön—revealer of hidden treasures, concealed mainly by Padmasambhava and Yeshe Tsogyal.

Thrangu monastery—one of the main Kagyu monasteries in Nangchen; seat of the Tralek Jamgön and Thrangu Rinpoche incarnations.

three inner tantras—Mahayoga, Anu Yoga, and Ati Yoga.

three kayas of buddhahood—dharmakaya (body of enlightened qualities), the first of the three kayas, is devoid of constructs, like space. Sambhogakaya (body of perfect enjoyment) is the semi-manifest form of the buddhas endowed with five perfections: perfect teacher, retinue, place, teaching and time; perceptible only to bodhisattvas on the ten levels. Nirmanakaya (emanation body or form of magical apparition) is the aspect of enlightenment that can be perceived by ordinary beings.

three levels of precepts—*see* triple-vow vajra holder.

Three Roots—guru, yidam and dakini. The *guru* is the root of blessings, the *yidam* of accomplishment, and the *dakini* of activity. They are usually three types of sadhana practice.

Three Sections of the Great Perfection—(*Dzogchen Desum*); terma revealed by Chokgyur Lingpa. See *also* Mind, Space and Instruction Sections.

three times—past, present and future.

throne holder—current head of a major monastery.

Tilopa—great Indian siddha, teacher of Naropa, and father of the Kagyu lineage.

tishi—imperial preceptor; Chinese title for highest religious rank. Below the tishi are two masters of the *pakshi* rank, and each pakshi oversees two dignitaries with the position known as *goshir*. [tur]

Tishi Repa—Darma Wangchuk's disciple; early master in the Barom Kagyu lineage.

tokden—full-time meditators who never cut their braided hair; often they are monks.

Tölung valley—location of Tsurphu in Central Tibet, some 70 km west of Lhasa.

torma—implement used in tantric ceremonies; can also refer to a food offering to protectors of the Dharma or unfortunate spirits.

town yogi—lay practitioner.

Tramdruk—(Traduk), early temple in the Yarlung valley near Lhasa, built by Songtsen Gampo.

transmission—direct imparting of knowledge from master to student in an unbroken line of succession spanning centuries.

treasure revealer—*see* tertön.

Treasury of Dharmadhatu—one of Longchenpa's famous Seven Treasuries. Translated by Richard Barron as: *Precious Treasury of the Basic Space of Phenomena* and *A Treasure Trove of Scriptural Transmission*, (Padma Publishing).

Treasury of Knowledge—(*Sheja Dzö/Sheja Kunkyab*), Jamgön Kongtrul's unique encyclopedic masterpiece embodying the entire range of Buddhist teachings. See *Myriad Worlds*, (Snow Lion Publications).

Treasury of Nyingma Songs—compilation by Kyungtrul of spiritual songs by masters of the Nyingma lineage.

Treasury of Oral Instructions—Jamgön Kongtrul's compilation of the most vital instructions from the eight chariots of the Practice Lineage.

Treasury of Precious Termas—(*Rinchen Terdzö*), Jamgön Kongtrul's collection in 63 volumes of the most important revealed termas of Padmasambhava, Vimalamitra, Vairotsana and their closest disciples; gathered by with the help of Jamyang Khyentse Wangpo.

triple-vow vajra holder—outer level of ethical precepts, inner level of bodhisattva trainings, and innermost tantric level of a vidyadhara. Someone who observes all three is a 'vajra holder of the threefold precepts'.

Trisong Deutsen—*see* King Trisong Deutsen.

tromter—terma treasure revealed in full public.

Trulshik Rinpoche—chief disciple of Dudjom Rinpoche and Dilgo Khyentse Rinpoche; monastery (Tubten Chöling) in the Solu Khumbu, northeastern Nepal.

Tsagah—Tulku Urgyen Rinpoche's sister.

tsampa—staple of Tibetan diet comprised of roasted barley flour.

Tsangsar—family name of Tulku Urgyen Rinpoche and an ancient kingdom in Nangchen.

Tsangsar Dranang—the homeland of Tulku Urgyen Rinpoche, accessible only by horse, one day from Lachab, Fortress Peak, or Dechen Ling.

Tsang-Yang Gyamtso (b.19th cent.)—(Gebchak Tokden), chief disciple of the first Tsoknyi; founded numerous nunneries in Nangchen.

Tsari-like Jewel Rock—(Tsadra Rinchen Drak), located on the slope above the Palpung monastery in Kham; extensively described in *The Autobiography of Jamgön Kongtrul*'s and in Ngawang Zangpo, *Sacred Ground: Jamgön Kongtrul on "Pilgrimage and Sacred Geography,"* (Snow Lion Publications).

tsa-tsa—small clay image of a buddha or stupa, stamped from a mold.

Tsechu—monastery adjacent to the royal palace in Nangchen; seat of the Trulshik Adeu and Tsoknyi incarnations.

Tsele Natsok Rangdröl—(b. 1608) master of the Kagyu and Nyingma schools; reincarnation of Vairotsana; author of *Mirror of Mindfulness* and *Lamp of Mahamudra*.

Tseringma—female guardian of Chokgyur Lingpa's treasures; often depicted with her four sisters riding on various animals.

Tsewang Drakpa—*see* Wangchok Dorje, the second son of Chokgyur Lingpa.

Tsewang Norbu (1856-1915/6)—Chokgyur Lingpa's first son and lineage holder; teacher of Samten Gyatso.

Tsichu River—flows between Tsikey and Surmang monasteries in Nangchen.

Tsikey Chokling—*see* Chokling of Tsikey.

Tsikey monastery—one of the three main 'seats' of Chokgyur Lingpa; located at the confluence of the Tsichu and Kechu rivers ten minutes inside the Tibetan Autonomous Region east of Nangchen (Qinghai).

tsiu—spirit of recurring calamity.

Tsogyal—*see* Yeshe Tsogyal.

Tsogyal Lhatso—Life-Lake of Yeshe Tsogyal; situated at Drakda some 20 km from Samye.

Tsoknyi (1828/1849-1904)—Drubwang Tsoknyi the first; an emanation of Milarepa's disciple, Rechungpa, and the tertön Ratna Lingpa; contemporary of Khyentse, Kongtrul and Chokling.

Tsurphu monastery—(pronounced *tsur-pu*), monastic seat of the Karmapa incarnations in Central Tibet, situated in 65 km west of Lhasa.

Tukdrub—short for Tukdrub Barchey Kunsel.

Tukdrub Barchey Kunsel—Chokgyur Lingpa's most famous terma, revealed with Jamyang Khyentse Wangpo, consisting of more than ten volumes.

Tukdrub Trinley Nyingpo—sadhana of Padmasambhava.

tulku—incarnation, manifesting the spiritual qualities of a previous enlightened teacher.

Tulku Pema Wangyal—Taklung Tsetrul Rinpoche; Nyingma master living in Dordogne, France.

tummo or *tummo yoga*—practice to develop the blissful inner heat to refine the subtle vajra body, consume obscurations and to bring forth realization. One of the Six Doctrines of Naropa; practiced primarily in the Kagyu lineage.

Uddiyana—country to the north-west of ancient India where Padmasambhava was born on a lotus flower.

Uncle Sang-Ngak (1885/6-1949?)—uncle of Tulku Urgyen Rinpoche.

Uncle Tersey (1887/9–1955/7)—Tulku Urgyen Rinpoche's uncle; Tersey means son of the tertön.

Universal Panacea (*Karpo Chiktub*)—tantra that give liberation through hearing, touching, or tasting.

Vairochana—of the five families, the chief buddha of the tathagata family.

Vairotsana—sublime and matchless translator of numerous texts of sutra and tantra at the time of King Trisong Deutsen.

Vairotsana Dzogchen—(*Heart Essence of Vairotsana*; *Vairo Nyingtig*), synonyms for Dzogchen Desum.

vajra—as adjective connotes adamantine, diamond, indestructible; specifically it means of or pertaining to Vajrayana.

Vajra Club of the Lord of Secrets—(Sangdag Dorje Bechön), the deity Vajrapani from Chokgyur Lingpa's termas.

vajra holder—of the threefold precepts: *see* triple-vow vajra holder.

vajra master—master adept in the rituals and meaning of Vajrayana, from whom one receives tantric teaching and empowerment; can also refer to the master who presides over a tantric ritual.

Vajra Varahi—female buddha; sambhogakaya manifestation of Samantabhadri; one of the chief yidam deities of the Sarma Schools, as well as a wisdom dakini.

Vajradhara—dharmakaya buddha of the Sarma Schools; refers also to one's personal teacher of Vajrayana or to the all-embracing buddha nature.

Vajrapani—one of the eight great bodhisattvas; chief compiler of the Vajrayana teachings; also known as Lord of Secrets.

Vajrasattva—sambhogakaya buddha who embodies all the five families; source of purification practices.

Vajrasattva recitation—chanting of the mantra in hundred syllables; one of the preliminary practices.

Vajrayana—vehicle of tantric teachings; training in seeing phenomena as the display of primordial purity. The six classes of Vajrayana tantras teach this in an increasingly direct and profound way. The gateway to the Vajrayana is the empowerment, which is given by the spiritual master.

victory banner of realization—sign of having overcome all veils that cover the buddha-nature.

vidyadhara—realized master on one of four stages on the tantric path of Mahayoga.

view of the inner yogas—body is deity, voice is mantra, and mind is samadhi.

view, meditation and conduct (and fruition)—the philosophical orientation, the act of growing accustomed to that, the implementation of that insight during the activities of daily life, and the final outcome resulting from such training. Each of the nine vehicles has its particular definition of view, meditation, conduct and fruition.

Vimalamitra—Dzogchen master who was invited to Tibet by King Trisong Deutsen; one of three main forefathers of the Dzogchen teachings, especially *Nyingtig*, in Tibet. Vimalamitra means 'Flawless Kinsman'.

vivid presence—clear visualization of the deity.

wakefulness, original, luminous—(*yeshe*), intrinsic quality of knowing and its ways of functioning as the five wisdoms.

wang—religious dignity; see *tishi*.

Wangchok Dorje (1860/2-86)—son of Chokgyur Lingpa; incarnation of the Indian king Jah.

Wangchuk Dorje (1556-1603)—the ninth Karmapa.

Wangdu—Tulku Urgyen Rinpoche's brother-in-law; a Central Tibetan aristocrat.

Way of a Bodhisattva—The Indian master Shantideva's famous work on Mahayana training and realization.

wisdom protector—enlightened Dharma protector.

wisdom-body—ethereal form, beyond the confines of a material body.

Wish-Fulfilling Jewel—highly honorific way of addressing the Karmapa; also shows one's deep respect and devotion.

Yarlung valley—south of Lhasa in Central Tibet; associated with the early kings; cradle of Tibetan civilization.

Yeshe Tsogyal—close female disciple of Padmasambhava and compiler of his teachings.

yidam—deity used in tantric practice; could be Avalokiteshvara or Vajrasattva.

yidam practice—training in all sights, sounds and thoughts as being deity, mantra and samadhi.

Yölmo—(Helambhu), sacred valley three days walk north of Kathmandu.

Yönga—close disciple of Old Khyentse.

Yongdzin—Druk Kharag Yongdzin Rinpoche, aka Tokden Paksam Gyatso. Drukpa Kagyu master. Among his living disciples is Soktse Rinpoche.

Yongey Mingyur Dorje (1628/41-1708)—tertön at the time of the tenth Karmapa, Chöying Dorje (1605-74).

Yudra Nyingpo—Vairotsana's chief lineage holder; one of Padmasambhava's twenty-five disciples. The reincarnation of Lekdrub of Tsang, born in the region of Gyalmo Tsawarong, he was brought up by Vairotsana and reached perfection in both learning and yogic accomplishment. He is counted among the 108 *lotsawas* and is one of the main lineage holders of the Mind Section of Dzogchen.

Yutok Gönpo (708-833)—famous Tibetan physician and writer.

zhidag—local deity; powerful spirit of the region.

Ziling—Travelogues variously spell this city on Nangchen's north-eastern frontier of with China as Sining, Xining, or Xilling.

Activities and Information

www.blazingsplendor.com

Here you can find contact addresses for teachings and retreats, archives and publications, downloadable pictures to use as screen savers on your computer, biographies of the lineage masters, a more extensive glossary and suggested reading.